W9-BXS-880

Soviet Succession Struggles

Soviet Succession Struggles

Kremlinology and the Russian Question from Lenin to Gorbachev

ANTHONY D'AGOSTINO, 1937-

Boston
ALLEN & UNWIN
London   Sydney   Wellington

Samford University Library

Copyright © 1988 by Anthony D'Agostino
All rights reserved.

Allen & Unwin, Inc.
8 Winchester Place, Winchester, MA 01890, USA

The U.S. Company of
Unwin Hyman Ltd,
P.O. Box 18, Park Lane, Hemel Hempstead, Herts HP2 4TE, UK
40 Museum Street, London WC1A 1LU, UK
37/39 Queen Elizabeth Street, London SE1 2QB, UK

Allen & Unwin Australia Pty Ltd,
8 Napier Street, North Sydney, NSW 2060, Australia

Allen & Unwin (New Zealand) Ltd, in association with the Port Nicholson
Press Ltd,
60 Cambridge Terrace, Wellington, New Zealand

Library of Congress Cataloging-in-Publication Data

D'Agostino, Anthony.
  Soviet succession struggles.
  Bibliography: p.
  Includes index.
  1. Heads of state—Soviet Union—Succession.
  2. Soviet Union—Politics and government—1917–
  I. Title.
JN6540.D37   1987   974.084   87-1380
ISBN 0-04-497043-9

British Library Cataloguing in Publication Data

D'Agostino, Anthony
  Soviet succession struggles: Kremlinology
  and the Russian question from Lenin to Gorbachev.
  1. Political leadership—Soviet Union—
  History—20th century   2. Soviet Union
  —Politics and government—20th
  century
  I. Title
  351.003'4'0947   JN6541
  ISBN 0-04-497043-9

Set in 10 on 12 point Bembo by Paston Press, Loddon, Norfolk
and printed in Great Britain by Biddles of Guildford

JN
6540
.D37
1988

Contents

To Martine Noël

Preface

THE SOVIET UNION has no legal mechanism for leadership succession, a fact that Western observers have commonly seen as a source of latent weakness and political instability. Soviet history has been marked by terrible crises following the incapacity or the death of a leader, during which, lacking the guidance of a constitution, the succession could be achieved only by informal procedures—that is, by a struggle for power. Moreover the absence of rules of the game means that succession is not merely a moment of temporary indisposition for an otherwise stable system but the climax of an ongoing exercise in which even he who attains power must continually shore up his position. Personal ambition and conflict of interest are not unknown in the West, of course, but are better reported than in the East, where decisions are so often described as unanimous, or at least taken in a 'unified spirit.' Nevertheless the contentious nature of Soviet political life is widely recognized.[1]

This does not mean that, aside from personalities, the process is devoid of rhyme or reason. The bulk of famous Communist politicians defeated by Lenin, Stalin, Khrushchev, and their successors claimed that theirs had been no personal rout but more: a rejection of needful policies or even deathless principles. One need not accept these claims at face value to recognize in Soviet history a succession of policies alongside the succession of leaders. The moderation of the New Economic Policy of the twenties was followed by the furious foreign and domestic radicalism of 1928–1933. A period of relaxation followed, then disappeared in the Great Purge of 1936–1938. The party seemed to subordinate the state machinery in the early postwar period, but those who led the party revival were persecuted without mercy in 1948–1949. These were also occasions for foreign policy changes.

Violent turns in the official line, with the resultant ruin of important leaders, are not in my view deviations from the general flow of Soviet history but have instead a pattern of their own. That these turns are indispensable benchmarks for periodizing that history gives rise to the temptation (I hope pardonable in a historian) to suppose them to be keys to understanding the rhythm of Soviet political development in general. The following work, a political survey and a historiographical study, therefore attempts to shed light on the process of succession and the method of its explication.

My vehicle is examination of Western, mostly émigré, writing on Soviet succession, with special attention to those who, through journalism or biography, have influenced subsequent historical accounts. These include Leon Trotsky, the most celebrated exile, who made his views known in volumes of writings touching on every phase of Soviet political life; Boris Souvarine, like Trotsky a biographer of Stalin, and one of the most respected continental observers of Russian Communism until his death in 1984; Boris Nicolaevsky, influential chronicler of the post-Stalin succession struggle of the 1950s; and a number of other figures who have had a similar impact. In the case of Trotsky and Souvarine, I have noted writings that were not published or were distributed among a select readership in order to show the counterpoint with their more famous works and to provide valuable testimony that the authors themselves later suppressed. I have also paid attention to polemical exchanges, such as Trotsky-Souvarine (1929), Nicolaevsky-Dan (1943), and Souvarine-Nicolaevsky (1962).

Out of these writings emerge two distinct forms of analysis: one pertaining largely to the Lenin succession, searching for an answer to what I call here the Russian Question (What is the nature of the Soviet state and society?), and the other, which had its heyday at the end of Stalin's reign, attempting to divine in fragments of evidence the relative power of individuals at the top of the Soviet hierarchy, usually called Kremlinology. One task of this study is to describe the interplay between the two approaches. Chapter 1 shows their conflict as applied to the Lenin succession. The next three chapters look further into the facts of the case and contrast early pronouncements of Trotsky and Souvarine with their better-known later views. The next four chapters trace the waning and transformation of the Russian Question and the rise of Kremlinology, alongside echoes of the Lenin succession in the later faction struggles.

The stress I have laid on the Lenin succession results not only from the fact that the other successions must be studied from a paucity of material. It also underscores the rise of Stalin as a permanent factor in the shaping of Soviet politics and his ascendancy as the indispensable premise for everything that followed. As indicated in the last chapters of this book, I regard his influence as a continuing one even in today's Soviet Union. I hope this will excuse my devoting slightly less than one-half of this study to isolation of the basic patterns of Soviet succession that emerged under Stalin and the remainder to a discussion of the continuity of these patterns in subsequent factional struggles.

In this I have been guided by numerous historical studies of Soviet Russia and Communism and works of Western Kremlinology, many (but unfortunately not all) of which are referred to in the footnotes. Despite the just homage due these works, however, I intend here more than a critique and synthesis. A number of interesting sources, unused even by recent scholars, are now available to alter our understanding of many facts of Soviet succession as well as the positions of its participants and chroniclers. Among them is the former 'Closed Section' of the Trotsky Archive, open to researchers since 1980. I have used these and other materials to reorder some of the facts of the case but as a rule not to establish special legitimacy for any of the historical actors, least of all to depict any of them as the true heir of Lenin or the repository of Bolshevik continuity. I count it as unexceptional that one who attempts to understand Soviet thinking does so from the standpoint of 'Western biases,' but I would not like this work to be thought of as an application of any a priori notions, or as anything but an empirical examination. The conclusions are not those of any school of thought, and if I end by defending Kremlinology, this is not because I hold it to be wed to any particular approach to the study of Soviet reality.

I have discerned a pattern of alternance of party programs which I describe in terms of a Moscow line and a Leningrad line. Aside from making more explicit the periodization of Soviet history, alternance may also suggest evidence for pluralism in the institutional structure. But trying to conceptualize Soviet politics by analogy with parliamentary notions of program and constituency can be cruelly disappointing. Individuals change programs with disturbing ease, and the victory of a program often coincides with the political defeat of the leader associated with its advocacy. This prompts the conclusion that alternance is a useful idea only alongside a recognition of the power of the center in Soviet politics. The capacity to execute turns from one line to its opposite, in a Lenin, a Stalin, or a Suslov, indicates true mastery in this system.

As alternance suggests pluralism, moreover, centrism would seem to deny it. Yet Lenin, Stalin, and Suslov managed very different regimes, a fact that confounds our attempts to identify a single continuous technique of holding personal power.[2] Instead of producing a timeless model, then, I have had to be content to trace patterns of change connecting unique historical situations. This study, therefore, cannot pretend to solve all the riddles of Soviet succession, or to pronounce finally on the historiosophical problems of the Russian Question. I hope, however, that an examination of alternance may contribute something to the demystification of the struggle for power and at least clarify some of its mechanics.

Acknowledgments

IT IS A PLEASURE to acknowledge my debt to many who helped in this enterprise. Robert Conquest lent advice and invaluable encouragement at various stages in the process. Mikhail Agursky, Jerald A. Combs, Robert McNeal, and Pedro Ramet all read the entire manuscript, providing many helpful suggestions and making it less clumsy. A number of others read various chapters or drafts of material incorporated into the manuscript, furnishing useful comments. In particular, I wish to thank Robert Alexander, Gordon A. Craig, John Patrick Diggins, Leopold Labedz, George Lerski, Anne Morgan, and Moses Rischin. Jean Van Heijenoort and Ella Wolfe gave me the benefit of their recollections on many points concerning the Stalin era. My students stimulated my efforts by disputing on numerous matters, for which I am grateful. Also, I should acknowledge three of my teachers who first excited my interest in topics central to the theme of this book: the late Raymond J. Sontag for the international relations of the interwar period, Hans Rogger for Russian national consciousness, and Robert Wohl for the problems of the early Comintern. To all of the above I am greatly obliged. Errors and other shortcomings in what follows are, of course, my own.

The National Endowment for the Humanities supported the project with a summer research grant. The U.S. State Department provided a Title VIII Soviet and East European Studies Research Fellowship that permitted me to spend six months as visiting scholar at the Hoover Institution during the academic year, 1986–1987. I must thank its Associate Director, John B. Dunlop, for making that period stimulating and enjoyable. Generous support for the completion of the manuscript was given by San Francisco State University.

The staffs of several research institutions helped locate documents and in general eased burdens. They include Michel Dreyfus of the Bibliothèque de Documentation Internationale Contemporaine at Nanterre, Melanie Wisner of the Houghton Library at Harvard, Jacqueline Pluet of the Maison des Sciences de L'Homme in Paris, Giuseppe Del Bo of the Fondazione Feltrinelli in Milan, L. J. Van Rossum and Marie Huninck of the International Institute for Social History in Amsterdam, Keith Bush of Radio Liberty Research in Munich, Hilja Kukk and Linda Wheeler of the

Hoover Library, Elena Danielson of the Hoover Archives, and the staffs of the British Museum, New York Public Library, and the Bibliothèque Nationale. I am grateful to the Houghton Library at Harvard University for permission to quote from the Trotsky and Trotsky Exile Archives.

I have had the benefit of an understanding and patient editor in Lisa Freeman-Miller, and much assistance in word processing from Helen Friedman.

Finally, my most pleasant acknowledgment: Thanks to my daughter Martine for occasionally roller-skating by my desk, engaging in hysterical games of three-minute chess, and in general providing me with much-needed distraction and delightful torments.

1

Forging the Stalin-Trotsky Myth: Trotsky's Controversy with Boris Souvarine, 1929

'What is Truth?' said jesting Pilate, and did not wait for an answer.
—Francis Bacon

BEFORE THE Second World War, the subject of Soviet succession—that is, the Lenin succession—had not yet aroused great interest in the West. This was not, however, the case with other features of Soviet reality. A historical literature on the revolution and civil war began to appear during the regime's first decade. The memoirs of various pre-revolutionary figures and leading politicians of the Provisional Government of 1917 became available, as did reminiscences of diplomats and other individuals who had come into contact with the Soviet regime. The anarchists Alexander Berkman and Emma Goldman recorded their disillusionment with Bolshevism. Certain Western journalists, such as Michael Farbman of the *Observer* in Great Britain and Louis Fischer of *The Nation* in the United States informed their readers about important aspects of Soviet government policies. Yet analysis of the workings of Soviet factional politics remained the province of those émigrés who had personal knowledge of Russian communism and the activities of its leaders. The Russian Mensheviks maintained a journal, *Socialisticheskii vestnik* (*Socialist Courier*), that tried to keep abreast of Soviet politics, as did the anarchist *Delo truda* (*The Cause of Labor*). There were other occasional revelations. The American journalist and radical Max Eastman brought news of a Lenin Testament in 1925, a document said to contain strictures by the founder of Bolshevism against Stalin. And Stalin's personal secretary, Boris Bazhanov, slipped out of the Soviet Union in 1928 to give testimony about some episodes of the inner life of the Bolshevik Politburo.

This was not enough, however, to counter Western impressions created by the official Soviet version of Stalin's succession. Early accounts of Soviet communism accepted, on the whole, Stalin's claim as the rightful

1

heir to the mantle of Lenin.[1] They saw Stalin's victory as mainly a triumph over one principal opponent, Trotsky, in a conflict symbolized by competing slogans 'Socialism in One Country' and 'Permanent Revolution.' More will be said in the following chapters about the polemics in which these two ideas were explicated and criticized. Western readers generally understood Permanent Revolution to entail efforts by communists 'to overthrow the existing cosmos,' as one British parliamentarian put it. Socialism in One Country was contrasted as an implied renunciation of international communism in favor of efforts to meet Soviet domestic needs. There was widespread agreement with Louis Fischer's view that, because of its triumph, 'instead of concentrating energies on the overthrow of world capitalism, the Bolsheviks were bent on making good themselves.'[2] The suggestion was that peaceful coexistence, impossible in the past, could now be arranged between Russia and the West. Stalin did not at all mind having himself understood in this way in the West, but within the party he bitterly denounced the intimation that any backward step had been taken from revolutionary internationalism.[3]

Trotsky, for different reasons, would also permit the Lenin succession to be understood as a matter of Socialism in One Country versus Permanent Revolution. He wanted foreign Communists to believe that his expulsion from the Soviet leadership marked the liquidation of the revolution's international message for the sake of an insular national communism. Many serious and casual students of Soviet politics have generally accepted his interpretation down to the present time. There has been a temptation to see Stalin and Trotsky as unwitting agents of greater forces, subordinate to a higher law laid down by previous revolutions, according to which the original revolutionary spirit must inevitably give way to a more realistic consolidating influence that takes control of affairs and ruthlessly liquidates the more radical elements, amid cries that it has 'betrayed the revolution.' This view compares Trotskyists in Russia with the most radical parties in previous revolutions:

> The revolution stirs the people's dormant longings for equality. The most critical moment in its development is that at which the leaders feel they cannot satisfy this longing and proceed to quell it. They get on with the job which some of their opponents call the betrayal of the revolution. But their conscience is so uneasy and their nerves are so strained by the ambiguity of their role that the worst outbursts of their temper are directed against the victims of that 'betrayal.' Hence the extraordinary vehemence with which a Cromwell, a Robespierre, or a Stalin, each hit out at the levellers of his time.[4]

Trotsky and Stalin have normally been seen to personify revolutionary maximalism and revolutionary consolidation, respectively. But this interpretation has never fit the facts. The true representatives of Russian

maximalism, if by this term one understands the grandest hopes sum-
moned up by the revolution, were to the left of the Bolshevik party. The
symbolic heirs of the Levellers of the seventeenth century English Civil
War, who preached democracy, or of anarchists such as Gerrard Winstan-
ley, or of the Enragés and Hébertists of the French Revolution, who
preached 'socialism' and occasionally anarchism, these all ran afoul of
Bolshevism shortly after the October Revolution. The Russian
maximalism of 1917 had envisioned a society run by factory committees,
soviets, free communes, and the like, but not by a Bolshevik one-party
state. Trotsky had seemed to some anarchists and other radicals at the time
the best of the Bolsheviks to represent these moods, because of his
experience with the St. Petersburg Soviet of 1905. In power, however, he
quickly moved to sublimate these forces in the building of a powerful
state, abandoning maximalism for *étatisme*. Those who continued, after
1917, to struggle for the continuance of the maximalist spirit—the left
Socialist Revolutionaries, the anarchists, and the Kronstadt sailors who
rose in mutiny in the name of a Third Revolution in 1921—all came to feel
Trotsky's wrath.

Nevertheless, the Stalin-Trotsky myth has lived on even in the best and
most detailed historical accounts.[5] Stalin and his theory have been thought
to have transformed the Soviet Union 'from the epicenter of world
revolution to just another big power.'[6] However, in the course of relating
the Stalin-Trotsky fight, these accounts usually take note of various
discrepancies and loose ends in their narrative of shifting factional align-
ments. They mark well the occasions when Trotsky inexplicably fails to
give battle and Stalin gains a march without resistance. Why does not
Trotsky oppose Stalin, with all of Lenin's authority behind him, at the
Twelfth Party Congress in 1923? Why does Trotsky stir up controversy
with his *Lessons of October* in 1924? Why does Trotsky not come to the aid
of Zinoviev in the latter's fight with Stalin at the Fourteenth Congress in
1925? What constitutional weakness or chronic political ineptitude
explains these colossal failures of nerve? On the other hand, would we
have less to explain if we simply ceased to assume that Trotsky was in
opposition? Histories of science tell us that an existing explanation of a
natural phenomenon is usually not discarded even when multifold discrepancies appear, or even when it is widely criticized by dissatisfied
practitioners. This, it is said, is because the prevailing theory retains the
ability, despite its complication and many qualifications, to 'save the
appearances,' that is, to explain the phenomena, no matter how tortu-
ously. One can say this about the concept of the Stalin-Trotsky rivalry and
the rise of national communism. Hence the ongoing effort by various
scholars to revise this interpretation and to develop one with greater
economy.

One result has been renewed interest in the figure of Nikolai Bukharin, proponent of a fully developed notion of Socialism in One Country and, it has been argued with force, the genuine continuator of Leninist ideas about Soviet economic development. The point at which these ideas were discarded, the plunge into agricultural collectivization and the Five Year Plan in 1928–1929, is said to mark the divide between Leninism and Stalinism.[7] Another valuable suggestion is that the whole idea of Permanent Revolution be discarded in discussions of Trotsky's role. The locus of Trotsky's presumed programmatic opposition to Socialism in One Country is thus shifted from world revolution to the world economy. Trotsky is said to have fought Stalin not because he wanted to set the world aflame but because of his resistance to Stalin's neomercantilist schemes for a 'closed' economic system. Trotsky's position of principle is described as one on behalf of Soviet integration into the existing international market.[8]

Dissatisfaction with the traditional interpretation has helped illuminate various areas in the landscape of the Lenin succession. The intriguing question is: What happens when we abandon entirely the Stalin-Trotsky struggle or the antagonism between Permanent Revolution and Socialism in One Country as presumed keys to understanding the events of the 1920s? Does this not make possible a reordering of the events wherein the exceptions to the traditional line can be integral parts of a different one? In fact, what proved to be the decisive blow against Trotsky was delivered before Socialism in One Country had appeared. It was not Stalin but Grigorii Zinoviev, head of the party in Leningrad and president of the Communist International, who set against Permanent Revolution the 'Leninist' idea of the Revolutionary Democratic Dictatorship of the Proletariat and the Peasantry and the related notion that Trotskyism was 'hostile to the peasant.' This innovation created the polarity of 'Marxism-Leninism' and 'Trotskyism.' Socialism in One Country was a further subdivision of the Leninist heritage among the beneficiaries of the conquest of Trotsky. It was ostensibly aimed at Trotsky but actually provided a means of splitting with Zinoviev. Trotsky did not criticize Socialism in One Country, least of all with the heresy of Permanent Revolution. Once the Zinoviev faction was defeated with, as will be shown, arguments from Trotsky's arsenal, Trotsky made another attempt at reintegration into the Bukharin-Stalin bloc. When that failed, he joined Zinoviev to attack Socialism in One Country in the name of . . . the Democratic Dictatorship of the Proletariat and the Peasantry.[9]

The closest thing to a consistent opponent of Socialism in One Country, although he was rarely consistent in anything, was Zinoviev. In opposition in 1925–1927, he sketched the outlines of what is called in this study the Leningrad line. It combined stout assertion of revolutionary internationalism, calls for campaigns to coordinate agriculture into a general plan of quickened growth in industry, and, as it would develop later, a foreign policy emphasizing a confluence with German nationalism. After

Zinoviev was finished politically, the line reappeared with Molotov and Zhdanov in the thirties, with Zhdanov in the forties, and echoes of it were to be found in the views of Kozlov and Romanov after that. Zinoviev was thus the founder of a major policy line toward which the party periodically turned. In respect of this, and of his other contributions to the intellectual formation of the post-Lenin regime, Zinoviev has not had his proper share of recognition.

He also adumbrated what is called here the Moscow line, in his solicitude for the peasant, presumably underestimated by Trotskyism. Bukharin took up this theme, added to its neopopulism assurances that the state machine would be guaranteed its routine and its security from top-down rationalization campaigns, and suggested a foreign policy looking primarily to Western moral support, in the twenties from the British left, in the thirties from the French. Again, with the corresponding alterations, Bukharin's heirs were Malenkov and Kosygin.

The story has been told as a Stalin-Trotsky fight because Stalin and Trotsky wished it to be, but also because in the West we have assumed in Soviet politics too great an identity of men and programs. We are too much influenced by parliamentary models of responsibility wherein a leader whose program is defeated is expected to resign and those who wish to live on by changing their political clothes, as Ramsay MacDonald did in 1931, are exceptional. Bolshevism, especially as practiced by Lenin himself, was not at all like that. As he understood it, dialectic forbade the fetishizing of programs, which would have to be adopted and discarded in a timely fashion in order for the party, and often the party leaders, to be able to navigate hostile seas. I have devoted some attention in Chapters 2 and 3 to 'How Lenin Fought,' in order to illustrate the circumstances of Lenin's last turns. The most successful Soviet leaders have not been those who staked all on the justice of their factional 'cause,' but centrists, as Lenin and Stalin were and as Trotsky sought to be.

It is a peculiarity of Bolshevism that struggles over practical matters of policy (and over personal precedence) are conducted in a highly theoretical and Marxist form of discourse. Moreover, this is not entirely empty ritual. No leader can be really successful in gathering support unless he is perceived to be on an orthodox path. This is often overlooked in suggesting, as is sometimes done, that Stalin's victory was exclusively a victory of bureaucratic wire-pulling, accomplished while his foolish rivals wasted their energy on abstract disputes. This idea produces the triumph of the truly twentieth century man, the administrator, over the intellectual in politics. A 'patronage thesis' goes hand in hand with related notions of Stalin's indifference to the revolutionary cause. The chapters devoted to the Lenin succession take note of the way patronage gains were accumulated, but they seek to demonstrate how each conquest in the field of organization was preceded or bolstered by a conquest in the realm of ideas.

One of Stalin's crucial victories, for example, the Lenin Levy of 1924, which permitted him to appoint more than two hundred thousand new party members, was made possible by the campaign for 'Bolshevization' that came out of the dispute over the question of whether the events of 1917 are best explained by the Democratic Dictatorship of the Proletariat and the Peasantry or the Permanent Revolution.

This study seeks to tell 'how it happened' but also 'how it was told.' Alongside the exposition of the Lenin succession, which occupies the first five chapters, the reader can also follow a trail through the labyrinth of Trotsky's and Souvarine's various explanations. We begin with these in their most distorted form, in the debate between the two in 1929, not to confront the reader with a parody of *Roshoman* but to unravel two distinct but related myths: that of the Left Opposition's continuous struggle against the conservative Stalin and that of the golden age of pre-Stalin communism. By examining the stories of the two Stalin biographers as if they were characters in a detective novel, it may be possible to solve not only some riddles of succession but some riddles of sovietology as well.

Brandler and Zinoviev

The expulsion of Trotsky from Soviet soil, just as the Stalin regime was embarking on agricultural collectivization and the Five Year Plan, meant that the West could now consider the testimony of one of the leading figures of the revolution and the Communist leadership. This testimony would produce a counterweight to the views of Soviet life held by the most influential Western writers. His vantage point was extraordinary, certainly, but Trotsky also brought with him a prodigious literary energy, as great as any figure in this century, and a burning zeal to tell his side of the story. From 1929 until his assassination in 1940, he would produce an autobiography, a history of the revolution, several extended analyses of the fate of the revolution, and countless political tracts, circulars, bulletins and other communications to his disciples and followers. Trotsky was not merely a charismatic politician but a stern debater and tireless polemicist. He had the additional advantage of knowing more than most about the facts of the case, since he brought with him the vast collection of documents today known as the Trotsky Archive and housed at Harvard University. Trotsky wanted to argue his interpretation of Stalin as the usurper of the Lenin legacy wherever he found a forum. It was a detailed and formidable case. Moreover, despite the fact that he eventually failed in his efforts to extend the revolution westward and to overthrow Stalin, his interpretation of the Lenin succession appears, in its essentials, to have stuck. Even among those who considered his defeat by Stalin inevitable, or even fortunate, his discription of events has always had influence.

At the moment of his expulsion, when he was settling down for what was to be a four-year sojourn at Prinkipo Island, off the Turkish coast, and before his line on the succession had had enough time to congeal, he entered a discussion with Boris Souvarine. It is of interest for two reasons: first, because Trotsky's viewpoint did not enjoy at that time the chronological refinements and adjustments that it would acquire as his political position in the Soviet Union deteriorated. To be sure, he was hardly regarded with favor in Russia, but this was years before he would be described as the arch-fiend who masterminded the immense plot outlined in the Moscow trials of 1936–1938. Many of his opponents considered him a political rather than a criminal problem. Later they would be told that he plotted with fascist intelligence services to assassinate the Soviet leaders, sabotage industrial work, and enhance cattle mortality in western Siberia. But in 1929 Trotsky could still hope for a groundswell of opinion urging reconsideration of his case, especially if the policies of the present leaders foundered, as he was sure they would. While Trotsky hoped for this revival of his fortunes, he used restraint in interpreting Soviet politics. As the hope faded, his analysis would become less inhibited. The changes that Trotsky would make in his interpretation will help us to piece together a more accurate picture.

Second, his opponent was a figure of great importance in the history of French communism and at that time possibly the closest student of Soviet politics outside Russia. Souvarine had followed the succession struggle in his own articles for his periodical, *Bulletin communiste*. These would serve as the basis for his book *Staline*, which appeared in 1935 and has been widely regarded as the first serious work of biography on the dictator. Trotsky, despite his contempt for Souvarine's political views, may have been influenced by *Staline* in the writing of his own Stalin biography. His widow later recalled that he often consulted Souvarine's book, scribbling in great irritation his comments in the margins, while frequently noting that it was 'remarkably well researched.'[10] As with Trotsky, the changes in Souvarine's different accounts will be of interest. In the controversy of 1929 may be found suggestions of a clearer understanding of the Lenin succession in particular and Soviet succession in general.

Despite its other indignities, Trotsky's expulsion from the Soviet Union in February 1929 was a kind of literary liberation, which at least afforded an opportunity to tell his side of the story of Stalin's rise and his own defeat. He had already finished a series of short articles for Western newspapers, published in ensemble as *Chto i kak proizoshlo?* (*What Happened and How?*); by summer he would complete his autobiography and preside over the establishment of the *Biulleten oppozitsii* (*Bulletin of the Opposition*) and the French weekly *La Vérité*. In these writings he wanted to establish that he and a 'Left Opposition' had fought consistently since 1923 against the rise of a 'Thermidorean bureaucracy' led, only incidentally, as Trotsky had it, by Stalin. He called the bureaucracy 'Thermidorean' by analogy with the fall of Robespierre on 9 Thermidor (July 27) 1794, an event which marked a turning back from the most radical phase of the French Revolution. He wanted to show that he did not center his protest on the rise of tyranny in Russia but on its moderate and rightward policy drift. From his writings would emerge a version of the myth of the Stalin-Trotsky struggle, which animated his followers and sympathizers and contributed to an influential interpretation of the fate of the Russian Revolution.

The mystery was that there was no cohort of 'Trotskyists' or Communists who had stood with him in struggle against the Thermidorean tendencies in the Communist International. This was odd in view of the fact that the struggle was supposed to have been waged on behalf of internationalism against the national narrowness of Socialism in One Country. There were some who, while they did not call themselves Trotskyists, nevertheless viewed his plight with considerable sympathy. Even they, however, did not understand the issues of the succession struggle as did Trotsky, and had very different ideas about its 'lessons.' Virtually the first of them to challenge Trotsky was Souvarine. Their controversy, unfolding in the spring and summer, thus raised many questions that Trotsky never succeeded in answering about the international message of the Russian opposition and the internal contradictions of his version of communism.

Souvarine had been a major figure in French communism and a courageous defender of Trotsky. Born Boris Lifschitz in Kiev in 1893, he had emigrated to France to be naturalized in 1906. A Socialist during the war years, he had originally been a supporter of the center of the party led by Marx's nephew Jean Longuet. In the early days of the Communist International, Lenin and Trotsky had hoped to form Communist parties by splitting off the left wing of the Socialist parties. The rest of these parties they regarded with less sympathy than syndicalists and anarchists, who, they judged, might be worse Marxists but better revolutionaries. They viewed French syndicalism with particular interest. Syndicalists had preached antiparliamentarism and direct action by means of economic strikes, to culminate in the general strike. Their ideas had caught hold in the French trade unions when anarchists had introduced them in the 1890s, and syndicalism would be powerful down to the Popular Front era of the late 1930s, when it yielded much of its influence to the Communists.[11] Souvarine had accepted the argument about the continuity from syndicalist antiparliamentarism to Bolshevism, and had helped form the Parti Communiste Français (PCF). In its first years, Souvarine was an influential liaison with Moscow and editor of the PCF's theoretical review, *Bulletin communiste*.

He had been expelled from the PCF for 'Trotskyism' (an idea that mystified him) in the course of the 'Bolshevization' campaign that shook the entire Comintern in 1924. He had not, however, been expelled by Stalin, nor was he a victim of Socialism in One Country, a theory which did not make an appearance until the beginning of 1925. Souvarine's tormentor had been Grigorii Zinoviev, president of the Comintern and head of the Leningrad party apparatus. Souvarine could testify that Zinoviev, not Stalin, created the official doctrine, 'Leninism,' and the official heresy, 'Trotskyism,' acts which Souvarine judged to have destroyed the Communist International's independence and viability. Far from fearing the rise of Stalin, Souvarine had welcomed the duumvirate of Stalin and Nikolai Bukharin in 1925 as welcome relief from the scourge of Zinovievism. Outside the party, he retained *Bulletin communiste* as the organ of his own literary group, the Cercle Marx-Lénine.

By 1929, Souvarine's group stood among those of several other expelled French oppositionists. These included Souvarine's old comrades Alfred Rosmer and Pierre Monatte, working with the 'syndicalist-communist' *Révolution prolétarienne* and the group around Pierre Naville and Gérard Rosenthal, who had published the colorful surrealist review *Clarté*. The Russian oppositionist Piatakov had tried to unite these into one group in 1926, but Souvarine and the others gagged at the idea of joining with the Zinovievists as Trotsky, to their disgust, had done. Monatte and Rosmer joined the *Révolution prolétarienne* group and returned to syndicalism. Eventually there emerged a theoretical journal *Contre la courant*, directed by Maurice Paz, and the transformation of *Clarté* into *La Lutte des classes*, another theoretical review. Paz, Rosmer, Naville, Rosenthal, and numerous others made pilgrimages to Prinkipo in 1929, where Trotsky worked to fuse them into the staff of the weekly *La Vérité*.[12] He even attempted, later successfully at least for a time, to include Albert Treint, who had engineered the expulsion of most of the others. Himself out in the cold after the fall of Zinoviev in Russia, Treint had published *L'Unité léniniste* before attempting unsuccessfully to reintegrate with the Stalinists in 1928.

Trotsky wanted all of them to form a united Left Opposition. 'We are headed for such difficult times,' he warned, 'that every co-thinker, every *potential* co-thinker, is precious to me.'[13] This would not be a period of mass actions, during which disagreements tend to disappear, but one of 'ideological demarcation,' with 'differentiation, splits and internal struggles.' For Trotsky, this meant a fierce fight against 'centrism,' in which three issues were paramount: insufficient support by Stalin and Bukharin to the British Communists during the British General Strike of 1926, the disaster suffered by the Chinese Communists at the hands of the Nationalist Kuomintang in 1927, and the too-moderate economic policy of Stalin-Bukharin up to 1928—all this 'in conjunction' with the theory of Socialism in One Country. These were 'decisive criteria.'

Trotsky deliberately omitted what he called the 'Regime Question.'

Complaints about the character of the Soviet party regime and the oppressive features of the bureaucracy were not, in his view, exclusive to Bolshevism, and would not distinguish oppositionists from Mensheviks and liberals. Moreover, his arrangement and demarcation of the issues expressed a continuity with his struggle of 1926–1927, in league with Zinoviev against Stalin and Bukharin, casting maximum fire on the Bukharinists and distinguishing their tendency from that of the Stalin center. Despite his own expulsion from the party at the end of 1927, Trotsky was encouraged by Stalin's break with Bukharin and the beginnings of agricultural collectivization. Even while Bukharin was fighting for his political life against Stalin, Trotsky maintained the primacy of the 'Right Danger' posed by the Thermidorean Bukharinists. They might yet turn the tables on Stalin, he warned, and 'hunt down Stalin as a Trotskyist, just as Stalin has hunted down Zinoviev.'[14]

Trotsky was claiming paternity for Stalin's radical agricultural policy. By August, he would use this as justification for supporting the surrender to Stalin of his closest associate, Christian Rakovskii, which he must have hoped would open the way for his own return.[15] Only with the failure of the 'Rakovskii capitulation' did he shift the tone of his polemics to emphasize the chaos and bureaucratic arbitrariness of Stalin's policy. For the moment, however, the main attack was directed against the right and its international supporters, in Italy the Tasca group, in the United States that of Lovestone, and in Germany that of Brandler and Thalheimer.

Souvarine had a special interest in the German right oppositionists. The fall of Brandler-Thalheimer in 1924 had coincided with his own fall; the group around Albert Treint and Suzanne Girault in the French party had driven him off as part of the same campaign in which Arkadi Maslow and Ruth Fischer had ruined the Brandlerites in Germany. Behind all the 'Bolshevizers' of 1924 had stood Zinoviev, Trotsky's *ally* of 1926–1927. By the time Trotsky had been expelled from the Soviet party, Souvarine maintained, all life had long since been squeezed out of the International. Thus for him international communism had been ruined by the Zinovievists whom Trotsky was now urging serious efforts to win. And to attack the right was inevitably to perpetuate the myth of Brandler's 'treachery' at the time of the German Communists' bid for power in 1923.

That was precisely Trotsky's position. At Prinkipo, in the summer, he told Rosenthal:

> In 1923, chances of a victorious revolution were offered more strongly than ever in Germany. The [French] occupation of the Ruhr disorganized the bourgeoisie and the state. The mark fell daily at a more fantastic rate. Unemployment ravaged the proletariat and ruin seized the *petite bourgeoisie*. The Communist Party was more powerful and more active than it had ever been. Strikes became more and more

general. Then the leader of the German party, instead of guiding and leading the class toward insurrection, organized a conference of factory delegates at Chemnitz and awaited its decision. . . . The hour of victorious revolution passed. . . . Men like Brandler have no place at the head of a Communist organization. With the Brandlers, there will never be a revolution.[16]

Brandler 'neither saw nor knew how to exploit a revolutionary situation,' wrote Trotsky to Souvarine in April. In 1924, he continued, when the opportunity had already been lost, Brandler had still thought a revolution possible. In 1925, he had turned to the right and accused Trotsky of overestimating the chances for revolution. From 1925 to 1927, said Trotsky, he had echoed the line of Stalin and Bukharin. This included supporting Stalin and Bukharin on economic policy, China, and the British General Strike, and failing to criticize Socialism in One Country.[17]

Souvarine could not fathom the campaign against Brandler. He reminded Trotsky that the latter had shielded Brandler and Thalheimer from Zinoviev's wrath immediately after the failure in 1923. Trotsky, however, claimed that he had intended only to show 'that it would be inadmissible to make them scapegoats for 1923, while the real responsibility for the German catastrophe fell entirely on the Zinoviev-Stalin leadership.'[18] Souvarine disavowed any intention to defend Brandler's actions in 1923, nor even his positions on China and Britain, but insisted that the 'Thermidorean character and arbitrary methods of the struggle against "Trotskyism" from 1923 to 1927' formed the essential context of this debate and that Zinoviev must be seen as the culprit. Trotsky could not see any profit in that analysis, preferring to concentrate on the failure of the German revolution in 1923: 'This catastrophe forms the basis of all the leaps of German communism to right and left. It constitutes the political premise of the period of stabilization of European capitalism which followed.'[19] As for Brandler and Thalheimer, they were the equivalent of 'Menshevik liquidators' who were even at present supporting Bukharin against Stalin. The question of the 'regime' of the Zinovievists-Treintists-Ruthists in the International must not be mixed up with the question of Thermidor: 'The problem of Thermidor and Bonapartism is in essence the problem of the *kulak*. Whoever turns from this to the problems of bureaucracy is blind.'

The Regime Question or the Russian Question?

The arrangement of the issues offers a glimpse into the political mind of Trotsky at work. This was not for him a discussion among historians designed to clear accounts and put the decade into perspective. It was a political struggle in support of the left line of the moment, Stalin's line, for which every intellectual resource might be mobilized, giving the crucial emphasis to the arguments that fortified the political line and leaving the grander perspectives to sticklers for 'formal' truth such as Souvarine. The point was that concentrating on the Regime Question would have suggested a bloc with Bukharin against Stalin; emphasis on other issues could support a bloc with Stalin against Bukharin.

Both Trotsky and Souvarine had been converts to Bolshevism, and both had been victimized in 1924–1925 by a newly discovered creed of 'Leninism,' also by turns called 'Integral Leninism,' 'One Hundred Percent Leninism,' or 'Marxism-Leninism.' Largely the creature of Zinoviev's fevered imagination, it was designed to contrast with the 'Trotskyism' of the founder of the Red Army, or with that of Souvarine, or Brandler. Trotsky had never defended 'Trotskyism' and swore by 'Leninism,' but Souvarine felt differently. Now he responded to Trotsky's demands with a book-length epistle rejecting the latter's 'decisive criteria.' These were 'secondary questions of strategy and tactics.' By contrast, the actions of the 'Leninists,' he charged, 'represent a break with the inspiring and directing principles of our movement up to 1923.'[20] Trotsky was correct, he wrote, to have accused the Comintern of comprehending too late 'the reestablishment of a capitalist equilibrium, the American hegemony, fascism, the consequences of the Ruhr occupation, the Dawes Plan, and the new stage of the Chinese Revolution.' From that point on, 'everything happened without us,' because the Soviet leadership marched under the banner of the Soviet 'neo-communism of 1924.'[21] Bolshevism itself had originated, said Souvarine, as a 'simplification of Marxism to the usage of a poor country.' In the process, Western Marxism had been impoverished. Soviet 'State Bolshevism,' which regarded among its tasks the need to submit all of society to ideological dictatorship, had reduced Marxism to the status of myth. And the 'Trotskyism' that was now taking shape at the urging of Trotsky himself, in calling itself 'Bolshevik-Leninism,' became thereby the international apostle of this mysticism of a peasant country.[22]

The idea that 'left' communism was the real Leninism was the special myth of the Trotskyists, said Souvarine. Marxism had not always been to the left of its opponents. By comparison with the Blanquists and *carbonari* of 1848, Marx and Engels themselves had been on the right. Ferdinand Lassalle, the German trade union leader of the early 1860s and an opponent of Marx, had also appeared the more radical, with his talk of opposing the working class to the rest of society ('one reactionary mass'). In the days of the First International, Marx had been to the right of the anarchist Bakunin, and after 1905, Lenin had stood to the right of his own party. There was nothing magical about being on the left. Moreover, Trotsky's criticism of Soviet policies toward the English trade unions showed he knew nothing of the traditions of English socialism. English trade unionists who resisted transforming the 1926 General Strike into a revolutionary movement could not be accused of betraying a cause they had never embraced. Instead of hurling anathemas at them, one might better realize that Communists have never properly understood the aspirations of the non-Communist workers of the West, and as Karl Radek had once suggested, one should think instead of 'an honest united front on the basis of a minimum program.'[23] As for the Chinese revolution, 'I hesitate to offer opinions on the plane of the Chinese peasant, from the standpoint which has been so weak on the western worker.'

Blame for the corruption and degeneration of the Communist International could not be laid, said Souvarine, at the door of the Russian right. If, following Trotsky, one traced the process to origins in the German events of 1923, Brandler's 'betrayal' must be its source. But Brandler had enjoyed no independence at that time. He had been controlled entirely by the Comintern Executive, and finally by the Soviet Politburo. It was praiseworthy, Souvarine told Trotsky, that in 1924 'you resisted the tendency to blame Brandler.' From this it did not follow that there was cause to blame Brandler's failure on Zinoviev and Stalin. Radek, Trotsky's supporter in Soviet internal questions, had enjoyed the most authority in Comintern councils on German affairs. Stalin had counted for little, even less than the Poles. Between August and September 1923, the whole Politburo had imposed its authority on the Comintern Executive, and got general agreement. In Moscow in September, Brandler had been solidly 'left,' requesting that Trotsky himself be sent to Germany. Piatakov and Radek, who did go, had been agreed that the Chemnitz conference condemned the insurrection to defeat and that it was time to retreat. Only in January 1924 did Zinoviev discover that the whole fiasco had been the fault of Brandler. But if Trotsky were to blame all on Zinoviev, Souvarine continued, he had to find Brandler guilty as well. Brandler had certainly made mistakes, said Souvarine; certainly it was a mistake to have given so much ground to the Fischer-Maslow 'lefts' and to have permitted them to work uninterruptedly to undermine his position. But Trotsky's criticism *paralleled* that of the German lefts. Souvarine recalled that in the collection of *Pravda* essays appearing at the time of the Thirteenth Party Conference (January 1924), Trotsky had claimed that the German Communists' error had been their failure to make a 'sharp turn' toward a policy of insurrection between May and July, 1923. Radek, Trotsky's ally, had counseled moderation in that period. Then, in the *New Course*, in an essay written *after* the failure of the Communists' insurrection in October, Trotsky continued to foresee revolutionary chances in Germany.[24] 'Why refuse the excuse to Brandler?' asked Souvarine. He recalled that he and Rosmer had been alone in facing the wrath of the Zinovievists, who accused them of not 'believing' in the German revolution.

Attacks on the German lefts, argued Souvarine, had been conducted

exclusively with the Russian internal situation in mind. He recalled that
Molotov had accused Maslow of being in league with Miasnikov and the
'Workers' Group'—opponents of NEP expelled from the Russian party
after the Eleventh Party Congress of 1922—who had issued sympathetic
appeals to striking Soviet workers in the summer and fall of 1923. Molotov
had charged Maslow and Miasnikov with plotting to form a Fourth
International. Piatakov had proposed Maslow's arrest and had had to be
restrained by Radek and Souvarine himself. 'All this so that we would be
permitted to see Maslow and company recognized in 1924 as orthodox
Leninists by the Zinoviev-Stalin-Molotov leadership of the Russian party,
and as authentic Bolshevik-Leninists by the Trotsky-Zinoviev-Piatakov-
Radek leadership of the Opposition.' Trotsky proclaimed the 'betrayal' of
Brandler, Souvarine charged, in order to accommodate these German
lefts:

> Adventurers in 1922, splitters in 1923, Leninists in 1924, oppositionists
> in 1926, capitulationists in 1927–8, vulgar demagogues and dangerous
> bunglers always, Maslow and his consorts now have the confidence of
> the Russian Opposition insofar as they should desire it. By what right?
> Is it because they have caused the German party to lose two-thirds of its
> members, nullified its influence in the unions, turned two million
> electors away from Communism and succeeded in raising up Hinden-
> burg to the Presidency of the republic? Not to speak of their decisive role
> in the 'Bolshevization' that has bled our International white.[25]

Souvarine recognized only Trotsky's claims on the subject of Soviet
economic policy, and the fact that it was Trotsky's policy that was serving
as a point of departure for Stalin's current actions. Stalin had always
recognized Trotsky's ability and wanted him in the economic machinery.
'He opposed your exclusion from the party,' Souvarine told Trotsky, 'and
from all work in which you did not threaten his political hegemony, and
he sought to have you assume the highest responsibilities for economic
activities.'[26] Souvarine seemed to suggest that Trotsky's criticisms of
Soviet economic policy were the only aspects of the heritage of the Russian
Opposition worth salvaging. Here again Souvarine reproduced the position of the Brandler supporters: since the oppositionists no longer had
anything of value to say to the Western labor movement, Soviet economic
construction remained their sole contribution. For the whole international
movement, said Souvarine,

> There is nothing more important than the economic success of the
> Soviet State, whose state capitalism signifies the first attempt to organize
> production without private appropriation; this state capitalism is not
> socialism, but it represents an undeniable progress over capitalist
> imperialism, in its tendencies if not in its realization.[27]

Souvarine judged that Soviet economic development still held a claim on the loyalty of Western Marxists, who should remain its defenders. They could not do so as Communists, however. In the Communist parties, Souvarine concluded, there was 'no place for Marxists.'

Thus ended Souvarine's statement, an impressive bill of particulars, all the more imposing for being constructed, as Souvarine saw it, on the basis of the political practice of Bolshevism to 1923, by a loyal defender of Trotsky's role in the history of Bolshevism. It raised so many questions, however, that, had Trotsky attempted to answer them all, he could never have maintained the record of the Russian Opposition of 1926–1927 as the theoretical basis for an International Left Opposition. Now that the question of the degeneration of the Soviet regime had been raised, it became necessary to date the degeneration. Trotsky tried to have it both ways: the defeat of the Left Opposition of 1926–1927 was crucial insofar as it was a defeat of the only legitimate program, and yet the degeneration had its roots in the Thermidorean attacks on 'Trotskyism' since 1923. In that case, did the Opposition defend the 'Trotskyism' of 1923? Was it not Zinoviev, rather than Stalin, who had launched this 'counterrevolutionary' campaign, and was he not therefore the originator of the degeneration? In championing the record of the Opposition, was not Trotsky championing Zinoviev's record of opposition since 1925, rather than his own, more complex, record? Trotsky's response to these contradictions was characteristic. Without even seeming to be particularly disturbed, he wrote Souvarine to tell him how disappointed he had been by the latter's statement. Yours, he told Souvarine, is the pen of a *'journaliste mécontent.'* 'You treat the party of Lenin and the Communist International as a corpse.' This was really the most important thing from the standpoint of Trotsky's current plans. 'I have neither the possibility,' he continued, 'nor the desire to analyse the complicated chains of your paradoxes and sophisms. I will select only one case, but quite a sufficient one, as it involves a most important question.'[28] The question was 'state capitalism.'

Souvarine claimed that 'state capitalism' was the only progressive feature of Soviet reality that commanded the loyalty of the Western worker. 'This "state capitalism,"' argued Trotsky, 'lives and dies with the party. Moreover, the best proof of its life consists in the fact that the Soviet economy submits every day to the influence of the Opposition refracted and disfigured by the Stalinist apparatus.'[29] Trotsky's own position had been shown by Souvarine to entail a mass of contradictions, yet he was still able to strike at the central contradiction in Souvarine's position. As a Marxist, one could not speak of the proletariat in power without the idea of the party, and if there was still something healthy in the proletarian state, did that not mean that there was still life in the Communist party? And was that not the main premise of Trotsky's line of loyal opposition within the Comintern? To overcome this contradiction, Souvarine would have to abandon what he was later to call his 'naive fidelity to Marxism.' Trotsky did not seem to realize that this also implied an eventual contradiction in his own position on the same point, which he would not have to face until the advent of Nazism in 1933, when he proclaimed the death of the International, yet hesitated to proclaim the death of the Russian party.

This exchange seemed to puncture Trotsky's version of his struggle against the Soviet bureaucracy, but Souvarine was also propagating his own myth of the golden age of pre-1923 communism. Souvarine's complaints did not center on Stalin but on the role of the Zinovievists, Maslow and Fischer, Treint and Girault, in the degeneration of international communism. Souvarine was merely defending his own record and that of Brandler-Thalheimer from the Zinovievist charges that they had constituted an anti-Bolshevik 'right' in 1923. He guarded a kind of Bolshevik orthodoxy from which even one of its authors, Trotsky himself, had strayed. Souvarine thus attempted to save Trotsky from himself, and to preserve the heritage that he and Trotsky had in common from the years before 1923. Trotsky was interested only in asserting a line of continuity for the Opposition *since* 1923. He made his stand on the ground of the 'Integral Leninism' proclaimed by all of Lenin's successors in 1924, a Leninism which excluded 'Trotskyism' as a conservative strain within Communism up to 1926 and as a 'counterrevolutionary' idea after that date. Trotsky would not permit the debate to question the basis on which he and Souvarine had ever solidarized, nor would Souvarine have thought to do so. We shall have to look further into both men's claims.

Moreover, Trotsky avoided the troublesome problem of establishing the facts of the Lenin succession, a full account of which cannot be found in any one place in his voluminous writings, by raising what has been called the Russian Question: What is the nature of the Soviet state? The answer to this question determines one's loyalty, or lack thereof, to the Soviet state, so Trotsky, who remained loyal, was going to the heart of the matter. Yet the task of ascertaining the facts of Soviet succession has often been mixed up with the task of answering the Russian Question. As we shall see, these two tasks cannot be isolated from each other, and it is especially important that the student of Soviet succession avoid, as Trotsky failed to avoid, substituting one for the other.

2

How Lenin Fought: Problems of Original Communism, 1919–1921

The anarchists rightly pointed to the opportunist views on the state prevalent among most of the socialist parties.

—V. I. Lenin

Now I should like to ask what are the chosen organizations that are to reorganize the economic life of a society; some bourgeois elements that come together to form a party, who have no contact with economic life, or the elements that stand at the roots of production and consumption? Everybody must admit that only those organizations that stand in the closest contact with production are called upon to organize economic life and take it in hand. There can be no doubt—we see it in Russia too—that a gigantic role in economic life devolves upon the trade unions.

—Augustin Souchy

Industry is indispensable; democracy is a category proper only to the political sphere.

—V. I. Lenin

THOSE WHO FOUGHT for the mantle of Lenin knew that they could not accomplish their ends simply by marshaling votes behind closed doors. They needed to justify each of their actions with an ideological rationale which would be plausible, not only to the ranks of the Russian Communists but to the Communist International and its affiliated parties as well. This despite the fact that the Marxist training of the Bolsheviks was very different from that of foreign Communists. Men and women of Lenin's party considered themselves schooled in difficult faction struggles from the prerevolutionary years. Most of their comrades from the prewar Socialist movement regarded these as squabbles about which only

17

Russians could stir passion, but the Bolsheviks insisted that they were exercises in self-clarification which put their cause into sharper relief by means of Lenin's anathemas against Economism, Liquidationism, Recallism, Boycottism, God-Building, and other heresies. Foreign militants might regard the lessons as prosaic: Political ideas must be brought into the factories along with trade unionism; an illegal apparatus had been indispensable in Tsarist Russia; Bolsheviks must participate in almost every kind of parliament when necessary; no compromise was to be made with religious sentiment in peasant Russia. Yet these and many other major and minor disputes reassured the Bolsheviks, and Lenin himself, that their movement was principled in the theoretical sense—in fact, that their party was a vessel of theory.

Foreign Communists, however, had not rallied to the Comintern out of reverence for the ideological record of prewar Bolshevism, of which most knew little. Communists, they usually supposed, were those who had opposed the war and who now supported the Russian Revolution. Lenin went a step further by asserting that the revolution had an international message vindicating his party's struggle with the European Social Democracy. Russian Bolsheviks would have felt foolish claiming that the treason of the social patriots (invoking war credits for their governments) had been a bolt from the blue in August, 1914. Actually it was exactly that, but it seemed un-Marxist not to see deeper roots. No one could be sure what these were, but many hoped that all the various motives for criticizing the prewar Social Democracy from the left could be demonstrated as wholesome and as illustrating the need to 'rebuild' socialist continuity from Marx and Engels to Bolshevism.

Yet there was a disturbing anomaly. Prewar Bolshevism had not in fact opposed itself to the ideological mainstream of the Socialist International. The Bolsheviks had fought like demons with the Russian Mensheviks and with the opponents and critics of the Marxist orthodoxy preached by Karl Kautsky and August Bebel of the German party. And they had attempted, unconvincingly, to insist that their critics were somehow spiritually akin to Kautsky's, but never had Lenin fought against Kautsky, still less set himself up in opposition to the latter's 'opportunism,' as Soviet students are taught to this day. When in 1905 the liberal Peter Struve suggested differences between Lenin and Kautsky, Lenin responded by challenging Struve: 'When and where did I call "the revolutionism of Bebel and Kautsky" opportunism? When and where did I ever claim to have created any sort of special trend in international Social Democracy *not identical* with the trend of Bebel and Kautsky?'[1]

However, once in power, the Soviet leaders found it a psychological necessity to insist that they had always fought the opportunism of the Social Democrats. This they felt was even more required in Western Europe, where there were live Social Democratic parties, than in Soviet

Russia, where Menshevism was in eclipse. The idea of a universal message of the Russian Revolution led them to proclaim an imaginary continuity of their party's history. Foreign Communists found that it was not enough to solidarize with the Russian revolutionaries; one had to toe the line of 'Old Bolshevism.' By 1924, Lenin's followers took the next step by inventing 'Leninism,' presumably as legitimate heir to the traditions of Marx and Engels. Thus the post-Lenin leadership would be not only torn by bitter factional quarrels but also increasingly walled off from reality by their mythical constructions, which, they hoped, would establish revolutionary continuity and legitimacy. Candidates for power had to drape themselves in the garments of Leninism, which were only half finished. Popular Comintern leaders who thought themselves good Marxists found that they could not measure up as Bolsheviks, since the definition of Bolshevism seemed to change hourly with every shift of influence in the Soviet Politburo. Their prewar notions about Marxist ideas hardly seemed an adequate guide. As to the question of what genuinely revolutionary Bolshevism meant in terms of practice in their own countries, the real answer was: Whatever the men in the Kremlin said.

The contestants in Moscow, since they often grasped for Marxist things to say against their opponents, found that the mythical things said in Comintern disputes about the real meaning of Bolshevism often inspired their diatribes against one another. Since they insisted that theirs was an international movement, their relations were also affected by their opinions on Comintern questions. Each of them identified the cause of the revolution with his own cause; hence the obligation to fight to win. In this sense, it would be impossible to separate programmatic differences from personal ones. Furthermore, even while wandering in an ideological void, they had to face real problems and offer practical policies to solve them.

The core of their dilemma lay in the odd duality of ruling backward Russia while attempting to spread the revolution westward into more industrially advanced countries. They had won power by marching together with anarchists, syndicalists, and other radicals who wanted 'workers' control' of production and the abolition of the state. Experience in Russia showed that this sort of person would have to be won over in Western countries and that he, rather than the established leaders of Socialist parties, would be more likely to make a good Communist. In Russia, however, they were fighting hard to extinguish the radicalism of 1917, hiring bourgeois specialists to officer their army and to direct, through 'one-man management,' their industry. They were tightening discipline in the world of work and building the apparatus of a powerful state. Trotsky, who headed the Red Army during a time of vicious civil war, spared no effort to crush any who, in the name of the ideas of 1917, faltered before the task at hand.

Souvarine, however, was not in the same position. Hoping to build a

Communist movement in the West, he had to pay court to syndicalists and other extreme lefts and to justify before them Trotsky's and Bolshevism's ruthless suppression of their co-thinkers in Russia. Although complaints about Trotsky's arbitrariness and high-handed measures would later become common coin, Communists in Russia and outside applauded and encouraged him while Red Russia fought for its life in the civil war of 1918–1920. Lenin urged Trotsky on more than anyone else. After the end of the fighting, however, the founder of Bolshevism reconsidered, and finally decided, during the Trade Union Debate of 1920–21 that Trotsky's power must be limited. At first Trotsky's most vigorous supporter, Lenin came to organize a coalition of those who would prove to be Trotsky's future opponents, including Zinoviev, Kamenev, and Stalin, against the organizer of the Red Army. Lenin's supporters watched carefully and took note of a Lenin that was not a myth: one who guarded his counsel, acted at a distance, intervened only at the last minute, and did not fear to occupy the center position, shifting his weight now to one side, now to another, for maximum effect. Lenin taught them how Bolsheviks fight.

The communism on which Souvarine and Trotsky based their political solidarity did not and could not exist before the war. Souvarine rallied to the cause of the Communist International only with its founding in 1919.[2] Unlike the men who became his closest associates, Souvarine had not attended the Zimmerwald conference of antiwar Socialists in 1915 from which dated the development of a Committee for the Resumption of International Relations, one of the early precursors of French communism. During his stay in Paris, in 1914–1916, Trotsky had worked with Martov publishing *Nashe slovo* (*Our Word*) alongside other Russian émigrés — Rakovskii, Lunacharskii, Manuilskii, Radek, Lozovskii, Balabanova, Kollontai, and others — who would become well-known Bolshevik leaders. His best French contacts were with Pierre Monatte, Alfred Rosmer, and the militants of the *Vie ouvrière* group, opposed to the war, critical of both the Majority Socialists (for their *jusqu'au boutisme*) and the Minority (to which Souvarine adhered). They were convinced that the way forward for the left would come, not from French socialism, but from the direct action tradition of revolutionary syndicalism.[3] The *Vie ouvrière* welcomed, but did not trust, the growing pacifist tendencies among the French Socialists. The roots of *Vie ouvrière* did not lie in the prewar Marxist Orthodoxy of Jules Guesde, or in the reform-oriented tradition of Jean Jaurès. Instead, it was expected that the forces which would revitalize the revolutionary movement would come from the national trade union federation, the CGT, and even from the anarchist militants who had provided much help in organizing it. Rosmer recalled that, while Socialists had not been prepared for the outbreak of war, certain libertarians and syndicalists had read the warning signs. He pointed to Alfonse Merrheim's

L'Approche de la guerre (1911), with its description of the Anglo–German naval rivalry, and Domela Niewenhuis's *La Guerre anglo-allemande vue de Holland* (July 1914). These 'prophetic' works were in contrast to the work of the Socialist parties, and even their developing left-wing elements. The *Labor Leader* of the British ILP served as a rallying point for 'liberal imperialists,' said Rosmer, while *Avanti* gave 'a good example of a socialist daily that said during the war what it said before the war.'[4]

The cooperation between *Nashe slovo* and *Vie ouvrière* was a curious product of antiwar agitation. Russian Menshevik internationalism was led by men who did not follow Lenin in his call for a new International and thus had not been part of the 'Zimmerwald left.' Presumably this showed their hope that the Social Democracy was not beyond repair. Nor could they agree with Lenin's call for adoption of the slogan 'Defeat of One's Own Country.' In any case, wrote Trotsky in 1915, the line of Lenin according to which 'defeat is the lesser evil' becomes a 'substitute' for 'struggle against war on the basis of the conditions which gave it birth.'[5] For these thoughts Lenin and Zinoviev branded Trotsky a 'conciliator' of the prowar Socialists. This was the real meaning they claimed to see in Trotsky's use of the slogan 'Neither Victory nor Defeat.' Trotsky had oscillated between the internationalists and the chauvinists, said Zinoviev, as he had previously oscillated between the Bolsheviks and the 'liquidators.'[6] Zinoviev early showed a talent for connecting Trotsky's current positions to old ones of which the latter was not proud. Zinoviev was also eager to establish a continuity of Trotsky's political misjudgments, a 'Trotskyism' that went beyond this or that utterance of Trotsky's and encompassed an entire tradition of betrayal. On the assumption that Bolshevism was the one true church, this was not wrong. Trotsky had counted himself a critic of Bolshevism right down to the point of fusion of his and Lenin's organizations in the summer of 1917.

The *Vie ouvrière* group traced the policies which had led the Socialist parties into war back to their prewar parliamentary tradition. In this they still clung to the critique made by revolutionary syndicalism: Parliamentary socialism was a dead end for the trade unions, inherently revolutionary instruments which needed to carry the struggle against the class enemy by direct mass action, economic strikes, and the economic general strike. Prewar critics of parliamentarism, including anarchists, could feel vindicated, thought the *Vie ouvrière* militants, by the collapse of the Second International. This tempting association of parliamentarism and war led to the conclusion that, if a new revolutionary International were to be built, it might be like the First International, in which the anarchists had been prominent, as opposed to the Second, from which they had been expelled. Was the Communist International to symbolize a repeal of the verdict of the Hague Congress of 1872, by which Marx's followers had excluded those of the anarchist Mikhail Bakunin? Had the Russian Revolution caused a reevaluation of the record of the anarchists? This could hardly have been merited on the strength of the anarchist leaders' antiwar record. The major figures, Kropotkin, Jean Grave, James Guillaume, and a number of their disciples, had urged support for the Entente, but the many French libertarians had taken a pacifist position, publishing a manifesto, *Vers la paix*, in October 1914, and an antiwar weekly, *Ce qu'il faut dire*, distributed illegally at the front in 1916. The anarchist Sebastien Faure led a revolt against Jean Grave and blamed the war on French revanchism.[7] There was a kind of 'anarchist Zimmerwald' which looked to the Russian Revolution of October 1917 as a culmination of antiwar movements (the German Socialist deputy Otto Ruhle called it a 'pacifist putsch'), and regarded Lenin's *State and Revolution* as a manifesto against Marxism as they had known it. Inspired by this tempting and widespread reading of the meaning of Bolshevism, the French anarchist group of Raymond Péricat 'proclaimed' the Parti Communiste in June 1919, arguing in its first manifesto that the general strike would usher in a stateless society with production under the control of Soviets.[8]

Péricat's attempt came to ruin with the splitting of his group later in the year. Both splinter groups continued to work with the other groups seeking to build a French Communist party. They continued to hope that the new Communist International, if it did not build on the heritage of anarchist and syndicalist antiparliamentarism, would at least re-create a broad proletarian movement of the type of the First International. If these leftists were confused, they can hardly be said to be worse off than the Left Socialist *minoritaires*, led by Marx's grandson, Jean Longuet. They were critical of the war effort but could not embrace defeatism. They continued to vote war credits and kept their distance from the Zimmerwaldists. In the early days of 1917, Souvarine had defended Longuet and Trotsky against Lenin and Zinoviev. He changed his mind after the formation of the Comintern in 1919, but he continued to see in Trotsky the soul of the Russian Revolution. He did not break completely with the *minoritaires*, continuing instead to pursue the Comintern's aim of bringing the bulk of the Socialist party into the Comintern, as well as the bulk of the CGT unions. He helped write the terms under which the Socialists voted to join the Comintern at Tours in 1920.

In the early years of French and Russian communism, Souvarine was perhaps the most important interpreter of Russian conditions and party life in the Kremlin for the newly unified French party. In the pages of the party's theoretical journal, *Bulletin communiste*, Souvarine wrote widely of the emergent socialist construction in Russia and tutored his readers in the methods and ideas of Russian Bolshevism. He and his readers assumed that the French would have much to learn from the party of Lenin and Trotsky. Hardly emphasized, but no less true, was the fact that the Bolsheviks were, in the years after victory in civil war, themselves not really sure of their identity. Their party was also a product of fusion and regroupment and, while they of course felt their tradition vindicated by the revolution, they thought of themselves first and foremost as internationalists and had to fight off a gnawing sense of self-doubt about their lineage in European left politics. Were they heirs of left-wing socialism and the tradition of Rosa Luxemburg? Were they the offspring of the direct action tradition of anarchism and syndicalism, cleansed to be sure of its antistate and antiparty features but wed nonetheless to mass extraparliamentary struggle? Some might have fearfully remembered prewar Bolshevism as perhaps the most sectarian and mercilessly polemical party in the Socialist International. But the prevailing view was that the revolution had dissolved fractious tendencies. Hair-splitting and intrigue were perfectly natural among declining sects of émigrés publishing their papers in cellars, but the responsibilities of power would shatter all dogmatism and all residues of Carbonarism. Trotsky and Souvarine felt that they had nothing to fear from the most thoroughgoing struggle against centrism and opportunism, but they both deeply needed an atmosphere of regroupment and reconciliation. Otherwise the vacuity in the soul of historical Bolshevism was capable of devouring them as well.

Under Souvarine's direction, *Bulletin communiste* praised Trotsky's work in the civil war, in the Soviet economy, and in the Comintern. Souvarine's articles would ultimately serve as the raw material for his *Staline* of 1935. At first, the PCF's Bibliothèque Communiste sold more literature by Trotsky, Souvarine, and Klara Zetkin than that of other writers, including Lenin. The writer Victor Serge, himself the living proof that former anarchists can make good Bolsheviks, contributed sad articles on the fate of Russian anarchism but insisted that the repression of the anarchists would ultimately build a genuinely libertarian Russia.[9] The most famous of the Russian anarchosyndicalists, Daniil Novomirskii, now a Bolshevik and member of the Comintern apparatus, wrote on Kropotkin, mutual aid, and other subjects dear to libertarians, nevertheless insisting that the only real role for a contemporary anarchist was that of a Bolshevik. Russian anarchists had taken considerable liberties with doctrine in order to support the Bolshevik 'revolutionaries' against the Menshevik 'Social Democratic Marxists,' suggesting that the path to their utopia would have to traverse a 'transition period' of 'labor dictatorship.'[10]

The Bolsheviks kept in mind the advantages of their parallel struggle, alongside anarchists and syndicalists, against the Provisional Government, as they made their campaign to woo the ultra-left outside Russia. In the first year of the Comintern's existence Lenin urged that factory committees and Soviets be formed in order to circumvent the trade unions, in accordance with the Russian model of 1917.[11] The failure of the Hungarian and Bavarian Soviet regimes and the disaster of the Communist rising in Vienna convinced Lenin that Central Europe would not for the moment be a field for the application of the tactics of 1917. At the same time, the International Federation of Trade Unions — 'yellow' trade unions, as they were called by the Bolsheviks — was taking shape. More than seventeen million unionists from fourteen nations were affiliated. Lenin's response would be the Red International of Trade Unions (Profintern), organized by July, 1921, in order to keep the anarcho-syndicalist Spanish federation, the CNT, from following the CGT into the Amsterdam ('Yellow') International. It is usually supposed that these unfavorable events caused a change of orientation in Moscow, signaled by the appearance of Lenin's *Left Wing Communism: An Infantile Disorder*. True enough, Lenin took up a campaign against those sympathizers and new Communists who refused to work in trade unions, but he did not abandon his search among the antiparliamentarians for good 'revolutionary material.' He outlined two tasks: first, to split prospective Communists from the 'centrist' Social Democracy and recruit them from syndicalist and anarchist organizations, and second, to send them back into trade unions and parliaments for what the French syndicalists called *noyautage*, and the Americans, 'boring from within.'[12]

Trotsky had, with Lenin, campaigned to win the various syndicalist leaders to the Comintern. They had praised the excellent work done in training the workers in a spirit of hostility to parliamentary democracy, work that the two in their prewar incarnation would have condemned as sectarian. The only thing these revolutionaries needed at this point, according to the makers of the Russian Revolution, was the idea of the party. Against those who suggested that this lesson had been drawn decades ago — the founders of the Socialist parties were those who had been responsible — they responded that they did not have in mind parties of that type, but vanguard parties of the proletariat.[13] All that the lefts needed do was create a Bolshevik type of party, a party rejecting all previous experience save that of the only existing Bolshevik party, the Russian. Trotsky urged that the French syndicalists had already held this idea in embryo, in their notion that the workers must be led by an 'active minority.' 'What else is an active minority held together by unity of conceptions,' asked Trotsky, 'if not a party?'[14] The publication of Lenin's *Left Wing Communism* was not intended to change this line, with which Lenin and Trotsky continued to keep faith.

Left Wing Communism was instead a rebuke to the faithful, who took Bolshevism as a mentor on tactics, to warn them that the Russian Revolution was not so complete a break with the parliamentary labor movement as they had hoped. Herman Gorter, who, with Anton Pannekoek, had split from the Dutch Social Democratic party and formed a small Communist party, in much the same way as Péricat, had attempted to speak for the radicals in his *Answer to Lenin*. Gorter had been to Soviet Russia and spoken with Lenin, only to be shocked at Lenin's ignorance of

Western conditions.[15] 'This man I expected to be and to feel himself the generalissimo of the world revolution,' Gorter told Pannekoek, 'but I had to realize that Lenin thought constantly of Russia and saw things only from the Russian point of view.'[16] Gorter viewed the Russian Revolution as a democratic, not a proletarian, revolution, led by the Bolshevik party to be sure, but having as its driving force a military mutiny backed by a peasant war. In the West, these factors would not exert an influence, since the revolution was to be an affair of the urban wageworkers. Russia had shown, Gorter argued, that the factory committee was a perfectly adequate substitute for the trade union, and the soviet as much so for the parliament.[17] Gorter's prediction that the Russian proletariat would inevitably be forced to capitulate before the peasantry and petite bourgeoisie could only cause a chill in Moscow, for it echoed the worst fears of the Bolsheviks, of which Trotsky had already given eloquent statement in his *Results and Prospects* of 1906. Gorter's arguments expressed the views and moods of many newly converted Communists. German co-thinkers had already seceded from their Communist party, forming the Communist Workers' Party of Germany (KAPD).

Yet the door was not closed to the antiparliamentarians, or, as they have become known, Council Communists. Trotsky, disdaining Gorter as an 'aristocratic revolutionary,' nevertheless granted the truth of his condemnation of the Socialist tradition. 'The role of the Social Democracy,' he wrote, 'is in the final analysis reduced to managing bourgeois society and the state in the interest of the working masses.'[18] This reminded some that the German Social Democratic revisionist Eduard Bernstein had indeed put it as a goal for his party to learn to manage capitalism in periods of crisis.[19] Trotsky emphasized, however, that Communists have no faith in parliaments, but simply use them to destroy the faith of the workers, sunk in 'routine, deadly habits of thought, myopia,' that electoral activity will help matters.[20] An oddity of the radical turn of mind permitted this argument to be taken as a satisfying answer on the many occasions when Lenin or other Bolsheviks resorted to it. The image of Communists ruthlessly exposing the chicanery and corruption of the other parties had its appeal, but how could the Communist voters be content with this continual demonstration of a 'truth' that might be more forcefully, if more absurdly, expressed by political absention?

Trotsky questioned Gorter's views but kept well back from attacking him. In fact he was solicitous of Gorter, hoping that those who thought as he did might make their way back to the Comintern. The German Communists had been augmented by perhaps three hundred thousand members by the action of the congress of the Independent Socialist Party (founded in 1915) at Halle in October 1920. The most prominent personality in the United Communist Party which had emerged from the Halle congress was a follower of Rosa Luxemburg, Paul Levi. He was impressed by the establishment of Soviet power in Petrograd, and he took note of the Bavarian and Hungarian soviet regimes of 1918–1919, but he was equally convinced that nothing of the kind would occur in Berlin, at least not for a considerable period. To make of the Communists a mass party, he thought adhesion of the bulk, or perhaps only a section, of the trade unions would be indispensable. The Gorterites of the KAPD, of which he was only too glad to be rid, could only botch this task. Trotsky was of a different mind, expecting another outbreak of revolution in Germany in the near future. He therefore imagined a new reconciliation:

> If the organization of the KAPD, which embraces a good number of revolutionary workers, fears to enter the Communist Party, a party forming itself not by superficial methods of recruitment but by the pangs of revolution, long struggles, splits and fusions, this shows that the leaders still play too great a role in their own party.[21]

The KAPD militants were to be thought of as the Bolsheviks in 1917 had thought of the ranks of the Left Socialist Revolutionaries, or the anarcho-syndicalists, or even Trotsky's own Interborough Organization, or the way the Reichswehr would later think about the SA ranks in Germany. They were essentially 'good material,' if they could be pried away from the influence of their leaders.

Trotsky did not fear the KAPD's contempt for Western trade union politics. He was at the time engaged in his own struggle against the Soviet trade union leadership. His reorganization of the Soviet railways in 1920, carried out at a time when the war with Poland was going badly and the military methods of the energetic War Commissar seemed very much in order, had tred hard on the prerogatives of Soviet trade union leaders. Mikhail Tomskii, head of the All-Russian Central Council of Trade Unions, had enjoyed a position of growing power since the subordination of the revolutionary factory committees of 1917 to the new trade union structure. The assumption accompanying that major shift of industrial power, which had also opened the door for many ex-Menshevik trade union leaders and closed it for many anarchosyndicalists, was that the unions would have an important role in controlling the economy. Some radical unionists, who would soon be grouped under the rubric of the Workers' Opposition, hoped that decisions would be made by the unions rather than the party, an idea at which Lenin was aghast.

Tomskii and the trade union leaders felt they had much at stake in their resistance to Trotsky's measures. Trotsky was feared for his desire to 'shake up the unions from above' and to bring military methods under the control of the economy. The trade union debate of 1920–1921, broken only by the news of the revolt against the regime by the sailors of the Kronstadt fortress, was to be the arena for this airing of views on the role of unions in the dictatorship of the proletariat. It was also the occasion for a rally of the opponents of Trotsky, a rally having its dim origins in other events. There had been resistance to his hiring bourgeois military special- ists to command the Red Army (Zinoviev's follower Lashevich had called them 'serfs, orderlies, and squeezed lemons'), and when Red troops had got the upper hand over the invading Poles in 1920, there were those who criticized his reluctance to pursue the Polish forces all the way to Warsaw. The 'Lenin Faction,' which was to assume Lenin's functions in his illness, gathered together on these issues during the trade union debate and reached a certain peak of influence, cemented by fear of Trotsky's dicta- tion.

Trotsky's position was that, while the unions were the 'primary material from which the Soviet government was built' in 1918–1919, in 1920 the Soviet organs must take them in hand and remind them of their first task, production.[22] Instead, the fear of this guiding hand from above had led to a 'centrocracy' in the trade union leadership. 'They consider the union to be a little domestic organization,' said Trotsky, 'as it was in the past epoch.' Direction of the economy in the aggregate, however, called for a different approach. The state could only adopt forms 'transitional' to planning, but the old-style trade unionist would resist even these. 'The point of view of a trade unionist, that is, to sow hostility, is the ruin of his organization at present.'[23]

Trotsky asserted much later that his 'mobilization of labor' position in the trade union debate had been intended exclusively as a prong of the policy of War Communism, which sacrificed everything to the demands of military expediency in order to wage civil war. He would also later assert that he himself had proposed a change of line which would have introduced the policies of the New Economic Policy a year earlier. Rejection of this change, he would claim, had led to the 'productionist' line of 1920–1921.[24] Yet foreign Communists could not help but note that Trotsky's statements went beyond advocating the line as temporary military expediency, and seemed to sketch a philosophy of the role of labor in socialism. 'We should have favorite factories,' wrote Trotsky 'as well as factories which feel themselves dishonored in the opinion of Soviet Russia because their output is relatively smaller than others.'[25] 'The construction of a socialist economy,' he argued, 'is in reality a regroupment and well defined education of men in favor of production.'[26] Trotsky thus advo- cated 'socialist emulation' as a fundamental conception of socialism.[27]

Against this view was ranged the Soviet trade union apparatus, what Trotsky called 'unionists of the old mode.' Tomskii and the trade union council had not made careers as leaders of unions, of course. Unions had only appeared briefly in twentieth century Russian history, during out- breaks of revolutionary crisis. In 1917 the Bolsheviks had never really won the trade unions, instead exercising grass-roots influence in their working- class constituency largely through the medium of factory committees.

The 'old mode' to which Trotsky referred was not the Russian mode but his idea of the Western. 'Consumptionism' was a Western trade unionist outlook which was to be viewed as heresy in a workers' state. The workers must adopt a new attitude toward their 'own' state. In the socialist society of the future, the worker would no longer march to work 'timid and holding back, like one who is bringing his own hide to market, and has nothing to expect but a hiding,' as the prewar socialists could quote from Marx's *Capital*. Workers would feel differently about work in which they had a 'stake,' or so Marxists believed. Their 'alimentary' needs would be amply met in socialist society with an elaborate capitalistically developed industrial structure. No Marxist could have imagined such needs being met in a backward society, one reason why Trotsky was quite alone in foreseeing the possibility of a socialist dictatorship. Even his own theory of Permanent Revolution had pinned everything, not on socialist construction, but on 'state support' from the Western proletariat as the result of the spread of the revolution. In his 'productionist' views, Trotsky was improvising without benefit of experience or theory, yet characteristically lacking nothing in confidence and verbal grandeur. No Menshevik or other Social Democrat could agree with Trotsky's ideas, but neither, as it developed, could many Bolsheviks.

Moreover, Trotsky's ideas fell thunderously on the ears of Western trade unionists, so repugnant would they be to the rank and file. Many of the prospective Bolsheviks in the West were trade unionists or supporters of trade unionism, a category into which syndicalists would naturally fall. Were these latter not also 'unionists of the old mode?' The Bolshevik belief was that syndicalists certainly were not union bureaucrats but revolutionaries, who needed only to tack onto their previous views the idea of the vanguard party. Had they not formed their doctrines in reaction to the stifling embrace of bourgeois parliamentarism? Could a syndicalist be a mere trade unionist?

Actually the question had been debated before the war at an Amsterdam congress of anarchists, at which Errico Malatesta, speaking for the purest version of anarchist–communism as preached by Kropotkin, had challenged the syndicalism of Pierre Monatte. Malatesta seemed to reassert Lenin's distinction between a mere trade union official and a tribune of the people, with the anarchist as the ideal tribune in place of Lenin's Social Democrat.[28] Now Trotsky was eagerly wooing the same Monatte and glorifying the traditions of revolutionary syndicalism. 'It is evident to any conscious Communist,' he was to write, 'that the French syndicalism of the prewar period was a profound and important revolutionary tendency.'[29] The Charte d'Amiens, the 1906 declaration by the French unions of independence from political parties, was for Trotsky 'a very precious document' signifying liberation from reformism. Trotsky had not expressed such an opinion in 1906, but for him the Russian Revolution had illuminated these past events. Nevertheless, the element that Malatesta saw entirely in the context of anarchism, and Lenin entirely in the context of the Economist controversy in Russian Social Democracy, may have had wider implications. It would have made sense to put the Charte d'Amiens alongside the Mannheim declaration of the German trade unions of 1906, thus to see it as a declaration of independence from the industrial leadership of Socialist ideologues and in fact a distinct step in the direction of what the American followers of Samuel Gompers called 'voluntarism.'[30] Within the framework of a Socialist mass party, a declaration of this type could indicate the trade union leaders' desire to curtail party decisions about strikes or about the activities of a youth movement, and to mediate relations with the ideological party leaders by enhancing the role of more practical party men who led unions. In the Soviet party, this type was well represented by those such as Tomskii.

But Trotsky and the *Vie ouvrière* militants had a much more romantic idea of the trajectory of syndicalism. Contributors to Souvarine's *Bulletin communiste* frequently expressed the hope that the Communist International would continue in the tradition of defiance of bourgeois convention and sentimentality in morals, as had *syndicalisme révolutionnaire*. They invoked the figure of Georges Sorel, the prewar literary voice of the movement, who saw in the General Strike slogan a valuable 'myth' capable of shaking the workers from a deadly faith in bourgeois progress. Some militants rejected Sorel's mixture of Marxism and the vitalism of Bergson, but his influence was strong nonetheless. One major leader of the syndicalist CGT, Paul Delesalle, expressed the hope that 'the era of the great strikes, those revolutionary gymnastics of the proletariat,' was not over. 'And it is my opinion,' he wrote, 'that the Communist party could undertake to propagate the idea of the General Strike, which Georges Sorel saw as most likely to awaken the proletarian masses, and which is most neglected by reformist socialists and syndicalists.'[31] Former anarchist Amadée Dunois, who would, as a Communist, support Souvarine until his being driven out of the party in 1925, preferred Sorel to the reformists. 'Each time it is my fate to hear Blum talk, I always feel the need to re-read, for cheering up and invigoration, a passage, no matter which, from Sorel's *Reflections on Violence*.'[32] Syndicalist theorist Robert Louzon raised the objection that Sorel had no influence on the formation of syndicalism. 'The merit of Sorel,' answered Souvarine, 'lay not in what he did for the movement, but in what he added to the theoretical baggage of the revolutionaries. For Communists this means his puncturing the sophisms of democracy, denouncing the crimes of the intellectuals, and illustrating the fecundity of violence.'[33] Despite Sorel's reputation as a partisan of industrial workers, however, he was in fact never particularly interested in their welfare, but in the 'revitalization' of society according to the ethics of Nietzsche. To be sure, he hoped that syndicalism would shake the workers loose from their 'morality of the weak,' but more important for him was the shock of industrial 'direct action' which would 'restore to the bourgeoisie something of its former energy.' The real beneficiaries of socialist reformism were the intellectuals and white-collar workers, whose deadly grip could be broken only by proletarian *and antiproletarian* violence.[34] The passion for Sorel was misplaced among those who would not be willing to divide their enthusiasms equally, as would Sorel, between Lenin and Mussolini.

Lenin did not have a record as an enthusiast of proletarian violence as such. New Communists who were sent to his *What Is to Be Done?* (1902) to learn the case for the vanguard party found also that Lenin was opposed to 'Economism,' which was there defined as the idea that the workers need not struggle for political freedom but should confine their activities to economic struggle for wages, hours, and conditions. Lenin expresses the fear that the Social Democratic movement in Russia will take for a model, not August Bebel, political leader of the German Social Democratic party, who educates the workers in Marxist theory and prognosis, but Robert Knight, leader of the engineers' union in England, who fights for economic demands and parliamentary political action but who lacks the perspective of the total transformation of capitalist society according to Marxist prescriptions. The Economist heresy, says Lenin, is the Russian branch of an international tendency leading to participation in bourgeois cabinets (Millerandism) and revising Marxist theory (Bernsteinism).[35] Yet nowhere would these readers of *What Is to Be Done?* find Economism compared to French syndicalism, which it most clearly resembled.[36]

Trotsky's views from that early period in the history of Russian socialism would have been more congenial. In the beginning of his career, he had seen economic strikes as the essential expression of the workers' 'self-activity.' He was preceded in this by Rosa Luxemburg, in whose Polish organ *Presgląd socjial demokratyczny* (*Social Democratic Outlook*) Trotsky's characteristic ideas on Permanent Revolution were to appear. Luxemburg had argued that the Polish Socialists, in their pursuit of national independence, had neglected the economic struggle.[37] Trotsky learned more of this Economist criticism of Polish socialism from the Polish semianarchist Jan Wacław Machajski, whose essay *Evolution of Social Democracy* Trotsky had read during his first Siberian exile. Trotsky was impressed with the depth of Machajski's critique of opportunism, which the Polish revolutionary held to be a reflection of the class values of the intelligentsia, so that socialism became a vehicle whereby they might use the labor movement to take power. Machajski advised that the workers avoid parliamentarism and rely on the economic general strike to expropriate first the capitalists and then the intelligentsia.[38] Except for the anarchistic thesis of the 'expropriation of the intelligentsia,' which Trotsky could not accept but which he was to employ in the 1930s to urge his 'political revolution' against Stalin, Machajski's ideas may have been a push in the direction of Permanent Revolution.

Yet even before he propounded Permanent Revolution, Trotsky had criticized Lenin for the latter's advice to 'fight against spontaneity.' Trotsky had argued that Lenin preached 'class asceticism.' In his anti-Lenin polemic of 1904, *Our Political Tasks*, Trotsky opposed to Lenin's 'Blanquist opportunism' the preferences of leading Menshevik Pavel Akselrod for a broad labor party and popular institutions to unite all labor and democratic opinion. By 1905, Trotsky would see the Soviet as the fruition of these hopes.[39] The idea of Permanent Revolution, developed on the basis of the experience of the Russian general strike of October, 1905, held essentially that economic strikes would force any government, even a democratic one, to choose between breaking the strikes and nationalizing the plants. If it chose the latter, it would no longer be a democratic regime but a dictatorship of the proletariat.[40] Thus, Trotsky had predicted, the problem of democracy would be solved by socialism.[41]

The trade union debate of 1920–1921 thus saw the earlier positions of Lenin and Trotsky reversed. Trotsky, the defender of the 'self-activity' of the workers, now viewed the matter exclusively in terms of factory discipline in the spirit of production. Lenin, the enemy of Economism, now allowed that trade unions should not be controlled so rigidly but should enjoy a considerable measure of independence from the state. The reversal of positions was occasioned by the fact that both now saw the matter from the vantage of state power rather than opposition. Trotsky, holding the state to be genuinely proletarian, thought it contradictory for the workers to require protection from 'their' state. Lenin saw a role for independent trade unions because, he said, he harbored doubts that the state was truly proletarian. Perhaps he magnified these doubts because he needed them to fight the statist Trotsky. In any case, he asserted the idea of the dictatorship of the party, which had to represent two classes, workers and peasants:

> If one says: 'Why and against whom defend the working class, when there is no longer a bourgeoisie and the state is a workers' state?' — one commits an error. The state is not completely a workers' state. We have a workers' state with a bureaucratic deformation.[42]

From that theoretical position Lenin was carrying the day against the 'syndicalist' views of the Workers' Opposition, who wanted to concentrate all production in the hands of the unions and a 'Congress of Producers,' and against the Trotsky program, redrafted for the Tenth Party Congress with Nikolai Bukharin. Behind Lenin stood the same group that had opposed Trotsky on the Polish campaign, the most important figures among whom were Zinoviev, Kamenev, and Stalin.

The Bukharin line had something in common with his opposition to

Lenin in spring, 1918, which rested on the critique of Bolshevik policy of that period as 'state capitalist,' and to which Lenin had replied in his *Left Wing Childishness and Petty-Bourgeois Mentality*. Bukharin had criticized the signing of the Brest–Litovsk peace with Germany, the temporary cessation of the nationalization program, the state grain monopoly, and other measures, in the name of the 'commune state' referred to in Lenin's *State and Revolution*. Lenin defended precisely the 'state capitalism' which the Left Communists decried, recognizing that Left Communists were echoing the views of the left opponents of the party. No Bolshevik was immune to the fear that the party's change of course after taking power had pitted it against the same popular forces that had created the October Revolution. The maximalism of 1917, with its demands for workers' control, land to the peasants, freedom to the nationalities, democracy in the armed forces, and genuine rule by the Soviets, now continued, and would continue up to the Kronstadt revolt and beyond, directed anew against the Bolsheviks themselves. Leadership for a protracted campaign of maximalism would not be lacking. The Left Socialist Revolutionaries opposed Bolshevik policy on the Brest–Litovsk peace and the compulsory grain requisitions; anarchists and syndicalists opposed the 'statization' of industry and the formation of a Supreme Council of National Economy (*Vesenkha*); these and other radicals decried the subordination of the factory committees—in which they had joined the Bolshevik militants in fighting for workers' control and against nationalization of industry—to the trade unions, which had never been wrested from Menshevik control. Lenin feared most that this clamor would find an echo inside the Bolshevik party and cause a split. He was to regard all the Bolshevik oppositions of the next years as posing this threat. *Left Wing Childishness* had been in part an attempt to keep Bukharin from the clutches of the Bolshevik lefts.

In it Lenin had frankly compared German state capitalist economic policy with that of Bolshevism. He was referring to the kind of state and private mixed ventures essential in his view to pose against the small property economy brought about by the land settlement of the revolution. Bukharin was successfully separated from the Left Communists, but he never embraced Lenin's enthusiasm for 'state capitalism' as a term, preferring instead to lay emphasis on the socialist character of the nationalized sector of Soviet industry as a guarantee of the dictatorship of the proletariat. Although Bukharin's joint program with Trotsky at the time of the trade union discussion was designed primarily to compromise the differences between Lenin and Trotsky, and occurred only after the failure of his attempt to provide a 'buffer' between the two, it was natural that Bukharin and Trotsky would·find themselves agreeing on industrial policy. Neither gave voice to any doubt about the proletarian character of the Soviet state.

Lenin did not really disagree with the 'militarization of labor.' At the

Ninth Party Congress, in March, 1920, he had joined with Trotsky in defense of one-man management, disciplinary actions against refractory workers, piecework, and basing wages on 'socialist emulation,' to boot. The Congress had resolved that

> under dictatorship of the proletariat the trade unions cease to be organs for struggle against the capitalist ruling class. They become an apparatus at the disposal of the working class which governs.[43]

Tomskii's resistance was supported by the Democratic Centralist faction, which echoed the horror of the anarchists and syndicalists at these measures. Lenin was also offended by Tomskii's suggestion of a chain of command linking party members in the unions to Tomskii himself:

> The Russian Communist Party can in no case agree that political leadership should belong to the party, and economic leadership to the trade unions. This is a residue from the views of the bankrupt Second International.[44]

This had been Lenin's position against the Economist heresy in 1902.

After the debacle of the invasion of Poland, which made Trotsky appear wise for having opposed it, Lenin tended to go along with Trotsky's ideas—that is, until Zinoviev encouraged Tomskii to seek Lenin's support against Trotsky's stated intention to 'shake the unions up from above.' At the Fifth All-Russian Trade Union Conference, 2–6 November, Lenin vehemently attacked Trotsky's 'bureaucratic excesses' while continuing to support 'sound forms of militarization of labor.' In fact, Lenin wanted to balance Tomskii and Trotsky, perhaps because he feared that Trotsky was developing a reputation to eclipse his own, perhaps because he feared the state led by the army eclipsing the party in controlling the economy. His arguments against 'syndicalism' show that he felt the party must lead the economy to justify its existence. But he wanted to placate Trotsky. At the Central Committee plenum of 7 December Zinoviev took the lead in attacking Trotsky. Lenin continued to urge the controversy into quieter channels while it nevertheless continued to expand.

By the Eighth Congress of Soviets, 30 December, he had found a program, in the meager hints contained in Rudzutak's 7 November statement about a teaching function for the unions. Lenin said the unions must be 'schools of communism,' a 'link between the vanguard and the masses.' The error of *Tsektran* (the Central Committee for Transport, Trotsky's creature for militarizing the railways) lay not in using coercion, which was to its credit, but in not shifting to normal methods at the right time, that is, after the Polish war was over. The emphasis on Rudzutak's theses was apparently an attempt to deflect attention from Lenin's outbursts against Trotsky, whom Lenin opposed before he had a platform on which to do so. Now, however, he had found one.

The real problem for Lenin was that Trotsky was 'using Tomskii and Lozovskii as whipping boys' and calling them 'trade union bureaucrats.' Lenin, never one to look kindly on trade union officials, now took their side against Soviet 'bureaucracy.' The workers' state was an abstraction, he explained in a discussion on 30 December. In reality the Soviet regime was a 'workers' and peasants' state.' Hearing that, Bukharin shouted from the floor: 'What? What kind of state?'[45] A few weeks later, Lenin corrected himself; it was a workers' state with two peculiarities: It depended on the peasantry and was marked by 'bureaucratic distortions.' Trotsky could not fathom this issue of bureaucracy, which Lenin used as a bludgeon against him and his supporters.

The charge was again made by Zinoviev at the Tenth Congress in March 1921. He repeated Lenin's formula and proclaimed that the party was facing not a crisis of trade union policy but a 'general crisis.'[46] Zinoviev was now describing in effect a conflict between the general and democratic aspect of the revolution and its proletarian and socialist aspect. Moreover, by this time the Petrograd party organization had come out foursquare behind Zinoviev while the Moscow organization defended the Bukharin-Trotsky 'buffer' position. For his part, Trotsky did not think that Zinoviev had located a general crisis, 'only a general phrase for the crisis.'[47]

Because Lenin did not want it, this did not become a fight to the finish. He and Trotsky directed most of their criticism at the congress to the 'syndicalist' deviation. Trotsky, in coalescing with Bukharin, had adopted a call for a 'workers' democracy' which he now promptly dropped. Instead he accused the Workers' Opposition of 'making a fetish of the principle of democracy.'[48] Lenin was much harder on Bukharin than on Trotsky. He repeatedly urged that Trotsky had simply blown the issue out of proportion and should calm down; Bukharin, by contrast, was attacked for supporting syndicalism, distorting Marxism by reaching 'an all-time low in ideological disintegration,' and finally, not really understanding dialectics.

With the victory of Lenin's theses the factional meaning of his campaign against bureaucracy became clearer. The secretariat was purged. Krestinskii, who with Trotsky had called for the 'shake-up,' was removed. Preobrazhenskii and Serebriakov, who had supported Bukharin, also lost their jobs. Their places were taken by Molotov, Iaroslavskii, and Mikhailov.[49] Tomskii did not benefit. *Tsektran* was reinforced in authority over the union officials, and when Tomskii showed sympathy with their complaints about workers' democracy in a May meeting, Lenin had him shipped off to do penance with an assignment in Tashkent. Lenin had not reduced Trotsky's influence for Tomskii's sake, nor really because of the original issue of coordinating the unions. The issue, apparently, was the power of Trotsky, as power is often the issue when complaints about bureaucracy are heard.

The trade union debate of 1920–1921 showed the essential features of the post-Lenin factional lineup. In one sense, it had become a struggle between the prerogatives of party and state. Lenin's intervention was conditioned by the progress of the war with Poland, the exigencies of which had given rise to Trotsky's reorganization of the rail unions in *Tsektran*. As long as he saw a chance of extending the revolution westward by the force of arms, Lenin had supported Trotsky's militarization of labor. By the end of 1920, with defeat in Poland, Lenin turned against the encroachments of the military apparatus of War Communism. He became convinced that a shake-up of trade union personnel could only strengthen the new Soviet state at the expense of tested and trusted cadres of Bolshevism. Lenin's complaints about bureaucracy are best understood in this context, outside which discussion of 'bureaucratic deformation' in the straitened conditions of 1920 might seem somewhat ludicrous. Both Lenin and Trotsky recognized that the state and, to a considerable degree, even the ranks of the party had been molded by the civil war. In denying the fully proletarian character of the Soviet state, Lenin was not merely defending the interests of trade unionists and the peasantry, but ensuring the primacy of the party and the claim to legitimacy of prerevolutionary Bolshevism as well. Thus the purge of 1921, normally seen only as part of the backlash from the Kronstadt revolt, had as its targets all who would deny the primacy of the Old Bolsheviks, whether they had been heroes of the maximalism of 1917 or the campaigns against the Whites.

Other pointers from the debate were visible. The maximalist spirit of 1917 was decisively defeated in the party and out, never again to threaten Bolshevik prerogative. Despite the simultaneous defeat of Trotsky's militarization of labor, at least one Old Bolshevik, Bukharin, had shared his view of the proletarian character of the Soviet state and would be willing to defend it again in 1925, once Trotsky had been suitably reduced. Bukharin's opponent would again be Zinoviev, who would again show an ability to argue Lenin's views to good factional effect. Zinoviev's base would again be Petrograd (by then, Leningrad), and that of his opponents, Moscow.

Politically Lenin seemed almost able to occupy more than one place at a time, supporting Trotsky and then attacking him for not making the timely turn, attacking *Tsektran* in the beginning and reinforcing it at the end. Moreover, each turn of Lenin's revealed new theoretical gems, which no one else would have suggested but which quickly became orthodoxy. Lenin never seemed himself to be fighting but urging others not to fight. In the end, however, everyone else was reduced, and Lenin, who stood clear of the wreckage, was lifted to new heights. He was a master in this kind of struggle, despite his claim that he did not want it. In these faction fights, the greatest rewards would be reaped by those who could best emulate Lenin, as the future General Secretary and father of the peoples must already have understood.

3

Lenin versus Stalin, Trotsky versus Zinoviev

Lenin was a Columbus in reverse. Columbus, seeking a new way into Old Asia, found a new world; while Lenin, seeking a new world, found old Asiatic Despotism.

—Lev Kopelev

Russia is a country where everything is mysterious and nothing is secret.

—Boris Souvarine

A DISTRACTED Europe derived comfort from the idea that Red Russia was sobering up from its original revolutionary enthusiasm. The Anglo-Soviet Trade Treaty and the New Economic Policy seemed to bear this promise. They were seen by some as openings to a general détente with the Western states and a full Russian participation, once she had cleared her obligations, in the security system established in Europe by the Versailles treaty. Why Lenin should have wanted this was never explained; the tendency was to imagine that a dynamic was at work which, by means of a Russian Thermidor, would liquidate the sins of October. It should not be surprising that unreal expectations were harbored about the changes in Russia, in view of the utter destitution of the European balance, not even particularly stable in the prewar period. It was no more nonsensical to suppose that Soviet Russia could play a role in securing the Western powers than to see a new Poland as a substitute for Russia, or Czechoslovakia-Romania-Yugoslavia as a substitute for the Habsburg Empire, or, for that matter, to see France as the predominant military power in Europe.

For their part, the Bolsheviks sincerely wanted normalization of their relations with Britain and France, which would not detract in the slightest from Comintern activity in pursuit of the European revolution, generally assumed to be the only real guarantor of the security of the Russian Revolution. They were prepared to make deep and far-reaching changes in the Soviet economic system—changes they have not been willing to make since—in order to pay for these Western assurances. In the event that this project should fail, however, they were prepared to follow the logic of their defection from the Entente ranks in 1917 and make common cause with defeated Germany to subvert Versailles. Thus, when their negotiations with the British and French foundered, at Genoa in April 1922, they cemented their cooperation with Weimar Germany by the treaty of Rapallo. This relationship would have far-reaching implications for the policies and the personal fortunes of the Soviet leaders.

The turn toward Rapallo also marked the point of a turn toward Trotsky by his erstwhile opponent, Lenin. After his stroke in May 1922, Lenin increasingly focused his attention on reducing Stalin, in league with Trotsky. Virtually alone among the Soviet leaders, Lenin saw Trotsky and Stalin as the two most important figures. Others would probably have judged Zinoviev to be the most significant. Zinoviev himself kept up the fire against Trotsky throughout 1922, but they cooperated in Comintern affairs, largely because Trotsky was carrying out a campaign against the most prominent foreign Communists on almost exactly the same terms that Zinoviev had used to attack him. Trotsky was helpful to his enemies, but he also rewarded friends such as Souvarine, who rose to the top of the French Communist party by virtue of this campaign.

Applying the Bolshevik Model

In the first days following the proclamation of the New Economic Policy, it became clear that the reform had not been thoroughly planned in advance. First mentioned in February 1921, its first decrees did not appear until May. It was, nevertheless, associated in the minds of Western businessmen and statesmen with the Anglo-Soviet Trade Treaty of March 1921. Indeed, negotiations for the trade agreement had been carried on through the whole period of the Polish war, a fact which quickly gave rise to the notion that the Polish invasion of the Ukraine had delayed an inevitable NEP from becoming policy much sooner. As events seemed to have unfolded, it appeared that the rising of Polish youth sparking the national rally against the invading Soviets, the 'Miracle of Warsaw,' had turned back the tide of Bolshevism, and with an assist from the Kronstadt sailors, this tide would now reverse the course of the Russian Revolution. Precedent for the Russian case could be found only in the French Revolution, so great store was set by the seemingly analogous events of the 1790s as a prevision of those of the 1920s.

In the milieu of the French left, the analogy with the French Revolution was particularly stirring, and was bolstered by the historian Albert Mathiez, who was to complete by 1922 an influential history of the French Revolution. Mathiez believed deeply in the equation of the Jacobins of

1793–1794 and the Russian Bolsheviks: 'Two dictatorships, born of civil and foreign war, dictatorships of class, using the same means, terror, compulsory requisitions, and taxes, and proposing in the last resort a single goal, the transformation of society, not merely the Russian or French, but the universal society.'[1]

Both revolutions, thought Mathiez, were born of defeat, and both persecuted extremist elements depending on mass spontaneity. Mathiez chose not to emphasize the fact that Bolshevism had emerged from a national mutiny against war, while Jacobinism had galvanized mass protest against the military disorganization which had resulted in defeat, only to enter the foreign campaigns with redoubled energy. He passed by the anathemas that Robespierre had heaped on the English people, and the antipatriotism of the Bolsheviks. The internationalism of the Declaration of Rights of Man might also have been better compared to the pronouncements of Woodrow Wilson. Yet Mathiez's message to the French left was unmistakable: Bolshevik methods were by no means atrocious in light of the history of revolutions, and the Russian dictatorship was not that promised by the panaceas of the parliamentary socialist movement, but a relentless democratic dictatorship in an agrarian country without developed industry.[2] French readers were invited to draw a straight line from the Bolshevism of 1905, with its Revolutionary Democratic Dictatorship of the Proletariat and the Peasantry, to the Soviet regime. Zinoviev would emphasize the same continuity in attacking Trotsky's Permanent Revolution, during the 'literary debate' of 1923–1924. The analogy with the Jacobins had great potential for use against the ex-Menshevik who had attacked Lenin's Jacobinism as far back as 1904.

Mathiez did not pronounce on the question of Thermidor, the moment in 1794 when the Jacobins fell. Would the Bolsheviks also experience a reaction? Mathiez put the question entirely in terms of a split between Lenin and Trotsky, already threatening in 1920–1921. Others considered Thermidor already manifest in the NEP. Trotsky himself was said to regard the NEP precisely as a Thermidor carried out in the nick of time by Jacobins. The most persuasive proponents of the idea of a Russian Thermidor were the *Smena Vekh* (Change of Landmarks) group, whose leading theorist, Nikolai Ustrialov, spoke of the rise and inevitable triumph of National Bolshevism. Ustrialov could not resist seeing the civil war period as a new Time of Troubles like the period of chaos, foreign invasion, and near-partition that followed the reign of Ivan the Terrible. The maximalism of the early years of the revolution had thus threatened to put an end to the Russian territorial state as such, had the Bolsheviks not checked the vast peasant war and its proponents, the Antonovs, the Makhnos, and the Kronstadt sailors. National Bolshevism had first taken root in Russia with the hiring of former Tsarist military specialists for the army, while it had appeared in German communism with the Hamburg 'national communism' heresy of 1920, which sought to build a German Red Army marching under the banner of a 'proletarian Reich.'[3]

The Russo–Polish war in 1920 had fueled the impulse in both Russia and Germany to combine nationalism and Communism for a defense of the fatherland in the Jacobin manner. Ustrialov claimed to speak for a generation of the Russian intelligentsia when he cited the dictates of reason of state and pled for reconciliation of the émigrés with 'National' Bolshevism. The absence of legality in Soviet Russia need not be an obstacle. That state of affairs simply expressed the true national interest, a 'state logic,' and 'essence,' which even while it trampled underfoot existing law, as with Napoleon's Eighteenth Brumaire or Stolypin's coup of 1907, nevertheless lifted society to a higher stage of development: 'As the Germans say, Need knows no law (Not kennt kein Gebot) — the same with us.'[4]

Ustrialov was a right Hegelian who believed that the rigors of reasons of state would tame Bolshevism. He saw that even if the Bolsheviks had ridden the tide to power with their maximalist slogans of 1917, the revolution would consolidate, and the duties of the statesman and the merchant would impose themselves. After the 'bourgeois specialist' would follow the *kulak* and the 'NEPman.' The state organs would be staffed by the patriotic intelligentsia, who would support the Thermidorean and even the Bonapartist stage of the revolution, and eventually reap the benefits of the democratic republic that would follow, a republic which, it was to be assumed, would respect property.[5] Ustrialov believed that Russia would follow the iron historical laws laid down by the phases of the English Revolution from 1640 to 1689 and the French from 1789 to 1830. His ideas were to have a powerful impact on all who thought about the Russian Revolution, not least on the Bolsheviks. By 1925 the Leningrad opposition would write its program in Ustrialov's terms, as a warning of the danger of 'Mensheviko-Ustrialovism.'

Yet the Bolshevik leadership clearly welcomed National Bolshevism from its first appearance. Lenin was delighted at the demoralization it let loose in the ranks of the émigré White intelligentsia. He appreciated, moreover, the role that a loyal nationalist intelligentsia would play in the laborious process of 'cultural revolution,' which would elevate the illiterate peasant masses to a position where they would be able to undertake socialist construction. He criticized mercilessly all who thought that 'cultural revolution' implied merely the education of the toilers in the spirit of social equality. The workers and peasants of Russia must learn from bourgeois culture: German state capitalism, Prussian order on the railways, American technology and organization of industrial trusts, American public education, and the like — all these would build socialism, if guided by Soviet power and the lead of the party. The Soviet intelligentsia, while it was not part of the proletariat, was nevertheless indispensable; the party must tend to its care and feeding. Minister of Culture Lunacharskii congratulated the *Smena Vekh's* 'real, active patriots' on the 'warmth of their interest in the Soviet state and the destiny of Russian culture.'[6] But he would also later caution that 'National Bolshevism' was not Bolshevism, which could never be reduced to realpolitik. Communists did not want a 'Russland über alles.'[7] Lunacharskii's warnings against aggressive Russian nationalism may seem naive in view of the absorption, despite Soviet teachings about national self-determination, of many non-Russian areas formerly ruled by the Tsars, but Lunacharskii also warned that National Bolshevism might imply limiting the reach of Communism to the territory of old Muscovy. In this respect, Lunacharskii's naiveté seems a better guide to Soviet reality than the historical realism of Ustrialov.[8] Soviet Communism was realpolitik and a good deal more.

Had this not been the case—that is, had Soviet Communism really been transformed into Russian nationalism—the observer of Soviet and Communist affairs might have expected a turn in Comintern policy toward broader coalitions with potentially pro-Soviet and pacifist elements, and some relaxation of Moscow's stringent requirements for admission to the Communist parties. Some claimed to see evidence of an international Thermidor in the adoption of united front tactics in 1921. Yet the increasingly heavy-handed Soviet intervention in the affairs of Communist parties continued to result in the purge of centrist forces and the reinforcement of leftists in their leadership.[9]

In both France and Italy, Lenin and Trotsky had wanted to transform the majorities of the Socialist parties into Communist parties, even if that meant taking some established leaders—Marcel Cachin and L.-O. Frossard in the French Socialist party and Giacinto Serrati in the Italian—into the bargain out of respect for their constituencies, which alone could guarantee that the new parties would not be mere sects. A separation of these leaders from their following could be left for later. In this respect, the same general tactic was pursued with regard to the Germans at Halle, the French at Tours, and the Italians at Livorno.[10]

In the Italian case, things developed differently. Not that Lenin did not harbor a certain admiration for Serrati for his opposition to the war and his protest against Allied intervention in Russia. As with the French, the Bolsheviks were also willing to countenance a protracted fight to win the followers of Serrati's 'Maximalist' Center faction. The problem was that the Italian extreme left, led by Amadeo Bordiga, was in a position to force what the Bolsheviks considered a premature split with the PSI right, led by Filippo Turati. Lenin gave ample evidence that he detested Turati, who spoke of a 'thaumaturgy of the idea' among leftists who hoped for revolution, according to what he called a 'miracle of the will.' Turati valued what the PSI had built in Italy over decades, against the opposition of anarchism and syndicalism spawned from Bakunin's years in Italy.

Lenin, who saw in him a quintessential Social Democrat, wanted him expelled, but not without first denuding him of both his following and his associates in the leadership, including Serrati. Hence the 'test' Lenin continually referred to at the Second Comintern Congress, which Serrati would have to pass. Only by parting with Turati—which to Serrati meant also the bulk of the trade union constituency of Italian socialism—could he prove his revolutionism. Serrati complained that his party's record was superior to that of the followers of the pacifist and reformist tradition of Jean Jaurès, men who would soon be leading French communism:

> *Serrati:* One fine day the French Socialists told us: Yes, dear Italian and Russian comrades, we want to call a general strike in support of the Russian revolution. I do not deny I thought they were sincere when they made this promise.
>
> *Goldenberg:* They were not.
>
> *Serrati:* But my friend, we do not have a *sincerometer* in our pocket.
>
> *Lenin:* We will find this *sincerometer*.[11]

Lenin did not intend that Serrati, Cachin, or any others lacking in revolutionary qualities would last long in the Communist International. Despite the NEP and the Anglo-Soviet Trade Treaty, he had not ceased to believe that he could build revolutionary parties capable of taking power and that Moscow was the place to stand, thus to move the world.

Nor did he think the postwar revolutionary wave to be past. The Italian strikes in the spring of 1920 and the autumn factory occupations signified for all the Bolsheviks a revolutionary situation. The *consigli di fabbrica*, appearing in Turino, passed muster as harbingers of impending revolution. Actually they corresponded, not to the Russian soviets of 1917, as many Italian Socialists thought, but to the factory committees of the same year, grass-roots organizations circumventing the emerging trade unions in order to lead wildcat strikes and exercise 'workers' control' of production. The Bolsheviks had enjoyed greater support in these committees than in the largely Menshevik-controllecd unions, or, until the autumn, the soviets themselves.[12] While the distinction between factory committees and soviets is important, it should not be concluded that the Bolshevik code, by which the lessons of their revolution were applied, provided only for seeking power by way of soviets. In the dark days after the failure of the July uprising in 1917, Lenin had contemplated abandonment of the slogan 'All Power to the Soviets'—soviets which under Menshevik-SR leadership were hounding the Bolsheviks—and adoption of 'All Power to the Factory Committees.' He knew well that, if a central council of factory committees could be convened, it might easily duplicate the functions, and the governmental pretensions, of the Petrograd Soviet.[13] The Bolsheviks, unlike the anarchists, had no emotional or theoretical attachments to any of these institutions, seeing them only as springboards for the advance of their party.

It cannot be said that the Italian Left Socialists most favorable to the Comintern understood much about these 'lessons' of 1917. Bordiga wrote to the Comintern executive in the beginning of 1920 that, 'as for soviets, they exist only in several Italian cities and there only as factory councils.'[14] Actually Bordiga did not like the notion of soviets before the revolution had occurred, fearing that they might limit the party's power. Antonio Gramsci's enthusiasm for the Turino councils led him to warn that 'the party and the trade union should not impose themselves as tutors or ready-made superstructures for the new institution.'[15] The latter should develop, he thought, by a 'molecular process,' having the way cleared for them by a party which left them their autonomy 'and not a party which uses the masses for its own heroic attempts to imitate the French Jacobins.'[16]

At the moment Gramsci wrote, the Russian factory committees had long been subordinated to the Soviet trade union apparatus. The committees had been levers against the unions before the revolution and instruments of the unions thereafter. Lenin and Trotsky repeatedly asserted that the Italian factory occupations gave a clear signal that the 'Menshevik' trade union leaders of Turati's type, with their contempt for the councils, could never be men of the Third International. Serrati was increasingly pressed to make the break, but he was also increasingly convinced that his party was being subjected to undue indignities. Had the French not been permitted to 'interpret' the twenty-one conditions demanded by the Second Congress for admission to the Comintern? He thought it a mistake to consider the explosive situation in Italy reason for a special campaign to rout Turati. The factory occupations were probably not the prelude to revolution; unrest in the countryside would not turn into an Italian peasant war; in any case, even in the event of successful revolution, a blockade would soon bring revolutionary Italy to its knees.[17]

Lenin considered this attitude intolerable. He was angry that an article titled 'We Will Be Blockaded' had been published in the party paper *Communismo*. If a blockade should occur, Lenin told Serrati, the country doing the blockading would find its working class rising up in protest. During the war with Poland, the English government had been prevented from intervening on the Polish side by the trade unions' threat to set up Councils of Action. This would become the model for proletarian support to the Russian Revolution. But Serrati believed that no Communist party or sympathizer-party would be capable of coming to the aid of an Italian revolution. Can the Bolsheviks in Moscow have expected successfully to support their comrades in Italy? Radek did speak of a 'south-eastern tendency' in the Comintern executive which hoped for a revolutionary breakthrough in a country with an aggravated peasant situation, such as Hungary or Romania. This would stir the pot in the Balkans and provide an 'agrarian hinterland' for the Italian revolution.[18] And Zinoviev, who would outdo all the other Bolsheviks in 1924–1926 in his projections for East European agrarian revolution, was in this respect perhaps more 'Leninist' than Lenin.

The founder of Bolshevism had finally decided on a solution to the Serrati problem by analogy with his handling of the 'strike-breaking' of Zinoviev and Kamenev in October, 1917. He recalled that those two tested Old Bolsheviks had opposed the Bolshevik insurrection and had even protested it publicly, but had soon accepted the fait accompli and had joined in the work of the new government, gradually reassuming positions of importance. Perhaps Serrati should do the same. The real fight was not in any case against him but against Turati and the reformists. Instead of a split of the left, Lenin suggested, why not expel the right and persuade Serrati and his circle to resign? At some later date, Serrati might reenter the leadership, as had Zinoviev and Kamenev. Lenin was later to make the same offer to German Communist Paul Levi, as we shall see, and the method may also have been applied by Stalin to the case of Trotsky in 1925.

In this case, however, it was Zinoviev who was more set on a vigorous ideological confrontation. He cited Serrati's deviation on three matters: Serrati had opposed as opportunist Comintern urgings that the British Communists enter the Labour party; Serrati had disagreed with Comintern peasant policy calling for redistribution of estates[19]; finally, Serrati had failed to endorse the Second Congress's call for support to the struggle of colonial peoples. Zinoviev was insisting that Serrati was hostile to the peasant and a social chauvinist as well.

Where Lenin sought a gradual separation of Serrati from his constituency, by the same process already under way in France and Germany, Zinoviev was less patient. He was concurrently urging a split among the German Independent Socialists (a party founded in 1915) in order to give the German Communists some real support in the trade unions, where the Independents had influence. Many of the Independents' leaders feared that a split could make sense only if there were a revolutionary situation, which they doubted. Zinoviev, at their Halle conference in October, 1920, had repeatedly cited the Italian situation as evidence that revolutionary struggles were unfolding. He had reason to fear Serrati's influence on the Independents. He had also stirred the Muslim delegates to the Congress of the Eastern Peoples at Baku in September with his call for a 'holy peoples' war' against British imperialism. All this may have caused him to be somewhat full of himself in dealing with the mere mortal Serrati.

The Comintern representatives at the Livorno Congress behaved as if they intended to support Bordiga's campaign for a split. A Communist

Faction was already in place, and Bordiga had been preparing a showdown all along. His speech at the congress seemed even to look beyond a split to the ensuing struggle with Gramsci's Ordine Nuovo group for leadership of the PCI. Comrades should be patient with those who err, he intoned; 'Gramsci may be on a false road, while I am on the correct one.'[20] Lenin and Trotsky preferred Gramsci to Bordiga. They had encouraged the polemics against Serrati, but they could not deny the truth of the accusations made by Turati that Bordiga's Abstentionism rolled back the clock and unraveled the victory of previous decades against Bakunin's antiparliamentarism. Still, they could not keep the leadership of the Italian party out of the hands of Bordiga. They had all along stated their preference for ultra-leftism (a malady of a healthy movement in its infancy) over 'reformism,' without being able to imagine the German Communists under the leadership of the men who formed the KAPD. Yet Livorno and its aftermath had left them with a PCI firmly in the grip of the Abstentionists, who were perhaps even more resolute sectarians. Bordiga would soon show his intransigence, even toward left elements that the Comintern wanted to recruit, and his pride in the PCI's splendid isolation. 'The Italian party,' he latter told a PCF congress at Marseilles, 'is the party that most resolutely carried out the struggle against the opportunists and it struggles at this moment most resolutely against syndicalists and anarchists in living polemics and in action.'[21] The Italian proletariat, he added, would be united by the PCI, or it would not be united at all. This was less than a year before Mussolini's march on Rome.

Paul Levi was in some ways as much of an irritant to the Comintern executive as Bordiga, in the sense that his ushering the future KAPD out of the Communist movement in 1919—an act which precluded a German Livorno—took the Comintern down a path it was not sure that it wanted to follow. Not that there was any more than a groping toward an idea of what Communism was, a matter which became clearer only as it was decided what Communism was not. Lenin, in a speech to the Second Congress, argued that everything was traceable to the absence, in the 1892 Erfurt program of the German Social Democracy, of a commitment to the dictatorship of the proletariat. Lenin recalled that Plekhanov had complained about the matter at the time. That made Plekhanov a kind of founder of the Communist International. By the Second Congress, it was becoming more or less established that Communists were not Social Democrats, nor were they 'opportunists,' 'reformists,' anarchists, syndicalists, or even Abstentionists. Moreover, they were for anticolonial struggles even by ordinary nationalists, and for division of the land in the direction of a smallholders' utopia. The Bolsheviks were feeling their way toward the nonsensical assertion, now canon in world communism, of a continuous international Bolshevik platform of this kind against opportunism dating from the Russian Social Democratic program of 1903. They were also asserting a tradition of theoretical superiority of Russian Marxism over that of the Europeans.

Nevertheless, Moscow could not yet say black was white. Even those, including Kabakchiev and Radek, who actually said they preferred a smaller Italian party knew they had not gained a reliable instrument at Livorno. Their intemperance toward Serrati was fueled in part by younger German Communists, who for factional purposes may have wanted to convince the Comintern executive to identify Serrati with Rudolf Hilferding of the right German Independents. Hilferding had argued against the fusion of the Independents and Communists at Halle. To follow the logic of the argument against Hilferding, it was necessary to assert that the Italian Socialists could have, by their own efforts, spread the occupation movement and created a revolution by going on the 'offensive.' The occupation movement was the sole rationale for insisting that Serrati be treated differently from the French. Comintern representatives who knew that the trade union leaders, the 'opportunists' whom they maintained had to be expelled at all costs, had actually *led* the movement, admitted quietly that the opportunists were somewhat more left in Italy than in the rest of Europe. According to the psychological quirk that one defends an absurdity only by another absurdity, the Comintern executive and its nascent faction in Germany were led to make the claims for their chances in Italy on more general ground. Thus there grew a pronounced agitation for an offensive in Germany as well.

Levi stood to lose most by the ominous drift. He also seems to have known in advance that it would not pay him to be correct in criticizing the executive, any more than it had paid Longuet, Turati, or Serrati. Far from really taking a stand on the Italian question, Levi at first complained only that the Comintern emissaries, particularly Kabakchiev, had done their work with 'tactical rigidity.' Levi had also demanded the expulsion of Turati, but in elaborating his views he contrasted 'organic' methods (those dependent on the local situation) with 'mechanical' ones (those in keeping with the iron unity of the 'World' Communist party). He found he could not avoid challenging the basic organizational premise of the Comintern. Radek, who appears to have been decisive in his fall, already had a pro-Moscow faction prepared against Levi and succeeded in having him demoted.

Almost immediately, and almost simultaneously with the Kronstadt Revolt and the Anglo-Soviet Trade Treaty, there followed the German March Action. In response to emergency police measures taken by the Social Democratic government of Saxony, the KPD attempted a general insurrection. For the last two weeks of March, a series of confused strikes and street fights were undertaken, all of which ended in failure. Even with exhortations to come to the aid of the Soviet workers' regime, embroiled at the same time in suppressing the Kronstadt uprising, it proved impossible to galvanize the German workers into revolutionary action. Far from terrorizing the German government, the March Action proved to be an advertisement of the weakness of the KPD, which probably lost more than half its membership as a result of its failure. Momentum toward a Soviet–German trade agreement, which would materialize later in the year, was perhaps even quickened by the abortive March Action.

The debacle was a watershed for the KPD, in that it led to Levi's expulsion, after he had denounced it as the 'greatest Bakuninist putsch in history.' It was also important in Bolshevik politics, since it sprang from Bukharin's theory of 'the offensive.' Bukharin had argued that the chief obstacle to victory for the Western revolution lay in the failure of the revolutionaries' conscious will to action. This he ascribed to revulsion at the result of the world war which stirred nostalgia for the pacifist sentiment of the Jaurès tradition. Yet the Bolsheviks sought to revive the offensive traditions of the French Revolution, including that of Napoleon. Bukharin used the same arguments he had employed to advocate revolutionary war in 1918, at the time of the Brest-Litovsk debate. Even if the revolution had resulted from weariness with war, he maintained, the act of constituting a revolutionary state power was itself part of an offensive against world capitalism. Against the assertion that revolution could not be advanced abroad on the ends of bayonets, Bukharin asked: 'Was not our insurrection itself a "bayonet"?'[22] The theory of the Offensive had enthusiastic proponents among the pro-Moscow critics of Levi in the KPD, including August Thalheimer, Heinrich Brandler, Ernst Reuter (Freisland), and Paul Frölich, who had contributed a discussion document, *Offensive-Theorie*.[23] Even after the failure of the March Action, Thalheimer insisted that it had failed only for lack of more thorough preparation, and that the *Zentrale* had been fully justified in expelling Levi 'for his base treason to the party; and his disregard for party discipline.'[24] The March Action was not a putsch, said the pro-Moscow faction, but a 'step forward in the growth of the German revolution and the Communist Party. . . . It gave the party the possibility to gather serious military experience and training for future campaigns.'[25]

The right tendency in Bolshevik politics may have originated in the turn by the advocates of the Offensive, such as Bukharin and Thalheimer, toward the tactical line espoused by Levi in his Open Letter of January. Levi had called for a united front with the Social Democratic unions in industrial action and agitation for an alliance of Weimar Germany and Soviet Russia, both suggestions resting on the premise that revolution was not on the agenda. After the failure of the March Action, both became part of Communist policy, after their author had been discarded.

No one could decide whose responsibility the March Action really was,[26] but the Third Comintern Congress in summer 1921 abandoned the Offensive for the tactics of the Open Letter. Radek admitted that no significant voice had been raised before March against the theory of the

Offensive, and that a certain correction was perhaps due. But the case of Levi was quite another matter, in which the choice was clear: 'It must either be with us or with Turati!'[27] Radek quoted Zinoviev's attacks on Turati by analogy with his own on Levi. Lenin privately admitted to Klara Zetkin the wisdom of Levi's critique, which would be amply demonstrated by the Comintern's adoption of united front tactics. This did not keep him from justifying Levi's expulsion for indiscipline. He recommended the same course to Levi as he had to Serrati: Drop out of party affairs and begin a slow and humble reentry.[28] Radek's views on Levi implied that the latter's was no mere case of indiscipline, but that of a 'semicentrist' who must be got out of the way in order to carry on energetic action, even under the tactic of the united front. If Germany and the rest of Europe were not in 'October,' they were nevertheless still in their 1917. Communists did not recognize all this; yet they were learning how a leader might be separated from even his closest following, his course adopted without acknowledgment, his record condemned on principle, his name become a kind of curse. Soviet disciples of Lenin could hardly fail to notice the distance from which Lenin acted on major policy matters, a distance permitting action he was later free to denounce. The March Action was another case in which he used the position of the supreme centrist to become the supreme arbiter.

Lenin patiently explained to the German Communists the lessons of the discussion at the Third Congress. The experience of the October Revolution demonstrated, he said, that there were two kinds of anarchism, one which was irreconcilably anti-Communist and one which would work in concert with Communists to make the revolution. It was necessary to be patient with these latter, good revolutionaries, who would aid in the struggle for power. Germany did not have a large anarchist movement, but it faced the same problem in the form of the KAPD. These comrades must be treated patiently in the expectation that they would render valuable aid in revolutionary struggles. Lenin indicated that, in rejecting this tendency in 1919, Levi had set the KPD on the wrong course. The implication was that Communist leaders capable of tactical action which would build the party in a relatively quiet period might be incapable of leading it in a revolutionary one. Levi himself, said Lenin, was once a Bolshevik, even before the revolution. He, Lenin, could never fully trust those who came to Bolshevism *after* its great victories.[29] Again Lenin sounded an ominous note proclaiming Old Bolsheviks to be the only real revolutionaries.

Toward the United Front

Lenin gave his advice at a moment when the purge of the party rolls, following the decisions of the Tenth Congress, was getting under way in

Russia. Despite the expectation of a milder regime than that proposed by Trotsky, Russian trade union leaders were being subjected to severe impositions. *Tsektran*, the embodiment of Trotsky's militarization of labor, was resurrected, now under strict control of the Central Committee. Tomskii himself was banished for a time to Tashkent for *moderantisme* in disciplining his underlings. Everywhere the campaign was directed, not only against the 'syndicalist' Workers' Opposition, but also at those former Mensheviks who had come into the party when the factory committees were subordinated to the unions in early 1918. Like Serrati and Levi, these men were now suspected of not being Old Bolsheviks. The purge in Russia thus ran parallel to the purge in the Comintern.

Trotsky knew he would have to reassure those who had fought him in Russia. Of the adversity of Comintern trends he had no inkling. On the Fourth Anniversary of the Revolution, he reviewed the events of 1917, providing an anticipation of debate over the failed insurrection in Germany of October 1923. The October Revolution had not come, said Trotsky, at the end of a series of riots and insurrections. It had in fact a 'legalist' character made possible by the fact that the troops felt that Kerensky had gone over to Kornilov and were afraid to obey the former's orders.[30] The Bolsheviks thus became the most reliable defenders of the status quo. The revolution was accomplished, Trotsky wrote, on a fixed date, by means of the Military Revolutionary Committee of the soviet which had been called together to organize the defense of Petrograd after the Germans took the Moon Islands. Trotsky again told with eloquence the story of the October rising, to show how the insurrection sprang directly out of united front tactics. His continuing reference to these events was bound to make Zinoviev cringe, in view of the latter's opposition to the October insurrection. The better was Trotsky able to advertise himself as the Comintern's greatest strategist.

For it was perfectly true that the turn toward united front tactics was not a turn to the right at all, but really a mobilization of the new Communist parties in industrial and local action. This was immediately recognized by European social democrats, who, on the whole, did their best to avoid the stifling embrace of the Communist trade unionists. Even the Communists wondered what new responsibilities and dangers lay in store. In France, Cachin and Frossard wanted immediate assurance that the March Action would not be repeated in their bailiwick. Trotsky went so far as to deny that the order for the March Action had been given in Moscow.[31] And the French need not worry about 'artificially provoked, partial insurrections.' Instead, they should prepare for a 'Kerenskiad,' that is, a regime of a Radical-Socialist bloc, as a primitive national reaction to the war period. This would 'shake the state apparatus,' and the Communists should expect police persecutions and widespread suppression, which should prove to be 'an excellent school.'[32] There must be an intensive effort to achieve the 'conquest of the unions from within' by means of Communist groupings 'under the direction of the Central Committee of the Party.' Thus would the united front serve as a slogan under which the unions would be penetrated. Communists must remember, said the former president of the Petrograd Soviet, that 'the Soviet was the form taken by the united front at the beginning of the Revolution. The masses themselves imposed upon us this formula of the united front, and we accepted it, and more than that, we threw ourselves into these Soviets as a minority, with the certitude that we would vanquish our adversaries — and we have succeeded.'[33]

Trotsky doubted whether the leadership of Frossard was up to the task. The secretary general of the PCF 'lacks firmness and energy,' complained Trotsky.[34] Leon Blum and the former right, the 'Dissidents,' were enemies like the Mensheviks, yet there persisted the impression that 'the argument with them is a fraternal quarrel and not a struggle to the death. The opposite is the case.'[35] Communist propaganda under Frossard, said Trotsky, 'lacks bite, does not fight the Church hard enough, does not have enough on colonialism, uses too much social-patriotic terminology.' Frossard, a shrewd and supple politician, did his best to maintain a broad unity between his center group and the Communist Faction led by Souvarine, but found himself hemmed in by this hard conception of the united front. Souvarine pressed his attack against the party right in which he saw social-patriotism, a desire to keep clear of the whole trade union question, and insufficient international discipline.[36] The Marseilles Congress of December 1921 did not decide the matter or sort out the Babel of tendencies in French Communism. Frossard complained of its united front resolution that it failed to recognize the utility of accords with *leaders* of other labor tendencies, including those which led to electoral blocs. 'The actions which are undertaken with these leaders will necessitate, not provisional and momentary accords, but permanent and long-standing alliances.'[37] Frossard recalled the many efforts of the Bolsheviks, between 1905 and 1917, to find unity with the Mensheviks.

True enough. But Trotsky and Souvarine did not want electoral blocs of the type of the *cartel des gauches*, which would take power by 1924. Here is found an anticipation of the attitude Trotsky was to take toward the Popular Front of 1936. The united front for him and for Souvarine involved primarily the trade union question, and the suspicion that Frossard would never lead a campaign of industrial strikes such as those which had arisen in Russia in 1917. Frossard denied his own reluctance, claiming that the party crisis was a crisis of personalities and not of ideas, while Trotsky muttered darkly that this was yet to be determined.[38] Following the line laid down in previous discussions, Trotsky insisted that the syndicalists of the CGT, like the KAPD in Germany, contained promising elements. Communist cells in the unions would find them, thus *noyautage*, 'boring from within,' was 'the most natural form of struggle for ideological influence and for unity of front, without destroying the unity of the [party] organization.'[39]

The split in the unions, which resulted in the formation of the CGTU, showed that there lay a field for Communist activity. Important figures among the syndicalists, men such as Pierre Monatte and Robert Louzon, looked hopefully toward the PCF, but news of the Kronstadt rebellion, of the fate of the Russian anarchists, and that of Russian trade unions themselves made it impossible for anarchists and syndicalists to come toward Communism as they had earlier. The anarchists wanted the CGTU to look to the International Working Man's Association, the anarchist trade union international formed in Berlin in 1922. The PCF faction in the CGTU instead wanted affiliation to the Profintern, and got its way when the Saint-Etienne Congress of the CGTU voted in favor of affiliation, with the preservation of the traditional 'autonomy' guaranteed by the Charte d'Amiens.[40] Monatte would join the PCF shortly.[41]

Trotsky and Souvarine held that the chief danger to the French party was its slippage toward pacifism, in particular toward the pacifism of the Socialists. This was why Frossard sought to develop his contacts with trade union and political leaders on the left. 'It is menacing,' Trotsky wrote to Rosmer, 'that Frossard can cite the necessity to continue in the tradition of Jaurès.' The leadership of the 'Dukhobors' would leave the party in 'sombre ruins.'[42] Trotsky sought to comfort those who feared that the attacks on the center group in the French party would produce another Livorno by claiming that the Italian case was unique, and that the split with Serrati had been forced by the effects of the defeat of the factory occupations.[43] Even while France was approaching her Kerensky period, the party had not yet been defeated and was not yet in need of a wholesale 'shaking up.' Trotsky imagined that he foresaw the situation of April 1917 for the French Communists, and he was trying to prevent any temptation to support a future left governmental bloc—a temptation like that of the Bolsheviks before Lenin's arrival in Petrograd.

Lenin Turns

While Trotsky prepared an extensive discussion on French party affairs for the Fourth Comintern Congress, to be held in summer, 1922, his position in the Russian Politburo was not improving. The New Economic Policy itself was becoming a symbol of party repudiation of the 'Bonapartist' methods of War Communism, with which his name was inevitably associated, and the decrees outlining that policy to which Trotsky was adjusting himself were hardly promulgated when a kind of battle for the soul of NEP broke out. Building on Lenin's notion that NEP was a return to (and a vindication of) the state capitalism of 1918, Finance Minister

Grigorii Sokolnikov published a study with the title *State Capitalism and the New Finance Policy*, in which he outlined an approach to a fresh economic relationship with the world economy.[44] Sokolnikov judged the atmosphere among Western capitalists to be favorable to reconciliation with Russia. The Cannes conference of 1921 not only had recognized Russia's right to her own peculiar economic system but also had envisaged an international consortium for the economic integration of war-torn Europe, including Soviet Russia. According to this scheme, the Soviets would have to recognize extraterritoriality, relax internal labor laws, and establish a number of free zones and even treaty ports. Russia would have to pay her debts, grant foreign concessions on a regular basis, and compensate Western owners of property seized in the revolution. In return, credits and production assistance would help to get Russia on her feet and to establish her role as a producer of raw materials for the industrial countries and a consumer of their finished goods.[45]

Sokolnikov urged a series of reforms to prepare the way for acceptance of one or more of these propositions. A gold ruble, strictly for international payments, would be a start. The enlargement of the ongoing program of foreign concessions through 'mixed companies' would follow; the newly emerging system of Soviet industrial trusts could be structured with this in mind. Industry would, of course, have to pay its own way; that is, its efficiency and creditworthiness would have to be established in the traditional manner, without Russian credit facilities being forced to lend it special support. Under these circumstances, foreign loans could be got more easily and the countryside's need for consumer goods might be directly met from abroad without the delays and other agonies associated with Russian production for this need.

The favorable, if limited, reception of these ideas among Lenin and his faction of 1920–1921 shows that those who saw in NEP an evolution rather than a tactic were not entirely mistaken. Lenin had led in the direction now being pointed to by Sokolnikov. All eyes were fixed on the Genoa Conference in April, at which the arrangements with Britain and France were to be made. Even Trotsky, who was not at home with Sokolnikov's ideas, was forced to adjust to the drift.

His own position was a kind of muted continuation of his previous stance. In peacetime it would make little sense to extol the virtues of 'shock work' as he had in 1920. He contented himself instead with a defense of industry against finance, by attempting to strengthen the prerogatives of the fledgling planning agency, Gosplan. Against Sokolnikov's attempt to loosen the hold of the Monopoly of Foreign Trade, he defended the Foreign Trade Commissariat (*Vneshtorg*) under Leonid Krassin. Despite the clear continuity with his earlier views in defense of the state, Trotsky could not pretend to be fighting on a question of principle. Germs of more extensive notions were always in evidence, to be sure. The Trotsky of 1922

was still the War Commissar whose fight against pluralistic forces anticipated his defense of Stalin's initial industrialization measures of 1928–1929,
which will be described below. In Soviet politics, however, the positions
of leaders are always adjustable so long as they remain in the leadership. It
is only on their being removed from the leadership that these positions
tend to be transformed into matters of principle. Moreover, Trotsky
himself was on many occasions an enthusiastic proponent of the concessions program. Even within the framework of War Communism, he
had argued:

> These 'concessions' are part of our plan. It pays to abandon to the
> capitalists this or that fraction of our territory in regions which are today
> inaccessible to us for various military or economic reasons, as, for
> example, Kamchatka is destined to remain for a long time outside our
> gates. [46]

Nevertheless, he was still opposed in 1922 as the economic Bonaparte, and
he criticized Sokolnikov as the father of a system of Soviet 'capitulations.'

The Genoa conference held out great hopes for the Soviet leaders for a
détente which might provide a considerable period of decent relations
with the Western powers and something of an economic enmeshment of
the Western banks and industries in the Soviet economy. The failure of the
Genoa conference dealt a blow to these hopes. Coinciding with the onset
of his severe illness, this marked the occasion of another shift of Lenin's
considerable weight at the fulcrum of Soviet politics.

Stalin had been appointed to the new post of General Secretary by the
Eleventh Party Congress in April. Thus the campaign against Trotsky
begun in 1920 seemed to have culminated in the securing of the party
apparatus and economic policy for members of Lenin's faction. The
meaning of all this changed abruptly with the illness of Lenin, which
opened to both Zinoviev and Stalin the possibility of becoming the heir.
Even had they wished to alter the economic line of Sokolnikov after
Genoa, they would have regretted the loss of 'state capitalism' as a
prophylactic against Trotsky. Zinoviev was not unaware of the enormous
power that had been given Stalin, but, as his attempt to downgrade Stalin
the following year serves to indicate, he still felt Stalin to be a manageable
problem for the future, second in importance to the fight against Trotsky.
As Lenin began his convalescence, he saw the need to fight the Lenin
faction itself. For this he turned to Trotsky rather than Bukharin. But the
onset of his illness marked his political decline as well.

The triumvirate of Zinoviev, Kamenev, and Stalin first crossed swords
with Lenin because it supported Sokolnikov's version of state capitalism
and wish to see *Vneshtorg* trimmed back, in the understandable expectation
that relaxation of the Monopoly of Foreign Trade would stimulate
exchange with the industrial countries. Lenin, despite his general support

for the drift of policy leading toward the Genoa negotiations, now resisted and defended the trade monopoly. Friction with the triumvirs on this score had already been in evidence at the end of 1921, and was exacerbated in the spring of 1922. In defending *Vneshtorg* Lenin was actually in consonance with the protectionist traditions of the Tsardom, which had resisted the free-trade predilections of the liberal Russian landlords, in the knowledge that cheaper and better foreign goods would rapidly outpace Russian industrial products and weaken the state. Lenin complained that he feared an 'alliance' between the Western bourgeois and the Soviet peasant. This had to be balanced against his clear wish to bolster Soviet state capitalism with foreign arrangements. Not the Western capitalist but the Soviet peasant presented in his eyes the most powerful threat to the building of socialism.

In the early jousting, Stalin's reluctance to follow Lenin portended a more defiant attitude as Lenin's health weakened after the attack of May. It would be difficult, however, to see in Lenin's actions prior to that point a growing struggle against Stalin. It is true that Lenin had devoted much effort to criticizing the abuses in the Workers' and Peasants' Inspectorate (*Rabkrin*), but that was mostly complaint about inefficiency and general sluggishness, reflective of his continuous hope that through cultural revolution the party might modernize Russian bureaucratic life, just as a genuine materialism, not necessarily Marxist but merely that of the eighteenth century French Enlightenment, must dispel the religious obscurantism of old Russia.[47] A special animus against Stalin would have placed more barriers against the latter's appointment as General Secretary. The momentum from the Tenth Congress, at which the pro-Trotsky secretariat of Krestinskii, Preobrazhenskii, and Serebriakov was replaced by the future Stalinists Iaroslavskii, Mihailov, and Molotov, had culminated in the appointment of Stalin.[48] The future father of the peoples was advanced along precisely because of Lenin's struggle against bureaucracy.

Lenin's illness caused him to review all this. By September, before he was able to return to work, he had come into sharper conflict with Stalin. Now it was the question of the rights of nationalities, particularly the Georgians, and Lenin's emerging image of Stalin as a Tsarist gendarme (*dzerzhimorda*). As in the case of the trade union debate, Lenin's resolve appeared to gather momentum after he had conferred with those who felt victimized by the growing threat. In 1920 it had been Tomskii and other trade union leaders warning about Trotsky's 'shake-up'; at the end of September 1922 it was three members of the Georgian Central Committee warning him about Stalin's arbitrariness. Stalin himself was confident at this stage. He had reacted to Lenin's defense of the independence of the Georgians in a projected Union of Soviet Republics of Europe and Asia by a grudging acceptance, and responded to Lenin's very gentle remark about his 'hastiness' by referring to the 'national-liberalism of Comrade Lenin.'[49]

It may be surmised how much greater the complaints of the Georgians would weigh on Lenin's mind once he knew that his own thinking on the matter was characterized by the Gensek as a theoretical deviation from Marxism.

When Lenin returned to work shortly thereafter, he entered into discussion with Trotsky for a combination against Stalin. At this point the issues were the Monopoly of Foreign Trade, which was to be limited by the triumvirs after the fashion suggested by Sokolnikov, and the Georgian question. The issues must certainly have seemed trivial to those who knew how much Lenin valued Stalin's ability to apply pressure. But they were all that Lenin had, and there can be no doubt, in view of Lenin's Testament, dictated at the end of the year, that Lenin had resolved, as his secretary Fotieva put it, 'to crush Stalin politically.' In the addendum of 4 January 1923, Lenin stressed the 'decisive importance' of removing Stalin from the latter's post as general secretary. Lenin's problem was to justify this action in terms of issues which, to iron-hard Bolsheviks, scarcely seemed to warrant it. For Trotsky, the Monopoly of Foreign Trade was the symbol of his resistance to the whole general line of Sokolnikov and, together with the strengthening of the Gosplan, represented his means of reconciling himself to the NEP and even, to the consternation of those who called him an economic Bonaparte, making it his own.[50] The Georgians were another matter. Most would have expected Trotsky's position on them to be little different from that of Stalin. The Twelfth Party Congress was to prove this expectation to be perfectly accurate.

While Trotsky welcomed Lenin's campaign against Stalin, he continued to pursue his own ends, installing Antonov-Ovseenko at the head of the MPA, the army's political commissariat. The displaced head, S. I. Gusev, was quickly coopted by Stalin into the Central Control Commission, where he was to prove a splendid weapon against Trotsky, publishing a history of the civil war which detailed Trotsky's dictatorial actions and his 'lightmindedness about shootings.' Nevertheless, with Lenin's aid, Trotsky was consolidating both his authority on economic questions, by way of the defense of the Monopoly of Foreign Trade and the Gosplan, and his control over the military. The latter frightened the triumvirs profoundly, as they were to show in their complaints against Antonov-Ovseenko's 'politicization' of the MPA. So Trotsky's attempts at reconciliation on the concessions policy were met with continued hostility.

Trotsky nevertheless concerted his efforts with those of Zinoviev in trying to rearrange the leadership of the French Communist party and bring Souvarine's group into full control of affairs. Trotsky toyed with the idea of a coup against Frossard at the coming Fourth Comintern Congress, set for November. 'Should we establish at the congress a new central committee for the PCF?' he asked Zinoviev.[51] He wanted to eliminate some of the party's Freemasons (Frossard among them) and Paul Louis, a contributor, to Moscow's horror, to the nonparty press. He also solidarized with Zinoviev on the defense of united front tactics against the critique made by Bordiga.[52] By New Year's Day, his indignant campaign against Freemasonry, widely regarded as a pretext, had succeeded in hemming in Frossard to the point that the latter saw no other course than to resign. Frossard now joined the company of Serrati and Levi. However, as Trotsky assessed the matter three months later, after French troops had invaded the Ruhr, there had been no 'French Livorno.' Serrati's case had been unique, entirely dictated by the failure of the Italian Socialists in the 'storms of 1920.' Levi had traveled across the class line in making his critique of the March Action and the Offensive, a tactic which Trotsky admitted was 'clearly in error.' Yet, claimed Trotsky, there was a common essence in all these fights against 'semi-centrist' leaders such as Serrati, Levi, Friesland, and Frossard. These were all 'prisoners of the past' of the prewar socialist movement.

> Their opposition to the Scheidemanns and to the Renaudels was rhetorical, literary, formal, verbal, but it was neither effective nor revolutionary. When after the war an invincible movement drove the proletarian masses to the left, toward struggle with the bourgeoisie, the elements of socialist opposition thought that *their* hour had come, that the masses had approved *their* criticisms, and prepared to follow *their* instructions. In reality, their situation and their policy appealed mainly to the moderate elements of the revolutions.[53]

Trotsky must have thought that he was impressing the other Bolsheviks with this 'iron-hard' critique of the left-wing socialist tradition, the more so since this was precisely Trotsky's own tradition. The critique meant a certain burning of bridges for the eager converted Bolshevik. The balance sheet that Trotsky drew amounted to saying that there was absolutely no continuity in Bolshevism from the socialist left. Moreover, leaders of this socialist left could not even be redeemed by their participation in great events at the head of masses of people. The only really revolutionary position, and the only genuine antecedent of Communism, was therefore Old Bolshevism. Many Communists of that period believed that Communism had emerged from diverse sources, and that it.was, at least at first, what Engels had called the leadership of the First International, a 'naive conjunction of fractions.' Trotsky utterly rejected these notions. In doing so he assembled much of Zinoviev's future case against him. At its core was the idea that what counted most in Communist leadership was not a mantle of valor accumulated by this or that revolutionary episode but a record of service to the only consistent opposition to the opportunism of the Second International, Old Bolshevism. This myth, established in the Comintern and embellished in Russia by the purges following the Tenth Congress, would play a prominent part in the Lenin succession.

4

The Year 1923

For me there is no question that German humanity and Russian humanity are more close to one another than Russian and French, incomparably more close than German and Latin. There exist possibilities more grand that those between what we call humanism and the vulgar humanitarianism of the Roman peoples.
  —Thomas Mann, *Considerations of an Un-Political Man*, 1918

The Indian comrade is a personification of national Bolshevism, which will not only conquer Germany, but will win the whole of the East for Communism.
  —Karl Radek, speaking of M. N. Roy

THE EXCLUSION of Serrati, Levi, and Frossard drastically narrowed down the search for the identity of Communism. Now it was no longer described as a cause uniting Zimmerwaldists and defenders of the Russian Revolution. Instead, it was found in the ideology of Bolshevism, said to have opposed the opportunist currents of the Socialist International since well before the World War. Many sincere Communists now found that they were not genuine Bolsheviks. The Communists had always thought they had perceived a clear message from Red Russia: 'Do as we have done,' which they understood to mean 'unite the left, fight the Social Democrats, defend internationalism, prepare for the day when workers' councils will provide the means for the party to seek power.' Increasingly, however, the message came to say: 'Follow the example of the practice of Bolshevism from its earliest days. Heed the word of the Russian comrades. Beware of deviation.' And matters would go still further. The Bolshevik orthodoxy for which Trotsky strove in league with Zinoviev and the others would soon be displaced by Leninist orthodoxy defined in such a way as to exclude Trotsky.

This development took place without the contribution of Lenin himself, who could be only an obstacle to the process, and whose own preoccupation, a struggle to defeat Stalin politically, could not gather support. By the Twelfth Party Congress of April 1923, Stalin would have evaded Lenin's blows and Zinoviev would redouble his efforts against Trotsky.

57

However, Zinoviev and Trotsky continued their consensus on Comintern policy, which, while it contained excesses of zeal on Zinoviev's part in order to advertise the revolutionary role of the world peasantry, nevertheless managed to combine encouragement for German nationalism in defiance of French power with enhancement of Moscow's discipline over the other Communist parties. It was a triumph of fine-tuning. It was torn apart, however, by a rising of workers in Central and Eastern Europe in the spring and summer which upset all plans. Russian Communists who had been eclipsed by the regime of the Tenth Congress, increasingly dominated by Zinoviev and, to a lesser degree, Stalin, found an opportunity to make revolution in Germany and express opposition in Russia. They sensed a final chance for the Russian Revolution, which in their view must expand or decline. Russia, however, failed to spread the revolution, just as France failed to control Central Europe. As it would be in the winter of 1946–1947, the year 1923 would shortly bring the United States into European affairs, and into the plans and projections of the Soviet Communists.

National Bolshevism

At the time of Trotsky's victory over Frossard in January 1923, things did not look at all bleak for the commander of the Red Army. Aside from the advance of his influence in the French party and that of his associate Radek in the German, he could count on Lenin's continued opposition to Stalin. This situation would undoubtedly weaken Stalin's alliance with Zinoviev, who remained Trotsky's most implacable enemy. This was permitting a consolidation of his hold over the MPA and even allowing him attempts at reconciliation with the triumvirs. The latter, in league with Sokolnikov, the interpreter of Lenin's state capitalism, had been defeated by Lenin and Trotsky on the issue of the trade monopoly. Lenin was no longer leading a combination, as in 1920, to restrain Trotsky's economic ambitions. By the end of 1922, he was promoting Trotsky and cautioning others not to misunderstand state capitalism. Stalin, who had failed to secure what was increasingly seen as Sokolnikov's 'financial dictatorship,' seemed to be about to elevate the role of the Gosplan instead, despite its presumed closeness to Trotsky's pro-industry views. Thus Stalin, like Lenin, seemed willing to grant Trotsky the intellectual and even organizational pre-eminence in economic questions that the anti-Trotsky combination had most feared in 1920.

However, in return for Lenin's aid, the founder of Bolshevism wanted Trotsky's support against Stalin on the Georgian nationalities question. Trotsky, however, felt first that he had to look out for himself and second, that Stalin was not his greatest worry. Moreover, the Georgian question was certainly not the best one on which to make a stand, even had he desired to do so. He had written a strident justification of the sovietization by force of Menshevik Georgia in 1921. Lenin's complaint against Stalin involved the rude treatment and arbitrariness with which Georgian Communists were treated by Stalin and his cohorts. The Georgian Communists were to be accorded a certain special courtesy owing to the delicacy of the relations between Great Russians and peoples of the formerly subject nationalities. As he had with Trotsky in 1920, Lenin decided on a campaign against Stalin's bureaucratic abuses and only afterward went about assembling a platform for it. Lenin claimed to see a vast national chauvinism in the actions of Stalin and his people, and dictated notes on the Georgian affair in December 1922 just prior to the additional note of January 4, 1923 calling for the removal of Stalin from his post as General Secretary. By the time of his last, incapacitating stroke in March, Lenin had reached the point of entrusting to Trotsky his entire case against Stalin at the approaching April party congress.

Trotsky, however, never caught fire on the issue of the Georgian Communists. In communications to the Secretariat, Trotsky let it be known that he did not share its view of the Georgians' '"deviation" from the party line on the national question.' He did speak frankly of the 'incorrect policy of Ordzhonikidze,' as head of the Caucasian bureau of the party. Ordzhonikidze was under fire from Lenin for his high-handedness toward the Georgian Communists, and had even struck one of them at a meeting. Trotsky spoke of Ordzhonikidze's errors but made no threat to take the matter before the party congress.[1] He assured Stalin of his desire not to speak on the Georgian affair without prior agreement.[2] He lamented publicly that 'nationalist tendencies' had appeared among Communists of small nations, and compared nationalism among Communists to anarchism among workers.[3] No 'national liberal' he!

The idea often presented in historical accounts—according to which Trotsky went through wavering and soul-searching in his role as agent of Lenin's struggle against Stalin, and finally accepted a rotten compromise warned against by Lenin because of his political ineptitude—explains his behavior less well than the simpler supposition that he had his own fish to fry. To attack Stalin would deprive him of the possibility of deriving benefit from a split between Stalin and Zinoviev, presumably the form which any victory over the triumvirate would take. Lenin was opposed only to Stalin, not to Zinoviev. Lenin no doubt assumed his victory would not be a posthumous one, in which case he could also carry Zinoviev, as in the past. Trotsky's position was different. Fearing Zinoviev far more than Stalin, desiring fully to regain the ground lost in 1920–1921, Trotsky must, on the contrary, have found himself in a strong position by the end of the congress. His victory over Sokolnikov's version of Lenin's state capitalism seemed complete. He defended heavy industry in his economic report, calling it 'the only economic basis of the dictatorship of the proletariat.'[4] Against the temptation to lower the barriers to integrating the Soviet and European economies, Trotsky called for further vigilance:

> Only a system of socialist protectionism carried out in a consistent and determined manner can assure in the present transition period a real development of industry in our Soviet state, surrounded as it is by a capitalist world.[5]

It would be necessary, argued Trotsky, to make arrangements for further foreign investment in Russia, but this should not deter the Soviet government from favoring its own industry. To that end import quotas must be used to provide for it a more favorable competitive environment.

Trotsky once again appeared as the arch-industrializer who had boosted 'Primitive Socialist Accumulation' and as a neomercantilist who sought above all to prevent the linking of the Soviet peasant and European industry that he felt would inevitably result from the current interpretations of 'Leninist' state capitalism. Yet he did not set himself against NEP, but rather posed as its most resolute defender. Nor did he attack the regime of the gold ruble. 'It has created great difficulties,' he had explained to Rosmer, but socialism must manage accounts by the same methods as capitalism.

> When the peasant decides to buy calico from a public rather than a private factory because the product of the farmer is better and cheaper, the workers' state will have proved its superiority over capitalism in the language of capitalism.[6]

Therefore gold-backed currency must, despite the primacy of industry over finance, still serve as a barometer of economic efficiency. Moreover, industry must understand the need for such efficiencies as would be necessary to close the 'scissors,' the gap between rising industrial prices and falling prices for foodstuffs and raw materials. Who would pay for the closing of the scissors? Trotsky was loath to answer this question, but it is clear that for him it was the worker who would pay.

Thus Trotsky defended the NEP in what has become the time-honored fashion of subsequent Communist regimes. The issue had become more pressing because of the persistence of extensive strike activity in 1922–1923. It was inevitable that various Bolshevik and nonparty intellectuals would see these as a revolt against NEP itself. As the strikes developed thoughout 1923, reaching a high point in the strike wave of July and August with its centers in Kharkov, Sormovo, and Moscow, the rise of Communist strike leadership, in groups such as the Workers' Truth of A. A. Bogdanov and the Workers' Group of Gabriel Miasnikov, sounded an alarum for the Bolshevik leadership. These groups were fond of referring to NEP as the New Exploitation of the Proletariat, evidence of the intelligentsia character of the Bolshevik regime, as analyzed by the theorist Machajski.[7] Trotsky defended the NEP and denounced the 'Workers' Untruth.' By this time he had tempered the stridency of his old defense of 'one man management':

> In the epoch of war communism, the trade union leaders had but one response to make to strikers: 'You have no right to stop work, nor is the union required to defend your interests. The state of the soviets is a workers state and there is no need of special organs to defend the interests of the worker.' At bottom this response was just and remains so, but it can become a deplorable official formula if the unions have not defended against the workers' state's bureaucratic deformation.[8]

Trotsky had accepted the formula of Lenin from the Trade Union Debate. Yet he had regained with Lenin's help, and with his own ideological adjustments, the position of primacy that he had in 1920. Or so he thought.

Zinoviev, however, was not asleep. He and Kamenev stuck to the Sokolnikovist interpretation of Lenin's state capitalism and warned that Trotsky's notions on planning, with their implicit 'dictatorship of industry,' would ruin the *smychka* (union) between worker and peasant on which the revolution was founded. Trotsky had provided Zinoviev an opening with the 1922 preface to his book *1905*, in which he predicted that the workers' state would come into conflict 'not only with all the bourgeois groups which had supported it during the first stages of its revolutionary struggle, but also with the broad masses of the peasantry with whose collaboration it [the proletariat] had come to power.' This, Trotsky had written, was a problem 'soluble only on an international scale.'[9] Zinoviev continued doggedly in the orthodoxy of 1920. In lectures on the history of the Bolshevik party he intimated that Trotsky's disservice to the *smychka* had deeper historical roots in the theory of the Permanent Revolution, developed by Trotsky as editor of the Menshevik *Nachalo* (Beginning) in 1905:

> Its main delusion lay in the fact that it either ignored or seriously underestimated the role of the peasantry, and completely lost sight of the fact that the Russian Revolution could not be victorious if the working class did not establish firm collaboration with the countryside. In other words, the leaders of this tendency underrated the Bolsheviks' slogan which had been formulated as early as the middle of 1905, proclaiming the dictatorship of the proletariat and the revolutionary peasantry.[10]

This was the old slogan of the Democratic Dictatorship of the Proletariat and the Peasantry under which the Bolshevik party had marched since Lenin's *Two Tactics* of 1905 had put it forward. Lenin, however, had

discarded it by April 1917, suggesting for the first time a socialist dictatorship of the proletariat and earning the charge that he had been converted to
'Trotskyism,' that is, to the thesis of Permanent Revolution, which held
that the economic demands of the workers would break the bonds of a
bourgeois–democratic revolution and force even a democratic dictatorship
to choose between repressing the workers and taking full control of
industry as a socialist dictatorship. Trotsky had liked to say that the
democratic revolution could be secured only by a socialist government. In
April 1917, Lenin had brushed off charges that he was a convert to
Permanent Revolution and remarked that anyone who still insisted on the
democractic dictatorship slogan belonged in the 'museum of Old Bolsheviks.' He accepted the Trotskyists into the Bolshevik party, but he
never clarified the arcane question of the fate of Permanent Revolution. He
encouraged Trotsky to publish his *Results and Prospects* of 1906, which had
explained the slogan, but he never intimated that he had adopted it.
Trotsky had wanted fusion into a new party with the Bolsheviks but with
another name, on the idea that the 'wavering' of the Bolsheviks on the
defense question before April 1917 had discredited the tradition of Bolshevism. Lenin had allowed only entry into the Bolshevik party. How
could he have known that he was opening the door for Zinoviev's cult of
Leninist orthodoxy?

Zinoviev had decided that he could rout Trotsky on the slogans of
pre-1917 Bolshevism, refined into the current charge that 'Trotsky is
hostile to the peasant.' The temptation to put the agrarian tactics of
Bolshevism at the service of the Russian power struggle was understandable. Moreover, this question had been prominent in the skirmishes in the
Communist International. Refusal to consider adoption in Italy of the
Russian peasant program had been a factor in the expulsion of Serrati in
1921.[11] That Communists should put themselves at the head of radical
peasant movements had seemed to follow from the Comintern's colonial
theses. The departure from Marx was sanctioned by the experience of the
Russian Revolution. Nevertheless, application of the Bolshevik tactics
toward the peasant in industrial countries seemed at first to be anomalous.
The unfolding of the NEP, however, was helping to break down resistance
to the idea. Bukharin's extraordinary speech at the Fourth Comintern
Congress in November 1922 set the tone by asserting that 'the problem of
a new political economy is an international problem,' necessitating a turn
toward the middle class and the peasant.[12] Ernst Meyer of the KPD was
sufficiently impressed to conclude that 'the proletariat of other countries
and perhaps even that of those highly developed in the capitalist sense,
could itself, under more or less modified conditions, be led to have
recourse to the NEP.'[13] There were some adaptable Communists who
were prepared to promote an international NEP.

The Comintern, in adopting united front tactics, had already accepted the corollary of a possible coalition government with Social Democrats. The slogan of a 'workers' government' was therefore suggested by the Fourth Congress, calling forth the objection from the Fischer-Maslow left that this was a mere 'united front from above.' Ernst Meyer defended the bloc with the leaders. His fall by January 1923 would recall the experiences of Serrati, Levi, and Frossard. It seemed that division among the Germans might reflect difficulty between Radek and Zinoviev, which would in fact come to a head by the end of 1923. But the Fischer-Maslow group had established contact with the Russian Workers' Opposition and Zinoviev hesitated at this time to take it in tow. Everyone therefore agreed that a provisional step toward power might be taken by a Labour victory in England, a coalition in Germany, or a number of other means. Lenin had been seriously shaken at the turn of the century by the idea of an Australian Labour government that was not a dictatorship of the proletariat, but his associates were not at all daunted by the present formulas. Trotsky endorsed the idea of a possible workers' government in France as 'simple, clear and convincing,' even if a bit 'algebraic.'[14]

It was easy enough for the Fourth Congress to take the next step and advance the slogan of a 'workers' and peasants' government' for certain East European countries, in the spirit of the 'hinterland' theory of 1920.[15] Just as it was now deemed permissible to give critical support to a workers' government from a position of opposition, Communists might now contemplate giving the same support to a peasant government. The case that sharpened the issue was that of the Bulgarian government of Stambulisky's Peasant Union, in power since 1919. The Communists, whose poll in the elections of 1920 would have indicated that they could provide the peasants with a majority in a future coalition, endorsed the Peasant Union, but with all the reservations imaginable to those who had held out at the Fourth Congress for a 'united front from below.' The Bulgarian Communists were agitated by the cooperative attitude Stambulisky showed toward the Western powers. When his government was overthrown by a *coup d'état* in June, the Communists declined to defend it. For Zinoviev this was a clear indication that not only Russian Communists required instruction in the revolutionary role of the peasantry. By October, he and Bukharin had helped to establish a Red Peasant International (Krestintern), which had an ephemeral existence for the next two years. In doing so, Zinoviev invoked the international applicability of the NEP.[16] The cult of the peasant was helping to establish him as the best interpreter, at home and abroad, of what he was soon to call 'Integral Leninism.'

The agrarianism of the founders of Leninism was of course no hindrance to their campaign against Trotsky, the hero of the proletariat and of Permanent Revolution. It seemed as well to be in keeping with the increasingly East European character of their supposedly universal doctrine and the shrinking options of an isolated Red Russia. When Walter Rathenau was asked to define the Soviet regime in March 1922, he could think of no better phrase than 'a rigidly oligarchic agrarian republic.'

However comforting his emerging Leninism in the struggle against Trotsky, Zinoviev nevertheless could not find in it any new ideas for ending the isolation of the revolution. Outside Russia everything began with the German question, in respect to which the Bolsheviks had not succeeded in improving on their inheritance from Paul Levi. It was Levi who had stressed the importance of combining agitation for a united front with the idea of alliance with Russia. The former had been decided on from the Third Comintern Congress and the latter had emerged from the treaty of Rapallo issuing from the failure of the Genoa conference. Yet these two ideas were never to be compatible. The Social Democrats, with whom unity was to be sought under terms outlined by Levi's Open Letter, were the most faithful servitors of the cause of peace with France and violently anti-Russian. The Rapallo arrangement had a much different support among the industrialists who saw some possibilities in Russian trade, with nationalists who sought backing for defiance of the Versailles *diktat*, and with army officers who were ready for a pact with Mephisto in order to reassemble the makings of a German army. Soviet contacts with this last constituency centered on Radek and seemed to lead naturally to Trotsky. The organizer of the Red Army was very much admired in the German officer corps for his administrative talents and for his help in establishing relations between the military forces of the two countries.

For his part, Trotsky thought of relations with the German military in terms of the German revolution. He had organized the Red Army from military specialists (*spetsy*) who had fought in the Tsarist army, including even former chief of staff Brusilov. He knew that patriotic appeals were not lost on career military men if the need was pressing. When the Germany military had attempted to seize power, in the Kapp-Luttwitz putsch of 1920, the Communists had remained aloof from the general strike which defeated the putsch. In view of widespread sentiment in favor of a purge of the officer corps, an action which could only strengthen the influence of Social Democrats and others who aimed to abide by the Versailles conditions, many military men had regarded Communist abstinence as a godsend. The Soviet invasion of Poland also seemed to be in general consonance with German objectives. It went without saying that the military regarded Communism with loathing and even, after the fiasco of the March Action, with a certain disdain. Yet if the Communists should serve the cause of resistance to the French and if they should be successful in staging a revolutionary insurrection, the skeletal Reichswehr might be compelled to realize that only through the KPD would it be furnished with a 'people's army.' Seekt would thus become the German Brusilov.

The Hamburg Communists Wolffheim and Laufenberg, in their pamphlet of 1919, *Revolutionary Peoples' War or Counter-revolutionary Civil War?*, had argued that the German nation was already 'proletarianized' by the Entente and needed to join Red Russia in a war to free the Fatherland. Radek had called their theory 'National Bolshevism' and, along with Levi, had rejected it.[17] Yet these ideas would not disappear. Béla Kun's Hungarian Soviet regime of 1919 seemed an excellent example of National Bolshevism. Kun had taken power during Hungary's partition with the support of the nobility. 'To exasperate the country to such a pitch that it was driven into the arms of Bolshevism,' wrote Kun's predecessor, the 'Kerensky' (pro-Entente) figure Count Karoly, 'was the only way for the old regime to regain power.'[18] Kun had enlisted the aid of Hungarian *spetsy* to command his military staff, had nationalized the land without redistribution to the peasantry, and had refused peace even when a negotiated settlement seemed possible, perhaps for fear that he would be driven out if he had accepted.[19] He had hoped instead for aid from revolutionary Bavaria and from a putsch to be engineered by his associate Ernst Bettleheim in Vienna. The Austrian revolution would link with the Bavarian and open the gates for National Bolshevism in Central Europe. But the Bavarian Soviet was overthrown, Bettleheim's putsch failed miserably, and Kun himself was driven from power. His failure did not call forth a search for scapegoats, as was to become the rule in the future. Instead, Radek defended Kun as the latter went down to intrepid defeat, maintaining that new victories would nevertheless follow.

If National Bolshevism had failed for the moment in Central Europe,[20] the Bolsheviks nevertheless reckoned that they must encourage 'national liberation' movements, even at the expense of local Communists, in Turkey, Persia, and Afghanistan. This campaign had been set in motion by the Soviet need to oppose the British in these regions during the civil war, and in its aftermath, it still seemed profitable to Moscow to pursue the line of the Baku Congress of 1920, for implacable holy war, led by the Central Asian peoples, against British imperialism. Thus the local radical forces, with which the Bolsheviks commiserated ideologically, were sacrificed in order to maintain good state relations between Soviet Russia and the national leaders, Kemal Pasha in Turkey, Riza Shah Pahlavi in Persia, and Amanullah Khan in Afghanistan. It was tempting for some Communists, for whom the movement signified first and foremost national self-abnegation, to see in this National Bolshevism a betrayal of internationalism,[21] but their sentiments found no echo in the Russian Politburo.

On the contrary, the Bolsheviks gained in self-assurance as a result of their success in foiling British plans in the Middle East. With Soviet and French support, the Turks were able to defeat British-backed Greek forces in October 1922, with the result that the government, and the career, of

Lloyd George came to an abrupt end. One month later, Bukharin told the Fourth Comintern Congress that the Bolsheviks were powerful and clever enough to ally with a bourgeois state to defeat or overthrow another bourgeois state. Moreover, in such a case, 'the proletarian state can and must be defended not only by its proletariat but by that of other countries.'[22] This idea, which called forth no protest, least of all by Zinoviev or Trotsky, was at the heart of the later doctrine of Socialism in One Country.

The idea of applying National Bolshevism to the German scene in the wake of the French invasion of the Ruhr, in January 1923, appears to have arisen without serious opposition. The Comintern immediately called for national resistance to the French. The KPD denounced the passivity of the German 'government of national dishonor.' Communist theorist Eugen Varga had already been popularizing the notion of Germany's reduction, through reparations payments, to the status of an industrial colony. Now Thalheimer promoted the thesis that 'the German Bourgeoisie had acquired an objectively revolutionary role in spite of itself.' He and Radek recalled that, at the time of the struggle against the Napoleonic occupation of the Germanies, the Prussian reformers Scharnhorst and Gneisenau had taken refuge in Tsarist Russia, whence they had led a national rally against the French. Having gone that far, they could not resist recalling the revolutionary role played by Bismarck's wars of national liberation in the 1860s, a role acknowledged by Marx and Engels themselves. It was forgotten that Plekhanov had cited that case to urge support for Tsarist Russia's war effort in 1914, and that Lenin had replied that in the era of imperialism, only defeatism would suffice as the policy of a true workers' party. The continuity from Bismarck to Rapallo was infinitely more attractive. When Radek made his famous 'Schlageter speech' in June, he was not, therefore, doing more than publicizing the line already in effect. Schlageter had been a Freikorps militant killed by the French in the fighting in the Ruhr, a soldier of the counterrevolution, whom Radek saw as a 'wanderer into the void' (after the title of a contemporary novel). Spiritually lost and cut off from effective national leadership, the Schlageters, said Radek, could find a way out only by union with Communists, who alone offered a way to defeat French imperialism. The Schlageter line was only a dramatization of the general approach the Comintern had taken toward Germany since the beginning of the French invasion, and the KPD tried in vain to balance it by antifascist activity in which it hoped to engage the Social Democrats. War Commissar Trotsky also argued this line and attempted to maintain its uneasy balance. Asked why Communists did not take advantage of the government's imposture to stage an insurrection, he replied that the Comintern must be more circumspect than in 1919:

> Certainly we are interested in the victory of the working class, but it is not at all in our interest that the revolution should take place in a Europe

exhausted and drained of blood and that the proletariat should receive from the hands of the bourgeosie nothing but ruins.[23]

Communists must, he insisted, work for peace; in the case of a war between France and Germany, however, they could not with equanimity view a Polish attack on Germany in support of its French ally. This would be 'a blow to the European economy and a strengthening of chauvinist reaction.'[24] Europe, he asserted, had been one economic unit before the war, but France was insisting on breaking it into fragments. East Central Europe had been torn apart and had lost its natural division of labor— Trotsky repeated the thesis of John Maynard Keynes's *Economic Consequences of the Peace*—and it would prove incapable of existing and developing except within some kind of federation. Yet the French sought to increase the disarray by 'Balkanizing Europe.' 'The invasion of the Ruhr,' wrote Trotsky, 'is a piece of violent insanity accompanied by far-sighted calculation—the final disruption of Germany—a combination not unfamiliar to the psychiatrist.'[25]

Trotsky's remedy was, he thought, truly 'European': a revival of the 'United States of Europe' slogan. This idea had a certain German pedigree from the prewar period. As early as 1902, the Kaiser had spoken of a plan for 'Les États-Unis de l'Europe,' to include both France and Russia, under German leadership. In 1912, the Kaiser had spoken to Walther Rathenau of a 'United States of Europe against America.'[26] Trotsky's advocacy in 1915 of the 'United States of Europe' had occasioned the quarrel with Lenin to which we have already referred,[27] a quarrel which was to serve as the theoretical foundation for Stalin's version of Socialism in One Country.

In 1923, Trotsky worried, as he had in 1915, that the slogan might take on the appearance of pacifism, but his was to be remedied by coupling it with the slogan of a 'Workers' and Peasants' Government,' or other formulations such as a 'Europe of Workers and Peasants.' Was this idea a description of the dictatorship of the proletariat? 'Only a conditional answer can be given to this question,' Trotsky admitted. The transitional character of both slogans must be emphasized. What, then, had happened to the idea of the Permanent Revolution, which insisted on the impossibility of 'transitional' democratic provisional governments such as that envisioned in Lenin's Democratic Dictatorship of the Proletariat and the Peasantry? Obviously, Trotsky had decided long since that he could not stand on the Permanent Revolution but would instead have to accept Zinoviev's revival of the pre-1917 Bolshevik position. Trotsky had already recognized that he could survive politically only as a disciple of Lenin.

Thus, he could make no real criticism of Zinoviev's and Bukharin's adventures in pursuit of a Peasant International. In 1923, these included a general Krestintern call for the formation of peasant parties. Exaggerated hopes would be placed in peasant leaders such as the Croatian Stjepan Radić. Trotsky would write of the opportunism of the latter's 1924 trip to the Soviet Union, that 'en route to Green Zagreb he thought it advisable to show himself to Red Moscow to strengthen his chances to become Minister in White Belgrade.'[28] Zinoviev's associate Josef Pogany, former minister in Béla Kun's Hungarian Soviet Regime, was dispatched to the United States, where, as John Pepper, he mastered the English language and the leadership of the Communist party. Pogany–Pepper argued for the revolutionary role of the American 'peasantry.' In respect of this, he directed a series of projects for a Farmer–Labor party to stand for the 1924 elections.[29] Trotsky would write later of those and other overtures to the 'world countryside' that they showed a fundamental error in attempting to form a 'two-class party' — essentially the criticism he was to make in 1927 of Comintern policy toward the Chinese Kuomintang.[30] However, he raised no such objection in 1923.

Trotsky had little reason to quarrel about the particulars of the slogans of the Zinoviev Comintern. He had consolidated his hold over the armed forces and had regained his primacy as maker of pronouncements on economic policy. The closing of the 'scissors,' as he had described it at the Twelfth Congress, was considered the first desideratum of economic policy. Yet the economic situation continued to deteriorate. The triumvirate dutifully followed the prescription to 'close the scissors,' to seek higher agricultural prices by opening up foreign markets, to seek lower industrial prices by eliminating waste, closing inefficient enterprises, and cutting costs, including labor costs, wherever possible. Trotsky emphasized as much as Sokolnikov the need for strict accounting in industry, and despite his pronouncements that planning must provide sufficient credit for industrial enterprises, he knew as well as anyone that closing the scissors would be paid for by the urban worker. In addition, inflation of the paper *sovznak* was driving the workers to desperation. In July and August, a wave of strikes hit Kharkov, Sormovo, and Moscow, at almost the same time that the strike curve was rising ominously in Germany and Poland.[31] The Moscow dialecticians apparently only partially recognized this message from the *Zeitgeist*: The workers were in effect demanding fulfillment in Germany and an end to the credit crunch in Russia. In Germany, the delicate balancing act between the National Bolshevist line and the united front was upset. In Poland, with nearly a million workers on strike (two-thirds of the entire industrial work force), the Communist party was taken completely by surprise.[32] In the Soviet Union, the leftist opponents of NEP, in particular the Workers' Group of Miasnikov, again sprang into action, sending out their powerful challenge to all who sought to close the scissors, including both the triumvirs, who controlled the party apparatus as Old Bolsheviks, and the leading outsider, Trotsky.

In the beginning of August, at the height of the German hyperinflation, a strike of the printers who manufactured the currency turned into a near-general strike and brought down the Cuno government. Gustav Stresemann, who was to be Minister of Foreign Affairs in a series of governments, assumed, in addition to that post, the leadership of the government. He was widely perceived in Moscow as an opponent of the policy of resistance to reparations by means of currency inflation, as he indeed turned out to be. His rise meant that the Soviet policy of encouraging such resistance was ruined. The Bolsheviks began to refer to him as a 'Kerensky' — which held the dual meaning that he was a tool of the Entente imperialists and, as well, a prelude to October. At the end of August, serious plans for his overthrow were set in motion.

As the pot boiled in the Soviet Union, party meetings increasingly concerned themselves with the loss of contact between the party and the proletarian masses, and the problem of suppressing any potential leaders of the revolt. It was at one of these meetings in October that Trotsky was challenged to intervene, on an odd pretext. A call was given to report any subversive groups within the party. Trotsky answered by stating that since this was ABC for Communists, the necessity of the call revealed a deeply unhealthy situation. Was Trotsky choosing the right moment for combat against the triumvirs? He thought that by neglecting Lenin's charge to fight Stalin at the Twelfth Congress he had gained considerable ground, at least in terms of his prestige in economic matters. He knew, moreover, that the crisis was causing disunity among the triumvirs and that both Zinoviev and Stalin sought his aid against the other. At the resort town of Kislovodsk in September, Zinoviev had convened some Politburo members and tried vainly to coopt Trotsky into the Secretariat. Stalin also sought to deflect any difficulty with Trotsky in Zinoviev's direction. Yet the period after the Twelfth Congress had not seen any progress in reconciling Trotsky with the leadership. Zinoviev was mobilizing Petrograd continuously with an ideological campaign against him, calling the Gosplan a 'nest of the *spetsy*' and planning itself a Menshevik idea. In May, his closest associate, Christian Rakovskii, was posted to the embassy in France. There seemed little reason to coalesce with the triumvirs in the face of the collapse of their economic and social policy. The policy was also his policy, but he could always claim that they were implementing it incompetently. This was certainly the case with regard to any matters dealing with personnel. Perhaps this was the time to use the crisis to get himself back into the inner leadership circle.

His letter of 8 October broke the ice. On the eve of revolution in Germany, wrote Trotsky, the party had still not found a way out of the crisis of its own mismanagement. The economic and social challenge was caused by failure to bolster the Gosplan, thus the better to carry out the rationalization of industry and to close the scissors.[33] The triumvirs were thus told that the policy that had caused the crisis was its remedy. The only way to make intelligible Trotsky's economic critique was to understand it as a demand for new generalship in the economy, the achievement of proportion among various branches of industry by the use of special dicta from above. These were not to be, Trotsky hastened to add, in imitation of the methods of War Communism. It must be recognized, however, that the problem originated, and was alone soluble, at the top. The crisis engulfed the party because Trotsky was not leading it.

This argument was attached to a general complaint about the appointment of provincial secretaries, which related directly to the building up of Stalin's patronage apparatus. However, Trotsky did not appeal instead for a broadening of 'workers' democracy,' a demagogic idea in view of 'the incompatibility of a fully developed workers' democracy with a regime of dictatorship.'[34] He wanted only a loosening of the regime and an end to the attacks on his administration of the armed forces. The reference was presumably to Stalin's attempt to enter the Military Revolutionary Council and Trotsky's categorical refusal to permit it.

A week later, the Platform of the Forty-Six was published. A curious document directed toward the economic crisis and the abuses of the party regime, it was apparently crafted by prominent Bolsheviks who had been increasingly pushed into obscurity after the decisions of the Tenth Congress in 1921, including Preobrazhenskii and Serebriakov, who had been removed at that time from the Secretariat. It emphasized that the crisis was not to be explained by 'the political incapacity of the leadership' but that the Tenth Congress had given rise to factional behavior by the leadership.[35] The signatories affixed their names only after making various qualifications and disclaimers. Some said they did not agree with the description of the problem, but recognized a problem. Thirteen signatories excluded absolutely any struggle in the party. Three complained of exaggeration in the critique of the leadership, and one asserted that no one could 'lead in a manner superior to those who now lead.'[36] The triumvirs were not likely to be impressed with this protest. They were, in fact, more likely to read it as a series of pleas for reconsideration of the individual cases.

Moreover, Trotsky did not sign the protest. His subsequent dispute with the triumvirs, extending into January, was never concerted with the Forty-Six. He would not have considered for a moment having his name appearing alongside Sapranov, Ossinskii, or other veteran dissidents, or being associated with the Democratic Centralists or other previous oppositions. Souvarine, following the controversy in *Bulletin communiste*, cautioned his readers, 'There is no one opposition in Russia. Trotsky fights alone.'[37] By his own later testimony, Trotsky strove to assert that his main opponent in 1923 had not been Stalin but Zinoviev. The mass of the Leningrad party, he wrote to Bukharin, 'was muzzled more than was the case elsewhere . . . everything in Leningrad goes splendidly (one hundred per cent) five minutes before things get very bad . . . the traits of apparatus bureaucratism peculiar to the whole party have been brought to their extreme expression in the regime of the Leningrad party.'[38] After he had joined Zinoviev's opposition in 1926, Trotsky spoke and wrote of the continuous struggle of the opposition against Stalinism, from 1923 on, a characterization accepted in many historical accounts, but highly dubious in view of his own record.

The German October

While the inner party controversy over a new course for Bolshevism was raging, preparations for the German rising went forward. KPD head Heinrich Brandler came to Moscow at the beginning of September, with the leaders of the party's Berlin left, Ruth Fischer and Arkadi Maslow. The latter had made a running critique of the Schlageter line but were now delighted to see the KPD preparing the German October. Discussion centered on the tactical problems of insurrection, or what Lenin had called the art of insurrection. It was decided, unanimously, that the KPD should not call on the workers to form soviets. The factory councils, it was held, which had played such an important role in the August strike, could play the role played in Russia by the Soviets.[39] The Petrograd Soviet had vied with the Provisional Government for the loyalty of the garrison, had won over many units, had created a military revolutionary committee which had directed the October insurrection. Centering their hopes on Saxony, the Bolsheviks planned for the KPD to enter the Left Social Democratic Zeigner cabinet, help themselves to arms from its arsenals, establish a Saxon 'workers' government,' and march on the capital. The timing was left to Brandler, although Trotsky had insisted on setting a date.[40] The moment arrived on 20 October, when, after Brandler and two other Communists entered the government, General Müller of the Reichswehr announced preparations to march on Dresden. Müller was cast as General Kornilov, with Zeigner as Kerensky; therefore, Zeigner should have given arms to the Red Guards (in the German case Proletarian Hundreds) with which to foil Müller, as the Bolsheviks had foiled Kornilov, after which the soviet (in the German case, a conference of factory council leaders and trade unionists meeting at Chemnitz on 20 October) would empower the KPD to take power. This was the abstract October 1917 model, with which the Bolsheviks took many liberties and made generous substitutions, especially with the schedule. To put it mildly, the model robbed the German October of its "organic' quality. The KPD did not get its arms, the Chemnitz conference (which was not a soviet) did not empower effective action against General Müller, and Brandler did not make the German October.

News of the success of the Reichswehr troops and the crushing of the Communist insurrection shocked both the opposition and the troika. But neither resolved to blame the other as yet. By the Comintern Executive (ECCI) meeting and the Thirteenth Party Conference in January, the course of action would be resolved. Zinoviev, who lost so much by the defeat, wavered as long as possible and then decided to throw his weight behind the interpretation given by the German left: Brandler had over-estimated chances in Germany, turned the bloc with Zeigner into a 'banal parliamentary coalition,' and thus betrayed the revolution. Zinoviev had not taken this position immediately, but he was prodded by Radek's threat that, if the troika should censure Trotsky, it would lose the support of the German and French parties, a suggestion that the crisis in the Russian party and the International were linked. In the first of a series of articles titled 'Problems of German Revolution,' Zinoviev did not blame Brandler. But Ruth Fischer's letter of 22 November and a document by Maslow attacked the strategy of joining in the Saxon government.[41] It did not take Zinoviev long to conclude that an amalgam of all his potential and real critics would serve him well. From this point on, he inveighed against the right deviations of Brandlerism and Trotskyism in the name of his one-hundred-per-cent 'Integral Leninism.' The German lefts thus made an effective intervention in the Russian faction struggle.

To be consistent, Trotsky might have argued that the fiasco was no one's fault, attributable instead to objective factors—that is, roughly the line that was taken on the failure of the Hungarian Soviet regime of 1919. Alternatively, he might have offered a critique, as Thalheimer later did, of the 'speculative plan of action,' imposed on Brandler (that is, had he really, as he later insisted, had nothing to do with its formulation).[42] But Trotsky did not defend Brandler. As much as Zinoviev, he feared being blamed for the German fiasco and knew that blame would be assigned to someone. He needed it to be assigned to Zinoviev and Brandler.

From early 1924, and especially from the time of his *Lessons of October*, Trotsky promoted the myth of their betrayal. In his *Third International After Lenin*, he referred to the responsibility of Zinoviev and the 'comedy of Saxony.'[43] He called the German failure the 'premise' for the degeneration of the Soviet Communist party. In 1930, he told his French adherents that the German events had prompted his own struggle. 'It was on that basis,' he wrote, 'that the opposition was formed.'[44] To some German semi-Brandlerists, he complained about the 'capitulation' of 1923.[45] The author of the capitulation was Brandler:

> In 1923, chances of a victorious revolution were offered more strongly than ever in Germany. The occupation of the Ruhr disorganized the bourgeoisie and the state. The mark fell each day at a more fantastic rate. Unemployment ravaged the proletariat and ruined the petite-bourgeoisie. The Communist party was more powerful and active than it had ever been. Strikes became more and more general. Then the leader

of the Germany party, instead of leading the working class toward insurrection, organized a conference of factory delegates at Chemnitz and awaited its decision. Naturally, in the presence of the irresolution of the leaders, this had the effect of forcing each to look to his own responsibilities. The hour of the victorious revolution passed . . . men like Brandler have no place at the head of a Communist organization. With the Brandlers, there will never be a revolution.[46]

Trotsky weakly claimed later that he had not been informed about the preparations.[47] Yet Brandler would later claim that Trotsky had been the most eager of all the Bolshevik leaders to convince him of the rectitude of the Saxony strategy. 'I spent a whole night with Trotsky,' Brandler would tell Isaac Deutscher, 'who tried to persuade me that I should submit to the decisions of the Comintern.'[48] And in 1939, in a discussion with an American follower, C. L. R. James, Trotsky also related that he had 'had many interviews with Brandler . . . Brandler took many notes during many discussions with me. But this very boldness of his was only a cover for his secret fears.'[49] Trotsky asserted to the end of his life that Brandler, together with Zinoviev, had ruined a splendid opportunity in 1923 and that this failure, somehow connected with the 1923 Russian opposition's defeat, laid the basis for the further degeneration of Soviet Communism. When the moment seemed opportune, he even tried to blame Brandler on Stalin:

> Stalin claimed that in 1923 Trotsky supported Brandler. Who I supported in 1923 is clear from documents before the then politburo. Stalin himself was the true Brandlerite.[50]

But he was never able completely to convince the most inquisitive of his followers.[51]

It was clear enough why Trotsky attempted to dissociate himself from the 'Saxon comedy.' At the time, however, the policy of the Moscow Politburo on the formation of a coalition government in Saxony had his explicit approval. In a speech to a meeting of Moscow metalworkers on 19 October 1923, he answered objections to the policy:

> At one meeting the question was put to me whether the entry of the Saxon Communists into a government of conciliators was not an act of opportunism? This is not opportunism but a revolutionary measure![52]

In a speech the next day, he called the coalition 'an entirely correct step' and argued that 'the mere fact of a coalition cabinet in Saxony meant a mortal blow to the German Social Democracy' and 'shook the organizational conservatism of the Social Democratic workers.'[53] In fact, when one reviews the numerous statements about the German October in Trotsky's later writings, including the *Lessons of October* (1924), one finds a curious reluctance to be explicit about the exact source of the failure of 1923. Yet he steadfastly criticized the missed opportunity. Ultimately it came down to generalship, in much the same sense as his economic critique of the troika in his letter of October 8. If Trotsky had been permitted to manage the affair, he seemed to be saying, he could have done better. He had been refused a chance to go to Germany, on Brandler's request, by the Politburo, which elected to send the 'Trotskyists' Radek and Piatakov instead. If he had been permitted to go, one might imagine Trotsky saying, the twentieth century would have had a more pleasant course. However, that would be another way of saying that there was no genuine programmatic difference between him and the troika. Essentially there was only the 'regime question.' And that was the point of the controversy with Boris Souvarine in 1929.

The regime of the troika was by no means loosened as a result of the crisis of the New Course, as it came to be known. A Politburo resolution of 24 December 1923 promised to emphasize production by light and consumer goods industries, but again stressed the crucial importance of bolstering discipline. The troika described the struggle as an attack on NEP, led by extremist elements foreign to the party, in which the Forty-Six and Trotsky tried to intervene, in order to restore the pre–Tenth Congress regime—that is, the regime of War Communism. Party members were again warned about the Bonapartist ambitions of the War Commissar. Although he had only played the role of an intermediary in the debate, Trotsky showed, they were told, that he was willing to stir up the youth against the old guard. That he had been able to make appointments to the MPA showed, they insisted, that the party's influence in the armed forces was threatened. There would soon follow a rash of dismissals of Trotsky appointees and their replacement by Zinovievists and even former Decemists. That the New Course controversy was a struggle between Party and Army, NEP and War Communism, was a constant theme. Even the 'Easterners' in the German Foreign Office, who sought to bolster German-Soviet relations, saw it that way, hoping for a victory by the War Commissar which, they thought, would serve their cause and avoid future interference in German affairs.[54] It was fantastic to think of the position of head of the armed forces as a liability, but Trotsky would within a year come to exactly this conclusion. In that time, Zinoviev would strive still more mightily to defeat Trotsky and to conjure the world revolution out of the depths. The setting would be drastically altered. On 21 January 1924, the party and the world received news of Lenin's death.

5

Moscow and Leningrad,
1924–1928

Zinoviev acts almost on Luther's principle. But whereas Luther
said, 'Here I stand; I cannot do otherwise.' Zinoviev says, 'Here I
stand . . . but I can do otherwise, too.'

—L. D. Trotsky

THE CONFLUENCE of the three events—the failure of the German
rising, the defeat of the 'Forty-Six' and of Trotsky, and the death of
Lenin—set Zinoviev even more firmly on the path he had been attempting
to cut since the Tenth Congress. Zinoviev appeared to be Lenin's successor, at least in 1924. After Lenin, he had been the central rallying force in
the group which had opposed Trotsky on the invasion of Poland in 1920
and in the Trade Union Debate. His adoption of Sokolnikov's program for
the financial manipulation of 'state capitalism' had unfortunately run up
against the opposition of Lenin himself, but with Lenin stricken, Zinoviev
had been able to resume the construction of Leninism by reviving the
slogan of the Revolutionary Democratic Dictatorship of the Proletariat
and the Peasantry. Zinoviev's problem lay not in defending these positions
against the counterattacks of the 1923 opposition, which proved to be far
from formidable and easily parried administratively. His real vulnerability
lay in the unchallenged premise that the Russian Revolution was only a
prelude to the world revolution, which would start in Germany or some
other Western country. As head of the Comintern, he was in effect charged
with producing that revolution. The defeat in Germany therefore weighed
more heavily on him than on any other Bolshevik. He could not treat it
with the magnanimity shown by the Bolsheviks in the face of the defeat of
the Hungarian Soviet. The clamor of the Berlin left against Brandler
demanded a decision, and Radek's insinuations that the German and
French parties supported Zinoviev's critics in Russia forced the issue. So
Zinoviev, having extended an ideological umbrella under which all those
who feared Trotsky might gather, was now forced to venture into the rain
in order to defeat Radek and Trotsky in the Comintern. His response was
the 'Bolshevization' of the Communist parties in 1924, complete with a

rationale for the hard times the Comintern had been suffering, the theory of international social democracy as the vanguard of fascism. Zinoviev claimed that Europe was in its eleventh hour—from here on it would be either Communism or fascism. His prognosis would be undermined, not by European events, but by the American Dawes Plan, whose loans eased the crisis of reparations and war debts and, like the later Marshall Plan, opened the way to economic recovery. Russian Communists soon took note of a stabilization of the situation in the West, which seemed to refute decisively the theoretical basis of 'Bolshevization.'

Zinoviev found it easier to coordinate the Communist parties than his Russian partners in the anti-Trotsky coalition. Stalin collected his gains in patronage power in 1924–1925, and Bukharin staked out a theoretical position from issues raised by Zinoviev in his campaign to designate Trotsky hostile to the peasant. By 1925, Zinoviev, having abandoned the middle ground, found himself isolated in his Leningrad bastion by a Stalin-Bukharin bloc. His opponents in the International, including Souvarine, hailed his defeat as a victory for sobriety and saw the Stalin-Bukharin bloc as a hope for reconciliation with Trotsky and a more predictable future for Communism. Yet by 1926, they would be thunderstruck by Trotsky's adhesion to Zinoviev's opposition coalition, an amalgamation which seemed to deny all political logic. By 1927, this opposition would be broken, with Zinoviev capitulating to Stalin, himself now breaking with Bukharin to adopt many of the old positions of the Zinoviev coalition. By the time of Souvarine's controversy with Trotsky in 1929, these twists and turns had left the former in disarray. Trotsky demanded of him that he agree to tell the story of the defeat of Stalin's rivals in a way that violated everything he had observed in Russian politics since his own fall. In Trotsky's 1929 position he saw essentially a restatement of the views of Zinoviev, his old tormentor. Souvarine would reject Trotsky, but would, like Fischer-Maslow, Treint, and others, seek a literary compromise between his own experience and the fables told by Trotsky.

The Patrimony of Anti-Trotskyism

In the course of the polemics on the New Course, Stalin and Zinoviev each layed stress on themes particularly important to his own bailiwick: for Stalin, the party's patronage machine; for Zinoviev, the Comintern. Trotsky, said Stalin, hoped to justify discussion without limit because he was not an activist, but only a talker, who had been quoted as saying that

> The party is a 'voluntary union of like-minded people.' I search in vain for this formula in Trotsky's writings but if it is there it is not correct.

The party is not only a union of the like-minded, it is a union of those who fight in the same way, champions of the same cause. . . . There must be an error here, because I know Trotsky to be one of those members of the Central Committee who has emphasized the active side of the party's work.[1]

Zinoviev, said Stalin, had been wrong to criticize the political level of certain party cells. If that were true, it was only because of so many recent retirements. 'It is necessary,' Stalin therefore concluded, 'to renounce excessive formalities for admission to the party.' This plea of Stalin's, from a speech to the Krasnopresnenskii raion committee in December, indicates what he was seeking even before Lenin's death and his call for a 'Lenin Levy.' With the great leader fallen, however, his own interest in building his patronage machine could be disguised as a final tribute.

Zinoviev underlined the need for activism as a major lesson of the New Course controversy, and explained to foreign Communists that Leninism demanded a resolute fight against *déclassé* intellectuals of Trotsky's type. He recalled the strike of government employees that had broken out when the Bolsheviks took power, a strike whose suppression had been one of the first acts of the Bolshevik regime.[2] This was how the working class must deal with a refractory intelligentsia. Zinoviev and Stalin would return to this theme in further contentions with Trotsky.

Zinoviev's greater burden, however, was to explain away the fiasco of the German events. At the Thirteenth Party Conference in January 1924, he reiterated the treason of Brandler and the betrayal of the Social Democrats, and added his own twist. On the assumption of power by Mussolini in Italy at the end of 1922, Zinoviev had referred to those socialists who offered Il Duce a bloc on foreign policy matters as 'social fascists.' In early 1923, he told the Comintern that Italy was being ruled by a 'fascist-reformist bloc.'[3] At the Thirteenth Party Conference, he again referred to Turati as a 'socialist of the fascist type.' 'His party,' said Zinoviev, 'is only a wing of fascism.' The German events, he thought, gave further proof of a general tendency. 'It is necessary to tell the workers,' said Zinoviev, 'that social democracy has become an element of fascism.'[4] Foreign Communists who understood these words issuing from the feverish imagination of the president of the Comintern could only react with horror. Those at fault for failure in Germany, in their 'banal parliamentary bloc' with the Social Democrats, were actually in league with semi-fascists.

Only one conclusion could follow: The united front as practiced had been false. It was necessary to break with the socialist leaders and pursue a 'united front from below' as preached by the Berlin left. The campaign would reach its height at the Fifth Comintern Congress in summer 1924, the 'congress of Bolshevization,' which celebrated the triumph of Fischer and Maslow in the German party and Treint and Girault in the French.

For his part, Trotsky tried to explain to his foreign supporters that he was not, as Comintern representatives were claiming, repeating the views of Miasnikov and the critics of the NEP. He tried to put the 1923 struggle into perspective by reminding his friends that 'a more serious disagreement arose in the autumn of 1917 over the question of taking power.' He also referred to an 'anecdote' to the effect that, at the time of peace negotiations with Germany and Austria at Brest-Litovsk in 1918, Bukharin had considered his differences with official policy severe enough to contemplate arresting Lenin.[5] Trotsky had never mentioned this before, but in view of Bukharin's attacks on him in 1923, there was no reason for him to treat Bukharin better than Zinoviev. The effect was to alert all that differences in the Russian party were indeed at the breaking point.

Souvarine did not know which way to turn. His admiration for Trotsky knew no limits, but he was slow to sense the need to choose sides. His most entrenched factional and personal opponent, Albert Treint, saw the opening and denounced Trotsky. Treint was not deterred by the considerable support Trotsky had given him, support which had aided his rise to a position in the French party analogous to Stalin's in the Russian.[6] Treint was as much a product of Trotsky's struggle against Serrati-Levi-Frossard as was Souvarine. Treint had never criticized the Comintern line, nor was he, prior to this, in solidarity with Fischer-Maslow as part of an international Zinovievist bloc. In German matters he defended Radek's policy.[7] But this opportunity was too good to miss. By March, Treint had managed to combine his numerous disagreements with Souvarine on the nuances of united front tactics — Souvarine had criticized Treint's reference to the socialists as 'chickens to be plucked' (*volaille à plumer*) — with the more general charge that Souvarine, Rosmer, and their associates represented, with Brandler and Trotsky, an international right deviation, seeking the 'de-Bolshevization' of all the Communist parties.[8] Treint's organizational struggle with Souvarine thus became cloaked in the garb of the Russian anti-Trotsky campaign. Souvarine complained of the ancien régime of 'Captain Treint' (he had held that rank during the war).[9] Treint saw that as evidence of indiscipline. Moreover, Treint said, the 'international right' was soft on the new British Labour government.

What Zinoviev and Treint saw, or claimed they saw, as a rise of social fascism was actually a kind of preview of the Popular Front period. An English Labour government under Ramsay MacDonald took office in January, and the *cartel des gauches*, in the wake of the failure of Poincaré's Ruhr policy, won the French elections in May. Both decreed de facto recognition of the Soviet Union. Moreover, during the summer, the Dawes Plan, extending American loans to Germany and resetting the schedule for reparations payments, was also put into place. Trotsky tried as sharply as possible to show that there was no broadening of the Mussolini model, but instead the long-awaited intervention of the United

States into European affairs. The center of world finance would now rearrange the affairs of the Old World, putting Europe, in his famous phrase, 'on rations.' The Social Democracy was the vanguard not of fascism but of the Wilsonian pacifism of the American republic, eager to reorder the world market, liberate the colonies held by the Old World, and ultimately train European craftsmen to refashion its mass-produced goods to the tastes of the non-European world. Would the former arbiter of the world market, mighty England, accept this reduction to the position of a poor relation? She would have to, said Trotsky, unless the revolutionary tradition was revived.[10] England would either resist America by means of Bolshevism or end by carrying the bags of the bumptious Americans. Trotsky would repeat this theme in *Where Is Britain Going?*, published in 1925. The National Bolshevism of the British was now counted on to breathe new life into the slogan of the United States of Europe.

Treint objected that Trotsky was wrong to suppose an Anglo-American antagonism to be at the center of world politics, when the British gave ground all along the line. Trotsky was preaching, he continued (with a logic worthy of the Mad Hatter), a kind of 'Kautskyan super-Imperialism,' a utopia of a perfectly managed world capitalism.[11] It would have been impossible to predict both a perfectly managed world imperialism and an Anglo-American war. Treint, however, was less concerned with the danger of contradicting himself than with the chance to harmonize with the line of Integral Leninism. Profintern chief Lozovskii wrote in the PCF daily *L'Humanité* in December 1923 that the Labour victory in England was a triumph for the British bourgeoisie. Treint went the next step and accused Rosmer, Monatte, and Souvarine of treating British Labour in a '*manière douce.*' The eager would-be Zinovievists were en route to the construction of a worldview out of the social-fascism epithet.

Yet it was too fantastic for even Zinoviev to sustain consistently. In fact, British Communists did not sever their ties to the British Labour movement, nor did Zinoviev discourage talk of amalgamating the Amsterdam International of trade unions with the Profintern. Profintern chief Lozovskii's hard line was in fact generating opposition from Tomskii, who wanted greater trade union cooperation and broader united front tactics—in effect, a return to the approach of Paul Levi. More shall be said about this below. Zinoviev's actions, even at the height of this campaign against the 'international right,' show that he veered wildly to the left only to dislodge Trotsky's Comintern supporters.

Trotsky fought back with his 'Lessons of October,' the preface to a newly published edition of his 1917 writings. The central burden of the essay was to string together (in the same manner that Zinoviev had strung together his case against Trotsky) the wavering, semi-defensist policy of the Bolsheviks in 1917 before Lenin's return, Zinoviev's and Kamenev's opposition to the October insurrection, the defeat of the Bulgarian party in 1923, and the German October. The current talk about Bolshevization, the Revolutionary Democratic Dictatorship of the Proletariat and the Peasantry, and the Leninist orthodoxy of the Old Bolsheviks, should not obscure, said Trotsky, the failure of the leadership evidenced in all these cases. Zinoviev, Kamenev, and Lozovskii were mentioned by name; Stalin's role, in the case of the pre-April, 1917, wavering, only implied. Trotsky admitted later that he was deliberately casting more fire on Zinoviev and Kamenev than on Stalin: 'When I wrote my "Lessons of October,"' he related in 1928, 'that is, in the summer of 1924, it seemed to me that Stalin held a position further to the left (that is, left-centrist) than Zinoviev in the autumn of 1923.'[12]

Trotsky demonstrated that in sheer obfuscation, he could compete on a level with Zinoviev. Historical accounts sometimes consider the 'Lessons of October' a tactical error and further evidence of his political ineptitude. It is more likely, however, that Trotsky knew what he was doing. He could not have failed to read the signs of the weakening of Stalin's solidarity with Zinoviev. Stalin had corrected Zinoviev on small matters having to do with defining the essence of Bolshevik discipline. He had never endorsed Zinoviev's 'overestimation' of the peasants. He echoed Zinoviev on the social-fascism theory, no doubt to encourage him. 'Social Democracy,' wrote Stalin in September, 'is objectively the moderate wing of fascism . . . they are not antipodes, but twins.'[13] At the same time, however, having got his Lenin Levy, he undermined Kamenev's control of the Moscow party machine, replacing its leader I. A. Zelenskii, with N. A. Uglanov, a Leningrad critic of Zinoviev.[14] Instead of simply stumbling with the 'Lessons of October', Trotsky may have been attempting to lead the critics of Zinoviev's Comintern tactics, those, like his old adversary Tomskii, who were to get the upper hand a few months later.

At any rate, 'Lessons of October' provoked a torrent of attacks from all the leading figures of Russian and world Communism. Every major Communist in agreement with the troika weighed in vehemently against Trotsky. Zinoviev's contribution to the onslaught showed how badly wounded he was by Trotsky's charges. He was forced to defend at length, before cadres not entirely familiar with his position in October 1917, his 'October error.' He described the hesitation of many workers and ascribed his mistake to their influence, so that the error was 'neither a personal nor an accidental one.'[15] He had broken a Marxist taboo and blamed the workers, which was bound to strike the veteran Communist as rather like blaming the sea for bad navigation.

Moreover, said Zinoviev, Trotsky was 'a classical type of the intellectual revolutionary,' who tended not toward the vanguard party but toward a 'broad labor party' as envisioned in the prerevolutionary days by Pavel Axelrod. This was perfectly correct as intellectual biography. That was the origin of Trotsky's thinking in the 1904–1905 period, thinking which seemed to be realized in the appearance of the St. Petersburg Soviet. Zinoviev went still further: Trotsky, he said, spoke for a new Soviet intelligentsia now manning the state apparatus, fond of planning and ultimately Menshevik in outlook. That must have made many party officials in state positions cringe, and wonder if Trotsky's 'Axelrodism' were as bad as Zinoviev's 'one hundred percent Leninism.'

Trotsky, said Zinoviev, had never thought differences with Rosa Luxemburg to be important. This again was true enough, but, in view of Rosa Luxemburg's murder in 1919 and her place as a martyr of Communism, little stress had been laid on, for example, her dispute with Lenin on nationalism in 1914. Now that Zinoviev had brought it up, however, one could imagine the possibility of fitting alongside Trotsky's underestimation of the peasant, an underestimation of nationalism, akin to that of Rosa Luxemburg. Trotsky's Permanent Revolution was said to have wagered all on 'state support' (that is, revolution) from the Western workers, and would thus have 'postponed' the October Revolution. All this Zinoviev wrote with a straight face, hoping to hurt Trotsky more than Trotsky had hurt him. The effect however, was doubly ruinous for Zinoviev, in that the Marxist arguments he was using against Trotsky, because of their very ingenuity and the particle of truth they contained, could serve as a point of departure, by way of the notion of Socialism in One Country, for attacks on the Zinoviev Comintern.

Stalin's contribution was, if the adjective has a place in describing this sort of skulduggery, quite brilliant. He excused his pre–April, 1917, wavering simply by saying that Lenin had rallied him to the correct position. He cultivated the image of the modest pupil of Lenin. Yet he dwelled at length, to Zinoviev's discomfort, on October 1917, claiming that the insurrection had not been led by Trotsky's Military Revolutionary Committee of the Soviet but by the party's own center, the 'practical central commission for the organizing direction of the revolt.'[16] Stalin claimed no special role for himself and denied any to Trotsky. The party, he intoned, and not special individuals, was alone responsible.

At the end of the controversy Stalin gathered up the available threads of claims and insinuations to fashion, in the manner of the day, an attack on Trotsky which was already a document of split with Zinoviev. In 'The October Revolution and the Tactics of the Russian Bolsheviks,' he returned to Lenin's 1916 controversy with Trotsky on the United States of Europe slogan. Zinoviev had already harped on the anti-Leninism of Trotsky's 1916 position, but Stalin breathed new life into the question of 'state support':

It goes without saying that we need support. But what does support of our revolution by the West European proletariat imply? Is not sympathy of the European workers for our revolution, their readiness to thwart the imperialists' plans of intervention—is not all this support, real assistance? . . . Up to now, has this moral support, coupled with the might of our red army and the readiness of the workers and peasants of Russia to defend their socialist fatherland to the last—has all this been sufficient to beat off the attacks of the imperialists and to win us the necessary conditions for the serious work of construction? Yes, it has been sufficient.[17]

Zinoviev had provided the opening by his interpretation of the Lenin-Trotsky quarrel of 1916; he had claimed that Lenin's critique of Permanent Revolution had been a critique of Trotsky's alleged expectation of 'simultaneous' revolution. Stalin only followed the obvious implications. If revolutions did not occur 'simultaneously' then there must at some point be a socialist revolution in one country. Thus Lenin became the author of Socialism in One Country. Stalin's most important embellishment was to assert the sufficiency of 'moral support,' for lack of 'state support.'

What did Stalin mean by 'moral support'? Perhaps he was thinking of the Black Sea mutiny in the French fleet in 1919, led by André Marty, which had thwarted the French invasion plans. Marty's rise in the PCF was a feature of the next few years. Or perhaps Stalin was thinking of the action of the British trade unions, at the time of the Polish war in 1920, in forming councils of action to resist British plans for intervention on the side of the Poles.

Here Stalin's notions were in tune with a changing mood in the Politburo by the end of 1924, and impatience with the excesses of Bolshevization. When Treint succeeded in driving Rosmer and Monatte—the *Gauche ouvrière*, the old guard of French Communism—out of the party, a protest, led by Bukharin, rose up in the Russian Politburo.[18] Treint was, he thought, fighting syndicalism, but his action was tearing up the delicate synthesis wrought by Trotsky and his French associates which alone had made the PCF a mass party. The reaction in the Politburo showed that Bukharin and Tomskii were not prepared to permit the campaign against Trotskyism, however much they were committed to it in Russia, to reduce the Comintern parties to tiny sects. Stalin's Socialism in One Country was his inspired attempt to merge with this groundswell against Zinoviev.

Much effort was later expended to prove that Stalin was really asserting the possibility of building socialism in Russia, against Trotsky's Permanent Revolution, which required waiting for the world revolution.[19] Later this developed into an even less interesting dispute over whether Russia could begin or complete socialist construction. Trotsky's foreign supporters knew, and were less afraid than his Politburo comrades to assert, that he had spoken dozens of times about the importance of 'socialist construction in a country encircled by capitalist states.'[20] Nor did Trotsky ever defend, as long as he was in the party, the theory of Permanent Revolution. Quotations against the theory were taken from his pre-1917 writings, or from his oblique description of his prerevolutionary ideas in 1921, which omitted the term.[21]

And this was not mere mental reservation. As is indicated above, Trotsky adopted Zinoviev's 'Leninism' more than he would ever admit, as already indicated in respect to the slogan for a workers' and peasants' government, and he would adopt still more of Zinovievism. The strictures against Trotskyism did not reflect real competition of ideas, but the distortions of polemics suited to the faction fight. This applied as well to Trotsky's later defense from exile. Strictly speaking, 'moral support' had large implications, as Zinoviev, and later Trotsky, were to assert. Rather than making revolution in their countries, the Communist parties could be said to have been reduced to the role of lobbies for Soviet foreign policy positions. Stalin never admitted this, however, and in fact warned that too much 'diplomatic' thinking about the country's problems would liquidate the foreign policy of the workers' state and the October Revolution. Socialism in One Country did not provoke a storm of controversy, or even the criticism of Zinoviev or Trotsky, until the factional situation prompted first one, then the other, to action.

In fact, the odd thing about the controversy that began with the 'Lessons of October' and ended with Socialism in One Country was that it effected a *reconciliation* of Stalin and Trotsky. Trotsky saw that the party was as solidly set against the army, that is, against 'Bonapartism,' as it had been at the time of the trade union debate in 1920. To deflect criticism, he resigned from his post as War Commissar. It has become customary to speculate at this point about Trotsky's failure to stage a coup d'état, or at least to use the army to intervene in the party, as Khrushchev, with the aid of Marshal Zhukov, did in 1957. Trotsky has protested the unthinkability of such a thing for a Bolshevik, an explanation which evidence does not permit us to dispute. Yet he had lost control of the MPA by the demotion of Antonov-Ovseenko, and his friend Sklianskii had been removed from his post as deputy commissar, making a putsch even more remote. Moreover, his position was not desperate. In fact, he was about to gain in influence as a result of the dispute.

Some indication of this was given by Stalin's interview in February 1925 with the German journalist Wilhelm Herzog. In view of the 'relative stabilization' created by the Dawes Plan, revolution, said Stalin, was not on the order of the day. The policies of parties which were expelling 'all who contradict' were obviously false.[22] Lest this hint be missed, he clarified it in a speech in March to the Comintern executive on the situation in the Czech party, where Trotsky's supporter Kreibich was defending the Russian critics. Stalin called for an ideological recital against Kreibich but reminded the Czechs that Trotskyism was 'the right wing of Communism' rather than Menshevism, as Zinoviev had been insisting.[23] This was a way of disclosing that Zinoviev's demand for Trotsky's expulsion had been rejected. Stalin would later tell the Fourteenth Congress:

> It was at the end of 1924 when the Leningraders proposed first to exclude Trotsky from the party. . . Some time later, at a C. C. plenum [on January 20, 1925], the Leningraders, in concert with Kamenev, suggested the immediate exclusion of Trotsky from the Politburo. . . We did not agree with Zinoviev and Kamenev because we thought that the policy of amputations is the greatest of dangers for the party, and the method of amputations as that of blood-letting (and they wanted blood) is dangerous and contagious: today it is one who is amputated, another tomorrow, a third the day after. What then would remain of the party?[24]

Stalin, whom Zinoviev had called a 'semi-Trotskyist,' now appeared to be making common cause with Trotsky, in his own fashion. Maslow, in prison in Germany since his arrest several months earlier, complained to Stalin with alarm. Stalin replied that Maslow was exaggerating the importance of the Herzog interview and that the left leaders of the Berlin party must keep up the fire against Brandler-Thalheimer, the German 'Trotskyists.'[25] Stalin felt confident that he could reap the benefit of defending Trotsky while urging others to attack Trotskyism.

The task of restraining Zinoviev and defending Trotsky was rearranging the Politburo consensus by the end of 1924. Increasingly the consensus was that Zinoviev would never produce anything of value for the Comintern. As we have seen, Zinoviev's policy toward the English Labour government was by no means as hostile as that of Treint-Girault or Fischer-Maslow.[26] Nevertheless, the affair of the 'Zinoviev Letter'—allegedly containing Zinoviev's instructions for an insurrection in England—which helped bring down the Labour government in October, had come as a great shock. The impact of the document, since proven a forgery, nevertheless gave at the time an indication of the impact of Zinoviev's reputation on Soviet foreign policy. And in December, a putsch was attempted, apparently at Zinoviev's direction, in Estonia. It involved only a few hundred men and was crushed within hours. After this, it would have been a rare Bolshevik outside Leningrad who retained confidence in the president of the Comintern.

After the fall of British Labour, Tomskii's analysis, rather than that of Lozovskii and Zinoviev, took center stage. Tomskii looked to close cooperation between the British Communists and the Trades Union Congress, making himself moreover the architect of the Anglo-Russian Joint Action Committee, which linked British and Soviet trade unions. Tomskii favored international contacts among unions and Soviet contacts with Western labor leadership. He represented a decisive return to the policy lines laid down by Paul Levi, lines with which the leading theorist of the new Politburo consensus, Bukharin, could only concur. There was, for a time, an attempt to support a pan-European trade union conception in 1926. Béla Kun, having switched from Zinoviev to Stalin after the beginning of the former's eclipse, advocated a 'Pan-Europe against the hegemony of the United States,' a way of reviving the United States of Europe slogan.[27]

Bukharin saw eye to eye with Tomskii and the advocates of broadened trade union connections. He and Aleksei Rykov, the amiable, alcoholic head of the Soviet state machinery, also saw eye to eye on the need to reassure Soviet officialdom against new 'shake-ups' which all would have expected from an opposition victory. They concurred on the NEP reforms of 1925, which removed many barriers to private initiative in the country-side. Bukharin's famous enjoinder to the peasants to 'enrich yourselves' was shocking only in its frankness. Most leading Bolsheviks, beginning with Zinoviev, saw the need for a more prosperous peasantry. Bukharin was schooled by Zinoviev's 'Face to the Village' slogan and the other elements of the anti-Trotsky campaign, including the revival of the slogan of the Revolutionary Democratic Dictatorship of the Proletariat and the Peasantry, which he was to apply with a vengeance in the Comintern. Thus, succeeding Zinoviev ideologically did not involve the presentation of broad programmatic alternatives. Rather, it was a matter of picking up ideas developed by others after they had veered away from them in practice. For Bukharin this would apply not only to Zinovievism but to Trotskyism as well. It went without saying, or should have, that this process of intellectual appropriation could go on only as long as the manipulations of the General Secretary pushed the previous owners aside and, from the outside, they made wilder claims in order to get back in.

Trotsky's ideas were part of the new consensus. In his large pamphlet *Where Is Britain Going?* (1925), he extended his previous observations on American hegemony, which he thought was now expressed in terms of a vast American store of gold and a vast British war debt, underpinning confidence in the dollar. Thus England, eager to return to the gold standard, must compete for short-term funds with the strongest currency on earth, and must suffer grave consequences for her industries when this competition spurred ever higher interest rates. Opting out of the competition meant a declining position in world markets, but participation meant punishment for Britain's domestic economy.[28] British Communism was the sole force capable of ending this slavery. National Bolshevism was again applied to Britain.

Trotsky urged that British Communists look to their own Cromwellian revolutionary tradition rather than to the traditions of Methodism, Fabianism, and gradualism.[29] This did not appear calculated to give Tomskii's appeals to the English union leaders greater credibility.[30] Trotsky even discussed the weapon of the general strike, for use against a future fascist threat. Yet, his prescription for the CPGB was to play, within the Labour party, the role of a 'ginger group,' such as had been played up to this point by the Independent Labour party.[31] Trotsky thus hoped for the CPGB to combine an extremely revolutionary mental set with the most prosaic of political commitments. Except for this mental set, his prescriptions were perfectly in line with those of Tomskii.

Moreover, Trotsky also shifted his ground on the economic issues. He was accused, falsely, of advocating energetic industrialization measures of the kind advocated in the past by Preobrazhenskii, whose ideas were shortly to clash violently with those of Bukharin. Yet, as we have stressed here, Trotsky's economic ideas since the trade union debate were by no means so sharply etched, and he was in no sense an opponent of the economic arrangements of the NEP. He had merely asserted that he could manage the economy better than others. As the rift between Stalin and Zinoviev widened and the eclipse of the latter loomed, Trotsky saw the opportunity for an appropriation of part of the legacy of Sokolnikov. In 1925, speaking for *Vesenkha* and the concessions committee, he made his the most prominent voice in favor of a policy of extensive foreign investment in Russia. As was so often the case with shifts in Trotsky's positions, he was not actually contradicting an earlier opinion but merely shifting the emphasis within his considerable repertoire of positions. He had always supported concessions. Even under War Communism he had admitted that 'these concessions properly so-called are part of our plan.'[32] In 1923, he had advocated further foreign investment in Russia under conditions in which industry was guarded by 'socialist protection.'[33] Now, in 1925, Trotsky continued to offer further to implant foreign investment in the land of the soviets, provided that capitalist influences be held in check once again by 'an all-round system of socialist protection.'[34] Trotsky was maintaining the cluster of positions on economic questions that characterized his essentially centrist views, in keeping, in 1925, with the centrist political position he had adopted.

He was attempting to use Russia's need for capital to divide its enemies. Britain's effort to restore the gold basis of the pound, with the inevitable raising of interest rates, was for Trotsky a clear sign of the subjection of Britain before the United States. Winston Churchill as the Exchequer had become the living symbol of this process. And Britain, Trotsky complained, continued to threaten Russia. 'Why?' he asked, 'under what pretext? It is not because she wants to take it out on somebody else because of the affronts dealt her by America?'[35]

In these circumstances Trotsky adjusted his concessions policy to fit the needs of American capital. 'No matter what statesmen who do not like Bolshevism may say,' wrote Trotsky, 'the capitalist circles of America will become convinced that for them there is no more fruitful and promising market for goods and capital than the USSR.'[36] If foreign loans were forthcoming, the Soviet Union could take two or three times the current foreign investment. The Dnieprostroi power facilities and the Ural-Kuznets metal and coal complex could accommodate foreign partici- pation. 'And since these are carried out at the initiative of the state,' Trotsky added, 'their internal connections are insured in the highest degree.'[37] This was no doubt an assurance about labor discipline. How- ever, Trotsky had not sounded this note at the right time. American capital was not prepared for this venture, still wary about the denial of rights in Soviet Russia, Communist propaganda in America, Soviet failure to pay its debts, and, as Elbert Gary of United States Steel stressed, Soviet reluctance to relax the Monopoly of Foreign Trade. The détente sought by the 'normalization' regime of 1925 was still premature. Ameri- can interests also passed up a chance to intervene in the Soviet succession struggle.

Trotsky increasingly isolated himself from those who would have sought his support and solidarity in order to keep his peace with the Stalin-Bukharin grouping in the Politburo, and to benefit from the split between it and Leningrad.[38] When Max Eastman published an account of the struggle against Trotskyism, on the basis of documents appearing in the Menshevik *Sotsialisticheskii vestnik,* Trotsky repudiated him and denied the existence of a Testament of Lenin. Trotsky later explained this, while admitting the Eastman account to be correct in essentials, by the exigencies of his line 'at that time oriented toward conciliation and appeasement.'[39]

Trotsky's alignment with Bukharin and Stalin put him in the position of disavowing Souvarine and the *Gauche ouvrière* as well. Treint and Girault had taunted Souvarine with the prediction that Trotsky would drop him. Treint had denounced Souvarine-Rosmer-Monatte as a 'syndicalist' devia- tion, a charge that Souvarine was quick to answer. Syndicalism, he replied, had been the principal source for the major militants recruited to the Communist International, not simply in the case of his group in the PCF but with Foster, Haywood, Reed, Eastman, Minor, Shatov in the American party; Mann, Larkin, Tanner, Murphy, Bell in the British; Maurin and Nin in the Spanish.[40] It was the current 'Leninism' which had no parents. Yet even with the 'normalization' that developed from the end of 1924, Trotsky still did not think it politic to defend Souvarine-Rosmer- Monatte. Treint demanded that Trotsky declare himself. Trotsky admit- ted that he had not objected to their expulsion and asserted that their activity since that time, in publishing *Révolution prolétarienne* as a 'syndicalist-communist' organ, 'justifies the exclusion.[41] Souvarine answered by reminding Trotsky that

the Communist International was formed by a regroupment of revolutionary forces, under the influence of the war and the Russian Revolution. Left Social Democrats, revolutionary syndicalists, anarch- ists, submitting their previous ideas to a necessary revision, all rallied to a common platform.

'Today,' Souvarine continued, one can no longer be a 'Communist' but must instead by an 'Old Bolshevik.'[42] After the departure of the *noyau* (as Souvarine-Rosmer-Monatte were called), further opposition to Zinoviev and Treint was led by Fernand Loriot, Maurice Paz, and others. They would succeed in dethroning Treint, but not in elevating themselves.[43]

Contrary to the expectations of the Zinovievists in the Comintern, their leader turned out to be their least ardent supporter. Zinoviev thought, or hoped, that he had other options. As he had led Bolshevization, he decided he could also lead normalization, probably because of Politburo pressure and his desire to save his Russian position at the expense of his Comintern supporters. In this sense he behaved no differently from Trotsky. In the German party everyone sensed a return to united front tactics in the style of Levi. Ernst Meyer reported that Zinoviev was encouraging him against Fischer and Ernst Thälmann.[44] In August, Zinoviev sent the Germans an open letter, acknowledging that the ultra-left policy of the year before had torn up the KPD's links to the public and to the unions, and attaching all responsibility for that state of affairs to Fischer. She was pushed aside in favor of Thälmann. Meyer's group, calling itself a 'center' faction, was brought into the leadership but was continuously referred to as a right tendency—and a 'dangerous' one, to boot. Stalin and Bukharin had succeeded in weakening Zinoviev in the Comintern even before they had done so in Russia. And Stalin's victory over Zinoviev already contained seeds, in propaganda against the Right Danger, of a campaign against Bukharin. When the same course was taken in the French party a year later, Treint and Girault were forced to yield, not to Loriot and those who had protested Bolshevization but to Maurice Thorez, like Thälmann a man of common origins and a faithful adept of Stalin's.

With the ground slipping beneath him in Comintern affairs, Zinoviev resolved to attack the Bukharin-Stalin-Trotsky bloc. In September 1925, he assembled the requisite arguments, with the help of Professor Ustrialov's newly published book.[45] He decided to adopt the approach of Ustrialov: There was an objective tendency for the two classes benefiting most from the NEP, symbolized by the *kulak* and the NEPman, together with the bureaucrat in the state apparatus inherited from the Tsardom, to form a constituency of degeneration. Were they to succeed, a restoration of capitalism would follow. As Ustrialov had predicted in 1921, they would create a Russian Thermidor. Ustrialov had seen all this as an inevitable result of NEP, had applauded it, and had urged support under the rubric of National Bolshevism. National Bolshevism, thought Zinoviev, was being preached by the present leadership through the slogan of Socialism in One Country. Generations of students of Soviet affairs were to associate this line of argument with the Trotskyist case against Stalin, but Zinoviev first used it to prove the Trotskyism of Stalin-Bukharin.

The views of Bukharin appeared to be chiefly responsible, in Zinoviev's reading, for this backsliding toward Trotskyism. Bukharin was accused of failing to recognize the danger in the 'state capitalist' elements of the Russian economy. Zinoviev thought that he would take advantage of a terminological dispute of long standing between Bukharin and Lenin. Bukharin had always thought it an error to use the term to describe elements of socialist economy. Zinoviev would therefore, in another display of Leninist orthodoxy, force Bukharin to dispute Lenin. At the Fourteenth Party Congress in December, Zinoviev punctuated his lengthy attacks on Bukharin (he exempted Stalin from criticism) by the claim that the growth of state capitalism (*goskapitalizm*) 'undermines the very basis of Leninism.'[46] Bukharin would retort that 'if state industry is a system of exploitation and if our power reposes on it, our state is therefore in no sense a proletarian dictatorship.'[47] Bukharin had restated an important element of his and Trotsky's position at the time of the trade union debate: the assertion of the proletarian character of the Soviet state. When Bukharin spoke of Socialism in One Country, the stress was as much on the word 'socialism' as on the more controversial phrase 'in one country.'

Bukharin's insistence on the socialist character of the commanding heights of the Soviet economy was said to have an air of complacency about it, in view of his ideas about harnessing industry to move at a pace comfortable to agriculture. And in order to make such a charge against Bukharin, Zinoviev was forced to abandon part of his own work, the slogan Face to the Village, which he now passed on to Bukharin.

Moreover, warnings about state capitalism might seem ridiculous in view of Zinoviev's close association with Sokolnikov, whose far-reaching ambitions for managing state capitalism had provided an important ideological bridge for the anti-Trotsky troika from the Trade Union Debate into the later struggles against Trotsky in 1921–1922. The true ring of his economic critique would be provided only when he had coalesced with Preobrazhenskii, Sokolnikov's polar opposite in economic thinking. Both Zinoviev and Bukharin still shared the 'Leninist' patrimony of the Revolutionary Democratic Dictatorship of the Proletariat and the Peasantry. Zinoviev, however, was now prepared to mix criticism of the pro-peasant line of the present leadership with charges of its being soft on Trotskyism.[48] This sort of problem did not bother Zinoviev, who had not only not lost the confidence that he could work ideological miracles but seems to have imparted some of the same confidence to Bukharin as well.

Between them, they had managed to take from the old and new ideas of Lenin, Trotsky, and others an assemblage of programmatic positions and slogans which they christened Leninism. They had proceeded to divide it in such a way as to provide the basis for what would have been, in an ideal regime of inner-party democracy, two permanent, competing platform factions, each with a considerable constituency in the main institutional centers of the Soviet regime. In this ideal regime, these platforms might have coexisted and succeeded one another for alternating periods. Conditions for a parliamentary alternance were not to emerge. But an alternance of policies has been in evidence, although owing to the special features of the developing Stalinist regime, leaders associated with those policies would enjoy neither power nor recognition.

Nevertheless, one can see a Moscow platform, urging solicitude for agriculture, assurance for the denizens of the state machine (especially the Moscow economic bureaus and the trade unions), a policy of foreign participation in the economy, and détente in foreign policy. Zinoviev's and Bukharin's neo-populism, Rykov's and Tomskii's care for the cadres, Sokolnikov's and Trotsky's notions about Russian participation in a world market, and a Marxist recognition of the persistence, even under a dictatorship of proletariat, of the law of value—all these contributed to the formation of the platform. By 1925, the utopia of unity, under these formulae, in which all the major leaders had basked since the success of the fight against Trotskyism, was about to vanish.

A Leningrad platform was also emerging, claiming the mantle of continuity from the traditions of Bolshevism-Leninism. The platform would appeal for the primacy of industry and planning (whatever that might mean for the 'independence' of the unions and managerial routine), a striving for liberation from the influences of the world market, to the point of seeking autarky, and a National Bolshevik foreign policy opposing the Treaty of Versailles, coupled with a revival of revolutionary internationalism and increased militancy in the activities of the Comintern parties. Preobrazhenskii's and, to a certain extent, Trotsky's notions of Primitive Socialist Accumulation and Socialist Protectionism, the conceptions of Trotsky and Radek on the uses of nationalism against Versailles, the radical Zinovievist Comintern line of 1924–1925, and a general spirit of voluntarism would contribute to this line. The clash between Moscow and Leningrad programs would be an important feature of future struggles, even after Stalin had attained supreme power, and would be a factor in the disputes among his successors.

The prize of the succession, however, would not be won by leaders who stood on either of these platforms. The center position would always claim that victory. Yet the policies would continue in their dance of alternance, specifically at the command of the primus at the center, as in 1945–1953, or in a struggle for a new primus, as in 1953–1957. The center could force the programs to compete, as Stalin would do, or it could even dull the violence of the alternance, as would Suslov. Movement around the center, however, would be the key feature, and the unlucky leader caught in a too rigid stand would be shaken loose as the train rounded a sharp bend. That was how Trotsky had described the fall of Paul Levi.

Trotsky Rallies to Zinoviev

Why, then, had Zinoviev broken with the Politburo synthesis of 1924–1925? He had hope to dislodge Trotsky from the War Commissariat (and perhaps to expel him) and Stalin from the Secretariat at the end of 1924. Stalin had shared Zinoviev's wishes in respect to Trotsky's post at the head of the Soviet armed forces, but he could not afford to remove Trotsky entirely, for fear of Zinoviev reducing him, Stalin, to the position of faithful executor of Politburo decisions. Stalin wanted to be a Lenin, not a Sverdlov. Therefore he had to slow down Zinoviev's campaign against Trotsky and, after the emasculation of 'Trotskyism,' use Trotsky against Zinoviev. Zinoviev saw the problem. The rise of Bukharin moreover demanded that he act promptly. In accusing the rest of the Politburo of Trotskyism, Zinoviev could hope for two possible gains: an immediate rally of the middle ranks of the Central Committee to him or, failing that, a rally of Stalin to his struggle against Bukharin and Trotsky. Historians commonly judge all these struggles to be meaningless in view of the inexorable buildup of Stalin's patronage machine, which rendered debate at conferences and congresses a formality. Yet it did not appear that way to the participants at the time, Stalin among them, who obviously took great care to avoid a political slip which might weaken their positions.

Zinoviev's initial campaign against Moscow occurred in the fall and winter of 1925, culminating with the Fourteenth Party Congress in December. Perhaps out of nostalgia for the 'Leninist' positions of 1921–1922, Zinoviev still had Sokolnikov in tow. The Finance Minister had no rationale for opposition from the standpoint of his economic ideas, which, since his rebuff on the question of Monopoly of Foreign Trade at the end of 1922, had not been much at variance with the rest of the leadership. Stalin, however, was attempting to advance at the Finance Ministry his candidate, Kuibyshev, at Sokolnikov's expense, and that forced his hand. Sokolnikov was by no means a useful ally to Zinoviev; his well-known enthusiasm for state capitalism was ludicrous alongside Zinoviev's warnings of its dangers. Stalin simply dodged the question of Leninist orthodoxy on state capitalism by admitting that Lenin had seen state capitalism as the predominant form in 1921, but insisting that since then socialist industry had reduced it considerably, to the point of their exchanging roles.[49] The importance of foreign investment, he added, was now 'minute.'

Bukharin carried the attack on the Leningraders on most of the theoretical issues. Stalin advertised himself as the preserver of collective leadership, defender of Trotsky, Bukharin, and other indispensable leaders. With the overwhelming majority vote against the Leningraders given him at the congress, Stalin set about to break their power, first in the Politburo, from which Kamenev was demoted, with Molotov, Kalinin, and Voroshilov added. Bukharin's group knew that Molotov was Stalin's man but thought, wrongly as it would develop, that they had some leverage on Kalinin and Voroshilov. Zinoviev lost control of Leningrad to Kirov.[50] Other of his supporters in the Urals, the Ukraine, and the Caucasus lost their jobs. Moscow ended the carping criticism of *Leningradskaia Pravda* by changing its editorship, and it renewed the ban on a separate theoretical organ. The era of Zinoviev seemed to have come to an end.

Souvarine could hardly conceal his delight. He was somewhat dismayed by the opacity of the polemics: Stalin-Bukharin were now being denounced as 'Mensheviko-Ustrialovites.' He thought that complaints about the *kulak* danger were so much rubbish. If things had reached such a sorry state, it was because of 'the insensate struggle of Zinoviev against Trotsky.'[51] Stalin was setting things right, judged Souvarine. 'The measures taken by Stalin have isolated Zinoviev and Kamenev and made possible joint work with Trotsky.'[52] In an article titled 'Some Strong Words from Stalin,' he suggested that

> the extraordinary columnies directed by Zinoviev and his agents against us, against the revolutionary opposition of all the International, count no better than those directed against Stalin. Who accepts one must accept the other; who condemns one must repress the other.[53]

When Souvarine wrote these lines, his application for readmission to the PCF and the Comintern had been submitted (in December) and was under consideration. It was shortly to be refused.

Trotsky had reason to be satisfied with the results of the congress, but the accretion of Stalin's power could by no means promise him more maneuvering room. Everything now hinged on Bukharin—specifically, on getting his help for an improvement of the regime. Clearly, no political considerations, in the programmatic sense, were dividing the two. To be sure, they had a range of disagreements which could justify lengthy disputes, but even with their different ideas, they had got on well enough for more than a year, and especially well while Zinoviev was charging Bukharin with Trotskyism. So, with Zinoviev vastly reduced in influence, Trotsky sought to make the next step on the Regime Question.

As was the case in January 1925, the first move was a mere attempt at restraining the victors from running roughshod over the province of the vanquished. The occasion was a meeting at which Kamenev asked why Bukharin was so ardent to bend Leningrad to the will of the central committee when he had not been so keen to do the same to Moscow after the New Course controversy of 1923. Trotsky interjected: 'He has acquired the taste.' Bukharin sent him a note protesting that this taste 'makes me tremble from head to foot.'[54] Trotsky thought he saw an opening. In a note to Bukharin, he stressed their agreement about the abuses of the Leningrad regime. He had, he said, recognized that already in 1923: 'I said then and repeat now that the traits of apparatus bureaucratism, characteristic of the whole party, have been brought to their extreme in the regime of the Leningrad party.'[55] The role of party secretaries in the rural provinces—appointees, for the most part, of Stalin—would of course loom large, wrote Trotsky. but he counted this 'inevitable' and even 'progressive.'[56] Leningrad, however, was another matter. Moreover, since apparatus bureaucratism had gone so far there, perhaps the best method of combatting it would be, not its coordination from above by Moscow, but an easing of the regime, to permit open discussion and inner party democracy in Leningrad. It was an offer to make the campaign against Leningrad a campaign against bureaucracy. Trotsky did not dare to criticize Stalin to Bukharin, but the implications were no doubt clear enough to the latter: a bloc with Trotsky on the Regime Question, ultimately, despite the talk about 'progressive' rural secretaries, against the regime in Moscow and the provinces as well.

Bukharin was put to the test. He was not, however, 'out' and in need of a bloc, so he hid behind the political issues, his humanism, his neo-populism, his ideas about the *smychka*, and of course his relationship with Stalin. Trotsky continued desperately: Could not Bukharin at least ease the impositions of the Moscow local machine led by Uglanov, on the pretext of combatting its anti-Semitism?[57] Trotsky had heard that complaints against Trotskyism had lately been emphasizing that Trotsky was a Jew. Would Bukharin go to the cell in question with Trotsky to investigate the matter? This might have started the ball rolling against Uglanov. The Moscow party ranks who had supported the 1923 opposition would be unmuzzled. But would Bukharin and Trotsky benefit from that, or merely Trotsky? We have no record of Bukharin's reply, but no campaign on the Regime Question, in Leningrad or Moscow, ever materialized.

Trotsky was genuinely desperate. A future of kowtowing to the 'Quadrumvirate' (of Stalin, Bukharin, Rykov, and Tomskii) now yawned before him like a chasm. He took a few weeks to consult physicians in Berlin on his lingering bouts of fever. Once in Berlin, he also decided to consult Ernst Meyer on an important matter: Trotsky asked him, 'What do the German workers think of Zinoviev?'

'I am convinced that if Lenin were alive he would have him hanged for the harm he has done the German movement. Yes I mean what I say: physically destroyed.'

'Is that your private opinion or that of the German workers?'

'I am their representative and hope to express correctly their thought and feeling.'

'I think you are exaggerating, Comrade Meyer.'

'As you wish, Comrade Trotsky.'[58]

At this time Trotsky must have made his decision: a bloc with the Leningraders, revolutionary internationalism against Socialism in One Country. Up to this point Trotsky had never publicly criticized the famous slogan of Stalin and Bukharin.[59] Nor did he have much of an attraction to the infamous 'internationalism' of the Zinoviev Comintern of 1924–1925. Zinoviev's continued association with Sokolnikov and their joint emphasis on the existence of Soviet state capitalism did not promise much in regard to an economic program. There was every expectation that friends and supporters in the West would consider a Zinoviev–Trotsky combination to be unprincipled.

Trotsky could hardly accommodate Sokolnikov's views on the economy. Saving the Monopoly of Foreign Trade against Sokolnikov's plans to drop it had been one of the proudest moments of Trotsky's career. However, when Zinoviev had realized the magnitude of his defeat at the Fourteenth Congress, he had called for conciliation with former oppositions. With many Democratic Centralists and Workers' Oppositionists, the authors of the Platform of the Forty-Six began to heed the call. This would bring into the Zinovievist ranks Preobrazhenskii's economic critique of Bukharinism, according to which Primitive Socialist Accumulation would have to be accomplished at the expense of the peasant. As Trotsky saw clearly at the time, this economic analysis could be joined to a program of autarkic development under the slogan Socialism in One Country.[60] Stalin might turn from Bukharin to Preobrazhenskii.

It would be an understatement to suggest that the political position of this bloc was confused. It would have been hard enough to struggle on the basis of Trotsky's subtle centrist positions, but to graft these onto those of Zinoviev and the oppositionists whom Zinoviev had routed in the past was really impossible. Stalin had a field day with the charge of an 'unprincipled bloc,' actually, thought Stalin, referring to Trotsky's 1912 grouping against Lenin, 'the August bloc in a new form.'

Nevertheless, neither of the major proponents of the Joint Opposition had an alternative. They would never again be presented an opportunity to join their forces and seek to shake the grip of Stalin and Bukharin on the apparatus. Yet they did not open with both barrels, but instead proceeded rather more cautiously. The international side of the program took shape in May, 1926, when the British general strike broke out. The Trades Union Congress leaders who were associated with the Anglo-Russian Joint Action Committee (ARJAC) called the strike off after twelve days. Trotsky and Zinoviev called that treason, demanding a dissolution of ARJAC. They had never objected to the committee before, but now they called it an inferior substitute for the British Communist party. The coup of Marshal Piłsudski occurred the same month, in this case with the tacit acceptance of the Polish Communists, who, quite understandably, thought Piłsudski to be an agent of the Revolutionary Democratic Dictatorship of the Proletariat and the Peasantry.[61] Stalin saw Pilsudski as an agent of bourgeois 'rationalization' in accordance with the wishes of Western finance. He agreed that Ernst Thälmann was right to criticize the mistaken estimate of Piłsudski.[62] The criticism of an 'opportunist united front,' which would blossom the next spring in connection with events in China, was aired in a 'Declaration of the Thirteen,' which broached an *implicit* critique of Socialism in One Country by complaining that the victory of socialist construction was inseparable from the 'progress and outcome' of the world revolution.[63] The crisis in Anglo-Soviet relations caused by the General Strike would destroy Stalin's thesis on the 'moral support' rendered by the Western proletariat, but the oppositionists were at first afraid to pounce on this, for fear of seeming disloyal to Soviet foreign policy.

Yet Trotsky's assessment of the ruling faction was becoming sharper and more focused. In a series of private memoranda, he begun to reflect more and more on Lenin's Testament and its suggestion to find a way to remove Stalin. The apparatus regime would inevitably consolidate under a single dominant will. As soon as this thought crossed his mind, however, the Bolshevik in him rejoined that 'one can be reconciled to any regime as long as it accomplishes some purpose.' A deadly thought: Criticism of the regime could only proceed on some 'political' basis, lest one be ranged into an 'unprincipled bloc.'

Even these first steps of Joint Opposition gave Stalin his chance to threaten expulsion. He laid down the line on 11 October: The opposition could escape expulsion only by resolving to obey the leadership, which would in return refrain from ordering Zinoviev and Trotsky to speak publicly in defense of the majority position, as Lenin used to require. However, they would have to disavow the Workers' Oppositionists and the Fischer-Maslow group in the KPD.[64] The opposition accepted the terms and apologized to the party, renouncing its supporters in the U.S.S.R. and in Germany, and throwing in another disavowal of Souvarine for good measure.[65]

With this it bought a winter of rueful rumination. Sokolnikov left the opposition before its capitulation; thus its economic ideas could only be clarified, although they still reflected the uneasy mix of Preobrazhenskii and Trotsky. The critique of Bukharin's neo-populism and 'opportunist' united front was now in place. But the status of the critics in the party leadership was further eroded. Trotsky was removed from the Politburo and Kamenev lost his candidate member status. Zinoviev, already out of the Politburo, had been forced to relinquish the Comintern to Bukharin. The replacements for purged oppositionists were followers of Stalin rather than Bukharin. Kuibyshev took over Vesenkha and entered the Politburo, and Ordzhonikidze took over the Central Control Commission. Stalin, moreover, insisted, as he had in the case of Maslow in 1925, that the ideological campaign against Trotskyism continue. More and more, Stalin smoked out criticism of Socialism in One Country. Trotsky finally rose to the challenge and, in a speech to the Fifteenth Conference in November, openly and explicitly criticized Socialism in One Country for the first time. In the same speech, however, he admitted its major premise: The sufficiency of 'moral support' by the European workers, as opposed to 'state support.' He called attention to a statement he had made in May 1917 to the effect that a Soviet dictatorship could not hold out against 'Conservative Europe.' This Conservative Europe, he contended, was dealt a mortal blow by the German revolution of 1918. Thus, 'that we have continued to exist is due to the fact that Europe has not remained what it was.'[66] That is, Soviet Russia was surviving on 'moral support' from the European workers—revolutionary support to be sure, but not the 'state support' of a socialist dictatorship in an advanced country.

Not for nothing had Trotsky dodged for so long this problem of the 'contradiction' between Permanent Revolution and Socialism in One Country. The 'contradiction' had no practical meaning whatever, in the absence of a revolutionary atmosphere in the West. Yet it had meaning in the factional sense, since it seemed to indicate Trotsky's unsuitability to lead Russia, maddeningly, on the 'premise' of his suitability to lead a nonexistent revolutionary movement in Europe. In pressing this issue, Stalin may have known that he was talking nonsense, but he grasped perfectly the psychological strength of his position. In dodging the issue for so long, Trotsky may have known that he was living in a world of 'Leninist' illusion. That he survived in this world as long as he did should be considered evidence against the thesis which ascribes his defeat to ineptitude. He was, as Stalin correctly pointed out after the capitulation of October, 1926, merely awaiting the onrush of major events which would put the rhetorical points of the faction struggle into perspective.

Everyone could see that the events were in the process of unfolding. Stalin and Bukharin had wagered much on their prognosis of a period of peaceful socialist construction, made possible by peaceful coexistence with the West, especially with Britain. The 'moral support' of British Labour would prevent intervention and support for further development of trade and financial contact with Russia. Stalin and Bukharin were relying on their ability to 'intervene' in the British parliamentary alternance. The general strike, by providing fuel to the anti-Soviet Conservatives—the 'Diehards,' who combined the Curzon tradition of containment of Russia with ideological anticommunism—had ruined the Soviet strategy. The notion was taking root in Britain, not simply because of Diehard agitation but by the impact of events, that Bolshevism was not amenable to diplomatic and commercial arrangements of a lasting character, but was instead an implacable foe of 'the existing cosmos.' By the end of 1926, the Diehards centered attention on Soviet cooperation with the xenophobic movement of the Chinese Kuomintang and its northern campaign to defeat the warlord regimes. In February 1927, a protest note on the deterioration of Anglo-Soviet relations, largely because of Soviet activity in China, was handed to Russian representatives. Moscow clumsily replied by suggesting that improvement of relations would require suppression of the Diehards. But some, such as Chicherin, ill in Berlin and yielding more and more to his assistant, Litvinov, saw that a complete break in relations was coming. In April, Chiang Kai-shek reached Shanghai and crushed the Communist movement there, as he had done at the beginning of his expedition in Canton in March 1926. By May 1927, the British government had broken diplomatic relations with Soviet Russia. The wager on the power of 'moral support' had proven an utter failure.

The debacle of Communist policy in China renewed the campaign of the Zinoviev-Trotsky opposition. At the end of May, the oppositionists restated their case in a 'Declaration of the Eighty-Three': Economic policy was a capitulation to the *kulak*; the opportunist united front was still in evidence, as Stalin-Bukharin had failed to dissolve the Anglo-Soviet Joint Action Committee; the Chinese revolution was being crushed because of the bankruptcy of the policy of entry into the Kuomintang; the Stalin-Bukharin bloc was under the sway of the anti-Leninist theory of Socialism in One Country.

> Attacks on the Left Opposition [the declaration continued] have for a logical conclusion the victory of Ustrialov in the name of the neo-NEP. Ustrialov is the bitterest, the most logical and principled enemy of Bolshevism. The self-satisfied administrators, the petty-bourgeois parvenue bureaucrats who regard the masses from a lofty pinnacle, sense the earth more and more firm beneath their feet . . . Behind them stand the Ustrialovist specialists, the NEPmen and the Kulaks, the last in the guise of 'economically strong peasants.' From this quarter comes the greatest, the true danger.[67]

The ominous references to the 'Ustrialovist specialists' took Trotsky's criticism into the vein that Zinoviev had been mining. Trotsky's original complaints about bureaucracy had spoken essentially to the problem of party life and the effect of his exclusion on party leadership. He had stopped short of predicting that defects in the party regime were a preparation for usurpation of power by an alien class, still less by a 'new class' unforeseen by Marxist theory. In the party, the Zinovievists had been the first to warn, in 1925, of a Thermidor, after the theory of Ustrialov, and the rise of the class of intellectual workers, which Machajski had called the real ruling class of socialist society. Here they were making use of a staple of anarchist and ultra-left propaganda. Before Trotsky had ventured into opposition in 1926, he had poured scorn on the notions of Ustrialov and Machajski. He, after all, had been the first to provide a special place in the Soviet state leadership for 'bourgeois specialists.' Even now that he had become a Zinovievist on this question, he still rejected the thesis of an already accomplished Thermidor, a thesis which he was to take up in later exile. The issue of Thermidor was to serve as a barometer of opposition attitudes to the Soviet regime. Oppositionists could speak of an accomplished Thermidor only at the point, which they felt had not been reached, when reform of the party was no longer possible.

The oppositionists were fierce in their castigation of official Soviet policy on China. They recognized the power of the issue and wanted Stalin and Bukharin to bear full responsibility for the immense defeat which seemed in prospect. Again, however, as was the case with the defeat of Brandler in the German October, it was not so easy to pinpoint exactly where the policy had gone wrong, and far easier simply to fix the blame. Even the oppositionists had not objected to China policy until its defeat was recorded. The opposition could not claim that they had conceived policy in a manner different from Stalin and Bukharin. All of them had marched in Asia under the banner of Lenin's theses on the National and Colonial Question, from the Second Comintern Congress of 1920. Lenin the revolutionary democrat, the Jacobin, had advised broad anticolonialist alliances with national bourgeoisies. M. N. Roy had urged independence of the Communist parties and noted the anticommunist potential of Asian nationalism. The amended theses of 1920 had reflected the compromise of these two ideas, for Lenin essentially a tactical problem which would have to be solved in practice. This uneasy synthesis had not called forth active opposition within the Bolshevik party. It had appeared that the tension between the 'democratic' tasks of the revolution and its proletarian content, a tension on view in the Trade Union Debate, for example, was not serious enough outside Russia to provoke major criticism, much less a split. Trotsky had never been moved to invoke the Permanent Revolution as a guide to action in Russia or the colonies.

The Comintern China line represented another arena for application of the perspective of National Bolshevism. Bolshevik policy had assumed almost from the beginning that the two 'sick men' of pre-1914 international politics, Turkey and China, should not be further partitioned and their defense would serve the interests of Soviet Russia.[68] None of the Bolsheviks had ceased to hope, at least in public utterances, that the troubled nations around their periphery would become an arena for proletarian revolution by way of soviets, as Lenin and Roy had imagined, and that anticolonial nationalism would be the lever to pry open capitalist encirclement. They also knew that, in practice, dealings with nationalists would momentarily involve 'sacrifices' by local Communists, and they turned a blind eye toward suppression of local Communists by nationalists whose foreign policy they hoped to influence. Neither Trotsky nor Zinoviev visibly championed the persecuted Turkish or Persian Communists. Their defense of this cause in China may be measured by the rise of their opposition in Russia. Zinoviev offered tepid objection to the policy of Communist entry in the Kuomintang after Chiang Kai-shek's massacre of the Communists in Canton in March 1926, suggesting an assertion of independence from the Kuomintang by 'transitional formulae.'[69] Yet the opposition, in the Declaration of the Eighty-Three, explicitly denied calling for withdrawal, as the official press had charged.[70] Trotsky later claimed that he had been for withdrawal but had been outvoted by Radek and Zinoviev.

If Trotsky's later statements are to be believed, he resolutely opposed the Stalin–Bukharin China policy from its inception.[71] However, as in the case of Brandler and the German fiasco of 1923, Trotsky claimed credit for private misgivings and votes which cannot, without the availability of Politburo minutes, be independently verified. 'You are quite right,' Trotsky admitted to Max Shachtman in 1930, 'when you point out that the Russian Opposition, as late as the first half of 1927, did not openly demand the withdrawal from Kuomintang.'[72] In fact, Trotsky's 'opposition' included neither Radek, nor Zinoviev and his followers, nor Rakovskii, nor Piatakov, but instead what he called a 'center' made of 'younger members of the Opposition of 1923,' which nevertheless compelled him to suppress his misgivings and follow Zinoviev publicly. Even if one judges this testimony in a light most generous to Trotsky, it may still be asked why the report of a commission on China policy on which Trotsky sat, a report issued days after the Canton coup of 1926, placed emphasis not on the policy of Kuomintang entry but on the diplomatic problems posed by pro-Japanese and pro-British warlords in Peking and Manchuria. 'The Chinese revolution,' it stated, 'is in a stage where the question of its relations with Japan take on a great significance.'[73] Appeasement of Japan, permitting Japanese-supported warlord Chang Tso-lin to operate Manchuria as an autonomous principality, was the recommendation of the committee. Japan was thus to be won from a possible new cooperation with Britain in North China, and a possible renewal of the Anglo-Japanese alliance, broken in 1922. News of the Canton coup could not have reached the commission, yet Trotsky was still not notable among its participants for his great confidence in the CCP and its revolutionary prospects. '[The commission members] were even opposed to my attitude, which was considered pessimistic' he remarked in an interview in 1939. Voroshilov, Chicherin, Dzerzhinski, and the other members had entertained greater expectations for the Chinese revolution. Trotsky recalled that 'they were anxious for its success.'[74]

The opposition critique of Kuomintang entry, as shown in contemporary documents, was by no means as clear as Trotsky later indicated. After his expulsion from the Soviet Union, he would maintain that Stalin-Bukharin had consistently overestimated the Kuomintang: They had been wrong to admit it to the Comintern as a sympathizing party and especially wrong to describe it as a 'workers' and peasants'' party (rather than a bourgeois party) capable of exercising a 'democratic dictatorship of the proletariat and the peasantry.' By 1928, when Trotsky was in exile in Alma-Ata in Soviet Turkestan, he would recall bitterly Lenin's 1917 advice about relegating proponents of the Democratic Dictatorship to the museum of Old Bolsheviks.[75] The slogan, he would conclude, was merely a 'cover for a *petit-bourgeois* conception of a revolution as a transition.' The opposition had consistently fought for establishing soviets in China. Yet the major pronouncements of the Trotsky-Zinoviev opposition including the *Platform of the Left Opposition*, published in September, 1927, called soviets the best form for the Democratic Dictatorship of the Proletariat and the Peasantry. Trotsky would have had a clearer record of opposition had he not abdicated the Permanent Revolution for the Zinovievist formulae of pure 'Leninism'—that is, had he been more of a Trotskyist.

Despite all the disarray in the opposition's pronouncements, however, as it saw things, the essential fact was that it called failure by its proper name and demanded that those responsible for the failed policy be called to account. Whether the opposition stood for anything different, whether it could claim to have foreseen dangers and advised wise remedies, was less important. It had put formidable pressure on the official strategies and would even change them. Yet all those who had power and who fought for power in the Bolshevik party knew that it was by no means necessary to face ignominy and loss of position because of failed policies; they could instead respond as had Lenin in similar circumstances, by recognizing the end of a period and the necessity for a turn. No policy was 'correct' in the abstract. Policies could only serve limited and temporary purposes, and, when they were exhausted, new policies that were incorrect yesterday would be essential today. This was the essence of dialectic. Moreover, knowing that the series of policies for the building of Socialism in One Country, with the 'moral support' of the proletariat abroad, were almost entirely exhausted, Stalin reached for alternatives. He had followed Bukharin's Moscow line up to now, and the moment had come to take up the positions indicated by the Leningrad line.

The turn began in Comintern affairs, in which Bukharin, having replaced Zinoviev at the seventh ECCI plenum in November, 1926, held sway. Zinoviev had been embattled in that position long before he lost it, having to face criticism in Moscow of the excesses of his Bolshevization campaign of 1924, and having his own moves checked, from the end of 1924, by Politburo pressure for a regime of Normalization in the International. Indications are strong that, before his removal, these pressures had forced him to carry out actions detrimental to his own closest associates. Such may have been the case with his Open Letter to the KPD in 1925, which weakened Fischer and Maslow in preference for Ernst Thälmann, who would become for a while the German Stalin.[76] Stalin liked to isolate his opponents from their supporters before defeating them in detail. By the time Bukharin had assumed the leadership of the Comintern, the regime of Normalization was under attack by the Joint Opposition. With Stalin distancing himself from the 'Bukharinist' positions, Bukharin himself felt obliged to forestall criticism by moving nearer the center. This meant moving to the left, competing with Stalin to demonstrate the inexorable tendency of the European stabilization to lead to new revolutionary chances. This resembled the verbal gymnastics about the degree to which Soviet Russia could complete socialist construction. Bukharin called for changes in the electoral tactics of the French and British parties.[77] Out of these recommendations came the slogan 'class against class,' a staple of what came to be known as the Third Period line. The 'second' period of stabilization would be proclaimed over at the Sixth World Congress in 1928. The Third Period would be one of increasing 'contradictions' in the world economy and sharpening of the 'general crisis of capitalism' must lead to wars and revolutions. As in 1924–1925, this would mean a return to violent opposition to the kind of united front activity prescribed by the Third Congress in 1921. 'Class against class' would be used in tandem with the designation of Social Democrats as 'social fascists,' therefore the primary enemy. Yet Bukharin's 'class against class' implied only its literal meaning, and no break with united front tactics.

Stalin's Comintern maneuvering was more dogged and far-reaching. Preparations to expel the Joint Opposition were going forward. In July, Victor Serge informed Trotsky that a national conference of the PCF had been told that Zinoviev and Trotsky had already been expelled, a sure sign of Stalin's plans.[78] In the same month, however, Stalin called for soviets in China and dispatched 'Besso' Lominadze to China in order to replace Chên Tu-hsiu, the Communist leader whose ideas seemed to harmonize with those of the opposition.[79] Plans for a rising in Canton were laid apparently after the July coup against the CCP by Wang Ching-wei and the Kuomintang left, who had won Stalin's support after the Shanghai massacre. At the same time, Mao Tse-tung received Comintern permission to stage the Autumn Harvest Rising in Hunan. 'On hearing this,' wrote Mao, 'I jumped for joy. Objectively China has long since reached 1917, but formerly everyone held the opinion that we were in 1905. This has been an extremely great error.'[80]

Both Stalin and Bukharin trumpeted this left turn, which would lead to the abortive December rising in Canton, timed to coincide with the Fifteenth Party Congress in Moscow and the expulsion of Trotsky from the party (Zinoviev capitulated and approved the measures against Trotskyism). But Stalin wanted the turn to shake loose Bukharin as well. Increasingly his Comintern supporters signaled the extent of the change of line by a change of vocabulary in condemning Trotsky: Now he was no longer an 'ultra-left' but merely a 'counterrevolutionary.' Stalin was going to occupy Trotsky's ground on the left. In the French and German parties, support was lined up by Stalin and Kuusinen on one side, and Bukharin, Manuilskii, and Humbert-Droz on the other. A key issue was reconciliation with the Brandlerites, in particular the return of Thalheimer to the circles of the KPD leadership. Meyer was in favor; Thälmann, referring to the succor it would give the Russian opposition, was against. Ruth Fischer, despite her adherence to Zinoviev-Trotsky, supported the position of Thälmann.[81] The German left still lived by the record of Zinoviev's denunciation of the Brandlerites for the fiasco of 1923. Conciliation was not, however, being affected, and, despite Bukharin's left talk and admonitions about the 'relativity' of stabilitation, the turn was becoming a reversal of all the policies associated with his name, under the banner of policies he had opposed for years. But no matter: Bukharin strove to show he had mastered dialectic and prepared to struggle against his own work.

Bukharin was prepared to make minor adjustments, toward the left in this case. He went along with the slogans that established the Comintern's infamous Third Period line but dug in for a kind of struggle for the soul of the Third Period, in keeping with his idea of the new opportunities available because of stabilization. That view would soon be pushed aside contemptuously by the Stalinists. The factional needs of the latter were similar to those of 1924–1925, when Trotskyism had been first anathemized, and a break with Zinoviev was on the agenda. But it was easier to turn right in 1925 than to turn left in 1928. The crisis and bankruptcy of the 'moral support' version of Socialism in One Country helped things along. The war scare occasioned by the break of relations with England, coupled with the mild measures recently taken to reduce the private sector's share in the national income, created a near panic in the countryside. The peasants withheld grain and, at the Fifteenth Congress, the ruling coalition began to assert itself against a 'grain strike.' By January 1928, this had resulted in 'extraordinary measures' to procure grain, the opening of the campaign for the collectivization of agriculture, and the First Five Year Plan.

The Rykov-Bukharin group reluctantly accepted the special measures, seeking to limit them by underlining their extraordinary character. They seemed to have won a respite at the July Central Committee plenum, which gave to the countryside assurances that NEP was not ended.[82] This only caused Trotsky to reassert his claim that the 'left zigzag' would end only in a further lurch to the right. The Stalin-Bukharin bloc had not broken up; Stalin's centrism would continue its 'semi-Ustrialovist' course.

Struggle against the *kulak*, thought Trotsky, required a struggle in the party against the right. Every step in that direction, he promised, would be supported by the opposition. The Shakhty trial of 1928 seemed to him to be such a step. A group of engineers in the coal industry had been accused of 'wrecking' activities disruptive to the industrialization of the country. The court condemned eleven of them to be shot, and five actually were. When the verdicts came in July, the press stepped up its attacks on the Ustrialovist intelligentsia, the 'bourgeois specialists.' Trotsky did not criticize the trial and seemed to accept the validity of the charges.[83] Oddly, Ustrialov himself had endorsed the turn to forced industrialization and urged patriotic compliance.[84]

The July plenum had also been the occasion for a meeting between Bukharin and Kamenev, in which Bukharin sought the aid of the former Leningrad leaders against Stalin. On what basis? The political programs were hopelessly at odds, so the cooperation could result only from a recognition that the programmatic differences were less important than the Regime Question.[85] Stalin was a 'Ghengis Khan,' cried Bukharin, a tyrant who changed positions according to the enemy of the moment. He would bring them all to ruin. When Trotsky got word of Bukharin's 'offer' to the Leningraders, he was immediately asked by supporters for a response to a possible grouping with the right against Stalin. Trotsky then spoke of a return of legality, 'giving the party back its rights,' as one modest base of agreement. It was a recapitulation of Trotsky's position in his letters to Bukharin in spring 1926: a left-right bloc on the Regime Question. Yet, in view of what had occurred since then, Trotsky could have little confidence in such a coalition. He had come to regard Bukharin as one who was at least partially an architect of the current regime. He also assumed that in the major disputes on collectivization, Rykov had led the right, with Bukharin wavering.[86]

Trotsky's position in his Central Asian exile was that only the center stood between the party and Thermidor. We can interpolate and assume than any offer to return and join Stalin against the right, without recantation, would probably have been accepted. Thus matters stood at the time of Trotsky's controversy with Souvarine. At the same time, Trotsky was freed of loyalty to the letter of the 1926–1927 program by the capitulations of Zinoviev and Kamenev. In letters to fellow oppositionists, he repudiated the 'obsolete' slogan of the Democratic Dictatorship and disparaged the Zinovievist left course of 1924–1925. Some followers, such as Pierre Naville, adhered to a kind of Trotskyism of the Permanent Revolution, a Trotskyism which might have been. The hallmark of their politics was rejection of continued joint work with Zinovievists Treint and Girault and even something of a critique of Trotsky's 1926–1927 bloc.[87] But Trotsky would in due course quash this sentiment. The door must remain closed for the Brandlerists and other rights, and open, under certain conditions, to the Zinovievists. The difficulty would lie in reconciling this view with his closest foreign admirers, people such as Rosmer, who would end by having almost as much conflict with Trotsky as Souvarine.

In spring and summer 1929, after his deportation to Prinkipo, Trotsky's position hardened all the more. The apparent victory of Stalin over the right confirmed his quest for party reform. When an international crisis over the Chinese-Eastern Railway arose in July—Soviet troops were to best Chinese troops in skirmishes over the next months—Trotsky again showed his Soviet patriotism, backing Stalin's actions and breaking ceremoniously with all who spoke of 'Soviet Imperialism.' This included people such as Paz, originally recruited by Rakovskii, and Zinovievists such as Hugo Urbahns. A high point was reached in August with the 'Rakovskii Capitulation.' Rakovskii and other well-known oppositionists made a declaration from Saratov emphasizing the importance of the party's struggle against the Right Danger. They proclaimed themselves in accord with the Comintern's Third Period line. Implementation of the Five Year Plan, they argued, was crucial. They declared themselves willing to join with the party leadership in a 'regroupment of forces,' prepared to dispense with 'factional methods' and to submit to party discipline. They pledged to 'eliminate the bitterness' of the recent expulsions, a bitterness which might be more quickly dissipated if Trotsky were permitted to return.[88] Trotsky endorsed the declaration by an Open Letter. The cooptation of left slogans by the center, he found, 'greatly facilitates the reconstruction of the unity of the party on a Leninist basis.' The essential problem of the October Revolution, he said, in an apparent bow in the direction of Socialism in One Country, is the transformation of the bourgeois society into a socialist society. He continued,

> A Marxist can refuse to sign your declaration, only in the case that he concludes that Thermidor is accomplished, the party is a cadaver, and that the road to the dictatorship of the proletariat can only be found by a new revolution.[89]

Several years would pass before this judgment of Trotsky's would be altered and the period 1923–1925 fixed for the onset of Thermidor. The great task of Trotsky's future historical writings would be a reduction of the struggle over the Lenin succession to a contest between revolutionists and Thermidoreans, ultimately between Trotsky and Stalin, with the other actors slipping into minor roles. Aside from this characterization's advantages to future assessments of Trotsky's historical role, it would establish Stalin's work as conservative throughout. Historical accounts of the future would appreciate the comparison with revolutions of the past, after which radical maximalists, hell-bent on preserving the revolution's utopian goals, must inevitably be pushed aside by more sober and prosaic individuals adapting to a more practical course against the inevitable cries that the revolution has been betrayed. This would be an alteration of Trotsky's message as historian of the Lenin succession, but by no means a violation of its fundamental contours. Souvarine's magisterial biography of Stalin, despite his disparagement of Trotsky's assessment of Bolshevism's role in the history of Marxism, would also stress the Thermidorean side of Stalinism.[90]

The 1929 controversy between these two historians of Stalinism, along with their previous polemics, seems to have been ignored in their later and more famous writings. Yet it is still of interest, for in the earlier writings we are able to see Stalin's importance for each of the actors in the struggle, if their programmatic aims were to be achieved. Trotsky's stress on the 'three issues' seems to verify Souvarine's suspicion that Trotsky intended to march under the banner of the Zinovievist cult of Lenin. Souvarine, despite the fact that he, no doubt along with Trotsky, saw Stalin as a savior against the depredations of the same Zinoviev, did not take the 'three issues' seriously. Perhaps one who did not have an immediate factional stake in the struggle could recognize that the Regime Question was always the only question of importance. Had Lenin lived, the same arguments, or fiercer ones, would no doubt have been aired, but the defeat of the programs of the various actors might have been no more injurious to their future fate than, say, Bukharin's defeat on 'Left Communism' in 1918. The menace was never in Stalin's program or in his prognoses, but in his regime, from which all our actors sought support against one another.

Perhaps they did so out of belief in the idea, as Trotsky put it, that 'one can be reconciled to any regime as long as it accomplishes some purpose.' They thought, no doubt, that to complain about the regime was less than truly Bolshevik. Yet Lenin's turns, against Trotsky in 1920 and against Stalin in 1922, seem to have been animated more by concern for the Regime Question (a 'personal' concern according to one-hundred-percent Bolshevik-Leninists) than by the program issues. He claimed to be fighting, first, bureaucracy in the state machinery, then bureaucracy in the party. Stalin's turns, against Zinoviev in 1925 and against Bukharin in 1927–1928, were of course driven by the desire to build rather than to limit a regime. It was Stalin who was called by the oppositions the architect of bureaucracy. Yet in these turns the issues were vastly more important. As it turned out, Stalin needed the policy alternance between Leningrad (Zinoviev) and Moscow (Bukharin), not only on the way up but even after he had settled the Regime Question to his satisfaction.

Trotsky's 1929 assessment of Stalin as a centrist was discarded later, but it was probably superior to his later judgments. A reassessment of the Lenin succession necessitates not only departure from the tale of Stalin versus Trotsky, as has been in progress among historians of recent years, but a closer look at the idea of centrism in Soviet politics, and what goes with it ineluctably, the idea of alternance.

6

Stalin and Alternance: The Second Centrism, 1929–1933

> If the country perishes, we all perish. If the country manages to recover, he twists around in time and we still perish.
> —N. I. Bukharin
> (to Kamenev, 1928)

WITH THE CAPITULATION of Bukharin and Rykov after the struggle of 1928–1929, it may have seemed that Stalin had finally got to the pinnacle of power. Trotsky nevertheless judged this primacy to be unstable and temporary. It was not just a question of clamping an iron discipline on the party but satisfying it that the problems of the revolution, now defined in terms of socialist construction, were being solved under Stalin's wise leadership. That is, Trotsky still regarded the Regime Question as derivative and his increasingly subtle corrections on programmatic issues as fundamental. Any other approach, for a Bolshevik, would be unprincipled. At the same time it was impossible to ignore the onset of Stalin's personal dictatorship and only reasonable to expect resistance to it to develop as the chaotic collectivization campaign in the countryside demonstrated to all the abyss into which Stalin was leading the nation.

Trotsky was also digging himself into a hole intellectually and politically. Up to this point, he had opposed, with the Leningraders, not Stalin's faction but the bloc of Stalin and the right, that is, the *program* of the right, which he judged to leave the country open to Thermidor. Now that program had been vanquished by a Stalin faction marching essentially under the program of Preobrazhenskii in economic affairs and Zinoviev, that is, the Zinoviev of 1924–1925, in Comintern policy. On the one hand, Trotsky was compelled to acknowledge in some measure the correctness of Stalin's programmatic initiative in internal affairs. But if he was not to follow the many oppositionists who counted that a justification for capitulation, and if he was to maintain continuity with the principles of

1924–1927, he would have to assert the continued threat of the Right Danger. Stalin must be condemned as a centrist, for his empirical 'zigzag,' which must ultimately open the door for the Thermidoreans. Trotsky was thrust, unwilling, into a fight against centrism, which in terms of personalities had narrowed for the first time to a struggle between Stalin and Trotsky.

It would have been more accurate to say that the Lenin succession had introduced a sharp programmatic alternance, Moscow versus Leningrad, Bukharin versus Zinoviev, with the position of greatest influence in the center. It was precisely this centrism that prevented the competing programs from becoming competing political parties. And those who maneuvered from the center position could with justice identify the cause of their personal triumph with that of the 'hegemony' of the Bolshevik party itself. Thus Lenin shifted his weight toward the 'militarization of labor' slogan before August, 1920, and afterward against; toward relaxing the Monopoly of Foreign Trade until May 1922, and afterward against. Lenin was not above applying the prerogative of the center to the case of both Trotsky and Stalin as individuals. In Lenin's party it violated dialectic to fall in love with a program and to cling to it while conditions, often factional conditions, undermined its usefulness. Stalin may not have enjoyed a reputation as a Marxist philosopher, but he understood that much. In this respect, he was what he strove to be, a faithful student of Lenin.

Trotsky, Bukharin, and even Zinoviev would have loved to be centrist in the manner of Lenin, but their positions in the factional fight did not permit it. So they were condemned to defend programmatic principles. Stalin lacked the accumulated intellectual authority to subdue them in Lenin's genteel fashion, but he had the administrative position, and he, too, was condemned to do battle with the weapons at hand.

Centrism, then, was a fundamental fact of Soviet succession politics. Trotsky did not recognize this at first, and later he sought to disguise the fact. Stalin's centrist zigzags for him showed that the Stalin faction had no firm basis in Soviet political reality. That analysis would have been good enough had the Russian political scene been a democratic one with a competition of parliamentary forces, each with its own constituency. In a regime of dictatorship the argument was ludicrous. It becomes intelligible, if not plausible, only if we translate it to mean: Stalin lacks the theoretical tools to lead the party of Lenin—he can improvise for a time but his crudeness will only lead him to ruin. Between the capitulation of Bukharin and the advent of Hitler to power in Germany, Trotsky criticized Stalinism, built an international opposition, and, as will be shown, contributed mightily to Stalin's most morbid suspicions about those around the supreme dictator. He continued to suspend discussion of Thermidor, still only a danger as he saw it, and argued instead in terms of the programmatic issues. He could not ignore the Regime Question, however: 'You might say,' he had told his followers from his Alma-Ata exile, 'that the bureaucratic maneuvering is unimportant, but you would be wrong. This is the epoch of the omnipotence of the apparatus which accelerates the dual power in the country, therefore we must consider the disposition of the bureaucratic actors.'[1] Trotsky thus recognized the value of Kremlinology, of which he was to become a skilled practitioner.

Those who considered the disposition of the actors unimportant would continue to analyze Soviet society up to the war in terms of the Russian Question: what is the nature of the Soviet state and society? Trotsky felt most at home on this path. He would contribute to the Russian Question. But the other path—the analysis of the Regime Question, which leads toward Kremlinology—promised, instead of a reconciliation of Soviet reality with Marxist theory, an identification of the unique features of Soviet succession politics.

Trotsky Turns Right

Stalin's great turn of 1928–1929 was, Trotsky thought, only a centrist zigzag, which showed that the Stalin faction and the bureaucracy behind it had no real moorings in the party of the working class. It was proof that the Stalinist bureaucracy was not a class with its own historical interests. 'Centrism,' he argued, 'is always moving to the left or to the right. It is never "just itself." '[2] If Stalin aimed to govern in the long run by means of these zigzags, he would be rudely reminded that his credit was limited. The party and the working class had not simply disappeared but would soon call Stalinism to account. Indeed, Stalin's turn to the program of the Left Opposition was proof of the vitality of the dictatorship of the proletariat. At the same time, centrism prepared the way for new defeats:

> Soviet centrism is the most natural means by which to slide toward national-reformism. The reign of centrism is a political symptom of Thermidor. The power, however, has not passed to the bourgeoisie and cannot without violent class battles.[3]

The Thermidorean reaction of the French Revolution had paved the way for Bonaparte. Did that mean that the restoration of the Soviet bourgeoisie would only be safeguarded by military dictatorship, or that the military would lead the way? Trotsky seemed unable to choose. On the one hand, he claimed that 'Stalinism is preparing Bonapartism,'[4] but he also argued that there were Thermidorean *and* Bonapartist types of overthrow, the former incremental and the latter sudden as the result of a military coup at the hands of 'adventurist-praetorian elements' such as Tukhachevskii, Blücher, Budenny, or Voroshilov. The Soviet generals, feeling the pressure from their peasant ranks as they carried out the brutal measures of agrarian collectivization, would seek relief by overthrowing

Stalin. Trotsky's ideas on the analogy with the French Revolution would not be sorted out until years later, but it is noteworthy here that he was ostensibly not looking to the military for help, but rather offering help to the party, even to Stalin, against these dire threats.

Trotsky's strategy was to criticize but also to prove the loyalty of his tendency to the party and its support of every measure of Stalin's against the right. That was essentially the line of the Rakovskii Capitulation.[5] The result was a considerable shakeout among his supporters. In the case of the groups of Urbahns and Paz there may have been a certain reluctance to plunge back into Communist party politics (the line of the Rakovskii declaration was ardent for reentry) after they had begun to breathe fresh air. They were certainly not keen enough Soviet patriots to please Trotsky. He had experienced few qualms in backing the Soviet recapture of the Chinese-Eastern Railway in 1929, but many of them spoke of defending China.[6] Urbahn's paper *Fahne des Kommunismus* had argued essentially that the Chinese-Eastern was a foreign concession to Russian imperialism, by no means patrimony of 'Red imperialism.' There was nothing worse, said Trotsky in reply, than 'formal lefts' who pursue tactics of the type of the offensive of 1921 or those of 1924–1925 with Zinoviev and Maslow, but who still think sentimentally about 'national fairness.'[7]

The source of ultra-leftism on the Chinese-Eastern question was not Urbahns, said Trotsky, but his mentor, Robert Louzon, an Allemanist (the tendency that had preceded and contributed to revolutionary syndicalism) at the turn of the century, who had worked with *Vie ouvrière*, had been a Socialist official, and then a Communist until his expulsion, and who now, like Pierre Monatte, was returning to syndicalism. His thinking would have a considerable influence on Trotsky's ideas about Soviet-American relations.

Like Trotsky, Louzon was impressed by the newly won preeminence of American finance, with its 'Dawes-ization' of Europe. Only a heroic effort by the British to defend the pound at $4.86 had kept them abreast of the United States. Together, the Anglo-Saxons projected their axis with Germany as the centerpiece of the international economy. Dreams of German *Weltpolitik* had evaporated with the development of a close relationship with the United States.[8] Thus, the postwar world of 'fulfillment' (faithful disposition of Germany's reparations payments) was a world in which Anglo-Saxon finance and Social Democratic pacifism sought to exorcise the demons of prewar national rivalry. At the same time, however, this was a world *rentier* economy in which the sources of profit were rapidly disappearing. Only areas such as China and, to a lesser degree, Russia held out the promise of sufficiently high rates of profit.[9] Therefore, if peace could be assured on the European continent, the natural propensity of the Americans would be to drive West, a march which, Louzon imagined, 'leads straight to China.'[10]

A healthy international economy depended, said Louzon, on stable currencies, but economic nationalism, yielding to domestic political pressures, constantly tended toward inflation. That was a boon for the labor aristocracy, but the illusory 'progress' weakened the resolve of the proletariat:

> An international economy, on the contrary, if it presents the disadvantage of suppressing certain internal antagonisms of capitalism, brings with it the inestimable advantage of suppressing at the same time the antagonisms within the proletariat, thus becoming a powerful agent of the internationalization of the proletariat.[11]

Thus real progress consisted in 'developing the productivity of labor,' which meant increased specialization across national boundaries. Economic nationalism went in the opposite direction. The foremost champions of autarky, 'national economy,' were the French. However, even they felt the pull of the international market because of Alsace-Lorraine, with its abundant coal, steel, and cast-iron industries and textile manufacturing.[12] These demanded export markets, so that 'by the forges of Lorraine imperialism penetrates France.'

This did not prevent France, in the view of Louzon, from continuing to Balkanize Europe, the better to unify it on French terms — that is, on terms of hostility to the Anglo-Saxons. Louzon was broadening the antipatriotic attitude of many French syndicalists into a worldview of internationalism. Not only Urbahns but Trotsky himself would harbor many of the same ideas. Trotsky saw French Premier Briand's 1929 call for a United States of Europe as a plot for a customs union against America. France also hoped for enmity between England and the United States. These hopes were not idle, said Trotsky, because the Anglo–American antagonism was the primary conflict in world politics:

> By means of the slogan of the Open Door America will incite not only China but also India and Egypt against British naval domination. Against the British bases America will find entry not by sea but by land, that is through the colonies and dominions of Britain.[13]

The fact was that Trotsky had the same position he ascribed to Briand: he advocated a United States of Europe (on the basis of 'Soviet' regimes) directed against the United States of America. Only five years later, he would drop this authentically Trotskyist idea entirely, in order to incite the United States against Hitler. However, before the advent of Nazism to power, he wanted, if anything, closer relations for the Soviet Union with Britain than with the United States. Anglo-Soviet economic undertakings could 'merge into one another like the bones of a skull.' Those English capitalists who recognized this would be able thus to defend against the coming 'outburst of Yankee truculence in every sector of the planet.'[14] Hitler's regime would cause him to look more kindly on this truculence.

The left line pursued by Trotsky in 1928–1929, according to the Rakovskii statement, emphasized support for the victories of the Stalin group against the right. Trotsky claimed that the timid Five Year Plan adopted in 1927 had been radically revised by Stalin 'only under the action of our critique.'[15] The basic ideas of the new plan came from the Left Opposition platform.[16] Even with the aid of socialist countries, wrote Trotsky, problems with the peasant would have been difficult. The 'democratic' revolution of 1917 had given them surcease from redemption payments; now, however, they paid even more to support socialist industry, since the Monopoly of Foreign Trade forced industry to produce goods which would be more efficiently produced elsewhere. The 'scissors' of industrial and agricultural prices stemmed ultimately from the Monopoly of Foreign Trade.[17] Trotsky seemed to acknowledge that the fundamental problems were not entirely due to defects in economic policy, while he never failed to suggest that he could do it better.

The left course of the Rakovskii declaration led in the direction of reconciliation with other lefts. Some of the difficulties with former Zinovievists have already been described. Trotsky had renounced much of his own thinking for a better identification as a Leninist. The combination with Zinoviev in 1926–1927 had deepened his disavowal of 'Trotskyism.' In exile, however, he felt less constrained by this etiquette, and undertook a defense of the Permanent Revolution theory in a polemic against Radek.[18] The former Zinovievists tried to rein in this 'Trotskyism.' Treint restated the line of 1926–1927:

> Trotsky recognized that it was Lenin who was right against him and notably in the questions of Permanent Revolution and relations with the peasantry . . . Lenin refused to admit the antagonism between the proletariat and the peasant masses after the conquest of power . . . Lenin showed that the proletariat could keep power and progress on the socialist path even if the world revolution was late in coming.[19]

Trotsky vastly overestimated his polemical powers and the coherence of his ideological record, continuing the debate with the Zinovievists in the hope that the capitulation of their leader would weaken fidelity to their line. But the Zinovievist version of Leninism, up to this point the same as that of Stalin and Trotsky, proved too resilient.

Trotsky then made an attempt to enlist the Italian followers of Bordiga, once again in the hope that his rendering of the Lenin succession and its Comintern ramifications would prove convincing. Trotsky thought he could isolate Bordiga's 'positive elements.' Bordiga had a record of defense of Trotsky in the Italian Communist party. Indeed, the amalgam Bordiga-Trotsky was well known to PCI militants. Bordiga had in fact disapproved of Zinoviev's liberties with the 'fundamental Marxist line,' and criticized Zinoviev's version of Bolshevism as 'a revolutionary ideology of the proletariat allied to the peasants.'[20] The anti-Trotsky campaign had only broken out in the PCI in February 1925 when the opponents of Bordiga, claiming the similarity in the views of Bordiga and Trotsky, had raised the amalgam. Actually Trotsky had objected to Bordiga's harsh criticism of united front tactics, but Bordiga had joined Trotsky in denouncing the German fiasco of October 1923 and had endorsed Trotsky's 'Lessons of October'. Bordiga's *Rome Theses* against the united front had been the main target of Palmiro Togliatti and Antonio Gramsci in their anti-Bordiga fight,[21] and it had been too tempting not to join this criticism with accusations of Trotskyism. In the course of the dispute which removed him from the leadership, Bordiga had actually defended Trotsky. He had sought common ground on the issue of Brandler, underlining, with Trotsky, the failures of October 1923. Bordiga, however, had reminded Trotsky of the latter's support for the line of the Comintern and for Brandler's tactical line in Germany as well.[22] This was because Bordiga had never endorsed the turn to the united front taken by the Third and Fourth Comintern congresses. Trotsky's call to unify the Left Opposition elements on the basis of the first four Comintern congresses was bound to run aground here.

So Trotsky approached Bordiga on other matters. The idea of the vanguard party, suggested Trotsky, surely divided Bordiga and his followers from those such as Monatte, Louzon, and Souvarine, who still entertained syndicalist ideas.[23] Moreover, the Bordigists' conception of the 'absolute independence' of the Communist parties implied, argued Trotsky, hostility to the 'Sun Yat-sen-ism' that had led the Chinese party aground in 1927 and to the capitulation to the English trade unions that had hurt the British party the year before. Similarly, Trotsky continued, the Bordigists must be agreed, against Urbahns, Louzon, Souvarine, or whomever, that the Soviet Union was still a workers' state. With so much in common, and with a common 'centrist' opponent in the Stalin–Togliatti leadership, there should be no reason not to coalesce.

Trotsky's relations with Bordiga were working their course when another group of expelled Italian Communists made contact with him. The group, led by Leonetti, Tresso, and Ravazzoli, calling itself the Gramsci *nucleo*, opened a correspondence with Trotsky, suggesting that the Gramsci tradition and the Trotsky opposition were at one in their record of resistance to the rise of the current Comintern leadership. Trotsky found that there was indeed a great deal of common ground with the Gramsci *nucleo*.[24] Thus was born a powerful myth exerting influence on the Italian left up to the present.[25]

No sooner had Trotsky made contact with the Gramsci *nucleo*, which called itself the Nuovo Opposizione Italiano (NOI), than his relations with Bordiga began to deteriorate. Further discussion with the Bordigists revealed that they were eager to pursue the Brandler question, on which they thought Trotsky's protestations unconvincing. They rejected the united front line of the Fourth Congress and felt that it was responsible for the fiasco of the German October. It could not be a case, as Trotsky had striven to prove, of a bad application of a good strategy.[26] Instead of accepting the first four congresses as a common platform, they wanted a fierce critique of the first five congresses. That is, they wanted to discuss the Fifth Comintern Congress of 'Bolshevization' in 1924, presided over by Zinoviev. That would have ruined any chances to win Zinovievists, such as Treint, on whom Trotsky had not yet given up.

With the abdication of the Spanish king Alphonso XIII in 1931, the NOI began to argue on the basis of a Spanish revolutionary situation. As they held with regard to the Italian situation under Mussolini, the agenda should include a democratic program rather than a socialist one according to the Permanent Revolution. The Bordigists, they held, would be incapable of dealing with either the Italian or the Spanish situation. On the other hand, a broad democratic front, with appropriate accommodations for the peasantry and small business classes, would galvanize the anti-Mussolini struggle, and a civil war would introduce *kerenskismo italiano*. Trotsky agreed with the NOI:

> The Italian revolution must have a more or less prolonged democratic preface prior to the struggle of the proletariat for power. During this preliminary period the proletarian vanguard will not be able to ignore the problems of democracy. The position of the *Prometeo* group, in refusing on principle to issue democratic slogans, in the light of Spanish events appears theoretically inconsistent and politically ruinous.[27]

Leonetti insisted that Bordigism had been ever thus. Eager to blend the old Gramscian critique of Bordiga with current resistence to the Third Period line, Leonetti accused Bordiga of inventing the term 'social fascism,' which had been picked up by Zinoviev and used during the 'Bolshevization' campaign of 1924. Thus the old affinity for this idea, thought Leonetti, would cause the Bordigists to oppose a united front against German fascism as well.[28]

Trotsky could only agree with that, and counting the NOI a big gain for the international opposition, he sharpened his criticism of Bordiga. Did his agreement with the NOI rest on anything more than temporary convenience? Were they veterans of the Trotsky position in the Lenin succession fight? To be sure, they had opposed Bordiga's tactics on grounds that Trotsky or almost any other Bolshevik would share. But when Bordiga had defended Trotsky in 1926, they had not said anything on Trotsky's behalf.[29] Even during their friendly approaches in correspondence with Trotsky, they put Permanent Revolution between inverted commas. They had actually rejected Permanent Revolution from the time that Zinoviev had put it on the agenda with 'Bolshevization.' Gramsci had criticized Trotsky's thesis of 1925 about the power of the United States as unduly pessimistic.[30] Without ever supporting Trotsky, Gramsci had urged unity on the Russian Politburo at the time of the Zinoviev-Trotsky opposition fight of 1926.[31]

As the NOI admitted in correspondence with Trotsky, they had supported the Comintern line, 1926–1929. So much for the all-important 'three issues.' Moreover, they had made a 'little mistake' in supporting Togliatti against the Italian right led by Angelo Tasca.[32] But Togliatti's campaign against the right had become an ultra-left zigzag, with Togliatti proclaiming a 'catastrophist perspective of immediate insurrection.'[33] The NOI had helped introduce the line of Third Period Stalinism, but had found themselves in turn pushed aside by Togliatti. That was the basis for their approach to Trotsky. The entire episode of Trotsky's recruitment of an Italian section for the International Opposition demonstrated that the Russian succession struggle had as little resonance for the centrists of Comintern 'normalization' as it had for Zinovievists. That Trotsky ignored this fact so blithely demonstrated that he himself could not take his rendering of the succession struggle seriously.

Trotsky gathered support internationally not as a left opponent of Thermidorean Stalinism but in the same way that he had in 1925, as a pole of normalization and refuge for those who could not follow the Comintern's ultra-leftism, in the guise of either Bolshevization or the Third Period.[34] Thus the 'three issues,' which seemed to offer a choice between Trotsky and Thermidorean Bukharinism, grew less and less important. While his supporters generally endorsed his version of the events of 1926–1927, few of them had been following Russian politics closely enough to have formed a genuine opinion, and in most cases, the Comintern line of that period had not been nearly so hard to take as that of the Third Period.

Isaac Deutscher, the future biographer of Stalin and Trotsky, whose historical studies have had an enormous impact in the West, became associated with Trotskyism out of such a reaction. The Polish Communist party's factional life had been dominated by two groups: The Warski-Walecki-Wera Kostrzewa group, known as the 'Three W's,' had come under criticism from Zinoviev and Stalin in 1923–1924 for alleged 'Trotskyism,' which they had understood no better than Souvarine, Brandler, or any of the others caught up in the net. As a result of 'Bolshevization,' Zinoviev had replaced them with a group led by Domski, Lenski, and Sofia Unszlicht, by analogy with Treint-Girault and Fischer-Maslow. But the 'lefts' were dislodged by the Bukharinist Normalization, which returned Warski and Kostrzewa to power at the end of 1925. In the KPP there was Zinovievism and Bukharinism, but no Trotskyism. Warski-Kostrzewa drew the blame for the 'May Error,' the KPP's support, under the rubric of the Democratic Dictatorship of the Proletariat and the Peasantry, for Marshal Piłsudski's coup d'état in

1926. This was apparently not on orders from Moscow (Piłsudski as the opponent of 1920 was not confused in the Kremlin with Chiang Kai-shek, who was thought to be a protégé) but the result of a local application of the line.[35]

When Deutscher had been first introduced to the Polish theater of the 1926–1927 dispute, he had spurned the Zinovievists and favored the Bukharinists.[36] Deutscher counted himself a critic of Trotskyism. After the turn to the Third Period line, however, he sent a memorandum to the Comintern in 1931, criticizing the ultra-left tactics.[37] At first the Polish leadership was reluctant to bring in Russian issues, but Deutscher built a following by propagating Trotsky's writings on the German situation.[38] No Polish group before this time had called itself Trotskyist. The same might be said for the British Trotskyists of the Balham group, who had preferred the more moderate line of the Bukharin period and who resisted the Third Period line.[39]

Trotsky had hoped to build a Spanish section of 'Bolshevik Leninists' around Andrés Nín, but ran aground on Nín's reluctance to break with the workers' and peasants' bloc led by Joaquín Maurín. The bloc was a mass organization, rather than a Communist party. It admitted communists and anarchists of every confession, and acted 'as a kind of permanent united front.'[40] Trotsky wanted Nín to stand against the others on the basis of the former's telling of the Russian struggle, but Nín apparently made little headway. The different dissidents did not see their positions as ones based on principle and felt that the divisions had been imposed on them from without. Nín assured Trotsky that he was bringing the bloc members to adhere to his program, but 'in Catalonia,' he said, 'we adhere to the bloc. There is no other way, as we don't exist in Catalonia.'[41] Nín was bothered by another consideration. Rosmer and Naville had appealed to him against the leader of the French Trotskyists, Raymond Molinier, who had used undemocratic methods against them, apparently with Trotsky's support.[42] With Kurt Landau of the German opposition, they were already working, or so Trotsky suspected, to create a second international left opposition. Trotsky was finding little echo of his version of Russian events, and moreover, in his enthusiasm for men of action who could apply pressure, he seemed to make the same sort of errors that Lenin had made with Stalin.

In truth, Trotsky could not call his opposition to Stalin a 'left' opposition at all. Despite the credit he claimed for the influence of the platform of 1927 on Stalin's industrialization and collectivization policies, and despite his applause for attacks against the Bukharinists, by spring, 1930, Trotsky was drawing away from the line of the Rakovskii declaration. He may have been following Stalin's moves, or Stalin may even have been influenced by his. At any rate, Trotsky's shift in emphasis from his left line was clear enough. He had had rather bad luck with the Zinovievists, especially while he called the Third Period line 'an attempt to rerun the errors of Zinoviev in 1924–1925 on a higher footing.'[43]

In early 1930 Trotsky began to say that Stalin's policy in both domestic and Comintern policy had changed 'from a left zigzag to an ultra-left course.' He sounded a cautionary note. Resources for economic development were not inexhaustible, and the tempo could not be determined by the administrative whip alone. Then came news that Stalin, under heavy Politburo pressure, had spoken of 'Dizziness with Success' and had chosen to slow the pace of collectivization. Within days of Stalin's speech, Trotsky published an article claiming that 'we have never held the socialist transformation of the rural economy to be possible except in the perspective of several decades.'[44] The scissors of industrial and economic prices, only recently thought by him to be inevitably open because of the consequences of the Monopoly of Foreign Trade, now were said to be open only because of Stalin's impetuosity. They must be closed at all costs. The moment had come, he wrote a week later, to 'evacuate in good order' the adventurist economic positions.[45] A 'timely retreat' was now imperative. In the West, the call must be for economic collaboration between countries suffering unemployment and the Soviet Union.

Trotsky must have sensed that his campaign was paying off, or at least that it was coinciding with a revolt against Stalin. This was implicit in its dark hints about 'elements of dual power' in Russia. To those who remembered his thoughts about dual power in 1917, this could only mean that the armed forces were not entirely reliable. Trotsky had only an inkling of the disaster on the Russian countryside, with Stalin's 'civil massacre' wiping out thousands of peasants, losses in livestock that would not be made good for decades, and after the 'Dizziness with Success' speech, an exodus from the collective farms. When Stalin resumed the attack months later, he joined it with renewed purges and ideological attacks on Trotskyism. In fact, each effort made by Trotsky to solidarize with a Stalin move against the 'Thermidorean' threat seems to have provoked, not softening, but renewal under even more harsh terms, of anti-Trotsky propaganda.

The obvious conclusion was that Stalin was deeply frightened, not simply at the impasse into which he was driving the country, but at his inability to find a way out by shifting sides. A turn to the right was no solution, for he could not simply restage the Fourteenth Congress. He had chosen a hard road to the building of his regime through Zinoviev's Comintern policy and Preobrazhenskii's agrarian policy. He was at this point the most extreme Leningrader in terms of program, yet the Stalin regime had not yet accorded him the place he coveted. In fact the clearer it became to those around him that he was not even a Bukharin or a Zinoviev, the more he burned with the desire to be recognized as a theorist. At the moment, he built on a combination of ideas taken from

Bukharin and Zinoviev. That this 'heritage' was defined exclusively in terms of opposition to 'Trotskyism' was not a particular problem. Lenin had defined Bolshevism in terms of opposition to 'economism,' 'boycot-tism,' 'recallism,' 'liquidationism,' 'social patriotism,' and the like. But Stalin wanted to make his own contribution to the analysis of Trotskyism, and to have it recognized nationally and internationally.

In a sense, Stalin had already begun by building on his appropriation of the attitude of Zinoviev toward the intelligentsia. Zinoviev had stressed the base among the *spetsy* of Trotskyism. He had called the Gosplan, at the time of Trotsky's efforts to reinforce its powers, a 'nest of the *spetsy*.' His political fight, against those symbolically represented by Rykov and Tomskii in the state and trade union machinery, and Bukharin in academic circles, was put in terms of a struggle against 'Mensheviko-Ustrialovite' specialists. Stalin had appropriated this heritage programmatically in 1928 and had expressed it in the early show trials. The Shakhty trial of 'specialists wreckers' in the Don Basin in 1928, the trial of the 'Industrial Party' of technical specialists allegedly doing the bidding of French intelligence, and other trials were attempts to rally the youth against the intelligentsia and Ustrialovism (although Ustrialov enthusiastically sup-ported Stalin). By 1931 Stalin put on the brakes by arguing that the old intelligentsia, inherited from the Tsardom, had to be disciplined sharply, but the new Soviet intelligentsia would have a key role in socialist construction. Stalin thus sketched out vistas for the youth whose allure would silence many doubts about the revolution he would unleash in 1936–1938. The ideas of the perceived patron saint of the intelligentsia baiters, J. W. Machajski, were revived in order to be condemned by warning that 'every ruling class must have its own intelligentsia' and the proletariat was no exception.[46]

Stalin also sought to deepen Leninism by defending the continuity of Bolshevism from the prewar years. *Proletarskaia revoliutsiia* had published an article by a certain A. G. Slutskii showing, correctly, how close Lenin had been to the German Social Democracy and its main theorist, Karl Kautsky, prior to 1914. Slutskii noted the fact, not yet admitted by Soviet scholars, that Lenin had not criticized Social Democratic opportunism in Kautsky's case, and from the viewpoint of 1914 and after might be said to have 'underestimated' the latter. Stalin saw a chance to contribute. He denounced Slutskii's 'rotten liberalism' and 'Trotskyism,' with an original rationale. Lenin, wrote Stalin, could not have solidarized with the German left Socialists such as Rosa Luxemburg, who criticized the German party's opportunism, because these lefts had worked together with Trotsky to concoct the theory of Permanent Revolution just after the 1905 revolution. In short, all that had been said against Permanent Revolution was valid for the Luxemburg tradition in German socialism as well. Moreover, Rosa Luxemburg was now a Trotskyite.[47]

Stalin may not have been pursuing an abstract question. While the dispute was going on, there was a split in the German Socialist party led by a left group which considered the Social Democratic attitude to the onrushing economic depression too passive. The Socialist theorist and statesman Rudolf Hilferding had already offered the opinion that he who advocates state intervention to cure the ills of a capitalist society abandons Marxism. Despite this, the Socialists had decided to seek international aid for the German economy. In October, 1931, a group of left Socialists split from the KPD to form the Sozialistische Arbeiterpartei (SAP), reaffirming the tradition of Rosa Luxemburg and calling for a united front with the KPD, that is, approximately the same line that Trotsky was then advocating. Stalin's intervention in the *Proletarskaia revoliutsiia* affair thus buffered the KPD from this contagion.

On the German Question, Trotsky was on solid ground. His criticisms about the dangers of the 'social fascism' line, his warnings about the unique dangers of Nazism, his call for a united front for common struggle against Hitler, all this had resonated in the International and in the Soviet Union. Among the Italian oppositionists he had debated the matter by way of quarreling with Bordiga's view of Mussolini as the revenge of finance capital *tout court*. The question was easy to confuse, since the Comintern's struggle against Permanent Revolution had led it to pronounce the necessity for intermediate, prolonged 'democratic dictatorships' as transitions from bourgeois society to the dictatorship of the proletariat. But could one tell the constituency of a 'Jacobin' regime from that of a Bonapartist? The Italians thus pondered the Polish 'May Error' and Piłsudski. Gramsci insisted that fascism had a mass popular constituency and compared Mussolini in that respect to Piłsudski.[48] August Thalheimer had questioned that view at the Sixth Comintern Congress, denying that fascism should be thought of as an attempt to stabilize capitalism in an agrarian country. The starting point, he argued, must be Marx's analysis of Bonapartism, the latter with its appeal to bohemia, to '*déclassés* of all classes.'[49] Many, including Isaac Deutscher, thought that the Trotsky theory of fascism took Thalheimer's theory as a point of departure, one which led Trotsky to conclude that fascism was based on a constituency of 'human dust':

> The main army of fascism still consists of the petty bourgeoisie and the new middle class: the small artisans and shopkeepers of the cities, the petty officials, the employees, the technical personnel, the *intelligentsia*, the impoverished peasantry.[50]

The social categories of Trotsky's 'human dust' comprise the Marxist term 'petite bourgeoisie,' here rendered in its most pristine, nineteenth century form, embracing categories supposedly being pushed from the historical stage by the onrush of industrial development. But the intelligentsia of white-collar workers, civil servants, professionals, administrative and technical personnel—could one pit the proletariat against this mass of the nation? Trotsky was interested in the matter only for the purpose of devising tactics, which could in no circumstances be electoral tactics. However, he was contending not only with the problem of Comintern policy but also with the exhaustion of classical Marxism.

Trotsky was not theoretically inclined to try to sort out this problem. In any case, a united electoral front between Communists and Social Democrats would clearly not hold the key after Brüning had initiated rule by decree in 1930. The tactics of the united front were for him the tactics of 1917, in which soviets were the highest form of united front. One got there gradually, starting with purely defensive measures against the Nazi gangs, but eventually the solution must be to introduce 'dual power' effected by the pressure of the workers in direct extraparliamentary action. 'Today,' said Trotsky, 'the fundamental problem of the German situation may be formulated thus: on Russia's path or Italy's? . . . The position of Thälmann in 1932,' he added, 'reproduces the position of Bordiga in 1922.'[51]

In works on this period, it is a commonplace to note the wisdom of Trotsky's pleas for a united front with the Socialists, in contrast with the seemingly suicidal line of the Third Period Comintern, according to which the Socialists were the first enemy, even when they were attacked by Nazis. A Socialist-Communist bloc, in this view, seems a formidable obstacle in Hitler's path. It is usually not taken into account that the arena of struggle was not parliament but the street. The prospect of protracted extraparliamentary class war with the Nazis appealed very little to the Socialists, who, under those conditions, would likely have lost leadership to the Communists. It was, moreover, just such a prospect that created the feeling among the coalition's potential opponents that they could not get along without the Nazis.

The Third Period line, designating the Social Democrats as 'social fascists,' asserted that they would betray any common action such as Trotsky was urging. That they were not true revolutionaries was the reason that they were Social Democrats and not Communists. It was among the enemies of the Social Democrats, in the nationalist movement, that more real revolutionaries were to be found. And, unlike the Social Democrats, whose real spiritual support was in the West, German nationalists could hope for sustenance from important sectors of German business and the military. This thought was the temptation to which Stalin and Molotov succumbed.

It has been argued that Stalin pursued the disastrous Third Period line in order to isolate further those in the Comintern who sided with the rightist opponents of collectivization in the U.S.S.R.[52] It has also been tempting, in view of the supposed ascendency of Socialism in One Country over proletarian internationalism, to argue that Stalin's *realpolitik* really best explains the Third Period line. The German Social Democrats were probably the party most friendly to the Western democracies and most desirous of 'fulfillment' of the provisions of the Versailles treaty. This made them the sternest critics of Soviet-German military cooperation. To call them the first enemy of the German working class was only, it might be argued, to use German communism as an instrument of Soviet foreign policy. Thus German nationalism can be judged as much of an ally during the Third Period as it had been in 1922–1923, and the Third Period can be seen as a continuation of National Bolshevism.

Franco-Soviet relations had their ups and downs during this period, but in general the enmity was quite sharp. The Soviets had expected the French to goad Poland and China into attacking them in 1928–1929. They did not improve matters by their obvious sympathy for a revolt against France in Indochina in 1930. A French hand was thought to be behind the Japanese invasion of Manchuria in September, 1931. Even when the Soviets succeeded in getting a nonagression pact with France in 1932, they had to resist a French attempt providing for abrogation in the event of 'an attack by a third power,' which in the circumstances could only have meant Japan.[53] Moreover, the Japanese threat argued strongly in favor of cementing ties to Germany on the other flank.

The conviction was widespread, among Stalin's advisers and spokesmen, that the German bourgeoisie could never be satisfied with fulfillment, could never accept the Young Plan (the rescheduling of reparations payments promulgated in 1929), because at bottom they wanted *Anschluss* with Austria, boundary change in the East at the expense of Poland, and a program of rearmament. Men such as Kuusinen had long been convinced that Soviet power would expand in the future not by revolutionary means, but only by 'armed force and conquest.'[54] Radek, who worked closely with Stalin during these years, was known to favor a political line which would dovetail with anti-Versailles sentiment.

As much as he resisted any of the temptations of National Bolshevism (during these years) and urged the united front with Social Democracy, Trotsky was never moved to accuse Stalin of forsaking the German revolution. At the end of his life, some of his supporters suggested that Stalin might have 'sabotaged' the German revolution, a charge he rejected: 'I would say that Stalin sincerely wished the triumph of the Communist Party in Germany in 1930–1933 . . . Stalin wanted to show that he was no Menshevik.'[55]

The social-fascism line also wavered during this period, with common work in local elections in Saxony showing that Trotsky's urgings had some resonance in the KPD. This coincided with the pause after Stalin's 'Dizziness with Success' speech. The Comintern executive called for a right turn on March 15, days after Stalin's speech, reproaching German and Austrian leaders for 'sectarianism' and failure to make appropriate defense measures. That was close to Trotsky's position. At the end of the year, however, with the Brüning government's declaration of rule by decree (and with resumption of the Russian collectivization drive), the cry was that fascism had already arrived and some sort of new front was needed to combat it. The result was the slogan of 'People's Revolution,' declaimed most enthusiastically by Heinz Neumann.[56] A certain Lieutenant Scheringer, after an assiduous study of the classics of Marxism, switched allegiance from the Nazis to the KPD, with a celebration recalling the 'Schlageter line' of 1923. German-Soviet relations warmed in the summer of 1931 with a trade agreement negotiated by Piatakov. The Berlin Treaty of 1926 was extended. A Nazi referendum to remove the Social Democratic–led coalition government of Prussia was supported by the Communists. This 'Red Referendum' was the most notorious example of Communist-Nazi cooperation.[57] Trotsky, in his most indignant tone, as if he had opposed the National Bolshevism approach in 1923, warned against the new adventure of 'People's Revolution,' which, he said, 'reconciles part of the working and middle classes to the ideology of fascism.'[58] Stalin and Heinz Neumann, and, no doubt, Radek as well, must have thought it would work in the reverse direction, with the KPD as the heir of Nazi popularity. Otto Strasser, a prominent exponent of Nazi anticapitalist revolutionism who had broken with Hitler in 1930, was invited to Moscow to discuss common action for the KPD with his youthful followers.[59] A joke of the period referred to 'Nazi beefsteak,' which was brown (the color of the stormtrooper uniform) outside but red inside.

Stalin's motives cannot be determined with precision, especially if it becomes necessary to distinguish whether actions such as the Red Referendum were designed to stiffen German resolve against the West or merely to worsen the situation in Germany.[60] Here, as in later cases, it may be useful to appreciate Stalin's capacity to move toward a goal by various routes. We need not assume that Stalin, having presumably forsaken international Communism for Socialism in One Country, was sacrificing German communism on the altar of anti-Versailles realpolitik. The KPD steadily increased its poll during 1930–1932 from 13 to almost 17 percent. In the elections of November, 1932, during the explosive Berlin transport strike (which both Nazis and Communists supported), it increased its share by more than 2 percent, while the Nazis lost 4 percent. The impression was given that Nazism might be fading and ultimately ceding to Communism. Each street battle saw hundreds of militants change sides afterward to join the victor. Stalin may have thought that he could present the hesitant army and business people with a choice between Hitler (and war) and the KPD (and continuation of Rapallo).

This might not have been incompatible with toleration of the Schleicher government, which was trying various anti-Hitler combinations, including a possible deal with the trade unions and with SA leaders such as Gregor Strasser.[61] It may be that Stalin and the KPD did not fear fascism because of the Reichswehr's reassurances, especially since Schleicher was considered an enemy of Nazism and a proponent of Soviet-German cooperation.[62] This may have contributed to the loose talk in the KPD about Hitler as 'the springboard,' or of fascism as the 'father of revolution.' What lay behind these musings, given voice both in the Comintern and the KPD, was the vague hope that the hold over the German workers exercised by the Socialists, which could not be broken by the KPD, might be broken by the Hitler 'revolution.' The KPD would be better able to withstand a white terror and would in its illegal activities draw to it the former Socialist workers, after their unions and party organizations had been destroyed. A few months of a Piłsudski-like dictatorship would be the worst case. The Reichswehr could be relied on either to keep Hitler from power as the KPD advanced or, in the event of his taking power, to control him. At the same time, the pressure of the Berlin transport strike raised the specter of a repetition of the general strikes of 1920 and 1923, and caused the Papen-Hitler combination to emerge as the only alternative to the impossible situation of the Schleicher cabinet. Stalin was, in effect, tightening the noose around a victim whom he thought, wrongly, to be without alternatives. Perhaps this was because he shared the illusions of the Reichswehr about controlling Hitler.

The 'Economic October'

Hitler's elevation to power crashed about everyone's ears, providing the most damning commentary possible on Stalin's Comintern policy. It closed a historical period during which Stalin, having got to the top, found it impossible to consolidate and stabilize his rule. The Lenin succession was seemingly completed, but the Stalin who had succeeded was not yet the real Stalin. More obstacles would have to be cleared before he could reach his full height. The Stalin-Trotsky rivalry, which we have been taught by Trotsky and others to see in the 1920s, was emerging in its finished form only in the years between Trotsky's expulsion and the arrival of Hitler. During these years it was never a matter of the leftist-internationalist Trotsky and the Thermidorean Stalin. Stalin's sin was not *moderantisme* and the Third Period was not the most logical and obvious accompaniment to Socialism in One Country. In fact, the centrism Trotsky attributed to Stalin, a formula which he would soon drop for less useful ones, was also fully attributable to Trotsky himself. Trotsky went left with Stalin in 1928–1929, and right in 1930. When Stalin resumed the collectivization campaign in autumn 1930, Trotsky declared that 'successful socialist construction is proceeding in the Soviet Union.' Trotsky veered less wildly than Stalin; had he been in power, his personal and intellectual authority would not have necessitated any more. But Stalin, who derived his only 'authority' from bureaucratic means, had to make the turns as sharply as possible, in order to demonstrate that those who challenged his personal regime did so only to sabotage his feats of socialist construction. Stalin had more need of programmatic alternance than did Trotsky.

This was still more confirmation of the irrelevance of the three issues and the importance of the Regime Question. At first Stalin's bold initiatives toward agrarian collectivization, industrialization, and even his Comintern line drew seasoned Old Bolsheviks to him. 'One must compromise to get to the helm,' Zinoviev had said. Trotsky had answered that they were all well compromised but the helm was nowhere in sight. The stifling and humiliating character of the regime very soon caused efforts against Stalin from within his own entourage. In these years the only one of Lenin's former compatriots who daily spoke his own mind was Trotsky. Evidence suggests that Stalin made constant efforts to profit in his own way by what he could glean from Trotsky.

And Trotsky mixed his criticism with many gestures of support. The Shakhty trial of 'engineers-wreckers' in the coal industry of the Don Basin in 1928 was an attack on the intelligentsia very much in the spirit of Zinoviev's rantings about the 'Ustrialovist *spetsy*.' Many of the elements of later trials were already present: the 'conveyor' system of continuous interrogation, the miserable confessions of wrecking and contacts with international capital, the death sentences.[63] Yet Trotsky generally accepted the findings of this and other political trials. Rather than question the truth of the verdicts, he tried to use them to bolster his own critique of the leadership. The trial of the 'Industrial Party,'[64] he wrote,

> gives incontestable evidence that, just as much in the period of economic *tailism* before 1928 as afterward, the economic direction of Stalin worked under the influence of a center of saboteurs and agents of imperialism.'[65]

Nor did he show sympathy for the defectors from Stalin's regime. Grigorii Bessedovskii, Soviet chargé d'affaires at the embassy in Paris, defected in 1929 and published a number of intriguing and contradictory stories about the workings of the Soviet government. He claimed that 'Stalin is the only one among the Old Guard of October, 1917 who continues to believe in the immanence of world revolution.'[66] Trotsky centered attention on the fact that the 'traitor' Bessedovskii had replaced Rakovskii in Paris. This, he said, was the kind of man produced by the purge of real revolutionaries!

At the same time, Trotsky carefully noted every sign of rumblings within Stalin's apparatus. These occurred first among the 'Young Stalinist Left' with the Shatskin-Sten group's call for a freer regime in the summer of 1929.[67] Rakovskii, in exile in Barnaul, thought the suppression of these 'left-centrists' showed the weakness of Stalin's grip.[68] We are not sure what sort of inner-party opposition forced Stalin's retreat with the 'Dizziness with Success' article in March 1930. In the fall came news that the Central Control Commission had expelled Mikhail Riutin, a secretary of the Krasnopresnenskii *raikom*. A former army officer, he had been editor of *Krasnaia zvezda (Red Star)*, the army paper, and was accused of a plot among the cadets of the Central Committee's military academy. Riutin, together with the Bukharinist Uglanov, had been censured by the October 1928 plenum for 'right opportunism' and was said by *Pravda* to have opposed collectivization. Yet he was expelled for 'underground work of propaganda for a bloc of the Right with Trotskyism' and for the suggestion that Trotsky had been correct to oppose the party 'regime.'[69]

Shortly after, Trotsky wrote an odd article speculating on the fall of Robespierre on 9 Thermidor and noting that 'petty-bourgeois revolutionaries . . . have always been forced to make a struggle on two fronts . . . the isolation of Robespierre permitted a bloc of his enemies on the right and the left to remove him with ease.'[70] In November the Syrtsov-Lominadze affair became known. S. I. Syrtsov had been chairman of Sovnarkom for the Russian republic and a highly regarded supporter of Stalin's collectivization. However, even in speeches demanding a quickened pace, he criticized local officials for their 'administrative ecstasy' and spoke of the need to cure 'disproportions.'[71] V. V. ('Besso') Lominadze was, with the Comsomolist Shatskin, a critic of Bukharin who had helped implement the Comintern's left turn of 1927 in China.[72] The two had combined in what was called a 'left-right bloc.' In exploding their plot, *Pravda* warned that the struggle against antiparty elements 'is continually waged on two fronts.'

It required little to see the encirclement of Stalin within his own faction, indeed within the inner core of his support. Stalin had been growing disillusioned with his Old Bolshevik cohorts and seeking the aid of a Stalinist youth. Now, however, even its major leaders were unhappy with him. Trotsky noted that

> there are those who vote against Syrtsov and Lominadze, demand the expulsion of Rykov and Bukharin, swear oaths of loyalty to the unique beloved leader, and at the same time have at the back of their minds: how to betray to their own best advantage.[73]

Trotsky articulated Stalin's innermost torments. But Stalin also fought back, striving to show that the struggle was not simply against the double-dealers around him but also their secret accomplices: the bloc of the 'Toiling Peasant Party,' the 'Industrial Party,' and the 'Union Bureau' of Mensheviks.[74] Taken together, these undoubtedly fictitious entities comprised the normal parliamentary spectrum of opinion for an East European country of the period. In making the country accept the trials, Stalin was trying to mask his own encirclement within the ranks of Bolsheviks as the encirclement of genuinely revolutionary Bolshevism, its heroic collectivization policy, and its magnificent leadership.

Still more serious opposition surfaced in 1932, at a time when the collectivization campaigns had produced a situation of famine and near-civil war without precedent. A 'national deviation' led by Ukrainian Commissar of Education N. A. Skrypnik was exposed ruthlessly by Pavel Postyshev, who would by 1937 be trying to slow the process of hunting down 'enemies of the people.' 'National deviation' was echoed in Armenia and other areas where resistance to collectivization was in evidence.[75] A group led by N. B. Eismont, G. G. Tolmachev, and A. P. Smirnov, and with alleged links to Rykov and Tomskii, was attacked for advancing moderate right views and calling for a revival of the soviets.[76] The party right was active throughout the year, with the most serious challenge coming from a program apparently written by the already exiled Riutin, a lengthy platform document of which there exist only scattered reports, but which apparently espoused the view that Bukharin had been right on economic policy and Trotsky on the party regime. Riutin had also called Stalin the 'evil genius of the revolution.'[77]

Reports from Moscow spoke of an 'economic October' for the Stalinist regime, with the Riutin program widely distributed and discussed. *Sotsialisticheskii vestnik* also told of party circles discussing a 'Letter of Eighteen Bolsheviks,' having issued from a 'New Opposition,' which it described as an amorphous bloc of former right and left oppositionists with the aim of replacing Stalin. To the party they had offered the slogan 'Replace the Leadership Responsible for the Wrecking of the Five Year Plan and the Establishment in the Party of a Personal Regime.'[78] The letter attacked an internal policy which, it complained, consisted only of maneuvers and zigzags. Comintern policy, scarcely mentioned by the author of the *Letter of an Old Bolshevik*, was severely criticized by the Eighteen: Stalin was accused of having stifled the Comintern for the sake of foreign policy freedom. The foreign policy, however, had failed in the East, with regard to China and the Kuomintang, and in the West, where 'decisive class battles' were shaping up in Germany, with the German Communists, in a 'highly favorable situation,' unable to give a lead.[79]

Biulleten oppozitsii spoke of a huge document, perhaps 165 pages, characterizing the economic and political situation as catastrophic. The document called for the liquidation of the *kolkhoz* system and described the bankruptcy of the leadership. Originating with the right, it contained a 'light polemic' against Bukharin, an indication that he remained loyal to Stalin.[80]

The *Letter of an Old Bolshevik* describes a confrontation between Stalin and a grouping of Politburo 'liberals' led by Kirov and including Ordzhonikidze and Kuibyshev. The issue was whether to consider the

Riutin program a call for Stalin's assassination and to try Riutin accordingly. Stalin has been assumed to have suffered a rebuff and Riutin to have been saved from shooting by the 'liberals.' This interpretation is not clinched by precise evidence but is certainly plausible in view of its concurrence with other evidence. We know that the issue of Riutin and the Eighteen came to a head either at the Central Committee plenum of 28 September–2 October or at a meeting of the Central Committee Praesidium shortly after. On 11 October, *Pravda* published a list of twenty party members to be expelled for 'complicity with the counter-revolutionary group of Riutin-Galkin-Ivanov and others,' in a program advocating destruction of collective farms, aid to the *kulaks*, and restoration of capitalism.[81] Riutin, already in exile, was not listed, while prominent Bukharinists A. H. Slepkov and D. P. Maretskii were.[82] The last two names on the list were those of Zinoviev and Kamenev, accused of organizing a 'bloc of opposition groups.' The remaining were no doubt the authors of the 'Letter of Eighteen Bolsheviks.'

Trotsky did not remain aloof from the right's campaign against Stalin. No matter how hard he strove to assert the program and record of the left opposition, he could not view with indifference any sign of hostility to Stalin's personal dictatorship. When Trotsky and his family were deprived of their Soviet citizenship in February 1932, he had addressed an Open Letter to the Soviet government, which ended by stating that

> Stalin has brought you to an impasse. You cannot proceed without liquidating Stalinism. . . It is time to carry out Lenin's final and insistent advice: Remove Stalin![83]

The first of the Moscow trials, that of Zinoviev, Kamenev, and others in 1936, was to describe this open appeal as a 'secret letter,' smuggled into Russia with instructions to assassinate Stalin. Trotsky and his son, Leon Sedov, would indignantly refute the charge by citing the true circumstances. But they also engaged in secret activity in 1932.

Shortly after the appearance of the 'Letter of Eighteen Bolsheviks,' Trotsky initiated contacts with Russian oppositionists. During his stay in Copenhagen in November, to deliver a radio address on the Russian Revolution, he gave a letter to an English sympathizer, Harry Wicks, urging his Russian followers to 'come out of their passive state':

> Keeping all precautionary measures, it is necessary to establish communication for: *information*, to distribute the Bulletin, aid with money, etc., etc. I am definitely depending that the menacing situation in which the party finds itself will force all comrades devoted to the revolution to actively gather about the Left Opposition.[84]

At about the same time, Sedov was conducting negotiations through his contacts for a bloc with a number of opposition groups. Trotsky expressed himself to be in favor, as long as it was 'a bloc and not a fusion (*verschmelzung*).[85] He was in the dark about the Eighteen Bolsheviks and wanted further information. Moreover, he was hoping the bloc could adopt an economic program 'sketched out' (*skizziert*) in an article by Ivan Smirnov, recently smuggled out and published in the *Bulletin*. Smirnov described a situation in which 'the tempo of economic growth is sharply decelerating,' due to 'disproportions' in every sphere of production. There was a 'catastrophic' state of affairs in the livestock economy and in general an 'economic and political dead-end.'[86]

Trotsky's interest in the economic program shows that the bloc was intended for more than an exchange of information. Smirnov's article was published in the same issue that led with 'The Soviet Economy in Danger,' an essay calling for 'capital reconstruction' and action against the 'disproportions.' A 'temporary retreat' in industry and agriculture must be put on the agenda for 1933. Trotsky had complained about the expulsion of Zinoviev and Kamenev that they had been unjustly placed in an 'amalgam' with the rightists. Yet his economic program and that of Smirnov were much closer to the right critics of Stalin than to that of the 1927 Opposition. Trotsky was taking a position of economic moderation and pursuing, as in his letters to Bukharin in 1926, a broad coalition to address the Regime Question.

Sedov reported at about this time that a bloc had been formed. It comprised groups led by Zinoviev, Sten-Lominadze, Preobrazhenskii, Ufimtsev, and Smirnov.[87] In reporting the formation of the bloc, Sedov also had to report the arrest of Zinoviev and Kamenev, and the dispersal of the last three groups. Sedov insisted that the ranks of these groups were still at large and active. Zinoviev and Kamenev, who would perform still another recantation and apology before Stalin a few months later, were accessible to both the right and the left oppositionists, unlike the Safarov-Tarkhanov group, who clung to the original Leningrad program of 1925–1926. The isolation of the latter shows that the center of gravity in all the anti-Stalin coalition-building was on the right. Yet Jan Sten, whom *Pravda* called a left, was counted among both the bloc organized by Sedov and those punished with the Eighteen.[88]

Trotsky also must have desired a broad coalition between his bloc and the Eighteen. This is indicated by his sudden show of preference for the slogan 'Down with the Personal Regime,' which apparently concluded the 'Letter of the Eighteen Bolsheviks.' Sedov was not at all happy with the change:

> I think it perfectly correct to oppose the slogan 'Remove Stalin' [*ubrat Stalina*] to the slogan 'Down with the Personal Regime.' Of course, 'Remove Stalin' leaves a great deal unsaid, but 'Down with the Personal Regime' means above all to remove Stalin. 'Personal Regime' for the

workers is too abstract. To declare on this means to arrive at the question of the liquidation [*likvidatsii*] of Stalin (by no means a panacea but still a very serious beginning on the path of the liquidation of the personal regime).[89]

Sedov reminded his father of the Clemenceau thesis, invoked by the opposition in 1927, which applied especially at the present moment, 'when there is no war, but the danger is greater than war.'[90]

Trotsky, however, wanted to sound the same call as the Eighteen. He granted that 'if we were stronger, the slogan might make sense. But now the Miliukovs, Mensheviks, and a series of internal Thermidoreans would be only too glad to support the slogan 'Remove Stalin.'[91] 'Down with the Personal Regime,' on the contrary, left open the possibility of cooperation with those Stalinists who had followed the Master this far but feared both going further and turning against him. These 'liberals' were an important, perhaps the most important, factor in Trotsky's calculations. Sedov claimed that the 'liberals' had helped him in 'practical' ways. He and Trotsky thought they saw indications of 'active Politburo opposition to the plebiscitory regime.'[92] But the 'liberals' could not be unduly challenged. They chided the Trotskyists for being too moderate politically, which reminded Trotsky of Zinoviev's and Kamenev's similar attitude in 1926. At the moment they counseled patience, which for Trotsky meant that they had chosen the path of passivity. Yet he cautioned that the opposition must do nothing to create the impression that Trotsky would only return sword in hand: 'Conversations among bureaucrats, about whether Trotsky will make short work of us when he returns, are the most important instruments of the Stalinists.'[93]

The announcements following the plenum gave more indications of division in the Politburo on how to handle the Eighteen. *Pravda* was full of proclamations of the unshakeable unity of the Moscow and Leningrad party forces, already a sign that there had been some differences. Statements by the two cities' leaders to their own organizations gave further suggestions. Kaganovich, addressing the Moscow cadres, praised the work of the plenum in dealing a blow to 'capitulators and bourgeois degenerates from the counter-revolutionary camp of Trotskyites and Right opportunists.' But he warned that this was not the end of the fight, that the party could expect further struggle with 'the *kulaks* and their agents.' The victories already won only meant that now the class struggle would continue and assume 'other forms.'[94]

Kirov, in a speech to the Leningrad organization two days later, also praised the work of the plenum and the rebuff dealt to the Eighteen and to Zinoviev and Kamenev, who now found themselves in the camp of Trotsky, a 'man on the other side of the barricades.' But he seemed to regard the struggle with the oppositionists as a matter for the historians. 'There was a time,' he said, 'when we fought the left and right. Now all those questions are decided.' In fact he seemed to regard it as a curiosity that opposition could still leave traces 'now when the victory of socialism in our country has been secured, when the question '*kto-kogo*' (who-whom) has been answered decisively for socialism not only in the cities but in the villages. . . [95]

Kirov's words were later repeated, no doubt at the insistence of Khrushchev, in Molotov's self-criticism in 1955. After his defeat at the July plenum of that year, Molotov was forced to withdraw his seemingly innocuous formula contrasting the East European regimes with a Soviet Union that had already laid the foundations of socialism. Instead, Molotov wrote, 'the question of '*kto-kogo*' had been answered against capitalism' in 1932.[96] Khrushchev was forcing Molotov to retract his opposition to Kirov in 1932. The needlessness of the purges of 1936–1938, in a period when all the battles had already been won, would be a major theme of Khrushchev's secret speech against Stalin in 1956.

Kirov need not be depicted as soft on the opposition, or as a critic of agrarian policy, for one to appreciate his role as a center around which Politburo 'liberals' sought to rally. He had been the most vigorous executor of the left line, but in 1932 he sought to learn from the criticism and execute a turn to the right, to adopt a more moderate policy on the countryside and a more sensible foreign and Comintern policy, to which later he devoted several paragraphs in the postplenum speech. That is, he was in the position of a centrist, as was Stalin. It was Molotov who was arguing against relaxing the pace in economic policy and who was the most visible proponent of the Third Period Comintern line that would soon be judged to have contributed to the triumph of Hitler. It was Molotov who, after the turn in 1933, would suffer a period of eclipse.

Yet the turn would be terribly damaging to Stalin, not because of the change in policies but because the highest leadership of the party had in various ways discussed the modalities of getting rid of him, while the 'liberals' and Kirov proclaimed that all the victories had been secured. The bitterness of Stalin's defeat was capped by the death in mysterious circumstances of Stalin's wife Allilueva on November 9, 1932. This may have been the result of suicide, but it has also been claimed, by Boris Nicolaevsky and others, that she was murdered by Stalin. If Elizabeth Lermolo's account is to be believed, she had also been in sympathy with the Left Opposition.[97] In the circumstances of 1932, that would have made her a partisan of the views of the Eighteen. Stalin's wrath can be surmised in view of this invasion of his own household by his political enemies. Kirov could only dread the popularity that had fallen to his lot. Molotov could only effect a comeback by opposing the new policies and fighting to secure the leader. Trotsky would continue to 'terrorize' Stalin by speaking of the disloyalty of his entourage. Stalin would have to find a way to make new turns and defeat his enemies.

7

The Russian Question, the Purges, and Alternance, 1933–1939

Speaking of the use of words I must mention a man who doesn't have any professional dealings with words. Nevertheless, look how Stalin hammers out his speeches, how his words are wrought of iron, how terse they are, how muscular, how much respect they show for the reader. (applause) I don't suggest here that we should all write like Stalin, but I do say that we must all work at our words as he does.

—Isaac Babel, to a congress of Soviet writers, 1934

WITH THE DEFEAT of the Trotskyists, Zinovievists, Bukharinists, and the other oppositions and resistances, Stalin may have seemed to have completed the Lenin succession, but actually Stalin's position was still precarious in 1932, and perhaps more so in 1934. Only by 1937–1939 can the process of his rise be said to have reached an apogee. The last phase of Stalin's rise, to which we now turn, involved his substitution of a personal apparatus of repression for the punitive organs of the Soviet state, and the liberation of the dictator from all constraints against the use of terror, a freedom which would entail the near-liquidation of the party itself. This struggle was played out against the background of the rising threat of Nazism, whose leader epitomized an age of personal dictatorship. Hitler often made clear his animosity for Bolshevism and thus concentrated the minds of its leaders on the importance of state power, expressed, not simply in terms of economic success or even in quantities of military equipment, but also in the capacity of the supreme leader to dictate his will to the nation. In an age of personal power there was a terrible compulsion to imitate the most powerful.

Nazism also concentrated the minds of many Western intellectuals who had been sympathetic to Soviet communism. Previously, it was thought that the Soviet economy had little to teach Western Europe, but that Soviet ideas about revolutionary change would be relevant. With the onset of the depression, this was reversed: The Soviet economy seemed a demonstration of planned 'national economy' in an age that carried admiration for economic self-sufficiency to great lengths. But Communist militants in the West were now confronted, not with a decreasing and dispirited circle of men in top hats, as Marxist doctrine had prepared them to expect, but with a fascist mass movement which, they began to suppose, could probably be countervailed only by the Soviet state.

It was generally thought that Nazism's path to power had been rendered smoother by the seemingly suicidal actions of the Comintern. Communism, despite all its hollow protestations of an unique continuity, had been nevertheless widely seen as part of the European labor movement, whose center of gravity was in Germany. By the time Hitler had carried out his first revolution and crushed the German unions and left parties, some sensed that the whole experiment with Communism had produced nothing but nightmares in Europe and that Soviet Communism, especially the Communism of Stalin, might have turned out to be the exact reverse of the wildest expectations that had greeted the Russian Revolution.

Many European intellectuals who had knowledge of Soviet domestic affairs viewed the monster of Stalinism with incredulity, and asked themselves whether it was the apotheosis or the negation of Russian Communism. This was a way of inquiring into the Russian Question: What is the nature of the Soviet state and society? Merely to ask this question one assumes a discrepancy between the promise of the revolution and the system presided over by the General Secretary. Was Stalinism a judgment on the revolution, or Marxism, or ideology itself? The debate marked not only a crisis of conscience for all those who had sympathized since 1917, but also, in its own way, an attempt to discover the economic and social dynamic of Soviet society. Out of the discussion have come a number of notions that have held our interest down to the present, among them, for example, the idea of Totalitarianism.

Most pertinent from the perspective of this study is the relationship that developed between theoretical studies of the Russian Question and speculation about the actual disposition of the bureaucratic actors. As is still to some extent the case today, many of those interested in the broader questions found Kremlinology irrelevant and misleading. If the object of the inquiry was to determine whether Russia was a socialist or state capitalist regime, or a degenerate workers' state, or a 'state neither socialist nor capitalist,' as one popular formulation had it, it mattered little how Molotov was aligned with regard to Bukharin or Postyshev. Or so it was thought. At any rate, by this time it had become virtually impossible to get firsthand documentary evidence of the discussions among Soviet leaders on the most important questions. Party congresses, conferences, and even Central Committee plenums were becoming rarer. Differences among the leaders had been open to public and international scrutiny before 1928, but they were covered by seven veils thereafter. There was really no alternative to speculation on the basis of fragmentary evidence, rumors, irregularities in announcements from the Soviet press, and the like.

But for those who continued to try to fathom the great enigma, there were small rewards. And the effort was compulsory, in view of the importance of Soviet strength in a world clearly plunging headlong into war. Stalinism seemed even less sure of its identity than the Communism of the Lenin period. Centrism, which Trotsky would soon discard as an explanation in favor of less promising theories, continued to be a hallmark of Stalin's actions. A programmatic alternance of the type we have been describing—Moscow and Leningrad—continued, albeit with alterations and changes in personal representatives, to provide the framework for policy choices. Stalin, even after he had got to the pinnacle of supreme personal power, continued, as he had on the way up, to make turns. Eventually it would become clearer that these turns were really an essential feature of the Stalinist system.

A State Neither Capitalist nor Proletarian

Trotsky called the advent of Hitler the greatest defeat for the working class since the German Social Democrats voted for war in 1914 and initiated the process which destroyed the Socialist International. Referring to the day the German war credits were voted, he pronounced August Fourth for the Communist International. Even so, a break with the Comintern was not easy for Trotsky to make. Hitler took power in January 1933. Up to March, Trotsky did nothing, expecting that Hitler's first measures would provoke resistance and ultimately a civil war. When that failed to come, he addressed a last appeal to the Soviet Politburo, warning that 'the most pressing and dangerous problem is *mistrust of the leadership* [italics in original] and the growing hatred for it. You are not less well informed about this than I am.'[1] In the spirit of his previous appeals, he once again called for coexistence between the two 'historically rooted factions,' in order to revive party life. The signs were changing rapidly. Stalin was no longer a rootless centrist zigzagging between the Bukharinists and the Left Opposition, but now head of an 'historically rooted faction.' At the same time that he launched this (ultimately unsuccessful) appeal, Trotsky sent out letters to his friends in the international opposition calling for a new Communist Party in Germany, yet halting at that. 'It's not a question of the creation of the Fourth International,' he announced, 'but the salvage of the Third.'

Trotsky's own associates were pressing him to break with the Comintern, while at the same time themselves trying to resist the blandishments of those who wanted to condemn Soviet Russia as well. Albert Treint was one of the most persuasive of the latter. Treint had maintained his association with the Paris Trotskyists and continued the quarrel of the Rosmer group with Molinier, before deciding to split in the summer of 1932. He had published a paper, *L'Étincelle*, calling the Trotskyists too conciliatory toward Stalinism.

> After the German catastrophe, comrade Trotsky recognizes the need for a revolutionary party in Germany. But he does not want new parties in the countries where catastrophes have already been produced. The German case shows a party is necessary *before* a defeat.[2]

Treint was still thinking as a Zinovievist, along the same lines pursued by Urbahns earlier. 'The historic treason of the Soviet bureaucracy,' he maintained, 'began in 1928, not 1933.' With the defeat of Zinoviev-Trotsky, Russia had ceased to be a workers' state.

Trotsky had failed, said Treint, to recognize the 'bureaucratic counter-revolution' because of his sentimental idea that there could only be bourgeois or proletarian states. But intermediate forms in equilibrium had been known to Marx as well, who had applied the term 'Bonapartism' to Louis Napoleon in the 1850s and to Bismarck in the 1870s. Indeed, Treint argued, Trotsky was clinging to an outworn notion of Thermidor. The fall of the Jacobins in France had not meant a change of ruling classes but only a 'fixing of the revolution in its bourgeois phase.' Trotsky applied the analogy incorrectly, assuming that the impending bourgeois counter-revolution would require a civil war.[3] Thus he missed the Thermidor of the Stalinist 'bureaucratic class.' Remembering his lessons, Treint charged that Trotsky's 'dual strategy' would only legitimize Socialism in One Country and the real source of the catastrophe, the policy of National Bolshevism, the idea that had caused all the difficulties since 1923. Treint thus repeated the argument of Ruth Fischer against Radek.[4] He judged, however, that the bourgeois counterrevolution had failed because the representatives of Professor Ustrialov, the 'Industrial party,' had been crushed. Treint agreed with Trotsky in applauding Stalin's early show trials as an attempt to stave off Thermidor.

By the time Trotsky left Turkey for France in July, he had come most of the way toward the position of Treint, in favor of abandoning the Comintern and forming a new International. In August he collaborated in a Declaration of the Four, signed by representatives of Trotsky's own International Left Opposition, the SAP, with which he wanted the German Trotskyists to fuse, the Independent Socialist Party of Holland, and the Revolutionary Socialist Party of Holland, lead by Henk Sneevliet, who as 'Maring' had played a role in forming Comintern policy in the Far East. The declaration called for a break with the Second and Third Internationals, but for defense of the Soviet 'workers' state.' The former

Zinovievists still felt Trotsky and associates to be too timid. At a Paris conference in August, Urbahns complained that the Four had dodged the most important problems. 'They have failed,' he said, 'to analyze the attempts of capitalism to surmount the economic crisis through state capitalism and failed to make a Marxist judgment of the Soviet Union.'[5]

Urbahns and Treint considered the idea of state capitalism indispensable to the task. All major economies had been converted to state capitalism during the war thought Urbahns. Russia's economy still having failed by that time to 'saturate' her internal market, she was left to complete the development in peace after the war. The Soviet state had become 'a single gigantic collective capitalist,' reversing the proportion of public to private property prevailing in the West. Nowhere in the world, said Treint, had state capitalism attained the same purity as in Russia.[6] Some of this had been foreseen by Marxists. Engels had admitted a kind of bourgeois state property. Lenin had called the Soviet economy 'state capitalist' in 1918.[7] But Trotsky, said Treint, had never understood the matter, mistaking as 'the utopia of the closed economy what is actually the realism of the directed economy.'[8] 'In this sense, one can maintain,' thought Treint, 'that state capitalism develops to the maximum the rational and progressive capacities of the bourgeois regime.' Moreover, not only Soviet Russia, but Nazi Germany and New Deal America would be its models. Like Bruno Rizzi, whose ideas will be discussed below, Trient saw affinity between 'the Duce, the Fuhrer, and the Blue Eagle.'

This analysis would gain currency on the European left during the period of the Hitler-Stalin pact, with the United States not yet committed to the defense of the Western democracies. The British and French imperialists, it would be argued, led by the Jewish bankers, were the last outposts of decadence before the wave of progressive 'managerial' economics. Treint drew on the Zinoviev tradition of describing the nationalized property of Soviet Russia as 'state capitalist.' Ever since Lenin had used the term in 1918, left opponents of the regime, anarchists and followers of Gorter and the German KAPD had also used it. Zinoviev had employed it as a warning about 'Ustrialovite' trends since 1925. This had facilitated his reconciliation with Russian groups such as the Workers' Opposition and the Decemists who occupied much of the same ideological ground as the KAPD and the anarchists.[9] Treint apparently took the Zinovievist arguments seriously, and he continued to describe them as a coherent tradition of true 'Leninism,' with which Trotskyists had only occasionally intersected.

Trotsky could not brush away the Zinoviev tradition. It would have seemed that things would be easier with the tradition of Rosa Luxemburg, highly relevant because of the influence of the SAP, which revered Luxemburgism. Because of Stalin's attacks on Luxemburg in 1931, it would have seemed that Trotsky would simply defend and reap the benefit. Once again, however, the Russian Question proved difficult to manage. Lucien Laurat, a French Socialist who had read Souvarine's writings on the Soviet succession struggle and sympathized with his arguments against Trotsky, tried to uphold Western Luxemburgism against Russian Leninism. For Laurat, this began with a defense of Luxemburg's theory of imperialism, with its description of the drive to penetrate the world hinterland of natural economy, against criticisms made by Bukharin in *Pod znamenie marksizma* in 1924.[10] Bukharin's theory visualized a growing 'state capitalism' evolving into a 'single trust' and an 'organized economy' according to a 'national plan.' Bukharin was an heir, thought Laurat, to the Hilferding analysis, 'vulgarized by Lenin' and now used to predict broad vistas of stability in a completely organized international economy.[11]

The international economy was not so singly under the control of this cartel-forming process, argued Laurat, and monopoly was not its central feature. The Hilferding tradition to the contrary, the world economy was governed by a law of the 'diminution of labor,' which decreed that means of production must increase more rapidly than production of articles of consumption. This was, said Laurat, only the 'capitalist expression of the fundamental law of human labor.'[12] Bukharin, in his *Notes of an Economist* of 1928, had attributed the working of the law in Soviet Russia, said Laurat, to 'lack of proportionality' between various branches of the Soviet economy. Trotsky had made a similar argument.

In reality, claimed Laurat, the persistence of depression in consumer goods was a reflection of the rise of a 'new directing class' and its formation, in the process of constituting the revolutionary state, into a 'bureaucratic oligarchy.'[13] It would be superfluous, he argued, to speak of a Soviet Thermidor, since in France that had only meant the consolidation of the rule of the bourgeoisie. But others had done so. Karl Korsch had put the Thermidor in 1927 and called the U.S.S.R. 'state capitalist.' Souvarine had written of 'surplus value appropriated by the parasitic bureaucracy.' Actually, thought Laurat, the arguments used in the succession struggle had missed the real point because of their fascination with the threat of the *kulak* and the NEPman, whereas the bureaucracy's need to find the funds for continued industrial expansion was the key to Stalin's victory. The class needs of this bureaucracy necessitated its faith in the utopia of Socialism in One Country.

Laurat considered it an irony that Communist Russia, with its fidelity to the tradition of Marx, should have become a convert to the ideal of autarky, which he thought as utopian in Russia as in the West. Because of a rising tide of protectionism, world trade was collapsing, especially that of the major prewar European powers. Laurat argued that the new technocratic doctrines of economic nationalism then in fashion had already been disposed of by Marx in the nineteenth century, when they had been advanced by the German economist and 'conservative' socialist, Karl Rodbertus.[14] Marx's polemic with Proudhon, said Laurat, was in part an attempt to establish the theory of value against those who thought that the price of money could be established by decree.[15] After Marx's death, argued Laurat, Engels had shifted the ground and actually accepted the 'historic necessity' of German protectionism as a reaction to the 'intolerable' English dominance in industrial exports.[16] So the Marxists of the Second International had failed to appreciate the trend toward autarky and corporatism, which now sought the destruction of democracy and which, moreover, now had an eastern Soviet branch.

The rubric of 'state capitalism' was a broad one, under which one could include every complaint about the Soviet regime without damaging the Marxist tradition. A certain consistency could be lent by the assertion of Treint and Urbahns that state capitalism was progressive; Lenin had claimed it to be a transition to socialism. Other intellectuals wanted to take the critique further. Max Nomad, an old associate of Machajski in the revolutionary underground of prewar Russian Poland, spoke for his master's thought by reminding his readers that Marx had never promised a regime of equality. Nomad referred to the *Critique of the Gotha Program* of 1875, with its admonition against promising the workers any more than the dictatorship of the proletariat. Stalin referred many times to the *Critique* whenever complaints about salary differentials reached him. Nomad thought that Western socialists were in no position to object.

> This principle of inequality had been proposed by their common master Karl Marx in his famous proposition on the 'first stage of communism'—a euphemism for state capitalism under the direction of the socialist intelligentsia.[17]

Nomad argued that the intelligentsia was therefore the real winner of the struggle that had already concluded with the suppression of the Kronstadt rebellion in 1921.

French essayist Simone Weil also stressed the significance of Kronstadt as a turning point. She preferred the analysis of Laurat to that of Trotsky. She decreed the 'radical falsity of the perspectives of the 1917 Revolution,' especially the idea that there were only two kinds of state: capitalist and proletarian.

> The workers' state has never existed on the surface of the globe, except for perhaps several weeks in Paris in 1871 and several months in Russia in 1917 and 1918. Instead there rules over one-sixth of the planet for fifteen years a state more oppressive than any other, which is neither capitalist nor proletarian. Of course, Marx did not foresee any of this. But for us Marx is not so dear as the truth.[18]

By contrast, said Weil, one can still find in the 'disorder' of the hated capitalist regime elements of 'freedom, initiative, and invention.' These appeared in a different light in a world being consumed by a voracious bureaucratism. Another French militant, reflecting on this trend, remarked that 'the Jesuits of Paraguay also lived in a regime of nationalization.'[19]

Trotsky was deeply pained by the various interpretations of Soviet state capitalism, and by characterization of the Soviet bureaucracy as a new exploiting class. Probably a good deal of this was because these theories had a certain appeal which, as we will indicate, Trotsky himself was not entirely able to resist. More important, they signaled a break with Stalinism more definite and final than he was willing to make. He pounced on Laurat with a vengeance.

> Laurat invests his revelations with the weighty formulas of *Das Kapital* ... obviously unaware that the entire theory has been formulated, with much more fire and splendor, over thirty years ago by the Russo-Polish revolutionist Makhaiskii, who was superior to his French vulgarizer in that he awaited neither the October Revolution nor the Stalinist bureaucracy in order to define the 'dictatorship of the proletariat' as a support for the commanding posts of an exploiting bureaucracy ... according to Makhaiskii, the author of *Das Kapital* deliberately covered up, in his formulae of reproduction (volume 2), that portion of surplus value that would be consumed by the socialist intelligentsia (the bureaucracy).[20]

This 'tribute' to Makhaiskii (Machajski) did not mean that Trotsky found any of the anti–intelligentsia position appealing. He was willing to admit that Soviet bureaucracy 'devours, wastes, and embezzles,' willing to find it guilty of 'social parasitism,' but never 'class exploitation.' Socialists and Communists who have debated this question from the earliest days of the Soviet regime have not lacked confidence that they could tell, whatever side of the dispute they supported, the difference between a 'class' and a 'stratum.' One can understand this resolute confidence, for on the distinction hangs the whole question of loyalty or hostility to the Soviet regime, moreover on Marxist grounds. Unfortunately, Marx did not leave instructions on how to define a class.[21]

If the bureaucracy were a ruling class, its overthrow would mean a social revolution. Since, however, Trotsky found the property relations established by the October Revolution still intact, he would soon judge that matters could be set right by a 'political' revolution conducted by a new Communist party. Thus the advent of Hitler had prompted the proclamation of a Fourth International in three distinct stages: first, a new party in Germany but not elsewhere; then a new International but no new party in Russia; finally, a Russian party and a new International.

The Neo-NEP

The agitation in Trotsky's mind was very much a reaction to the rebirth of theories proclaiming an end to the socialist experiment in Russia. But there was another reason to alter his previous views. The more he observed Soviet affairs in the Soviet press (he had no real contact with Russia after 1933), the more he became convinced that another major turn was taking place. The crushing of the German proletariat, he charged, was leading to a rightward lurch in foreign and domestic policy. He was no doubt impressed by Radek's *Pravda* articles, which warned for the first time that any attempt to revise the Treaty of Versailles would end in war. Soviet policy had, with varying enthusiasm, opposed Versailles since its inception. To alter that view undoubtedly suggested a rebirth of the Franco-Russian alliance.[22] This was coupled with what looked like a turn to the right in policy toward the peasant. The granaries were opened and measures were taken to alleviate hunger in the countryside. The *kolkhoz* peasants were permitted to cultivate private plots. A great deal of *sovkhoz* land was redistributed to the collective farms. It was a policy giving every indication of Bukharinist influence. Bukharin, Rykov, and Tomskii were themselves allowed to attend the Seventeenth Party Congress in 1934 as candidate members of the Central Committee, an occasion which Bukharin used to deliver a rousing anti-Nazi speech to the delegates. He and Radek would be charged to work on a new constitution, to be completed in 1936. Many other oppositionists were rehabilitated, and Bukharin's co-thinker Petr Petrovskii was even permitted to become editor of *Leningradskaia pravda*.[23] Rakovskii, much to Trotsky's chagrin, was moved to make a genuine capitulation and was returned from exile, free at least for the moment.

The right turn was a kind of confirmation of Trotsky's thesis to the effect that the left zigzag of 1928 was only a preliminary to a more decided and permanent lurch to the right. The assassination, in December 1934, of Leningrad party chief Sergei Kirov, was read by Trotsky as part of this turn. He did not pretend to be able to fathom the mystery surrounding Kirov's death. Nor was he able to judge the importance of Kirov himself to the turn. But Trotsky soon understood that the Kirov affair was being used to attack the Leningrad party apparatus of the Zinoviev period. And he was quick to predict that the regime of the 'neo–NEP' would provide scant protection for the Bukharinists. After the Leningraders were destroyed, the turn for the right would come. It was in the nature of Stalin's Bonapartism always to wage its war 'on two fronts.'

Trotsky was not at all sure who, of those around Stalin, would be the beneficiaries of the turn. Kaganovich 'the Amsterdamer'[24] had been as close to Stalin as any of them since 1928. Had he displaced Molotov? After the moderate right turn of 1930, Trotsky had guessed that someone would have to bear responsibility for the previous left course, and that it would have to be someone who had taken the left turn and the Third Period seriously. This could only be Molotov. As the present right turn unfolded and news of the trial of the 'Trotskyite-Zinovievite Terrorist Center' in August 1936 became known, Trotsky continued these speculations. By that time he had been granted asylum in Mexico and had organized a counter-trial by a committee headed by the American philosopher John Dewey, a tribunal which would deliver a verdict as to whether he could have committed the crimes attributed to him by the Zinoviev-Kamenev trial. At the end of his own testimony he speculated about those whom the alleged conspirators were to have assassinated; the 'honors list' of 'the closest comrades of Stalin' included Voroshilov, Zhdanov, Kaganovich, Kossior, Ordzhonikidze, and Postyshev. At no point in the trial did any defendant name Molotov.

Apparently, thought Trotsky, this was a sign of friction between Stalin and Molotov, perhaps on the whole subject of the right turn itself, with Molotov left to assume responsibility for the leftism of the previous period. Molotov himself referred to a division in the Politburo between advocates of 'vigilance' toward Nazi Germany, then the official line in view of the Franco-Soviet pact of May 1935, and the 'Stalin group' seeking an accommodation with Nazism. 'There is a tendency,' Molotov told the Parisian daily *Le Temps* at the time of the reoccupation of the Rhineland in March, 1936, 'among certain sections of the Soviet public toward an attitude of thoroughgoing irreconcilability to the present rulers of Germany, particularly because of the ever-repeated hostile speeches of German leaders against the Soviet Union. But the chief tendency, and the one determining the Soviet government's policy, thinks an improvement in Soviet-German relations possible.'[25] It seems highly uncharacteristic for Stalin to have taken the lead in defending or opposing a line already agreed to. It may be more plausible to suppose that Molotov assumed the defense of the pro-German foreign policy line of 1929–1933 as well as the position of scapegoat for the Third Period Comintern line. With Molotov in the shade with the turn toward France, Stalin may have encouraged him, as he was not unknown to do, to continue the struggle for revival of the Rapallo foreign policy orientation. In this case, Molotov would have become the heir to Zinoviev, even while the latter was being liquidated, and the personification of the Leningrad line.

Trotsky's Return to Thermidor

Developments seemed to justify Trotsky's prognoses, at least on the surface. He had clung to the idea of opposing Stalin from the left, an idea that had seemed ridiculous during the Third Period, but now the Stalin regime was moving to the right in every sense. It was a return to the policies of 1925–1927, but on a much larger scale. Having issued warnings about the Thermidorean dangers of this course, Trotsky felt that he had to pronounce once again on the question of the Russian Thermidor.

In view of his previous statements he was in an impossible position. The internal controversies of the twenties had featured prominent warnings about the Thermidorean danger. In the general striving to follow Lenin it was frequently suggested that the founder of Bolshevism had noticed the tendency first. But even he had only been responding to the challenge posed by Professor Ustrialov. The Thermidorean possibility, according to the theorist of Soviet National Bolshevism, arose from the fact that the revolution had torn apart the entire fabric of Tsarist society, broken every loyalty and reduced Russia to a position of statelessness, the nationalities seeking their freedom and the historical process of 'gathering in the Russian lands' set into reverse. It was a kind of anarchy, from which any revolutionary government by definition would have to retreat. Simply to take up negotiations with other states assumed the beginning of the relearning of 'reason of state.' But it meant more. From the moment when the call had sounded to defend the Red Fatherland, the death knell of the egalitarian experiment had sounded. Ustrialov argued, from analogy with the French Revolution, that the most that could be done to satisfy the inchoate yearning for equality was a revolutionary terror, but even that could not hide the fact that private property had not disappeared. However much the new Jacobins might promise, there would come a Thermidor. NEP was a confirmation of the fact, providing for a constituency—the kulak, the NEPman, the bureaucrat—which would eventually force an evolution into a democratic republic on the French model.[26]

Ustrialov's Thermidor theory was another way of saying that backward Russia could never produce a socialist dictatorship, but only a vast jacquerie, which the revolutionaries preferred to call a 'democratic revolution.'[27] The NEP seemed to be proof. Yet, while Lenin was still alive no one quarreled with his description of NEP as a tactic rather than an evolution. In Soviet faction politics one sounds the alarm only after one is either in opposition or going into opposition. Thus Zinoviev issued a warning of the danger in 1925. The Democratic Centralists, after the defeat of 1927, proclaimed Thermidor an accomplished fact, Russia having changed, as they saw it, into a 'kulak democracy.' They dated the evolution from the moment that Trotsky had been accused of being 'hostile to the peasant.'[28]

Trotsky had accepted the analogy of Bolshevism with Jacobinism, but rejected the Decemists' notions about Thermidor, since that would have meant forsaking the party.[29] Now, in 1935 he had ended with something like their position on the party. Could he admit them to be right about the whole process? Instead of doing that, he abandoned the Ustrialov theory of Thermidor, with which the opposition had marched since 1926. Ustrialov, because he thought 1917 to have been nothing more than the theory of anarchism temporarily realized, had spoken of the survival, despite obstacles, of property and the state. The warnings of the opposition put this survival in terms of the *restoration* of capitalism. Either way, Thermidor meant the establishment of private property. Lenin, in *On the Syndicalist and Anarchist Deviation*, had warned that the extreme maximalism in the party (the Workers' Opposition) and outside the party (the Kronstadt rebellion) would restore capitalism by wrecking the party and thus the dictatorship.

Ustrialov had maintained that the Russian Revolution was a repetition of the French Revolution. But suppose one argued that Thermidor was not a repetition but merely an analogy? That is, suppose one assumed that a socialist dictatorship of the proletariat did exist, and that, by analogy with the French Revolution's bourgeois regime, there had simply been a Thermidorean passage from a radical, plebeian phase (Jacobinism, 'Leninism') to a degenerate form of the same class dictatorship? Trotsky had not previously argued this way. The victory of Bonapartism over Jacobinism, he said, had only meant 'in the language of the class struggle . . . the gradual change of power from the sans-culottes to the leisure class.'[30] Marx had never seen the Parisian crowd (the sans-culottes) as a class capable of transcending the bourgeois basis of the revolution, but only as agents of a 'plebeian method' of settling accounts with the old regime.

Trotsky was finally forced to break with Ustrialov's language. Previous discussions of Thermidor, he admitted, had served only to 'becloud rather than clarify.' Rather than bourgeois counterrevolution, he suggested analogy only. The Soviet bureaucracy and the 'conservative upper crust of the working class' had taken power from the vanguard but had preserved the property relations established by the revolution. Thermidor, therefore, was not ahead, but behind, actually dating from 1924.[31] Trotsky thus 'solved' the problem of the persistence of Stalinist 'centrism.' In the process, he invited analogy between the opposition and the Jacobins, which seemed to suggest the ephemeral character of the work of the opposition. In assuming a kind of historical permanence for the Stalinist bureaucracy, moreover, he had abandoned the language of Ustrialov for that of Machajski.

In the course of this reappraisal, Trotsky must have wondered about Rakovskii's famous formula 'a bureaucratic state with proletarian survivals.'[32] Rakovskii had only used this formula in 1930, in the manner that Trotsky was then doing, in warning about the dangers of a neo-NEP. However, he had seen bureaucracy outside the context of backwardness, as a phenomenon developing from inside the working class. Moreover, he had envisioned the process of coercive industrial and agricultural campaigns as an expression of the interest of the bureaucracy engaged in primary accumulation. Laurat had made the same argument. Trotsky gagged at the thought of the bureaucracy as the ruling class, yet his 'political revolution' formula was an imperative for creating a Fourth International with people who were convinced of the degeneration of the CPSU and the Comintern. It pained him to use the formulations he had previously rejected as 'ultra-left,' but the perspective of reform of the party was now a thing of the past.

Thus *The Revolution Betrayed* of 1937 contains a call for a 'political revolution' against the Soviet bureaucracy 'of several millions.' When anarchists and other revolutionaries had spoken of a 'third revolution' against 'the commissars' in the 1918–1921 period, they had contemplated the destruction of the entire state apparatus established by Bolshevism. Trotsky was now also calling for the overthrow of the soviet intelligentsia, millions of full-time state functionaries, but not because he was a convert to anarchism. Recognizing the need for state employees, he wanted to replace their 'bureaucracy' by his 'administration.' A slogan of democratic revolt would have been a logical next step, but Trotsky promised only an improved Bolshevism. He could not admit that lack of democracy had created this monstrous regime. He had to invest the formula with a larger social content because of his fidelity to Marxism. It may also be that, with so many newspaper accounts stressing what they assumed to be his hatred for Stalin, his adamancy in denying any personal animus prompted the larger 'sociological' interpretation. Not 'down with Stalin,' but 'political revolution.'

The Turn Within the Great Purge

It was Stalin's 'liberal phase' almost as much as the success of Hitler that caused Trotsky to change his ideas about Stalin and centrism. Although the latter term appeared occasionally in his writings from this point on, he would eventually discard it altogether. The earlier ideas of centrism were a surer guide to the maneuverings of Stalin, for just as Trotsky pronounced that the regime based on the 'new gentry' had found its resting point in the neo-NEP, Stalin changed course again, as he would continue to do down to the end of his reign. The turns were not an occasional vice for Stalinism but part of the essential legacy that it derived from early Bolshevism. Stalin was what he pretended to be, a pupil of Lenin.

Trotsky could never accept that, so he had to strain the facts through a particularly fine mesh to avoid recognition of centrism and alternance. Without possessing the information that has since come to light on the Kirov assassination, he recognized to some extent its importance both as part of a turn toward a more liberal spell and a prelude to future campaigns of vigilance.[33]

His *Biulleten oppozitsii* and the Menshevik *Sotsialisticheskii vestnik* had become by this time the main sources of information on the Soviet regime. Moscow sources in the latter's 'On Russia' column reported a consolidation of Stalin's position vis-à-vis the Bukharin-Rykov tendency on the one hand and the Zinoviev-Kamenev on the other, on the eve of Stalin's 1933 turn.[34] In fact, the 'cult of Stalin' championed by Kaganovich led *Sotsialisticheskii vestnik* to speculate on the possibility of Stalin's planning to liquidate the Communist party.[35]

Bukharin's visit to Paris in 1936 provided the occasion for an interview with Boris Nicolaevsky, material from which, along with other information, was published in Nicolaevsky's *Letter of an Old Bolshevik* later in the year.[36] This was to be the most influential account of the prelude to the Moscow trials of 1936–1938. In it, Bukharin (or Nicolaevsky) tells of the program put forward by Riutin in the summer of 1932.[37] The call contained in it for the removal of Stalin, according to the *Letter*, caused Stalin to demand the death penalty for Riutin at the end of the year. But the Politburo, rallying around Leningrad party chief Sergei Kirov, denied this to Stalin. It has been further speculated that the bloc of votes against Stalin included, in addition to Kirov's, those of Ordzhonikidze, Kuibyshev, Kossior, and perhaps even Kalinin and Voroshilov, with only Molotov, Kaganovich, and Andreev supporting him.[38] Stalin's failure on the Regime Question (in this case, his right to shoot those who called for his forcible ouster) was matched by a turn to the right in foreign and domestic policy. Stalin bent with the trend but continued to seek to free himself from the constraints, in the first place, by planning the murder of Kirov. This assessment seems plausible.

Yet this was not the assessment of *Sotsialisticheskii vestnik* in 1933–1934. Kirov was not described as a moderate on the Regime Question or a patron of the neo-NEP. He and Kaganovich were seen as taking up the cudgels for proletarian Leningrad and proletarian Moscow against the policy of concessions to the peasant, as evidenced by their resistance to the disbanding of the political sections of the Machine Tractor Stations.[39] Stalin's reorganization of the security organs was described as the 'liquidation of the GPU,' a necessary prelude to a 'stabilization of the Stalin dictatorship.'[40] Stalin himself was generally thought a supporter of the right course and was said to be in a tense conflict with Kaganovich.[41]

As he had in 1927, Stalin was preparing a major blow against the Leningraders while also preparing to shift over to a strike against the right. The murder of Kirov permitted the first chapter, which went on as the conciliationist policy of the right turn was deepened in the country at large. Trotsky saw that the 1935 trial of Zinoviev and Kamenev, in which the latter admitted 'indirect complicity' for Kirov's murder, was an attempt 'to deduce the terrorist act of 1934 from the opposition platform of 1926.'[42] Rightists were permitted to hold the posts they had gained as a result of the turn, Rykov as Commissar for Communications, Bukharin as editor of *Izvestiia*. Bukharin, along with Radek, campaigned vigorously for the pro-French foreign policy line. At the same time, Stalin characteristically must have held his counsel in the discussion about how to come to terms with the Nazis.

Stalin no doubt still felt that he required exposure to the views of intellectuals such as Radek and Bukharin. He seems never to have had bright people murdered precipitously, no matter how profound his grudge toward any one of them. He felt supremely confident of being able to reduce their influence, isolate them, demoralize them, and then learn what he could from them up to the moment of their very destruction. This extraordinary patience and capacity for measuring the 'dosage,' as *Letter of an Old Bolshevik* puts it, was Stalin's own. Yet some aspects of his method of dealing with lesser leaders must have been learned from Lenin, who could ask a comrade to resign, could send him to Turkestan to teach him humility, then slowly reinstate the transformed and domesticated former opponent. No doubt many who were by this time not yet shot but only undergoing the third or fourth degree of demoralization, imagined, wrongly, that they would be treated as in Lenin's time.

There seemed to be good reason to think so. None of the Bolshevik leaders had been shot as yet, and many who had fought Stalin had enjoyed a return to responsible work in return for ritualized recantations. Both Bukharin and Radek had intimate consultations with Stalin on foreign policy questions which they thought to outweigh petty regime matters. Radek had been for several years Stalin's closest adviser on foreign policy and a spokesman, during the 'liberal spell,' for Soviet views on the developing alliance with France.

Soviet foreign policy was attempting to adjust to the initiatives of the diplomatic offensive of French Foreign Minister Louis Barthou, who judged the Soviet Union an apt candidate for a broad alignment designed to pressure Hitler's Germany to renounce its claims in East Central Europe. Barthou was a believer in old-fashioned *realpolitik* who was impressed by the cordial nature of relations between fascist Italy and Communist Russia, relations to which Stalin had referred in his speech to the Seventeenth Party Congress in January 1934. His aim was to use pressure from these two dissimilar states to get Germany to agree to an Eastern Locarno, a recognition of boundaries on Germany's eastern flank comparable to its recognition of western ones in the Locarno Treaty of 1925. He built on the fact of Italian unease about the prospect of Austrian *Anschluss* with the Reich. Mussolini had signed the Rome Protocols, extending Italy's protection to Austria and Hungary, in March 1934. When the Austrian Nazis attempted a coup d'etat in July, Italian troops were dispatched to the Brenner Pass against a possible *Anschluss*. Barthou had reason to think that fascist ideology would not prevent Italy from common action with France to domesticate Nazi Germany. By September, Italy, France, and Britain had joined in declaring their support for Austrian independence.

Barthou was assassinated with King Alexander of Yugoslavia by Croatian terrorists in October, but his successor, Pierre Laval, continued in the same vein. He urged the Eastern Locarno on Germany, in return for which German rearmament would be accepted, while France and Soviet Russia drew closer together. But the strategy came unwound in March 1935 when Hitler announced that he had introduced conscription and, moreover, had achieved air parity with Britain. The latter had great impact in an era when statesmen generally believed that in any future war 'the bomber will always get through.' France, Britain, and Italy responded by forming the 'Stresa front' in April, promising joint action against future treaty violations, but this had an empty ring in view of the fact that Hitler had simply taken what they had previously planned to offer him. It was in this atmosphere that the Soviets made their alliance with France in May.

Hitler had little reason to fear the combination seemingly arrayed against him. The Soviet guarantee to Czechoslovakia, made at the same time as the Franco-Soviet pact, was contingent on prior French action. England broke the Stresa front in June by signing an Anglo-German naval agreement which, while it limited the German fleet to 35 percent of the British, actually permitted the German war industry to operate at full capacity for five years. It also gave approval to German violation of the Versailles Treaty. Stalin was himself hardly a steadfast ally. He sent feelers to Nazi Germany in July through David Kandelaki, and again in November and December through Kandelaki, Sergei Bessonov (who would be tried and shot in 1938), and Evgenii Gnedin. The French delay in ratifying the Franco-Soviet pact could only encourage Hitler's contempt for his opponents. By the time the pact was ratified by the French assembly in March 1936 Hitler marched into the Rhineland, making it a dead letter. It was at this time that Molotov revealed the existence of a faction in the Soviet government seeking to improve relations with Germany.

Radek and Bukharin, although they were generally associated with contrasting foreign policies (Radek with the Rapallo orientation and Bukharin with the anti-Nazi), appeared to be in a curious 'bloc' in 1934–1935, the years when the Barthou–Laval diplomatic offensive showed promise. Radek was associated with the view that Japan presented the principal threat to Soviet security and that, if some way could be found to limit that danger, coexistence with Germany could be arranged. Britain and France were seen as an encouragement to Japan, against which only Soviet-American unity would prove effective. The Entente imperialists could be balanced only by a trilateral combination of the United States, Germany, and the Soviet Union. Radek denounced British imperialism for seeking, on the one hand, to spur on the Japanese and, on the other, to give Germany 'a free hand to change the situation in eastern and south-eastern Europe.'[43]

Radek, however, wanted ententes rather than military alliances: a Pacific pact with the United States, Britain, France, and Japan, and an Eastern pact, negotiated perhaps through the offices of the League of Nations. Germany dodged the latter in 1934. Radek, however, was still optimistic at the time of the Stresa Front, which he claimed was 'not at all a means of encircling Germany and preparing war, but a defense of peace, which can hardly preclude the broadest discussion with Germany in the attempt to ensure its security.'[44]

Radek thus supported French foreign policy in the pursuit of détente with Germany. Preparing for war with Germany was quite another matter. He and Bukharin reminded their readers that in the final analysis the international activity of the working class, rather than diplomacy, was the best support of the Soviet state. The general strike that followed the Stavisky riots in France showed the political potential of unity between Socialists and Communists and provided a push from below for the French diplomatic offensive. It underlined once again the folly of the Third Period line and served as a prelude to the Comintern's turn to the Popular Front policy. Bukharin expressed confidence in a vast popular anti-Fascist movement throughout Europe.

Molotov, scapegoat for the disasters of the Third Period policy, expressed skepticism about a wager on the French. He allowed that, for the French, the Czechs, and others, the first desideratum was an Eastern pact rather than hostile containment of Germany. But Moscow could not bring that about: 'The Soviet government greatly desires to establish good relations with Germany. It would be a positive benefit for our people and the German people. However, this improvement of relations does not depend on us alone, but also on the German government.'[45] Moreover, if containment of Germany required that Italy be recruited, at the expense of giving her a free hand to conquer Abyssinia, the Western imperialists would find themselves tangled in the snarls of their *realpolitik*. The result of a 'new division of the world by the imperialists' would not provide security in Europe, but a new war.[46] Molotov saw no reason for the Soviet Union to participate in this war. Ultimately, Radek's views were closer to these than to those of Bukharin, who argued that the Soviet people must prepare for a historic struggle against an openly bestial philosophy.[47] The collapse of the French diplomatic offensive was required to set the two alternatives in sharp relief.

The first of the Moscow trials, that of the 'Trotskyist-Zinovievist Terrorist Center,' in August, 1936, was not an end to the 'liberal spell' but one of its expressions. There the whole case against the Leningraders was laid out for the Soviet public once more. Everything, it was claimed flowed from the political program of 1926–1927 and the infamous Clemenceau statement of Trotsky in 1927. In invoking Clemenceau, who had offered himself as an alternative to a floundering French war leadership in 1917, Trotsky, it was said, had revealed his desire to seize power with the aid of the military. After their political defeat in 1927, the Trotskyists-Zinovievists had turned to antiparty conspiracy in the Riutin platform and the 'united center' of 1932 with Lominadze, Shatskin, and Sten, heeding Trotsky's call to 'remove Stalin.' There followed the murder of Kirov and plots on the lives of Stalin, Voroshilov, Zhdanov, Kaganovich, Ordzhonikidze, Kossior, and Postyshev (but not Molotov).[48] The whole outline for all the Moscow trial accusations was laid bare, together with its future *dramatis personae*. Zinoviev said the conspirators had 'counted on' Bukharin, and maintained connections with Radek, Sokolnikov, Serebriakov, and Tomskii, principals (except for Tomskii, who killed himself) in the next two trials. Important intimations were made about contacts with the Nazis.[49] The conspirators, it was said, tried to follow the example of Lassalle, the German labor leader of the 1860s, who had cultivated Bismarck in order to further his own ends.[50] 'Lassalle-Bismarck' had become a kind of code for Third Period–National Bolshevism. The Bismarck tradition in German foreign policy had held it as fundamental to be on good terms with Tsarist Russia. Was this a suggestion that Communists could not cooperate with Germany, even with the latter under the influence of Bismarckians? Radek had encouraged the 'Easterners' among the German diplomats and military to look to the tradition of Bismarck. Now, it might seem, the Soviets had abandoned this view of things.

Sotsialisticheskii vestnik considered the paradox that, while these horrors were being unveiled, the optimistic atmosphere in Moscow was seemingly unaffected, with much excitement attending the prospect of a new Soviet constitution.[51] Some of the right opposition who thought themselves co-thinkers of Bukharin tended to accept the guilt of Zinoviev and Kamenev. Perhaps they remembered the vituperous article of Bukharin, 'Stern Words,' written shortly after the Kirov assassination. Bukharin had anticipated the entire case of the first Moscow trial, hooting about terrorists from the camp of the 'Zinovievist anti-party group' who, failing politically, had gone over to 'fascist banditism.' These 'anti-party double-dealers' were an outgrowth of the plots of 'Riutin-Slepkov' and the Trotskyists. These, in turn, were the result of Trotsky's 'Clemenceau thesis.' The plotters were a collective Charlotte Corday to the Stalin leadership's Marat. Most important of all, they were fighting the present domestic course, wanted to encourage the foreign enemy, and hoped to make the present foreign policy fail.[52] Brandler professed himself not too surprised by the abject tone of the confessions. The method of self-inculpation and humiliation, he said, was something specifically Russian, 'with numerous examples from that country's literature.'[53] When the Leningraders had lost their mass base, said Brandler, they turned to terror. We must recognize, he urged, that 'Zinoviev and Trotsky are guilty without reserve. Stalin is more progressive than his enemies and the Stalin leadership is right on all these questions.'[54]

Nevertheless, Bukharin, Rykov, Tomskii, and Uglanov, in addition to Radek, Sokolnikov, and a number of others, had been incriminated in the trial of the Leningraders. Tomskii committed suicide on news that a new investigation would be opened. The testimony of accused Reingold had connected Zinoviev and Kamenev to the plot of Riutin-Slepkov, so the indication was that new trials would be arranged for the leaders of the party right. However, on 10 September it was announced that charges against Bukharin and Rykov would be dropped 'for lack of evidence.' Some sort of organized resistance in the leadership to further trials must have materialized at this time. We do not know how the vote went or even the kind of meeting, but it has been suggested that Kossior, Rudzutak, Chubar, Postyshev, and Eikhe were the 'liberals.'[55] Stalin's response, as Khrushchev revealed in 1956, was to demand the removal of Iagoda as head of the NKVD and the appointment of N. Ezhov, who would preside over the next phase of the purge. A telegram sent to Kaganovich and Molotov by Stalin and Zhdanov, dated from the southern resort town of Sochi on 25 September 1936, spoke of the work of the police being 'four years behind,' apparently referring to the Riutin-Slepkov platform and the 'bloc' of 1932.[56] The same meeting or meetings that rescued Bukharin probably also decided to intervene in the Spanish Civil War.[57]

This decision was in no sense a normal extension of the foreign policy line of Litvinov in pursuit of collective security, which would have required greater harmony with the actions of Britain and France. The French had already decided on a policy of nonintervention, and under British pressure had closed the frontier on August 8, thereby foreclosing on even private aid to the Spanish government. It appeared that the Soviets were going to acquiesce in nonintervention. The 'liberals' in the Soviet Politburo who saved Bukharin were therefore also applying his international policy, which held that fascism would be defeated by broad mass movements of the type of the French and Spanish Popular Fronts. In this respect Trotsky and Bukharin agreed. Victory over fascism in Spain might be the best way to unhinge support for Hitler in Germany.

Moreover, the liberals must have thought their actions of September 1936 to be minor corrections of the line pursued since 1933. They must have excluded a return to Molotov's policies of the Third Period, for which there was so little support in the party and the country at large. For his part, Bukharin had taken great pains to stand aside from the murmurings among Bukharinists and others in 1932. But his name was inevitably associated with the course that had been followed since then. In moving against Iagoda, Stalin was clearing the way for a settling of accounts with the vast and variegated lot who had discussed the modalities of getting rid of him, as well as those who had protected them from punishment. This group would have included, not merely the 'bloc of rights and Trotskyists,' but the regional secretaries who may have voted against him at the plenum of September–October 1932, or at the Seventeeth Party Congress in 1934, and the Politburo liberals as well. In promoting Ezhov to unmask this vast cabal, Stalin and Molotov were also moving to restore their diplomatic freedom of action.

More details of the 'conspiracy' were provided by the trial of the Anti-Soviet Trotskyist Center, in January, 1937, with Radek, Piatakov, Sokolnikov, and others in the dock. The accused described their 'reserve center' as having been organized in 1932 around the Riutin platform. The conspirators wanted an arrangement with Germany and Japan for which they offered the Ukraine and Soviet Far East. For this, said Radek, Trotsky would require a war. Therefore all efforts had to be directed to 'hastening the clash between Germany and Russia.' To this end, Trotsky sought deals with Hitler and Hess. Quoting pretrial testimony, the prosecutor continued to harp on the idea that the plotters had needed war as a preliminary to the partition of the U.S.S.R.[58] Radek referred to a conversation in 1934 with a German diplomat who was anxious about the deterioration in Soviet-German relations:

I told him that realist politicians in the USSR understand the significance of a German-Soviet rapprochement and are prepared to make the necessary concessions in order to achieve this rapprochement.'[59]

The 'realists' were the 'bloc' of conspirators. Radek reports Trotsky lamenting that in his time better relations between the armies of the two countries prevailed, and he (Radek) mentions that he was always known as a defender of the Rapallo line.[60] Most important, to the 'honors list' of the victims of the conspiracy was added the name of Molotov. An elaborate plan to assassinate him was described.[61] The argument about the rapprochement with Germany was shifting toward his position, and another of Stalin's major turns was in process.

Perhaps the most dramatic signal lay in the sentences given those found guilty. While the thirteen major figures were sentenced to be shot, Radek and Sokolnikov were given prison sentences of ten years. This for people who had allegedly conspired in hair-raising treasonous acts. Trotsky read the lightness of the sentences as a retreat by Stalin before the pressure of world opinion, in view of Radek and Sokolnikov being well known in the West.[62] Stalin may have taken into account Sokolnikov's identification with the détente schemes of 1921–1922 and Radek as the personification of the Rapallo line. In this as in all things, he took the opportunity to equivocate and to appear approachable from both sides.

Coinciding with the turn now in progress, the Soviet effort in Spain wound down by spring 1937. Apparently the climax in the turn was the February–March Central Committee plenum, which finally took up the question of arresting Bukharin and Rykov, a plenum at which a kind of last stand was made by 'liberal' Stalinists who had been willing to purge the Leningraders and Trotskyists, but who also hoped that this would mean a halt to the hysteria. They were now in the same position as their victims. They had argued for the program of the 'liberal spell' and had not been able to answer the taunt: 'Will you do what is necessary to secure it?' For Bolsheviks, the regime question is always merely instrumental. Once they had voted to purge their 'political' opponents, they had no defense after their victims implicated them. Bukharin and Rykov were the symbols of this halfway position in the Great Purge.

The defenders of the status quo made a timid and equivocal last stand. Postyshev, who was to have spoken for Rudzutak, Chubar, Kossior, Eikhe, and Petrovskii—men who had presumably protected Bukharin in the past—was unhinged by Stalin's remark from the floor to the effect that the plans of his group were already known. Postyshev abandoned his objections. Rykov and Bukharin, it was decided, would be arrested immediately. This defeat was a key point in the turn, a point after which Stalin no longer bothered to seek support for the arrest of even his closest associates.[63] Stalin's victory on Bukharin–Rykov coincided with Yezhov's denunciation of the former Bukharinist Iagoda and the beginning of the most hysterical phase of the purges.[64] Apparently, it also meant the end of serious help for the antifascists in Spain and ruthless persecution of all who had been involved in the Spanish Civil War.[65]

Stalin's next step was the destruction of the most prominent of the Soviet military officers, with Marshal Tukhachevskii at their head. The announcement about a military plot, arrests, and executions was made in June, but the action of Stalin in framing the generals may have begun in December 1936.[66] Trotsky considered the possibility that there had actually been a military program for the overthrow of Stalin, or that Tukhachevskii was removed because of his connections with the German military, in view of what he judged to be the current pro-French orientation.[67] That is, he did not see a political turn in process.

The trial of the Anti-Soviet Bloc of Rights and Trotskyites, held in March 1938, broadened the implications of the Radek–Piatakov trial. This time the conspirators were said to be in touch with British and Polish intelligence. Accused Bessonov, who had worked in the Soviet trade delegation in Berlin, related a plot with Krestinskii and Trotsky to 'hamper, hinder, and prevent the normalization of relations between the Soviet Union and Germany along normal diplomatic lines.'[68] Rakovskii, relating his ties to the British and Japanese intelligence services, nevertheless also suggested another alternative:

Personally I thought the possibility was not excluded that Hitler would seek a rapprochement with the government of the Soviet Union. I cited the policy of Richelieu: in his own country he exterminated the Protestants, while in his foreign policy he concluded alliances with the Protestant German Princes.[69]

Hitler might be a Richelieu, but also, even with his vast persecutions of those who plotted with the Nazis, so might Stalin.

The sentences given the bloc again provided more curiosities. The major figures were shot. Professor Pletnev, who claimed to have plotted the medical murder of Gorky, was sentenced to twenty-five years. His name would figure in the Doctor's Plot of 1952–1953. Bessonov got fifteen years in prison and Rakovskii twenty. As in the case of Radek and Sokolnikov, the lightness of the sentences was striking. In earlier trials, going back to the Shakhty affair of 1928, the lightness of the sentence was usually taken by the foreign press to indicate the absurdity of the charges. In the Metro-Vickers trial of 1933, the last in which major claims were made about British involvement in skulduggery in Russia, the foreign press had tended to regard the charges as ridiculous and the intention of the prosecution as an attempt, for the benefit of the new Nazi regime, to show enmity between the Soviets and Britain.[70] To the casual observer who did not follow every turn of the accusations and confessions, it might still seem striking that Bessonov got fifteen years for plotting with the Germans while Rakovskii got twenty for plotting with the British.

Trotsky had by this time become convinced that Hitler and Stalin would come to agreement. When the idea had first been suggested to Trotsky, he had dismissed it as a 'White-Guard daydream,' but then he judged that it 'was not excluded' and a 'possibility' in 1937. After Munich, he expected 'with certainty' an agreement with Hitler, and in the spring of 1939 he observed that 'Stalin is completely ripe for an alliance with Hitler.' In July, he claimed that 'the objective of Stalin in international politics is a settlement with Hitler.' Once the agreement had been announced, he wrote that it had been Stalin's primary aim since 1933, and referred to the revelations of Krivitsky and Rauschning about Soviet feelers in 1934.[71]

Nicolaevsky and others later argued that Stalin wanted to use Nazi Germany as an 'icebreaker' to open up the West for Communism. Nicolaevsky had used this expression to describe the German Communists' presumed strategy of using Hitler to break up the Social Democracy in 1931–1932, and in the 1950's he applied it to Nasser in the Middle East. In this case, the icebreaker theory seems to give Stalin both too much and too little credit. He had to think not only about how to come to terms with Hitler but how to get him to influence Japan in the direction of better relations with Soviet Russia. After the German invasion of Prague in

March, the bellicose state of British public opinion no doubt seemed a powerful pressure to make the British honor their guarantees of Poland. Hitler was convinced that he could crush Poland without provoking a general war, but military discussions with the Anglo-French mission in Moscow must have convinced Stalin that there would indeed be war, perhaps a two-front war that Hitler would have to win before the heavy rains of late September created a quagmire for his military machine in Poland. The war danger he thought he saw looming was not one of *Blitzkrieg* and quick campaigns. In the Soviet armed forces tanks were parceled out among infantry rather than concentrated into tank units, obviously because no one thought that mobility had been restored to the battlefield. Khrushchev, in his memoirs, blames this on Soviet tank expert D. G. Pavlov, who did not understand *Blitzkrieg*. Stalin clearly expected a long, drawn-out trench war in Poland and the West, on the model of 1914–1918, in which all the contestants would be worn down. He treated Germany and France scarcely differently from the way he treated Zinoviev and Bukharin, from whose quarrels he had always profited. This was thinking well attuned to the cruel world of international politics. But Stalin reckoned without the tank.[72]

Trotsky did not recognize a turn in 1937, nor did he compare it, as seems reasonable, to the turn of 1927–1928. He had been executing his own turns. After Treint went into the Socialist party in 1934, he bade his followers carry out an 'entry.' This 'French turn' was ended in 1937 by another turn, out of the Socialist parties, preparatory to forming his Fourth International. Trotsky was, once again, making turns very similar to those of Stalin. He could not recognize Stalin's turn of 1937, however, because the Russia of the 'liberal spell' fit much better with his theory of the Russian Thermidor.

A World of Economic Blocs

A pact with the Nazis seemed the perfect climax to the degradation of the Stalinist regime, at least to a great many of those who had ever had any sympathy for it. Trotsky did not want to pass up .the opportunity to sympathize with this anti-Stalin indignation. He called the Hitler-Stalin pact 'treason.' In fact, however, he had never considered it beyond the pale to undertake something of this sort. Shortly after Hitler's taking power he had remarked that

> if the opposition of Bolshevik-Leninists were to find itself at the head of the Soviet State, it would be forced to proceed in its immediate acts from the relation of forces resulting from ten years of the policy of the epigones. It would be forced, in particular, to enter into diplomatic and economic liaisons with Germany and Hitler.[73]

While he wanted Stalin to bear the opprobrium, he could not count the pact, concluded from necessity, as one of Stalin's crimes. That things had been brought to this point, that was the crime.

Trotsky had long before foreclosed on the idea that Stalin's Russia could be of any assistance in stopping Nazism, no more actually than the fading democracies of Britain and France. The real hope against fascism, he had argued since 1934, was the United States. Arriving at this conclusion entailed for him a theoretical reversal as great as his conversion to the Soviet Thermidor. It will be recalled that after promising much for Soviet-American relations in 1925, he had seen the United States as a great threat against which a Socialist United States of Europe would be essential. Not strife with Germany but Anglo-American antagonism was the central 'contradiction' in world politics. By 1934 he viewed the entire matter differently. The United States was in the last analysis the only force capable of restoring the world economy against the disease of 'national economy based on racial community.'

> Everyone defends himself against everyone else, protecting himself by a customs wall and a hedge of bayonets. Europe buys no goods, pays no debts, and in addition arms itself. With five miserable divisions, starved Japan seizes a whole country. The most advanced technique in the world seems impotent before obstacles basing themselves on a lower technique. The law of the productivity of labor seems to lose its force. But it only seems so. The basic law of human history must inevitably take revenge on derivative and secondary phenomena. Sooner or later American capitalism must open up ways for itself throughout the length and breadth of our entire planet. By what methods? By *all* methods. A high coefficient of productive force denotes also a high coefficient of destructive force. Am I preaching war? Not in the least. I am not preaching anything.[74]

Was he preaching war? He was at any rate insisting on the inevitability of the reopening of the world economy, in the manner of Lucien Laurat. He counted inflation of Soviet currency as the pernicious effect of its closed economy, and monetary accountability, preferably based on a gold standard, as the first desideratum of economic and social progress. In his scheme the Soviet Thermidor coincided with the general result of the failure of the world revolution, a breakdown of the world economy into hostile regional blocs. He dated the process from 1924, but his recognition of it only dated from the onset of the Second Five Year Plan.[75]

Trotsky's proclamation of Thermidor gave birth to a curious dispute. If the regime had lost its revolutionism, one could ask: When had that occurred? This introduced a discussion on dating death, or perhaps death by dating. Miasnikov had put it in 1920 at the time of the Trade Union Debate. Most anarchists said 1921 with NEP. During the Dewey Commission hearings, Wendelin Thomas, a commission member and former Communist deputy to the German Reichstag, offered the view that the Bolshevik suppression of the Kronstadt rebellion had been the first real step down the road that ended with the Moscow trials. In arguing against these notions, Trotsky was forced to defend the actions of the dictatorship in terms of the right of any government to control over its military. Anarchist notions of a Third Revolution had threatened, he said, to ruin everything won since 1917. Resistance to this was ABC.

Discussion of Kronstadt had a terrible effect on Trotsky's followers, many of whom were unable to resist the identification of Stalinism with Bolshevism itself. Trotsky even admitted that Bolshevism, with its 1921 ban on factions, had provided a 'juridical point of departure' for Stalinism but that the main cause of Stalinism had been the numerous defeats of the Comintern since 1923. That idea had been his principal rationale since he first found himself in opposition. Yet for the public he sought to influence, the Moscow trials had really made it almost impossible to continue to maintain a distinction between Bolshevism and Stalinism.

Some became hostile to Communism by way of the discussion on dating Thermidor, others by way of analysis of the nature of the Soviet bureaucracy. Some tried to answer the questions posed by Ustrialov, some Machajski. Among the latter, the ideas of Treint, Laurat, Nomad, Weil, and others continued to fester. In the fall of 1937 one of the French Trotskyists, Yvan Craipeau, as if anticipating the Great Retreat thesis, concluded that 'in the last three years' the soviets had finally destroyed the dictatorship of the proletariat. He found the 1930 formula of Rakovskii the most accurate: 'Bureaucratic state with proletarian survivals.'[76] It was idiotic, said Craipeau in 1937, to have to denounce the French government, allied to the Soviet Union, as an unfaithful ally, while the Soviet Union itself was crushing the Spanish left by terror: 'a faithful ally of the Soviet counterrevolution would be imperialist.'[77] The Soviet Union, said Craipeau, did not need a political revolution but a social revolution. And should it be embroiled in war, the slogan in Russia should be the same as that of 1914–1917: 'Revolutionary Defeatism.'[78] Trotsky asked: If the Soviet Union were ruled by a new class, when did it appear? Craipeau's answer was: With the beginning of NEP.[79] This was the line of the Workers' Truth and the Workers' Group of 1922. Trotsky did not really know how to answer it. He called it emotionalism and appealed for dialectic.

The same question came up among the American Trotskyists, who were, like the French Trotskyists, venturing on a subject that would carry them to positions far distant from where they then stood. Many of the French militants would be attracted by the 'Neo-Socialist' ideas of Marcel Deat, and some would collaborate with the Vichy regime. Many of the Americans would return to liberalism and positions closer to the center of the spectrum. Perhaps it was this existential propulsion that produced such intense intellectual activity around the Russian Question. Unfortunately, the odyssey of this generation of intellectuals cannot be pursued here. It should be noted, however, that by 1937, American Trotskyists had characterized the Soviet Union as a 'bureaucratic state,' in the case of James Burnham, and even as a 'fascist state.'

> Russia should be the first state to attain the ideal form of totalitarianism, the form to which Hitler and Mussolini still aspire.[80]

Even Trotsky had remarked that

> Right tendencies are growing and even becoming fascist. The social basis is different in the masses. But if we take an isolated young bureaucrat—there is the totally fascist type with no tradition of the October Revolution. He is only disciplined to shoot and purge for the glory of the fatherland.[81]

Trotsky had used the word 'totalitarian' so often in describing Stalinism that his entire readership, not only his followers, had become well accustomed to it. In speaking of the NKVD he often spoke of 'fascists' or 'fascist methods.' Yet he wanted all these epithets suspended in his readers' minds as 'tendencies' which might take on meaning in the future. Still, many decided to take the next step, especially in regard to the idea that the Soviet Union was not 'Thermidorean' in his sense, but bureaucratic, in the sense of his opponents.

In addition to Craipeau, Burnham, Shachtman, Joseph Carter (who used the term 'bureaucratic collectivist'), and the others, there was also the grand theory of Bruno Rizzi, who had joined the Italian Communist party in 1921 and supported Bordiga. He had even lived in fascist Italy for a time, before moving to France. He was in correspondence with Trotsky in 1938 and 1939, hailing him as 'the chief of the revolution,' calling him 'comrade,' and seeming to support Trotsky's views against those of Craipeau.[82] Rizzi's famous book *La Bureaucratization du monde* reflects the 1939 version of his ideas on bureaucracy which, he claimed, failed to get a proper hearing on the French left. Rizzi held that the Soviet Union, with its 'new class' in charge, was the pivot of world politics.[83] Nationalized property in the Soviet Union played the same role as nationalized property in the fascist countries, that of providing a support for the new class. This gave the lie to the Marxist delusion that fascism was petit-bourgeois. Thus in Italy and Germany 'the capitalist state is being destroyed day by day.'[84] This even applied to 'Keynesian' state intervention in the economy of New Deal America. Everywhere one saw the promotion of the rising 'new class' in 'the four great autarkies' of Germany, Italy, Russia, and America.[85]

> We belive [he argued] that our planet will be divided into a small number
> of political units around a central vanguard cell. We would have a
> Latino-Mediterranean unit, a German unit, a Slavo-Siberian unit, a
> yellow unit with Japan at its head, an Indian unit, a North American and
> an Anglo-Saxon.[86]

Rizzi thus argued for the breakdown of the world into economic blocs, in
the fashion of the British protectionist and later fascist, Oswald Mosely.
There was no room, however, for the world influence of the Western
democracies, and no room at all for the Jews.

> The racist struggle of National Socialism and Fascism is at bottom only
> an anti-capitalist struggle led by the new synthesis. . . . Hitler is right and
> we are wrong. One must adjust and become anti-semitic in order to be
> anti-capitalist.[87]

The workers of the West, he urged, must press for 'an international
anti-capitalist bloc with Nazism, fascism, and Stalinism,' and 'they must
recognize the leading role of Italy, Germany, and Japan.[88]

   Thus one attempt of ideology to cope with two huge problems of our
century, bureaucracy and autarky, on which no help from Marx could be
expected. Trotsky's views were exactly opposite. He had not had any
truck with protectionism since his days in the Soviet Politburo, and he
counted the Soviet and the fascist bureaucracies as ephemeral, especially
with the approach of war. Yet his own views seemed scarcely more
plausible than those of Rizzi. Could it be that the Russian Question was not
the best guide to understanding Stalinism?

   On the one hand, the Russian Question was essential to Trotsky in
providing a theoretical understanding for the crushing of his historical
hopes. Revolutionaries were capable of beginning again; how many times
had Lenin done it? One had to return to the textbooks and build from the
bottom, knowing that the chaos of world politics entering world war
would provide anew. On the other hand, the Russian Question permitted
a certain intellectual and moral indictment of Stalin before the court of
world history. Despite all that was said about the hatred and bitterness of
Trotsky toward Stalin, Trotsky knew that he was the most powerful
influence on the writing of the history of the period, and that posterity
would vindicate him against the Moscow trials, as it has—even, to a
degree, in the Soviet Union. Posterity would also reduce Stalin, for that
was what Trotsky wanted, not to avenge himself on Stalin in the standard
sense but merely to show him as a man in elevator shoes.

   Trotsky lived for the idea that Stalin was a mediocrity, an idea that at one
time had influence among students of Soviet politics. By now the view has
been generally accepted that Stalin was no mediocrity, but rather a shrewd

practitioner of the art of factional politics, of 'dosage,' a man with a certain theoretical capacity, who moreover knew how to appeal to ordinary people without seeming to condescend. This idea is not much different from Stalin's own self-image. It contrasts sharply with our image of Trotsky as a brilliant, bold, vain windbag, who offended many with his patrician airs, and ultimately lost all because he could not operate politically in any way remotely to merit the mantle of Lenin. This, too, is not much different from Stalin's view.

Inevitably, Stalin and Trotsky will always be judged as opposites. It may even be that there is some merit, despite the current view, to the idea of Stalin's mediocrity as a way of explaining Stalinism. If one considers the role of Lenin in the intellectual life of Bolshevism—with a massive economic treatise, historical contributions on the populist movement and the organization question, a defense of the materialism of Diderot against Mach and Avenarius, notebooks on Hegel, and for posterity these and other works comprising over sixty volumes—one appreciates the problem of aspiring to his position of authority among the Old Bolsheviks. If one also considers that Lenin used every political and administrative device at his disposal to maintain his position of intellectual supremacy in a party that he liked to regard as a vessel of theory, one can appreciate not only the challenge but also the temptation presented to anyone aspiring to his position. And they all considered themselves his pupils.

Stalin, however, was not a great theorist, nor was he personally popular, or a good writer or speaker, or a man adept at quick verbal exchanges. In fact, when there was a dispute, Stalin usually held his counsel, out of his inferiority in debate but with the pretense that he was above it all, holding back, as Lenin did, to intervene at the right time or, in Stalin's case, when he could equivocate no longer. Lenin's intellectual authority was *sui generis*. No successor could realistically hope to match it, especially if one considers the splits that Lenin needed in order to build it up, splits that the ruling party could not afford. The Communists of the revolutionary generation seemed, on the contrary, to prefer collective leadership. To them a brilliant chief succeeding to the position of Lenin could only be a threat. This applied to the case of Trotsky and certainly to Zinoviev. This circumstance was a boon to Stalin. Only he was mediocre enough not to be feared until it was too late. And after he was on top, only he was mediocre enough to be thought reducible to a mere figurehead. When he attempted to be more, every day that passed under his leadership won new converts to the list of those who would remove him. Stalin killed so many because so many refused to see in him a Lenin. He had to conduct a social revolution, by means of arrests, to raise up enough virginal minds who would claim thus to see him. And since he was only mediocre, and nobody's fool, he could not really believe even them. Trotsky, who must have had an ordinary human capacity for hatred, nevertheless insisted, wrongly, that Stalin was only the creature of the apparatus. Consequently he refused to depict him as a monster or a devil, but only as a 'limited, wily boor.' Yet perhaps this, along with the other explanations, may help us to understand Stalinism.

8

The Third Centrism:
The Rise of Kremlinology,
1940–1964

Often the intellectual high command of the organic party does not belong to any faction but operates as a leading force standing on its own above the parties, and sometimes is even believed to be such by the public.

—Antonio Gramsci

AT THE SUMMIT of power with the pact with Hitler in his pocket, Stalin was still permitted no relaxation but had to face two years of tense intrigue and four of war before he could find himself in a truly secure position. He had triumphed over the party oppositions and then over the party itself. He had crushed any potential resistance in the armed forces and in the NKVD. It remained to triumph in war. This could not be done without again altering the form of the dictatorship in ways that posed new threats. The war with Finland in 1939–1940 raised special challenges to the civil-military relation bequeathed by the civil war period. The military command was not functioning well alongside the commissar apparatus, the party's wing in the armed forces. The Politburo meeting of March, 1940, decided to loosen political controls, giving command of the army to Marshal Timoshenko and removing Voroshilov. In addition, the commissar apparatus was abolished and 'one-man leadership' reconstituted to pursue one aim, the prosecution of war.[1] The party was now no longer cosigning orders, but merely keeping an eye on the command through the device of the Assistant Commander for Political Affairs (*zampolit*) in units down to the company level. With the German invasion, an attempt was made to reinstate the commissars, but abandoned again in late 1942. Not until the tide had been turned, that is, after Stalingrad, would the party bring the commissars back. This was done in April 1943. Stalin won his battle for political control of the armed forces in increments, as he had won his other battles. The last chapter in his struggle against 'Bonapartism' was the postwar demotion of Zhukov himself, but the issues personified by

159

Zhukov would be prominent in the struggle among Stalin's potential successors.

The last phase of Stalin's career should reveal for us a Stalin freed of the terrible faction struggles which form the identifying feature of his path to supremacy. Yet they reveal no such thing. In fact, the period 1945–1953 saw a reinstatement of the pattern of alternance which we have observed in the previous period. It would have been a reasonable expectation that, after Stalin's fight to get to the top, he would gather around him the veterans of the struggle, their loyalty to him tested by events, and rule in a relaxed manner expressive of his overflowing talents. But Stalin's talents never overflowed. Despite his insatiable appetite for public flattery, Stalin apparently did not desire to monopolize thinking about policy, but instead required real contention among his closest subordinates. The few evidences of this contention that were visible to foreigners were frequently interpreted as signs that Stalin was no longer in control. Using the model of Western parliamentary leadership, observers might conclude that Stalin's subordinates were really running things and had perhaps reduced him to the position of a figurehead. But Stalin did not like to devise plans for whose success or failure he would assume responsibility. Others had to be found to suggest possible approaches, and still others to put them under critical fire in anticipation of the moment when the policy line would be exhausted. With a new turn, those who had prompted the old line would have to take their punishment. Thus Stalin, always responsible for success, was never guilty of failure. Stalin needed alternance because it was the way he thought—or rather, it was a means by which he could expropriate the thought of others. More than an unpleasant necessity of his struggle for power, it was a durable feature of the unique system he gave to Soviet Russia.

It remains for this study to give an idea of how this alternance resounded in the period following the establishment of High Stalinism. A political history of the post-Stalingrad period is not intended; for our purposes it is hoped to demonstrate how the Western idea of the Soviet policy alternance developed, especially as indicated by the observations of Boris Nicolaevsky, Boris Souvarine, Isaac Deutscher, and some others whose writings had influence. Alongside the valuable insights and provocative suggestions one finds in these writings, one also finds a good deal of unsubstantiated speculation, for which Kremlinology has been justly criticized for its insider tone and for its air of omniscience. There would be little point in judging speculation of this sort against the more trustworthy works of historical scholarship, but it has a place in what might be called the intellectual history of Soviet studies, just as the thoughts of Robert Hooke have a place in the history of science, without our judging them against those of Newton. We continue to note the impact of the Russian Question. For after the death of the great tyrant, the Stalin succession also introduced a Soviet version of the Russian Question, in deliberations over de-Stalinization.

From the Stalin succession there emerged a third version of centrism far different from that of Lenin or Stalin. The centrism of party ideologue Mikhail Suslov would provide the most stable regime that Soviet Russia has known. Ensuring the cadres against a new reign of autocratic arbitrariness, he nevertheless shackled them with a commitment to the continuity of Stalin's, and his, ideas.

Zhdanov and Malenkov

Deliberation on the nature of the Soviet Union reached a high point in the first years of World War II, the Hitler-Stalin pact and the unleashing of hostilities having shocked interested participants into crucial choices. Could the Soviet Union still be regarded by followers of Trotsky as a state worthy of defense? Or rather, could one still defend Soviet conquests won by alliance with fascism? Trotsky, as we have seen, felt that one must. But many of his followers, echoing the analysis of Bruno Rizzi, decided that the Soviet state had changed its character and must now be seen as a bureaucratic empire. Unlike Rizzi, they found it to be lacking in 'progressive' historical features. Thus the line of Craipeau, Carter, Rizzi, and others led to the 'bureaucratic collectivism' description embraced by Max Shachtman, and the thesis of a 'managerial revolution' (a real repetition of Rizzi) espoused by Schachtman's former co-thinker, James Burnham. Bureaucratic Collectivism, as described by Schachtman, led him to a pacifist position which he maintained through the war, and which did not differ ostensibly from a position of Leninist defeatism. Schachtman would draw more conclusions after the war and eventually reconcile with the views of the Second International, without, however, ever bringing his Trotskyism satisfactorily to accounts. Burnham's 'managerial' position divided him more sharply from the Trotsky tradition and seemed, at least for a time, to urge recognition, in the Rizzi fashion, of the 'progressive' qualities of the 'great autarkies' as against the decadent Western plutocracies.[2]

Both these seemingly natural developments from disputes in the intellectual milieu of the left at the end of the thirties were anathema to Trotsky, who lived long enough to witness their beginning in disputes about the Soviet attack on Finland, Poland, and the Baltic states. Trotsky never thought of embracing the idea of autarky or of a New Class. Rather than this, he contemplated struggling on, should the war fail to advance the revolution or topple Stalinism, in a new environment historically fatal to his dreams of the proletarian mission, with a 'new minimum program' for the slaves of totalitarianism. But he was certain that more would come from the war being unleashed. He instructed his confused followers to oppose the war with the traditional defeatist position, modified by support for the Soviet degenerate workers' state. And, should the bourgeois states really fight Hitler, or come into alliance with Soviet Russia, this defeatist position should be implemented with prejudice against Hitler. In the antifascist camp, Trotsky explained, his followers should oppose the war, but report to the colors and fight as hard as the best, as 'proletarian socialist revolutionary militants.'[3] In the fascist camp, they should oppose with sabotage. Thus the defeatism that he preached was not what it seemed.

In fact he was entirely prepared to witness, if history so decreed, an end to the Communist dictatorship in Russia, which he felt must be accompanied by an outbreak of proletarian revolution in a necessarily more favorable place. This sentiment was an exact replication of Lenin's defeatism. War signified for the workers' state, he had suggested in 1935, what revolution signified for the proletariat in the West. That is, the Soviet workers might see it as their emancipation. After all, the victory of the anti-Napoleonic coalition had not meant the end of French capitalism.

> History teaches that when the conquerors find themselves at a technical and cultural level inferior to the conquered, they must take these into account. It is not military violence as such that menaces the USSR but the cheap goods which flow on the heels of the victorious capitalist armies.[4]

One can imagine Stalin's reactions to these sentiments. In 1939 Trotsky took matters further and advocated independence for a Soviet Ukraine.[5] This might be misunderstood for a while, he judged, but as war unleashed its centripetal tendencies, the folly of substituting for the world revolution the utopia of Socialism in One Country would become clear. He seems not to have heeded Angelo Tasca's famous remark that 'the Soviet Union is not a country, it is a continent.'[6]

Observers such as Boris Nicolaevsky did not have to wrestle with the problem of the 'degenerate workers' state,' as did Trotsky and those who followed on the Trotskyist path after their leader's death. Yet Nicolaevsky still found it difficult to arrive at a satisfactory answer to the Russian Question. Throughout the war he posed the question of Pontius Pilate to Menshevik readers. Jesus had told Pilate of his mission to bear witness to the truth. 'What is Truth?' was Pilate's ironic reply. Socialists, thought Nicolaevsky, now had to answer the question of Pontius Pilate. Should they agree with Mensheviks such as Feodor Dan, for whom socialism loomed as the only response for a faltering West and an emerging postcolonial world? Should the world seek salvation in the unity of socialism and the Russian idea? As Dan later put it,

> Through socialism to freedom—this, the former banner of Russian

'peculiarity' has every chance of becoming the universal banner of the development of all the peoples and countries of the earth.[7]

What was truth? Was it a matter of 'through socialism to freedom,' as Dan suggested? Had the nineteenth-century socialist idea, which had been inconceivable outside the framework of a democratic republic, now degenerated into a choice between Hitler's National Socialism and Stalin's Communism? Nicolaevsky concluded that Dan had been wrong, that socialism must avail toward freedom.[8] One must, in view of this, reject Rizzi and the admirers of socialist autarky, as well as Dan's Dostoyevskian vision of the Russian idea. Stalin and the Russified Comintern had removed all traces of the 'humanistic socialism of the Luxemburg tradition' from the Communist idea.[9]

Nicolaevsky was convinced that the Soviet system did not deserve to be called socialist. He shared the reassessment of the Russian Question made by Rudolf Hilferding in 1938–1939. For Hilferding, the idea of 'state capitalism' could not pass the test. In the absence of a market mechanism, one could scarcely speak of any variety of capitalism. On the other hand, the capacity for accumulation could not be denied.[10] Could this be, as Trotsky and others insisted, the work of the 'bureaucracy'? For Hilferding, Stalin had exploded the myth of the bureaucracy when he shot thousands of bureaucrats during the purges and thus demonstrated the independence of the state from this managerial 'ruling class.'[11] In place of a bureaucratic ruling class or neo-bourgeoisie, Hilferding found only an omnipotent state apparatus, freed of economic laws and mocking the Marxist analysis which had developed, as he put it, 'in a completely different period.'

Hilferding's 'totalitarian state economy' seemed to Nicolaevsky the best description of the structure of Stalinist Russia. Yet like Hilferding, he seemed to realize that acceptance of this idea meant abandoning the Menshevik analysis of Soviet Russia according to Marxist ideas. For years, he lamented, Mensheviks had taken for their specialty the description of the 'Thermidorean degeneration' of the Russian Revolution. Now they were speaking of a 'revolution without Thermidor,' or of a 'totalitarian revolution.'[12] Nicolaevsky could find no satisfactory answer to this problem, which may be too elusive for anyone to solve. Can one have both voluntarist totalitarian state supremacy and a managerial ruling New Class? From the standpoint of the Russian Question, there might seem to be nothing further to say until this problem was resolved, yet Nicolaevsky did not see the Russian Question as the end of analysis of Soviet Russia, but only its beginning.

The idea of the totalitarian state economy, a system perfected in the Soviet Union and one toward which the fascist economies were constantly moving, had its natural appeal in the wake of the period of the Hitler-Stalin pact. Nicolaevsky was moved to see further, more intimate identifications between the Nazi and Stalinist regimes. Following Krivitsky's suggestion of Stalin's intention to make a deal with Hitler as early as 1934, Nicolaevsky traced the tendency back to the Schlageter line of 1922–1923.[13] And perhaps further still: Lenin's line had always promoted 'national wars' against the security system laid down by the Versailles treaty, argued Nicolaevsky, referring to 'hints' of this in Lenin's prewar polemic with Rosa Luxemburg, in defense of the 'right of nations to self-determination.'[14] The Third Period line had been directed against the pro-Versailles German Social Democrats, who had criticized Russo-German cooperation under the Rapallo treaty. This was why the French Communists had supported Alsation separatism.[15] Stalin had banked on the Reichswehr, which had guaranteed him that Hitler would never attain supreme power. Even after Hitler had won, the army had continued to argue in terms of a pro-Soviet 'Bismarckian' foreign policy line which was only defeated by Hitler's army purge of 1938. It was no accident in view of this, said Nicolaevsky, that the anti-Soviet Nazis Hess and Rosenberg figured so prominently in the bogus plots described in the Moscow trials.[16] Kirov, Bukharin, and Gorky had also placed their heads on the chopping block by expressing antifascist views. Thus the Kirov affair came to be seen by Nicolaevsky as an important stepping stone toward the Hitler-Stalin pact.[17] The theory of totalitarianism seemed to be supported by reference to National Bolshevism in Soviet foreign policy.

This was also the case for Nicolaevsky's writings on the factional situation in the Soviet leadership, with Andrei Zhdanov, Leningrad party chief and chief beneficiary of the party revival that took place in 1945–1946, seen as the proponent of the National Bolshevik pro-German line that we have associated with the Leningrad orientation. Nicolaevsky was convinced that Stalin parted only with great difficulty from the views of Radek on the indispensability of German-Soviet understanding. Evidence for this idea was found in Stalin's 1941 interview with Harry Hopkins, in which Hitler's attack was described as the 'treachery of a partner,' for which only Hitler himself was said to be responsible, 'not Germany, not the German General staff, not the Reich as a body politic.'[18] Stalin thought the attack 'the act of a madman obeying a swift, murderous passion,' an act which must be followed, Nicolaevsky thought, by Hitler's break with Field Marshal Brauschitsch, chief of the army command and reluctant symbol of the Bismarck tradition.[19] In fact, Nicolaevsky later judged that Stalin had been completely convinced by the schemes of German geopolitical theorist Karl Haushofer for a bloc of Russia, Germany, and Japan against the Anglo-Saxons. Stalin had arranged the first part in 1939 with Hitler and the second in 1941 with Matsuoka.[20]

Zhdanov appeared to be in the position of heir to the approach taken on these matters by Radek and then Molotov. The Leningrad party chief was said to be an enthusiast for the Hitler-Stalin pact, for the absorption of the

Baltic states and the subsequent Finnish campaign of 1939–1940.[21] Along with Molotov, he went into eclipse with the Nazi attack in 1941, still playing an important role in the defense of Leningrad (and coming into conflict with Marshal Zhukov), while being excluded from the State Defense Committee in which Georgii Malenkov and Lavrenti Beria began to grip the controls of the war machine. Zhdanov continued to participate in the Supreme Naval Council, where he had fought for greater naval appropriations even during the 1939–1941 lull. Zhdanov had been a beneficiary of Kirov's murder, but nevertheless had made a number of attempts to slow down the Ezhov phase of the purge with appeals for legality. He must have hoped that Stalin, once defended against real enemies, could permit a kind of *Rechtsstaat* in the party regime.[22]

Malenkov had been brought into politics in 1925 by Poskrebyshev and worked with Yezhov in the thirties. He became a Central Committee secretary in 1939 and, after Zhdanov's eclipse, apparently enjoyed the central position in the wartime political leadership after Stalin himself. While Zhdanov had expressed the fear that the party would get lost in economic work and slide into a managerial outlook, Malenkov was critical of ideological blowhards who could not accomplish practical tasks. Stalin had favored the Malenkov view during the 'liberal spell' but turned in 1937 toward emphasis on theoretical education and a stricter division of labor between party and state. During the war, Malenkov's position was fortified. He seems also to have come into conflict with Zhdanov over his version of a 'Morgenthau plan' for Germany in 1944–1945. His scheme for the 'economic disarmament' of the captured territories was opposed by Zhdanov, along with Mikoyan and Mekhlis.[23] While Malenkov's line prevailed, up to summer 1945, he was able to replace Zhdanov's man, Vosnesenskii, with his own, Saburov, at Gosplan. His victory over Zhdanov was signaled by Zhdanov's restriction to the northern front and by the apparent barring of Zhdanov from ceremonies in January, 1945, celebrating the success of the defense of Leningrad. Zhdanov would only stage a comeback after Yalta. Nicolaevsky concluded as well that control over the affairs of the foreign Communist parties was at first entrusted to Malenkov when the Comintern was abolished in 1943.[24] The International Department of the Central Committee became the heir of the Comintern.

Yet Malenkov's ascendancy was ended by the time of the party revival initiated by Stalin at war's end. This important change, thought by some to be Stalin's opening salvo in the Cold War, was part of what now appears to be a general strategy of some complexity and nuance. Stalin was apparently attempting to blend a foreign policy emphasizing conciliation among the former members of the Grand Alliance with an attempt to open the door to possible revolutionary opportunities in the West. The cornerstone of foreign policy must have been alliance with France to achieve Soviet reparations aims in Germany. De Gaulle, reliant on the PCF's disarmament in return for entry into his postwar government, wanted to make 'a permanent Ally of the good and powerful Russia in the East.' Policy for postwar administration of Soviet-occupied East Europe was made to harmonize with this early postwar, pre–Cold War security arrangement. The former French allies of the interwar period were accorded considerably better treatment than the powers formerly dedicated to revision of the Versailles pact. Aside from the Baltic states, which became part of the Soviet Union, this applied to the entire French *cordon sanitaire*. Poland was granted its reclaimed lands at the expense of Germany. While the Soviets took back Vilna and Lwów and restored the Curzon line as the eastern frontier, the Poles would need Soviet help to keep Pomerania and Silesia. Members of the former Little Entente, the interwar alliance against Hungarian revisionism, were also treated well. Czechoslovakia got back South Slovakia, tossed to Hungary in 1938, and the Sudetenland, in compensation for Soviet annexation of sub-Carpathian Ruthenia. Romania got back Northern Transylvania, Hitler's 'Second Vienna Award' of 1940, from Hungary, and the Southern Dobruja from former revisionist Bulgaria. These compensated Romanian national sentiment for the loss of Bessarabia to the Soviet Union. In addition to Southern Dobruja, Bulgaria had to give up West Thrace, given her by the Treaty of Craiova in 1940; she lost areas she had fought for since the Balkan Wars. The territorial settlements arranged by the Soviets were designed to punish the former revisionists and reward the former French allies. They were designed to be appreciated in Gaullist France.

The party coalitions in occupied territories were initially composed to re-create the atmosphere of the Popular Front and the wartime national fronts. Peasant and bourgeois parties were permitted, and sometimes had to be resurrected where the Nazis had destroyed them. Wherever possible, their leaders were to be given a prominent place, as with Petru Groza's Ploughmen's Front in Romania, Ferenc Nagy's premiership in Hungary, and Stanisław Mikołajczyk's vice premiership in Poland. Sovietization was not on the order of the day. Land reform, rather than collectivization, was initially pursued. Communist discussions of People's Democracy recalled Mao's Bloc of Four Classes or even the Revolutionary Democratic Dictatorship of the Proletariat and the Peasantry of Zinoviev and Bukharin. Economic arrangements recalled those of the NEP period. Attempts at premature putsches were repressed ruthlessly. Stalin clearly wanted no emergence of 'sectarianism' in East Europe, and he appears to have taken the same position on China and Indochina. Genuine coalitions[25] were meant to echo those of Tripartism in France and Italy, except for Communist control of key internal security posts.

That was the diplomatic and political framework for the party revival. The Duclos letter of April 1945, in which the French Communist attacked the wartime dissolution of the American party under Earl Browder, was by no means a call to the 'offensive' like that of 1920–1921.[26] It merely urged an end to wartime liquidationism, applicable not only to the United States but to other parties of the international movement as well. These parties were not to storm the heavens but to pursue tactics in the tradition of Paul Levi. Nor should Stalin's attitude toward revolutionary opportunities outside the Soviet bloc be necessarily adduced from the Stalinist persecution of 'sectarians' who wanted to go faster. There is little reason to think that the bureaucratic motif in Stalinism had overcome the revolutionary.

On the contrary, in the days before the Marshall Plan, Stalin had good reason to compare the European situation to the days before the Dawes Plan. The problem was that opportunities had to be pursued through the Tripartite governments and moreover had to be balanced, on the one hand, with observance of the Stalin–Churchill 'percentages' agreement of 1944, allotting influence in East Central Europe with the British, and, on the other, with some show of conciliation toward the United States. Thus the party revival was accompanied by the promotion of an analysis of world politics in which fine distinctions were made and the dangers of the diplomatic thicket were kept in mind. Yet the opportunities were continually stressed. The nationalist energies let loose by the struggle against fascism would continue to have their impact.[27] And these should be encouraged. Eugen Varga's *Changes in the Economy of Capitalism as a Result of the Second World War* would by 1947 be pilloried as conceding far too much to the Western democracies, their Keynesian devices for dealing with the business cycle, and their capacity for planning. However, Varga also stressed that the Anglo–American antagonism was primary, that the United States would wrest the colonies from the grasp of the dying European empires, and that, until the inevitable intervention of U.S. capital export, the European economies would be in dire straits.[28] The analysis recalled certain elements from prewar Soviet prognoses.

The East European regimes 'of the type of the new democracy' were described by Varga in a way that suggested common features with NEP Russia of the twenties. Their economies were called 'state capitalist.' Varga's opponents would by 1947 correct him and emphasize the anticapitalist nature of these economies, in a manner reminiscent of Bukharin's 'correction' of Zinoviev in 1925–1926. At any rate, the anticolonial motifs of Varga's analysis, like his treatment of the problem of Germany's enslavement by 'Entente imperialism' in the twenties, were compatible with a National Bolshevik policy. Zhdanov's associates espoused a German line which would have cultivated traditional German national sentiment in the Soviet zone, a prerequisite for establishing influence among the German workers in the Western zones.[29]

Zhdanov was the principal beneficiary of the party revival, yet he seems not to have enjoyed genuine control of a revived Comintern apparatus. At the time of the liquidation of the Comintern in 1943, it passed, as has been noted, not into Zhdanov's hands but probably into those of Malenkov. And when Malenkov was relieved from his duties as Secretary of the Central Committee in 1946, the apparatus of the foreign parties came under Beria, who, Nicolaevsky thought, used it to stimulate conflict with Yugoslavia and, by implication, the Soviet Leningraders.[30]

Zhdanov's intimacy with Tito and the Yugoslav Communists has been generally assumed.[31] Thus, the fall of Zhdanov and the reinstatement of Beria and Malenkov has come to be associated inevitably with the failure of Tito's policy of support for a Greek Communist insurgency. This 'Comsomolist' adventure (as Stalin called it) violated the understanding that Stalin had made with Churchill in 1944 to the effect that Greece would be mainly a British sphere, and moreover, drew the United States, after the promulgation of the Truman Doctrine, into the defense of Greece against Communism. In the spring and summer of 1947, clear signs accumulated showing that the politics associated with the party revival and the ascendancy of the Leningraders were nearing exhaustion.

There had been reason to hope, during the first two years after the end of the war, that Communism might advance on many fronts. While Communists participated in the Tripartite governments of France and Italy, the East European coalitions would keep to their moderate policy, with the Hungarian Communists especially restrained (Churchill and Stalin had designated influence in Hungary to be divided fifty-fifty). Nationalization was not emphasized and only around one-third of the land underwent reform. Hungary appeared to be a hostage to Tripartism in the West. European Communists were not returning to the policies of 1919, but they worked carefully to fortify positions while the Soviets sought a share in the control of the Ruhr, loans from the West, and whatever gains might be offered by the economic dislocation. At the same time, weapons were left behind for the CCP as the Soviets evacuated Manchuria, another edition of the 'Ghilan republic' in Iran was essayed, and support in varying degrees was given to anticolonial and anti-Western movements in Indonesia, India, Burma, Malaya, the Philippines, and other areas. This was a many-sided policy appropriate to the postwar menu of opportunities.

Zhdanov's internal situation was precarious. He had been the beneficiary of Stalin's general disposition in favor of party control over the armed forces. This had presumably been a factor in his rivalry with Marshal Zhukov.[32] With the demotion of Zhukov at war's end, Zhdanov appeared to be at the height of his power. His rival Malenkov's demotion soon brought Zhdanov's supporters into positions of importance. A. A. Kuznetsov assumed control of the state security organs. N. A. Vosnesenskii, described by Khruschev as an 'economic wizard,' became chairman of Gosplan.[33] But Zhdanov's own demise was set in motion by the announcement of the Truman Doctrine and the Marshall Plan in early 1947. Churchill had already made his Fulton, Missouri speech, denouncing the 'iron curtain' that was descending across Europe, and opposition to Soviet plans in Iran had stymied Stalin. Yet Stalin must have supposed that the Anglo-American bond was not yet solid, and that as long as the United States did not support the efforts of the English in many parts of the globe, including, at this time, Palestine, the struggle against England could continue.

The German situation did not look as bright. The Soviets and the French still did their utmost to impede German reconstruction, in the spirit of the defunct Morgenthau Plan, but by December, 1946, the United States and Britain had fused their zones of occupation. 'Bizonia' became a symbol of Anglo-American unity and ultimately a refutation of the Soviet policy of 1945–1947 which reckoned without the full onset of the Cold War. The Marshall Plan unhinged the coalitions in East Europe, whose leaders would have to be prevented by strong-arm methods from taking its aid. Nor could Tripartism in France and Italy be saved by the Red Army, so those outposts too would be surrendered. With the crucial European stake lost, Stalin could no longer bear the risks of opposing a united Anglo-American coalition in Greece. The entire policy was a shambles. It was time for another turn.

Unfortunately for them, the closest of Zhdanov's associates were just sharpening up the theoretical basis of the party revival and heaping their attacks on the apparently beleaguered Varga. At the moment when the economist N. A. Voznesenskii was criticizing Varga for overestimating, in the manner of Kautsky's 'ultra-imperialism,' the capacity of the capitalist states for planning their way out of the inevitable postwar depressions, the Marshall Plan seemed to be arguing for the more nuanced position of Varga. Thus the apparent paradox that the Zhdanovists seemed to be on the warpath in 1947 as the premises for their radicalism were disappearing. Moreover, as Stalin's enthusiasm for the Leningrader line waned, he encouraged its author to press even harder for it. Tripartism collapsed in France and Italy in the spring. Then at the founding conference of the Cominform, at the Polish village of Sklarska Poręba, Zhdanov and the Yugoslavs took the lead in criticizing the leaders of the PCI and PCF for not doing enough to save their countries from 'enslavement' under the Marshall Plan. Malenkov and Suslov added emphasis to their strictures.

Yugoslav sources have insisted that this meeting, which apparently placed Titoism in a commanding position in the Cominform, was in fact designed by Stalin to undermine Tito.[34] The Cominform was not a revival of the Comintern. It included only European parties, and excluded those conducting insurgencies at the time of its founding, such as the Chinese, the Vietnamese, and the Greek parties. Zhdanov was believed by some to be in charge of the Soviet party's relations with foreign Communist parties,[35] but he showed little interest at Sklarska Poreba in the insurgencies, which were clearly subordinate in the Kremlin's policy to the strikes against the Marshall Plan being carried out in France. These, together with the 1948 Italian elections, appear to have been the last stand of the policy in place since the party revival. This was, in any case, the last stand of Zhdanov as heir apparent.

Nicolaevsky laid stress on the dispute between Zhdanov and Malenkov, and charted the former's fortunes alongside those of Tito and Titoism. He thought the foundation of the Cominform a probable disappointment for Zhdanov, who, he judged, would have preferred a revival of the Comintern. He noted the development of Tito's ideas on a Balkan federation, and the pacts Yugoslavia signed with Bulgaria in November, and with Hungary and Romania in December. Then, after Dmitrov's endorsement of the Balkan federation on January 16, 1948, *Pravda* disavowed the plan on January 28. Nicolaevsky, who saw Tito and Zhdanov as allies, thought this the first clear sign of the latter's fall. The Italian non-Communist press, girding for the general elections, the loss of which by the PCI must have put the seal on the fate of the international policy associated with Zhdanov, also feared that Tito would be marching on Trieste. Stalin's disapproval of that possible course of action was strong, in view of the united American-British-French policy in support of the return of Trieste to Italy.

To be sure, Zhdanov was by this time administering severe criticism to the Yugoslavs, no doubt at the bidding of Stalin. If he were to be the true heir he would have to demonstrate dialectic and the ability to make turns. Stalin in the past had used this requirement to force his victims to denude themselves of their own supporters, as with Zinoviev and Ruth Fischer in 1925. Now Zhdanov was apparently liberating himself from some of his co-thinkers. The break with Tito was complete by June; Zhdanov died, of a heart attack or by other causes, in August.

The unraveling of the policy associated with Zhdanov meant an entirely different approach to the East European coalitions. In May 1947, Hungary, a hostage of defeated Western Tripartism, underwent coordination. The independent peasant party premier Ferenc Nagy was forced out of office and sovietization proceeded. By fall, Mikołajczyk in Poland and Iuliu Maniu in Romania, both leaders of peasant parties, would also be pushed aside. The Czech government, in which Communists took a leading role by virtue of their 38 percent showing in the elections of 1946, would have preferred a hard line on Germany, and even an alliance with France to enforce it, but Stalin's French card was no longer worth much. Gottwald and Slansky were prepared by Moscow to tighten up the campaign against Marshall Plan aid. A few months later Czechoslovakia would undergo a coup, and its new Five Year Plan would reemphasize heavy industry production, perhaps as an attempt to make industrial Bohemia substitute in the Eastern Bloc for the share of the Ruhr's produce that Stalin's policy was unable to procure. French agreement on Anglo-American plans for the economic unification of Germany's western zones was yielded grudgingly through 1947 and 1948. With France reversing its policy, a united West began to loom before Stalin.

It seems clear enough that Stalin would have preferred not to see Europe divided into East-West spheres of influence and that his French policy was an attempt to preserve an open Europe, a poor Europe by necessity, which would have turned increasingly to the Communists for leadership. With the failure of that policy, the Soviets reluctantly abandoned restraint in Eastern Europe, at the same time that they began to call for the ouster of Tito's group in Yugoslavia.

When Malenkov was chosen to send greetings to the Japanese Communist party in May 1948, Nicolaevsky concluded that he had won the competition against Zhdanov. Nicolaevsky further concluded that the Czech coup was arranged by Malenkov with the use of Beria's Czech supporters. Zhdanov, he argued, had laid the plans to accompany these moves by a blockade of Berlin, but with the eclipse of the Leningraders, Malenkov assumed Zhdanov's work. The blockade had not come out of the blue. Motorists were required to have permits to go to Berlin as early as December 1947, and a number of intermediate steps preceded the full imposition of the blockade between June and August. Nicolaevsky later judged that attention had been kept on the blockade by Malenkov's design while the Chinese Communists went on a major offensive, taking Mukden in November and Peking by January, 1949. Malenkov had used the Berlin Blockade as a cover for the Chinese Revolution.[36]

Malenkov's work on a Central Committee Far Eastern Commission was said to have prepared the way for an onslaught of revolutionary insurgency in the East once Zhdanov's Western policy had failed. The revolution in the East had hung fire through the war because of the Soviet-Japanese neutrality pact of 1941–1945, which caused Mao Tse-tung and Ho Chi Minh to avoid battle with Japanese troops while husbanding their strength for future struggles. It has even been speculated that Ho cooperated with Subhas Chandra Bose, the pro–Axis Indian revolutionary who sought Japanese aid against the British in India.[37] Ho's armies did not engage the French and, while Ho sought friendly relations with the United States, he restrained his people through most of the Zhdanov period, a full fight with the French breaking out only at the end of 1946. As France turned toward Britain and the United States, the Indochina war became fiercer. With Mao's victory in China, the Soviets and the Chinese both emerged as material supporters of the Vietminh. There was even an element of Sino-Soviet competition for primacy in that role.[38]

Nicolaevsky supposed that Malenkov had imbibed Stalin's geopolitical view, as laid out by Haushofer, according to which Russia and Germany, with their Eastern alliances, would expand against the West.

Stalin's Last Turn

Zhdanov had been in favor of Western proletarian revolutions, and Malenkov in favor of Eastern guerrilla wars, said Nicolaevsky. Out of this estimate there developed further suggestions about the relation between Kremlin faction struggles and Chinese Communism. Nicolaevsky was later to cite H. K. Konar, a pro-Chinese Indian Communist, to the effect that Mao's quarrel with Khrushchev had begun because of the special favor with which the Chinese leader had regarded Malenkov and Beria. It has also been suggested that Mao considered Zhdanov responsible for the policy line designed to hold him in check in 1945–1947.[39] There was at any rate reason to think that the Chinese Communist would be pleased by the rise of Malenkov.

At first Malenkov presented the sharpest contrast with the urbane, ideological Zhdanov, who was as dapper in appearance as Malenkov was drab. But Stalin had indicated on numerous occasions a fondness for Malenkov—this despite the occasional charges to the effect that he was indifferent to matters other than production and even somewhat lax ideologically.[40] Nikolaevsky considered him the author of Earl Browder's liquidation of the U.S. Communist party in 1943. Malenkov's defense of the industrial managers suggests that he was a supporter of what was called the Moscow line, in the tradition of Rykov. His bitter relations with Zhdanov and his criticism of the ideologists in favor of practical managerial skill lead to that conclusion. However, Malenkov could do little programmatic trailblazing while Stalin was still on the scene.

The aging dictator retained most of his powers to the end. He may have suffered a stroke or heart attack in 1944 or 1945, which caused special attention to the state of his health, supervision of which was entrusted to Beria, Malenkov and Shcherbakov.[41] Khrushchev relates his increasing lapses of memory, his forgetting Bulganin's name, dictating ill-advised orders which his subordinates tactfully refrain from carrying out, with the result that Stalin would simply lose track of his original intention.[42] The impression of a doddering tyrant has prompted the view, expressed by some Western diplomats and politicians who saw him and, to some extent, by scholarly literature, that Stalin was out of control of affairs and in some ways a prisoner of his subordinates. Without denying the inevitable decline of his faculties, this view should be qualified. To refrain from taking part in the step-by-step formation of policy alternatives, and to abstain from their polemical defense, was the essence of his style of rule, his 'Leninism.' He had, moreover, lived for almost two decades under extraordinary tension, much of which was released by his victory in the war. At the pinnacle of his achievements, he seems to have been badly disappointed that he could not enjoy the orgy of adulation his subordinates arranged for him. Praise only bored him. He had long promoted the idea that his enemies were clever enough to hide behind expressions of unqualified enthusiasm for him and his projects. So whom could he believe?

Moreover, since plots against him derived from failed oppositions having no other recourse but terror, as the Moscow trials had instructed the nation in regard to the ecumenical bloc of 1932, one could expect the desire to kill Stalin to emerge from the slightest policy difference. Thus, when a policy turn was made, it no doubt made sense to Stalin to shoot those whose line was being abandoned, as a kind of preventive action. It also made sense for those around him to feed his fears, as Khrushchev says that Beria and Malenkov did in regard to the Zhdanovists, since *moderantisme* had long been regarded as a sign of disloyalty. It may be useless to ask if he really set store by the numerous conspiracies he constantly unearthed. Undoubtedly the habit of thinking and speaking about these to subordinates who agreed with every stray suspicion had sapped his critical faculties to the point where the purge became a kind of psychological dependency. He had arrested not only political opponents and other troublesome people over the years but also those of whose company he had grown tired. Beria obligingly arrested numerous members of his wives' families whom he no longer wished to see.

Of the disappointments in attaining such an exalted position of power, the greatest was that no body of theory that could genuinely be called Stalinist had been contributed by the leader of genius. Stalin lusted to make good this deficiency, seeking to create a theory of linguistics which would integrate into Marxism the idea of the primacy of language in general and the Russian language in particular, encouraging the campaign in behalf of Lysenko's biological theories and, most important, attempting to lay down for his successors an economic theory comparable in its effect to that of the last writings of Lenin on the problems of the NEP period. Because of the ideological prominence of the Leningraders, it was necessary that this effort be part of the campaign to rout them.

The fall of Zhdanov led to the Leningrad affair of 1949, in which thousands of party members were accused of a plot against the Central Committee. Malenkov and Beria had seemed to suffer most from the earlier promotion of Kuznetsov, Kosygin, Voznesenskii, and other associates of Zhdanov. Khrushchev tells of Malenkov and Beria manipulating reports to Stalin in such a way as to give evidence of a plot.[43] Beria is said to have been particularly worried about Voznesenskii. While chairman of State Planning, Voznesenskii is said to have sought a redistribution of appropriations that would have challenged the budget allocations for commissariats under Beria. This would have included the vast forced labor empire and perhaps the nuclear weapons program. Voznesenskii's critique of Varga's economic ideas thus loomed as a bid for theoretical primacy that would have put Beria in the shade both theoretically and practically.

Khrushchev relates the following about Voznesenskii as he was sentenced to death:

> Voznesensky stood and spewed hatred against Leningrad. He cursed the day he had set foot in the city when he came there to study from the Donbas. He said that Leningrad had already had its share of conspiracies; it had been subjected to all varieties of reactionary influence, from Biron to Zinoviev.[44]

From Biron to Zinoviev? What was Voznesenskii saying? Khrushchev professed to be dumbfounded and concluded that Voznesenskii had lost his mind. The Biron to which Voznesenskii referred was Count von Bühren, leader of the party of Baltic Germans who dominated court life and policy during the reign of Empress Anna in the early eighteenth century. The 'yoke of the Germans,' the *Bironovshchina*, continued through her reign, and featured a foreign policy designed to work with Austria to gain influence at the expense of Sweden, Poland, and Turkey. When the 'Germans' were finally swept aside in the 1740s by the 'Russian' party at court, the foreign policy line became more pro-French. Voznesenskii may have been thinking about the pro-German visage of the Leningrad line during the period of the Zinoviev Comintern, and comparing it to Zhdanov's National Bolshevism on the German question, or he may simply have been emphasizing the conspiratorial aspect of the Zhdanov faction's activities.[45]

Voznesenskii was, at any rate, unfortunate to have been associated with the Leningraders, and still less fortunate to have gained a reputation for being an 'economic wizard,' as Khrushchev put it, at precisely the time when Stalin was preparing an intervention in the field of economic theory. Voznesenskii had just begun work on a textbook, *The Political Economy of Communism*, when he was dismissed from all his posts in March 1949. He continued to work on the book while in the state of limbo described in Khrushchev's memoirs, during which he attended dinners at Stalin's dacha, but on its completion, in October, he was arrested.[46] Voznesenskii's discomfiture also provided an opening for Suslov to make his mark as his critic. Suslov, who had been brought up with the party revival, now demonstrated his political independence of ties to the Leningraders and his Varga-like talent for unobtrusively backing the Master in theoretical polemics. He had some background in disputation about economics, apparently having been among those Stalinists who had routed the Bukharinists at the Institute of Red Professors in the early thirties. As we know from a 1952 article of his, he called Voznesenskii's *War Economy of the USSR During the Great Patriotic War* an 'anti-Marxist book.' He may also have played a role in a secret meeting against the book in 1951, which served as a preparation for Stalin's own treatise, *Economic Problems of Socialism in the USSR*.[47] Thus the fall of the Zhdanovites was also the rise of Stalin's new theoretical synthesis, which would be unveiled by the Nineteenth Party Congress in 1952.

The notions contained in Stalin's last documents give indications that he was seeking at the end of his life to distance himself from formulations of the competing factions and to raise himself above all of his recent associates in the way that he had vis-à-vis the Old Bolsheviks in 1936–1938. The economic position was not particularly daring, or even, as he admitted in *Economic Problems of Socialism*, very original.[48] It was a mistake, he explained, to speak of changing or transcending economic laws, in particular the law of value, which in view of widespread commodity production, for example in the *kolkhoz* system, would be in effect for some time. On the other hand, it was wrong to make a fetish of the law of value by imagining it to govern the Soviet economy. That would mean the end of the primacy of heavy industry over consumer goods production. Stalin thus declared independence of those who, like Voznesenskii, extolled the virtues of state planning in terms of the miracles wrought by the wartime emergency measures. He also revealed his hostility to those who sought a turn to consumerism. Stalin indicated his disdain for Ostrovitianov, Gatovskii, and other critics of Varga. He limited and qualified his own statements about the dissolution of the contradiction between mental and manual labor. And he restated the central thesis of his essays of 1924–1925 on Socialism in One Country. Without unearthing that phrase, he stated unequivocally that the Soviet successes depended on 'moral support' from the world proletariat, specifically reminding his listeners that the peace movement would be the future locus for demonstrations of this moral support by proletarians of other countries. At the end of his life he was justifying his own brand of internationalism against the traditions of Trotsky and Zinoviev.

These departures in the realm of theory were being accompanied by a wave of purges that threatened everyone in Stalin's entourage. The purges of the Titoists and 'national deviationists' might be like the Leningrad purge of 1936 and serve as a prelude to an attack on the right. Stalin had originally intended that pro-Soviet elements in Yugoslavia would overthrow Tito, but Tito isolated and purged Hebrang and Zujovic, who had taken Stalin's side. Then in May 1949, Koci Xoxe, the Albanian vice premier, was put on trial for his leadership of a pro-Tito faction in the Albanian party. Xoxe was accused of building Trotskyism in Albania and of spreading the malicious idea that Stalin had encouraged Tito to annex Albania.[49] Hoxha was able to rid himself of an old rival. In September,

Laszlo Rajk, the Hungarian foreign minister, was put on trial, accused of a conspiracy which had originated during the Spanish Civil War. In December it was the turn of Traicho Kostov in Bulgaria. These and others fell in the European theater of the Leningrad affair. Real Titoism was less an issue in these trials of national deviationists than local rivalries,[50] but Stalin was exorcising the demons of partisan revolutionism, in favor of those who had spent the war in the institutes of the ex-Comintern.

These latter were Beria protégés, and at first it seemed that the purge would place Beria and his lieutenants in an excellent position from which to view the passing of the now frequently ill tyrant and perhaps, after that much-awaited moment, to liquidate the alliance with Malenkov much as Stalin had earlier done with Bukharin. The other old Stalinists seemed to be conveniently passing from the scene. Molotov, Mikoyan, and Bulganin all lost their government posts at the same time that the doomed Voznesenskii was removed from Gosplan, in March 1949. The most important of these, Molotov, apparently fell because of the shift of Soviet policy on Israel, and because of the activities of his wife, Polina. She was Jewish, corresponding regularly with a sister who had lived in Palestine for many years, and had been active on the Anti-Fascist Committee of Soviet Jews formed during the war. She was also highly respected by the leadership, the only woman, Khrushchev relates, regularly seen in the mostly male gatherings of the top leaders. Her being Jewish did not hurt until the victory of the fight for Israeli independence, originally supported by Moscow as a means of weakening British positions in the period when it was hoped that the United States was also anti-British.[51] In 1948, however, Golda Meir's visit to the Soviet Union prompted mass demonstrations of sympathy from Soviet Jews. Stalin was apparently frightened by this development and ordered the arrest of most of the members of the Anti-Fascist Committee, Polina among them. Molotov abstained on the vote to arrest Polina. That Polina had once been the intimate of Stalin's wife, Nadezhda Alliluieva, cannot have helped her cause, as she may have been suspected of knowing too much about the murky circumstances of Alliluieva's death.

So, with the Leningraders disposed of and the first-generation Stalinists on the wane, Beria seemed to be riding high. By August, he found his way to his greatest achievement. The nuclear program, which had been laboring under his supervision, finally conducted a successful test of a bomb-like device, ending the American monopoly. Beria could claim that his espionage efforts had made it all possible. There might also be hope for an eventual testing of a hydrogen bomb, work on which extended directly from the first nuclear test. Physicist Andrei Sakharov later reported that he was at work on a hydrogen bomb, which the Soviets were not able to test until 1953, already in 1948.[52] The United States had not made the program for the 'Super,' that is, the hydrogen bomb, an extension of the Manhattan project, and at the time of the Soviet test, was locked in a debate about the matter. Beria may have encouraged Stalin to think that they were going to pass America technologically by going directly to the Super.

There were reasons to think that Soviet Communism, if it measured its moves and did not succumb to adventurism, might soon have the military basis for considerable international gains. True, the Americans would soon embark on their own program for a Super, and the British had arrested Klaus Fuchs, who had been giving the Soviets information gleaned from his work on the Manhattan project. The Europeans, in the wake of the Berlin airlift, were looking to their defenses, and the Americans would look to a combined program of atomic armament and conventional mobilization. But they could not defend everywhere now that the greatest threat was no longer their monopoly.

During the early months of 1950, Stalin had meetings with Mao and Kim Il Sung. Khrushchev tells us that he gave the green light to Kim for a lightning campaign to unify the two Koreas.[53] Mao's role in this decision remains obscure. By the end of the year, Stalin's optimism was subjected to severe test. The campaign was met by American resistance, despite all rational calculation, and, after the Inchon landing, the American drive to the Yalu River had forced Chinese intervention. Mao may have been reluctant to antagonize the United States merely in order to shield the Soviet Union from direct participation and responsibility.[54] A year later, the lines had stabilized and the bitterest battles of the war commenced, battles which recalled the 1914–1918 war in their ferocity and insignificance in terms of terrain. This was not what Stalin had been led to expect. Moreover, the West was now mobilizing militarily, and anti-Communist vigilance dominated the American domestic scene. Soviet calculation seemed to have failed along a broad front.

Had too much confidence been placed in Beria? The question must have crossed Stalin's mind at this time. One way or another, Beria controlled the entire state security apparatus, the former Comintern, now under the aegis of the Ministry of State Security (MGB), the nuclear program, and much of Stalin's personal staff, down to the Georgian cooks. Khrushchev's being brought in to head the Moscow city apparatus at the end of 1949 seems to suggest that he was to be a counterweight to Malenkov and Beria. Khrushchev's schemes for agriculture, the amalgamation of *kolkhozy* and the plan for 'agro-towns,' had encountered the determined resistance of Beria. Khrushchev had, moreover, been brought immediately into the Secretariat along with Malenkov and Suslov, while Beria was outside. In the course of the wave of purges already under way, Stalin was making a turn, much as he had made in 1937. At the end of 1951, the purge began to menace Beria, its initial benefactor. This was not completely incomprehensible if one remembered the career of Iagoda.

Beria's man at the MGB, V. S. Abakumov, whom Nicolaevsky suspected of masterminding the Leningrad affair, was arrested. Slansky and Geminder, Beria's associates from the war years, were arrested in Prague. In Georgia, the Mingrelian affair was exposed and many arrests were being made. Beria attempted to take charge of the campaign with his customary brutality, but he must have known, from the experience of Zinoviev, Bukharin, and Zhdanov, that he who escapes by accusing his own supporters is on borrowed time. Nicolaevsky supposed that the turn had occurred because of the change of line on Israel, and that Abakumov, Slansky, and the others had come into disfavor because of their work in directing aid to Israel in 1947–1948.[55] Perhaps this explains Khrushchev's efforts in his memoirs to condemn Stalin for anti-Semitism and to deny that he shared this prejudice. He may have had difficulty facing the fact that this atmosphere worked very much to his profit at the end of Stalin's life.

The last phase of the purge, the case of the Doctors' Plot, centering on the charge that 'doctors-poisoners' had killed Zhdanov and plotted against Stalin and the other Kremlin leaders, was announced in January and continued until mid-February, 1953, days before Stalin's death. Nicolaevsky saw in the Doctors' Plot a purge of enormous dimensions, a 'second Ezhovshchina,' designed to promote a radical turn in domestic and international policy. The schemes for amalgamation of the *kolkhozy* seemed to recall the turn toward collectivization in 1927–1928. Nicolaevsky put it for a rule of thumb, one of the few to be found in his writings, that the more radical the agricultural policy, the more radical the foreign policy. He saw the U.S.S.R. preparing for war.[56]

In the eyes of Nicolaevsky, Khrushchev was and would henceforth remain a man of the Doctors' Plot, a representative of the radical policies of Stalin's last years or, in terms used in this study, a proponent of the Leningrad line. The revival of Zhdanovism at the time of the last anti-Beria purge seems to add weight to this view. Nicolaevsky was puzzled, however, about the role of Malenkov. On occasion he referred to Malenkov as the victim of the second Ezhovshchina, but eventually he settled on the view that the purge had been aimed at some of Malenkov's men but not at Malenkov himself.[57] Apparently, Stalin was simply trying to cleanse Malenkov, who remained the heir, of the influence of Beria. Stalin may have feared that Beria would dominate Malenkov one day and, while he still regarded Malenkov as the most cultured of his potential successors (as at one time he had probably regarded Zhdanov), he may have wished to place around the prince the best supporting cast. Khrushchev could not be regarded lightly, but was probably too *nekulturnyi* for the top job himself, and for precisely that reason he might have seemed the ideal 'counter-heir.'[58]

Yet Khrushchev was himself by no means secure. He later professed to have been baffled at the list of members of a new, enlarged Praesidium, designated by the 1952 Congress to replace the old Politburo. In the secret speech given to the Twentieth Congress in 1956, he left no doubt that Stalin's purpose had been to facilitate removal of the older members, but in his memoirs he claims that Stalin could not have known all the members and alternates on the list, and he concludes that the list must have been given Stalin by Kaganovich.[59] When one thinks of Kaganovich's actions in the thirties, it is not surprising that the major leaders were expecting the worst. Even before the purge could do its work, it became evident among the leaders who the chosen were. Stalin usually did not convene the enlarged Praesidium, nor even a smaller bureau of nine. Instead, he conducted business with four associates: Malenkov, Beria, Bulganin, and Khrushchev. Thus he had spurned the old Stalinists, and indeed all generalists, and preferred to meet with those who controlled the state, police, army, and party. He might determine the balance among these by the action of Poskrebyshev and his personal secretariat, who were weakening Malenkov and Beria at the end. Yet the delicacy of the balance among individuals does not suggest that Stalin was trying to prepare a smooth succession. On the contrary, fresh from his theoretical triumph at the Nineteenth Congress, he seemed to be taking moves to enhance his own prerogative. After his seven-minute speech to the congress, he had exulted in the wings: 'you see, I can still do it.' Most of his comrades nevertheless had to hope secretly that he was wrong and that the physical laws would prevail. Khrushchev was not one of these. 'Far from looking forward to Stalin's death,' he tells us, 'I actually feared it.'[60]

Malenkov and Khrushchev

The death of Stalin sharply focused the attention of the world on the politics of the Kremlin. Hopes were immediately raised for an improvement of East-West relations. Winston Churchill looked to a 'spontaneous and healthy evolution' in Russia and urged a conference at the soonest moment. He hoped for an 'easement of our relations for the next few years,' on the conclusion of an agreement on Korea and an Austrian treaty.[61] For many, the death of Stalin suggested the question of whether one could speak about totalitarianism without personal dictatorship. For others, the subtraction of Stalin would show decisively the institutional basis of Stalinist totalitarianism.

The closure of a historical experience seemed to demand of the authors of Stalin biographies some overall perspectives. Isaac Deutscher had provided his *Stalin: A Political Biography* in 1949 with its assessment of Stalin as a composite of Cromwell, Robespierre, and Bonaparte. 'Every revolution,' he wrote to the *Observer*'s David Astor, 'has gone through its phase of totalitarian degeneration, no matter what the moral philosophy of its leaders. The Puritan Christian Cromwell, the idealist–rationalist Robespierre, and the materialist Stalin were all totalitarian dictators guilty of similar crimes and responsible for similar achievements.[62] Deutscher continued Trotsky's incidental use of 'totalitarian' in the context of the latter's ideas about the comparison of the Russian and the French revolutions. Once Stalin's dictatorship was seen as a part of the Russian Revolution, it could no longer be properly grouped with the dictatorship of Hitler, which, Deutscher fervently believed, was connected with no revolution of any sort. For Deutscher, 'totalitarianism' signified simply a regime of excess, but never a historically specific, and historically recent, reworking of the relation of state to economy and society, as it had for Hilferding.

Moreover, the totalitarianism of the Soviet system, without Stalin's personal dictatorship, must soon give way to 'de-Stalinization by Stalinists,' by analogy with the attitude of the Tsar Aleksandr, in the 1850s, that it was better to abolish serfdom from above than to wait until it abolished itself from below.[63] Deutscher imagined a great pressure on the Soviet leaders to return to the pre-Stalin regime of Leninist internationalism. Deutscher also argued that Stalin had passed on to his successors the dynamic of the Russian Revolution, in a distorted form to be sure. Nevertheless, the postwar expansion of Communism was taken as proof of an idea of Deutscher's which, despite his fealty to the literary legacy of Trotsky, most estranged him from the Trotskyists: the idea that Stalinism was a continuation of the Left Opposition program of 1927. Through Stalin, by an irony of history, the program of Trotsky had been brought to fruition. While the Trotskyists clung to Trotsky's formula of Stalinism being 'counter-revolutionary through and through,' Deutscher thought instead that the postwar successes of Communism showed that Socialism in One Country had been buried for good.[64] For Deutscher, the analysis of Trotsky collapsed in the face of Stalin's left turns, such as the Third Period, 1928–1933, and the party revival of 1945–1946. No one at this time had thought to suggest an idea of 'dynamic bureaucracy,' so Deutscher felt he was on firm ground in recognizing the dynamic in Stalinism. Later he would judge it to reside in Maoism.

Despite his considerable influence on the eminent historian of the Russian Revolution, E. H. Carr, while the latter was writing his multivolume work on that subject, Deutscher could not convince Carr that the Soviet state was essentially the embodiment of the revolutionary hopes of 1917. Carr remained for Deutscher too much the devotee of *realpolitik*, inclined to view Russian Leninism as an infantile disorder of Russian Bolsheviks as they learned to manage the Russian state. Socialism in One Country thus became the crucial benchmark in this learning process. Much as he had derided the moralists of the thirties in *The Twenty Years Crisis* (1939) for failing to find a way to negotiate with Nazism, Carr sought to emphasize the possibilities of negotiation with a Soviet Union which had long since, in 1925, passed its sobriety test. Deutscher attributed this to Carr's Anglo-Saxon practicality. Carr was 'inclined to take note and learn from criticism,' Deutscher wrote to Brandler, but it was hard for him to 'get out of his skin, theoretically and ideologically,' so steeped was he in English empiricism.[65]

If Deutscher still sought the key to Soviet succession politics in the dynamic of the Russian Revolution, Souvarine was more and more seeking it in Russian and Slavic tradition. He was influenced in this direction by his friend N. V. Volskii (Valentinov), a former Menshevik who had known Lenin in Swiss exile and who had broken with him on his criticism of Mach and Avenarius in 1909, largely because he, Volskii, took their epistemology seriously and considered Lenin's criticism primitive. Volskii nevertheless wrote on Lenin with great authority and sensitivity.[66] An editor of a Soviet trade periodical until 1930, he knew many leading Communists and continued to write on Soviet economy, largely from a position of sympathy for the Bukharinist position, until his death in 1964. Volskii thought that Lenin's Marxism was antithetical to the Marxism of the First International, with the latter's easy accommodation to Western labour politics. Russian Leninism had been formed by the other Marx, the one who had written to Vera Zasulich in 1881 that socialism might be possible in Russia if accompanied by a Western proletarian revolution, the one who had been interpreted by Chernyshevskii, and through the latter, by Lenin.[67] Thus Bolshevism was long under the influence of native Russian radicalism, with its contempt for the patient evolution of Western traditions and its desire for an end to European tutelage. In Stalin, thought Volskii, this radicalism made its rendezvous with Russian traditions derived from her Byzantine past. For Volskii this included the fifteenth century idea that Russia was the Third Rome, destined to rally a world bereft of the leadership of Rome and Constantinople.[68]

Volskii was particularly fascinated by the affair of the Doctor's Plot, which had dominated Stalin's last days, because it shared so many common themes with the purges of the thirties. Volskii had good information on the latter from Valerian Mezhlauk, president of Gosplan and a Central Committee member, who had been shot in 1938. This led him to conclude that the affair of the Kremlin doctors was an extension of the purge of rights in 1938. The medical motif reminded him of two of the 1938 accused, Professor Pletnev and Dr. Levin, who had possessed information, supposedly, about Stalin's having killed his wife in 1932 and, in addition, had diagnosed the dictator clinically paranoid in 1938.[69]

The notion of Stalin's insanity had an influence on Souvarine, as did all of Volskii's ideas. Moreover, beginning in April, 1953, *Life* began to publish installments from the manuscript of former NKVD official Aleksandr Orlov, who had fled to the West years earlier. Orlov's book was one of the most detailed and suggestive sources of information on the conduct of the purges in the thirties, and contained references to the 'medical assassinations' of 1938.[70] For Souvarine, the suggestion of Stalin's insanity was an almost superfluous addition to the extended comparison he had made in *Staline* between the splendid Georgian and Ivan the Terrible. Where Deutscher saw the continuing influence of Westernizing trends introduced by the Russian Revolution, Souvarine saw the implacable revenge of a timeless Russia.

The Russian Question continued to have its fascination. Nicolaevsky maintained his interest in the nature and destiny of the Soviet system. But he seemed to be even more interested in the patterns discovered in Kremlin politics. It was, after all, the only politics taking place in the Soviet Union. Nor was he consumed by the issue of Stalinism without Stalin, de-Staliniz-ation, and the like, which so exercised the minds of other students of Soviet reality. There had been a continuous struggle for power under Stalin, even when Stalin towered over all those taking part in it, so there would be a struggle, perhaps in terms of the same programmatic patterns, once Stalin was gone. Nicolaevsky seemed to appreciate the pattern of Kremlin politics and to regard the post-Stalin struggle, as did many others, as the central focus of interest.

The factional struggle had raged under Stalin; it seemed reasonable to conclude that it would rage after Stalin. The contestants were legatees of a polemical tradition almost as old as the Soviet regime and had little choice but to continue in their fight to master the Soviet alternance. There was now, however, no longer any center. That position which every contest-ant cherished was now vacant, but no one could claim it. They would have to fight in their old programmatic trenches until one of them could reach the point of enjoying the luxury and feeling the necessity to change positions as Lenin and Stalin had. And the Stalin group would be suitably reduced, of course. Poskrebyshev disappeared; Suslov lost influence immediately. There could be no genuine continuity, unless the leaders were to designate one of their own as 'leader of genius.' Doing that for Malenkov would have solved the problem. It had apparently been pro-vided that Malenkov would head the state and party machinery on Stalin's death, and since Stalin's death also meant the liquidation of the affair of the Kremlin doctors, Beria's position could be secured by combining the MGB and MVD under his aegis. Molotov, widely considered a possible successor to Stalin, was saved from victimization in the 'second Yezhov-shchina' and given the foreign ministry, but at least for the present, the general intention seemed to be to bury him politically.[71]

Beria had been unable, or perhaps more likely unready, to seize supreme power in the first days, as he concentrated MVD troops in the capital. He may, however, have had a hand in the measures taken to concentrate Malenkov's power in the state machinery and to balance the latter in the party by Khrushchev. That Malenkov was willing to appear primarily as a spokesman for the government suggests that the atmosphere was not one of party revival. It is likely, as Robert Conquest suggests, that Beria moved to concentrate party and state machinery in Malenkov's hands, while he secured the police apparatus, on March 6, and then a week later combined with the rest of the leadership to remove Malenkov from control of the party.[72]

Beria's liquidation of the Doctors' Plot affair implied the dismissal of S. D. Ignatiev, who had prosecuted the matter up to Stalin's death, as head of the MGB. The Western press saw Ignatiev chiefly as an appointee of Stalin and Malenkov, so his fall was perceived as evidence of struggle between Malenkov and Beria. Nicolaevsky dismissed this idea, perhaps too quickly, by pointing out that Ignatiev had risen during the party revival of 1945–1946 as Malenkov slipped. Nor was Ignatiev a Zhdanovist, or he would have perished in the Leningrad affair. By a process of exclusion, Nicolaevsky made him part of Poskrebyshev's apparatus, destruction of which was the order of the day. The idea of a Poskrebyshev apparatus, appearing throughout Nicolaevsky's writings from this period, seems doubtful, but it was, in effect, a way of referring to a Stalin center independent of Malenkovists and Leningraders. While there is no reason to doubt Khrushchev's testimony on the oceanic nature of Beria's ambitions, the latter, as a Georgian and Stalin's most visible police figure, needed the protective coloration of collective leadership while he attempted to build a series of political positions for the fight ahead.[73]

These were positions in the spirit of what we have called the Moscow line. Beria followed the logic indicated by his counter-purge in Georgia to undo the Mingrelian affair; he reinstated local leadership not only in Georgia but in the Ukraine, Belorussia, and the Baltic states as well. The rule was that local nationals rather than Russians would hold the top posts. With this went a new course for the East German regime, emphasizing the production of consumer goods, with Beria protégés such as Wilhelm Zaisser threatening the rule of Walter Ulbricht. Nicolaevsky later judged that Churchill's call for negotiation with the Soviet leaders had been a result of feelers from Beria.[74] Beria had been the real author of both the de-Stalinization and the tenuous turn toward détente later associated with Malenkov.

The revolt in East Berlin in June provided the occasion for the rest of the Soviet leadership, who must have feared Beria (despite, or perhaps because of, his moderate actions), to solve the problem of Beria for good. Khrushchev relates his own efforts to build the cabal, his recruitment of Malenkov, and the assembly of a case against Beria, a case which already apparently mentioned the Leningrad affair—hardly an encouraging development for Malenkov. The arrest and execution of Beria, announced in December, thus strengthened Khrushchev's hand appreciably. In taking advantage of the antagonism between Molotov and Beria, dating to the period of the Leningrad affair, Khrushchev had put together a combination that would serve as well against Malenkov.

Nicolaevsky assumed a falling-out between Malenkov and Beria. He thought that Beria had been particularly eager to put an end to the anti-Semitic side of the Doctors' Plot purge, while Malenkov had been indifferent, his main intention drawn to protecting the managerial apparatus. With Beria gone, Malenkov struck out on his own, amplifying the promise of a new course; the apparatus of heavy industry had already been established, he said; now was the time to devote more attention to supplying the Soviet consumer with high-quality goods and better and more plentiful foodstuffs. Khrushchev did not seem to disagree. Even while the major thrust of Malenkov's policy would be maintained by the state machinery, Khrushchev would mobilize the party to implement the New Course. By February 1954, this took the form of the Virgin Lands program to increase grain yields in Kazakhstan and Western Siberia. This campaign was an ideal one for Khrushchev to use for a party revival among the local apparatchiks and youth. Whoever doubted the chances of this project could be denounced as a Bukharinite. Moreover, as in 1928–1929, the tour de force in agriculture required a tour de force in industry as well. Tractors had to be produced for the new farms, the production of which made further demands on heavy industry and undermined the consumerism of the New Course. It was party against state, Zinovievism against Bukharinism, Leningrad against Moscow.

Yet something new may have tipped the balance in this struggle: the intervention of the military, which had counted for nothing politically since 1937, or perhaps since 1925. The generals' participation in the anti-Beria plot may have been because of their alarm at the effect of the New Course on the occupation armies in Eastern Europe. They were no doubt also fearful of the effect of the consumer goods program on military procurement. All this was symbolized in a dispute over a statement by a military associate of Malenkov, M. Gus, shortly after the successful Soviet test of a hydrogen bomb in August, 1953. He had spoken of the 'paralyzing of the law of the inevitability of war.' Malenkov amplified this in March, 1954, to the point of demanding an end to the Cold War, judging it to be preparation for another world war, which would surely signal the 'destruction of world civilization.'[75] Communists liked to depict it as an argument over whether or not nuclear weapons observe the class principle: Do they kill capitalists only, or both capitalists and Communists? Malenkov apparently thought it perfectly safe to range himself with the second opinion.

This underlines the impression that the Soviets were at an important crossroads in foreign and defense policy, seeking an end to the tension of the Korean War and the standoff in Europe. The willingness of the leadership to discipline its Asian allies for the sake of its European security was demonstrated in May, 1954, after the Vietminh victory over the French at Dien Bien Phu. The Soviets induced Chou En-lai to persuade Ho Chi Minh to content himself with control over only the north of Vietnam. The Soviets wanted French Gaullist votes against the pending European Defense Community, votes which they hoped thus would retard German rearmament.

The Soviets were making a reassessment of Stalin's very primitive, Kutuzov-like war doctrines, which included the notion that nuclear weapons were not decisive in war. Stalin's successors immediately dropped that idea, and the military insisted, moreover, that it must be prepared to fight a war in which nuclear weapons were used at the outset, the factor of surprise thus being elevated to the decisive role. Khrushchev and the military men got their best reinforcement from the actions of the British and American governments, which adopted defense policies reliant on nuclear weapons in 1952 and 1953. Western policy seemed to show that, of the two types of crises it had faced since the war, it preferred Berlins to Koreas, that is, it preferred nuclear confrontations to conventional wars. The impression must have further developed in Soviet minds when the American use of nuclear weapons was broached over Korea (March–May 1953), Indochina (May 1954), and the Taiwan Straits (March 1955). Malenkov's natural dread of nuclear war may have seemed unexceptional, but Khrushchev was able to rally the generals to the proposition that the atomic bomb obeyed the class principle and that the nuclear war would result in the destruction of 'imperialism' only. After he had got to the top, he would feel free to make statements like Malenkov's, but for the moment, he knew he could appeal to the military with the idea that war-fighting and deterrence were related and that security was enhanced by optimism about victory in nuclear war.

It is not sure what issues finally produced Malenkov's resignation as chairman of the Council of Ministers in February, 1955. If one assumes, as Nicolaevsky did, a struggle between the beneficiaries of the Leningrad affair and the potential beneficiaries of the affair of the Doctors' Plot, the former no doubt won a victory with the arrest and shooting of Mikhail Riumin, a subordinate of Ignatiev, in July 1954. Nicolaevsky thought that Ignatiev might have been a 'cover' for Riumin, the real director of the second Yezhovshchina.[76] Malenkov may have got the upper hand temporarily, perhaps in a dispute over the implementation of agricultural plans. At any rate, this was soon reversed by the arrest and shooting of Abakumov, announced in December, for his role, the reports said, in the Leningrad affair. This seemed to follow the logic of the renewal of persecutions of Patrascanu and Ana Pauker in Romania and of the Czech Communists associated with Slansky. These were all people who had been under attack in 1951–1952.[77]

To gain this victory, Khrushchev must have had the support of Molotov and perhaps other of the old Stalinists. Molotov had been an architect of the policies of the 1928–1933 period, of which Khrushchev's policies were reminiscent. He may have been induced, in the spirit of Stalin's *Economic Problems of Socialism*, to resist the Beria-Malenkov consumerism and other efforts to relax the agricultural regime. He may also have had little choice but to combine with any forces capable of weakening Malenkov, that is, if he still entertained ambitions for himself.

Deutscher believed Molotov to be responsible both for the Korean cease-fire and for the Indochina deal at Geneva.[78] Soviet foreign policy no doubt had in mind obstruction of the task the United States had taken on, that of strengthening alliances in Europe and the Far East. The Geneva arrangement had the virtue of acting against NATO by striking indirectly at the EDC while at the same time restraining the Vietminh so that the Asian neutrals would not be frightened into the newly created SEATO. During 1954, Soviet propaganda began to heap praise on Nehru and his views regarding neutralism between the superpower blocs. Molotov could not have done this out of respect for Stalinist orthodoxy, which had usually described politicians such as Nehru as petit–bourgeois nationalists and therefore tools of imperialism. Molotov could only have acted from expediency in view of the threat posed by American alliance-building.

Yet there too was a logic which worked for Khrushchev in the next stage of his struggle to rise above both the Malenkov group and the old Stalinists. Khrushchev and Bulganin would simply ease their policy toward their allies and widen their contacts with neutrals, as if by logical extension of the policy pursued by Beria and Malenkov. Already in October 1954, Khrushchev promised Mao a Soviet withdrawal from Port Arthur, Sinkiang, and Manchuria, and agreed to an exchange of technical information on nuclear energy. To show their goodwill, the Soviets transferred to China control over their joint-stock companies mining uranium and thorium in Sinkiang since 1949.[79] They agreed with the Indonesian Communist D. N. Aidit's slogan for a coalition of Communist and national forces. They offered aid to both Indonesia and Burma. They discovered that the 'national bourgeoisie' in Asia was a progressive force. They encouraged Egypt and Syria against the British-sponsored Baghdad pact. They neutralized Austria. Finally, they made their bid to patch up the quarrel with Tito. If they could bring the world's Communists together again, they might regain the energy and momentum of the international movement and exploit the anticolonial spirit by speaking in its modern Cold-War language of neutralism and nonalignment.

Khrushchev seems to have considered Tito essential to opening up this path toward unity with the nonaligned movement. Unfortunately for him, he could not go back to the situation of 1948 to seek reconciliation. Titoism had continued to evolve, in its relations with the West and in its evaluation of the Russian Question. In the first days after the break with Stalin, Tito and his associates had reopened many of the old questions. A representative of the American Trotskyists who visited Tito in 1950 reported a 'friendly attitude' toward Trotsky and Trotskyism. Tito apparently offered the view that the Trotskyists were 'good people but a little sectarian.'[80] It was Djilas who was most hostile. He rejected as well Pijade's idea that a bureaucracy had usurped power in the Soviet Union, as did Tito, who held that the Soviet Union remained socialist.[81] Everything, Tito had warned, depended on antagonism between East and West, without which Yugoslavia would be lost. Only the Soviets could attack Yugoslavia, Tito judged, and as long as there existed a Western alliance, they would be deterred. In the meantime the Yugoslavs set about the task of creating a new International, in place of the Cominform. Yugoslav Communists hoped that a new organization would include the socialists of the Third World, militant neutralists such as Nehru, and some left Social Democrats.[82]

This was the mood of the Titoists when Khrushchev made his famous trip to Yugoslavia in May 1955. He was in effect seeking a means of combining with the Bandung group of twenty-nine Asian and African nations which had met the previous month. Tito was reportedly close to Burma's U Nu. Both Tito and Mao had influence in Asia. Khrushchev hoped to coalesce or perhaps compete, and he appeared willing to go a considerable way toward Tito's idea of a new International. Khrushchev also sought to blame the break with Yugoslavia on the Russian alternance, that is, on Beria. He reports his 'disappointment' at the reaction of the Yugoslavs, who insisted that the heart of the matter had been Stalin himself.

Khrushchev found himself confronted with the Russian Question and forced to break new ground in order to defend his ambitious new policy and, at the same time, the rationale for his entire political career. He did so by relying on continuity with the Leningrader line. Reconciliation with Tito was already a sort of revival of Zhdanovism; the next step would be to take Stalin under criticism. Khrushchev was spurred on in his campaign of de-Stalinization by the opposition of Molotov and some of the other old Stalinists, probably including Kaganovich. They had been allies in the fight to save heavy industry from Malenkov. Now, for the sake of continuity, they defended the break with Tito, in which Molotov had played a key role. They also resisted viscerally the Titoist ideas about a new International in favor of one controlled from Moscow.

Molotov, in an address to the Supreme Soviet in February 1955, still maintained that Tito had been at least partially responsible for the split. After an angry protest by Tito, however, *Pravda* corrected its foreign minister in March. After the issue was thoroughly debated at the July plenum, Molotov recanted. In a letter to the Central Committee theoretical journal *Kommunist,* he withdrew his previous reference to the Soviet Union's having 'already laid the basis of a socialist society,' while some people's democracies were only in the 'first stage' of the process. He recognized, he said, that 'the Leninist question of "kto-kogo" (who-whom)' had been answered in the Soviet Union against capitalism by 1932, and the transition to Communism begun in 1939. Therefore his February formula was 'theoretically mistaken and politically harmful.'[83] The Yugoslavs, while accepting the rubric of 'people's democracy,' had always maintained that theirs was a dictatorship of the proletariat building socialism as had the Soviet Union. They rejected Varga's notions of East European state capitalism. Now Molotov was humbly withdrawing the claim to criticize either their path or the path of his Soviet colleagues seeking normalization of relations. He was, moreover, forced to use the same language that Kirov had used against him and Kaganovich in 1932.

Malenkov had to welcome the breakup of the combination of Khrushchev and Molotov, which had been so effective against him. He would be drawn to Molotov by the same logic that had driven Sokolnikov to Zinoviev in 1926. But Khrushchev and Bulganin needed help as well. Together they represented the party and the state and worked together, observed Boris Meissner, in much the same way as Lenin and Trotsky had in the early years. Yet their weakness before Molotov and Malenkov was that they were only practical men who could do little more than 'rummage around in ideology.'[84] For the next step in de-Stalinization, they would have to lean on their party ideologists.

Thus, while Khrushchev and Bulganin improvised their way through the politicial thicket, certain basic features of the Soviet regime, entirely obscured by Stalin's personal dictatorship, were emerging with clarity. The struggle of 1953–1954 had shown the importance of the party as opposed to the police or the state machinery. Now the struggle unfolding would demonstrate the importance of theory within the party. The rise of Suslov was an important feature of this demonstration. Suslov had suffered briefly after the death of Stalin and the collapse of the enlarged Praesidium, but he had never lost his post in the Secretariat. He was brought into the Praesidium as well as by the July 1955 plenum. This fact is not easy to square either with Khrushchev's admission that Suslov had been 'particularly adamant' against reconciliation with Tito or with Seweryn Bialer's testimony that the plenum had seen a bitter conflict between Khrushchev and Molotov over Titoism and neutralism.[85]

Khrushchev had taunted Molotov about Polina's Stalinist orthodoxy and about the 1939 pact with the Nazis.[86] It would seem that Suslov had supported Molotov on the Yugoslav question. No doubt Suslov's views on the importance of Moscow influence among the Communist parties were also closer to those of Molotov than to those of Khrushchev. It may be that Suslov and Kuusinen supported Molotov on the character of the new International but criticized his 'sectarianism' toward the 'peace bloc,' as they called the neutral states. And during the period before the Twentieth Congress, Khrushchev himself had begun to warn against 'revisionism,' understood to mean Titoism, a suggestion that Molotov's view, or perhaps Suslov's, was in the ascendant.

Nicolaevsky thought Khrushchev to be a consistent defender of the Stalin line of 1952–1953. He could not reconcile the Doctors' Plot and Khrushchev's secret speech to the Twentieth Congress denouncing Stalin. He judged, therefore, that the secret speech had been 'Tito's price' for assisting Soviet accord with the Third World's peace bloc. Deutscher thought that Khrushchev and Mikoyan had waged a struggle on the Stalin issue, with Mikoyan fighting for de-Stalinization in principle and Khrushchev merely trying to find his way through his factional threats.[87] It may be that Khrushchev was faced in 1955 with the same factional lineup that was to oppose him in 1957, at the time of the Anti-Party Group's challenge to his authority. He appears to have been pushed on by Mikoyan and perhaps Zhukov, and to have relied on the ideologist Pospelov and the aspirant to Molotov's position, Shepilov.

Regardless of whether Khrushchev was forced into his attack on Stalin, the solution he offered to the Russian Question was a cautious one intended not to disturb the political basis of Stalinism itself. The secret speech maintained that Stalin had been correct against all the oppositions up to 1932 but had made the mistake of wanting more than their political defeat. The Fourteenth and Fifteenth Party congresses had been correct, but the Moscow trials, and especially the army purge of 1937, had not. This was, Nicolaevsky argued, essentially the position of Kirov in 1932–1934: Stalinism without terror or personal dictatorship. Those who had risen with Stalin but feared his whim of iron could scarcely argue differently.

Khrushchev's secret speech nevertheless ruined his personal alliances in East Central Europe. In Hungary, Rákosi had taken advantage of Khrushchev's ascendancy over Beria and Malenkov to oust the proponent of the Hungarian New Course, Imre Nagy. Leaders such as Rákosi had been confident of Khrushchev's support but were undermined by the swell of revolt against Stalinism that followed in the wake of Khrushchev's disclosures. Nicolaevsky thought that Rákosi was removed at Tito's behest. Bierut died during the congress but Berman was removed shortly thereafter. The events of 1956, the Polish and Hungarian revolutions and the Anglo-French-Israeli attack on Suez, demonstrated the inadequacy and the danger of Khrushchev's leadership. The Polish events gave the Chinese an opportunity to intervene, on behalf of Gomulka rather than the pro-Soviet Natolin group, for the first time in East bloc affairs. The Hungarian revolt demonstrated not only the perils of Titoism, but that National Communism quickly leads to Djilasism, that is, to the renunciation of Communism. Perhaps the existence of the reclaimed lands in Pomerania and Silesia had restrained the Poles, and the absence of this factor encouraged Hungarian nationalism to defy the Warsaw pact.[88] At any rate, Khrushchev did not appear to be gaining control of affairs but losing it. The Suez affair also caused the Soviets to make nuclear threats against London and Paris, but ended by drawing the United States more energetically into Mideast affairs, a development which must have made Khrushchev's policy seem a disaster to his Praesidium colleagues.

Accordingly, during the spring of 1957, reports circulated of a comeback by Malenkov. Molotov, who had been replaced as foreign minister by Shepilov (to coincide with Tito's visit in June 1956), also enjoyed a renaissance. Shepilov had advertised the importance of the 'uncommitted areas' in criticizing Molotov's sectarianism and had especially urged reconciliation with Egypt's Nasser, whom Nicolaevsky saw as Moscow's 'icebreaker' in the Middle East. The Suez fiasco was the apparent cause of Shepilov's dismissal in December 1956, with a Molotov protégé, Andrei Gromyko, replacing him. Khrushchev struck back in the Leningrader spirit by his plan for *sovnarkhozy*, regional economic councils designed to lessen the power of the Moscow economic bureaus, whose managers had looked to Malenkov for protection, and to enhance the party's control over the machinery of the economy. Khrushchev seemed to be on the verge of ultimate triumph over his two major rivals.

While they had little in common in the programmatic sense, Molotov and Malenkov could see what Khrushchev had planned for them, so they had little alternative but to form what Lenin would have called a 'rotten bloc.' By June they and their supporters forced a showdown, apparently gaining a Praesidium majority against Khrushchev, while the latter was on a visit to Finland. On his return, Khrushchev demanded a review by the full Central Committee. Zhukov helped with military flights for this crucial muster, denying, it was said, flights to probable Khrushchev opponents. The plenum reinstated Khrushchev and defeated what would henceforth be called the Anti-Party Group, a combination including all the Praesidium members save a 'healthy nucleus' of Mikoyan and Khrushchev's close supporter Kirichenko. Shepilov had deserted Khrushchev, as had, at the last moment, Bulganin. Even Suslov was absent from Khrushchev's side, according to Saburov's 1959 self-criticism. Lacking Bulganin, Khrushchev was forced to rely on Zhukov and his friend Ivan Serov, head of the KGB. For that reason it has seemed sensible to describe the resolution of the June 1957 crisis as a coup by the party apparatus, the army, and the security forces.[89]

The Ideologues

The struggle with the Anti-Party Group bears the closest resemblance, from the perspective offered in this study, to Stalin's 1932 crisis, in which a truly solid phalanx of opposition across the Soviet political spectrum—a right-left bloc—came up against the Leader on the Regime Question. According to the lore of Bolshevism, that is unprincipled, a repetition of Trotsky's wretched August bloc of 1912 against Lenin. To group with those who have little or no programmatic agreement in order to remove an onerous regime or person is unconscionable. The Anti-Party Group could summon fears of a personal dictatorship by Khrushchev, on the model of Stalin's response to the crisis of 1932. The resolution of the crisis must also have been particularly fearful, as Khrushchev had not hesitated to do what Trotsky had feared to do in 1925 when he stepped down as War Commissar: to use the army to intervene in the party.

Suslov apparently tried to stand aside until the last moment before supporting Khrushchev. Thus, after this point, he was in excellent position to raise his own stock in time-honored fashion, by limiting the victory of his ally. The first sign of this may have been the counter-coup against Marshal Zhukov, who made a speech in July in Leningrad in which he was rumored to have made demands that the Anti-Party Group's crimes of 'thirty years ago' be investigated.[90] Zhukov frightened the leadership and disrupted the delicate solution they had applied to the problem of de-Stalinization. This was sensed by party ideologists such as Suslov. Their subsequent action to demote Zhukov for 'Bonapartism' was a rally of the party against outside intervention, a rally which had precedents in 1920, 1925, and 1953.

The press generally interpreted the events of 1957 in terms of the full, untrammeled ascendancy of Khrushchev. It was common to speak of the end of collective leadership. Deutscher showed his *partiinost* by referring to Zhukov's Leningrad speech as a 'dramatic opening of what looks like Zhukov's bid for leadership, a test of his popularity in the country.[91] Khrushchev was said to have become alarmed at Zhukov's actions and to have alertly removed the threat by dismissing his erstwhile savior. More likely, Khrushchev deserted Zhukov because the latter stood on the ground of the Twentieth Congress, refused to attack Yugoslav revisionism, and instead concentrated fire on 'dogmatism,' that is, the views of Molotov.[92] Since his troubles in Poland and Hungary, Khrushchev had been retreating from the line of the Twentieth Congress and had been echoing Suslov's critique of the Yugoslavs. His victory over the Anti-Party Group in June, as much as his shock at the Hungarian events, was making him Suslov's ideological captive. The first result of this was his joining with Suslov to remove the 'Bonaparte' Zhukov.

In any case, from this point forward the fight for collective leadership was waged anew, at first only in the tepid terms in which Suslov and the others attacked the Anti-Party Group. As in the period of the Riutin program, the central matter was whether the group was to be denounced for political mistakes or for criminal activity. Khrushchev and his closest cohorts took the latter position, but Suslov and most of the others took the former.[93] They could scarcely afford to permit Khrushchev to raise charges against his recent opponents. They were very close to one-man rule of the type exercised by Stalin, and may well have reflected that if another Stalin were to rise to full personal power, he could only do it, as Khrushchev seemed to be willing to do, under the banner of anti-Stalinism.

Nicolaevsky saw a kind of rally around Suslov of the other leaders who feared this eventuality. He recalled the near-perfect Stalinist orthodoxy of Suslov's past, especially his struggle against Voznesenskii on behalf of the notions expressed in Stalin's *Economic Problems of Socialism*, and the fact that Suslov and Pospelov had consistently referred to the ideas of 'Marx, Engels, Lenin, and Stalin' up to 1956. Suslov's critique of 'Titoite revisionism' at the meeting of the sixty-four Communist parties in November had been supported by the Czech, East German, Bulgarian, Austrian, French, and Italian parties, perhaps, thought Nicolaevsky, an indication of an international Suslov bloc.[94]

Faced with the imposing front of 1957 and with the ensuing limitations on his freedom, Khrushchev apparently fought back in an attempt to undermine with policy initiatives the political base of his opponents. He had been a reasonably consistent Leningrader up to the crisis of 1957, but after this point he took the opposite tack: He proposed decentralization of industrial management, transfer of many functions of the Machine Tractor Stations to *kolkhoz* control, and a budget emphasis on the production of chemicals at the expense of steel.[95] Khrushchev was turning right, as Stalin had done after the crisis of 1932. In addition, just as Stalin had seemed to turn toward the Western countries during the 'liberal spell,' Khrushchev turned toward outward accommodation with the United States. He announced a plan for troop reductions and probably also argued for what Western writers would call a 'minimum deterrent.' When President Kennedy later remarked that the United States could destroy the Soviet Union twice over while the Soviets could do it only once, Khrushchev responded that 'once is quite enough.'[96] Khrushchev emphasized the need to compete with the United States by raising the standard of living of the Soviet citizen. Whether or not Khrushchev felt these policies, as opposed to those of 1953–1954, to be an expression of his deepest convictions, they were part of a turn that enabled him to annex some of the policy positions of his defeated opponents while challenging Suslov and his current rivals with a popular program.

Khrushchev and Suslov

Opposition to Khrushchev's ideas came forward immediately. Leningrad party chief Frol Kozlov criticized what he called an infatuation with détente, as did various military leaders. Suslov seemed to back them quietly. Moreover, much of the disputation among Soviet leaders hinged on issues on which the Chinese had sharply expressed themselves. Khrushchev had been uneasy about the Chinese intervention in the Polish crisis of 1956 and nervous about Chinese slogans in the Thousand Flowers campaign and the Great Leap Forward, lest the East Europeans begin to emulate Chinese models in their domestic politics. Nevertheless, he had accepted the Chinese call for unity in Communist ranks at the meeting of the sixty-four parties in 1957. He had completed preparations for the transfer of an atomic bomb prototype to China, even while he expressed disappointment at their lack of restraint in the confrontation with the United States over the offshore islands Quemoy and Matsu in 1958. Nor was he able to convince the Chinese to permit Soviet submarines to use Chinese coastal ports.[97] There is reason to suppose that the 1959 decision to cancel further aid to the Chinese nuclear program was linked to this Chinese decision. This turn of events was bound to make the Chinese more intransigent, a fact that Khrushchev seems to have understood immediately. Thus his attitude toward Mao's policies hardened, to be expressed by attacks against the Albanian Communists who supported Mao's line. This in turn provided Mao with the opportunity to broaden his critique of revisionism and eventually to make Khrushchev responsible for a 'degeneration' retroactively dated to Khrushchev's critique of Stalin in 1956.

The Chinese were thus permitted to intervene in the struggle between Khrushchev and Suslov-Kozlov. Not that anyone in the Soviet Union could openly agree with the Chinese criticism, but everyone feared the development of an open split on a permanent basis, and that fear could easily be transformed into a hope for a middle way, a compromise, with Mao. Kozlov failed fully to endorse Khrushchev's strictures against the Chinese in 1960, and the Chinese reacted violently to Khrushchev's speeches for détente, during and after his 1959 American tour. A trip to China failed to recruit Mao for the détente strategy and sharpened differences between the two leaders on military matters. In May 1960, when the U-2 spy plane was shot down over Soviet territory, the détente strategy exploded in Khrushchev's face. The two Central Committee plenums held in May and June removed a group of Khrushchev supporters, reducing the Secretariat to five members and increasing the influence of Kozlov and Suslov.[98] Khrushchev broadened his criticism of Mao's line at the Bucharest meeting of eighty-one Communist parties. In response, the Chinese gave indications of special displeasure, not with the whole of the Soviet leadership but only with Khrushchev in particular.

This sort of pressure from without and within may have prompted the impetuous Khrushchev to launch a campaign of nuclear threats on a scale not previously or since contemplated. His meeting with President Kennedy in Vienna in summer 1961 made his intention to step on what he called the Western 'sore toe,' Berlin, obvious to all. Chinese criticism had for some time pointed to a shift in the world balance of forces introduced by the demonstration of an ICBM in 1957, and the Chinese claimed that assertions against the West would produce clear gains. Having been on the short end of atomic diplomacy on so many occasions — the Berlin Blockade of 1948, the end of the Korean War in 1953, the crisis over Quemoy and Matsu — the Communist world was now in a position to threaten on its own. Nuclear diplomacy had schooled this response. Khrushchev, who felt that the West at its toughest was always calm enough to step back from the brink, began to take what he called 'certain unilateral steps,' denying access to Berlin, brandishing threats of nuclear war, and finally breaking his abstinence on nuclear tests, in effect since 1958, by detonating a sixty-megaton bomb. Unfortunately for Khrushchev, this succeeded in intimidating neither Kennedy, who stood firm on Berlin and forced Khrushchev to relent by November, nor the Chinese. At the Twenty-Second Congress in October–November, Chou En-lai demonstratively snubbed Khrushchev and shook hands with Kozlov and Suslov.[99]

Khrushchev succeeded in making the Twenty-Second Congress the second round of the de-Stalinization campaign, once more referring to the curious circumstances of Kirov's death in 1934, to Malenkov's role in the Leningrad affair, and to the perfidy of the Anti-Party Group with Molotov at its head. Khrushchev had remarked informally on his American tour that Western complaints about the Soviet one-party system should take into account that, if there were to be another party, it would probably be headed by Molotov and would take the position of the Chinese. His latest round of de-Stalinization had for its ultimate object the expulsion, or worse, of the Anti-Party Group, and apparently achieved it, as Suslov would intimate in 1964, in the case of Molotov, who lost his party card at this time. Khrushchev increasingly challenged Suslov's ideological primacy. His son-in-law Aleksei Adzhubei, editor of *Izvestiia*, spoke disparagingly of overpretentious ideologues. Ilichev, his counter-Suslov, was appointed to head an 'ideological commission,' presumably with the aim of deepening the investigation of the crimes of the Stalinists. Ilichev had been a member of the editorial board of *Bolshevik* in 1952, when Suslov had attacked it for praising Voznesenskii's book on the Soviet war economy. Ilichev again made favorable mention of Voznesenskii, an obvious stab at Suslov. Khrushchev intended to go still further and spoke of the need to move people between the ages of thirty-five and forty into the leadership. This would indicate the current generation of Soviet leadership of the late 1980s. One can imagine how this was received among those who remembered previous appeals to the youth, such as Trotsky's in 1923 or Stalin's in 1931.

Khrushchev's actions were, to be sure, actions under considerable external pressure. Not only was there constant counterpoint from the Chinese, but the strategy of minimum deterrence was almost entirely threadbare. Khrushchev had pinned his hopes on a prognosis that missiles were coming to outmode manned bombers and surface ships. Yet, after demonstrating a Soviet ICBM capacity in 1957, he eschewed immediate production of this first-generation missile in favor of orderly production of second- and third-generation missiles. Soviet strength in this area would not develop except at a measured pace. The question was: How would he cover the immediate inadequacy? The Western tendency to overestimate foreign strength, shown when a flyby of the Soviet Bison bomber, during a parade in 1955, fueled fears of a possible 'bomber gap,' provided Khrushchev with his answer. He would permit the United States to anticipate a 'missile gap' for the early sixties and thus enjoy a political relationship based on the American perception of great Soviet strength. When the United States decided that there was no missile gap, in summer and fall of 1961, Khrushchev's bluff had been called. This may have prompted the Soviet test of the super-megaton bomb, described by the Soviets as having a yield of one hundred megatons, not the actual sixty that Western estimates supposed. The Soviets claimed that these megatons could be delivered by submarines or by a standoff cruise missile, of the type of the Skybolt then projected for American sale to Britain in order to extend the life of the aging British bombers.[100] Khrushchev thus sought to hold off the Soviet airforce proponents of the manned bomber, navy proponents of surface ships, and even the proponents of an immediate program of first-generation ICBMs, not with weapons, but with an elaborate deception.

Signs of impatience with this strategy among the Soviet military multiplied in 1961 and 1962. Marshal Malinovskii, the defense minister, spoke at the Twenty-Second Congress of the need to thwart the aggressive plans of the imperialists with 'a timely blow,' a horrible formulation that threatened a surprise attack and that was not repeated in subsequent statements by Malinovskii. The marshal also ran afoul of Khrushchev by authorizing publication of Mao Tse-tung's military works. Moreover, every attempt by the new American president to explain to the public well-established policies on nuclear weapons was treated by the Soviet military as a novel threat and as renewed evidence of Khrushchev's inability to respond to American assertiveness. Khrushchev may have thought that his relative downgrading of conventional forces in favor of the minimum deterrent was only a Russian equivalent of what the British had done in their defense white paper of 1957 or the Americans earlier with their New Look. Yet the Soviet military rejected what they called reliance on one weapon. When Kennedy routinely reviewed with the press traditional policy on first use, Khrushchev, who was then in Bulgaria on a visit, had to answer to Malinovskii on this new 'threat.' In his memoirs he reported his response:

> It was during my visit to Bulgaria that I had the idea of installing missiles with nuclear warheads in Cuba without letting the United States find out they were there until it was too late to do anything about them. . . I knew that the United States could knock out some of our installations, but not all of them. If a quarter or even a tenth of our missiles survived—even if only one or two big ones were left—we could hit New York, and there wouldn't be much of New York left. I don't mean to say that everyone in New York would be killed—not everyone, of course, but an awful lot of people would be wiped out. I don't know how many: that's a matter for our scientists and military personnel to work out. They specialize in nuclear warfare and how to calculate the consequences of a missile strike against a city the size of New York. . . In addition to protecting Cuba our missiles would have equalized what the West likes to call 'the balance of power.'[101]

If this adventure had succeeded, Khrushchev would have won a margin of support for his other plans, including the division of the party into agricultural and industrial sections and renewal of de-Stalinization. He met with Bukharin's widow in September, an indication under what sign his economic reforms were proceeding, and he renewed his initiative toward Tito. But the Cuban affair was a miserable fiasco. In addition to the humiliation suffered by the leadership, they were subjected to brinkmanship on nuclear war to a degree that they had never had to suffer even under Stalin.

Khrushchev's retreat from the Cuban crisis was facilitated by the signing of a test ban treaty with the United States, in August 1963. He also benefited from the illness of his rival, Kozlov, which struck in April and would remove Kozlov from action until his death in the fall of 1964. It may be that the incapacity and death of Kozlov, 'the *de facto* second secretary,'[102] bought time for Khrushchev, or perhaps the subtraction of Kozlov gave Suslov the chance to concentrate coup plans around a more malleable candidate, Leonid Brezhnev. Suslov was also under the influence of Western Communists such as Togliatti, who feared the rise of the right in the United States, as represented by Senator Goldwater's presidential candidacy, and were doubly reluctant to follow Khrushchev in breaking with China.[103] Suslov had to appeal to the party 'democracy' in a Central Committee plenum in order to oust Khrushchev. When one considers the way Khrushchev had used a plenum to rescue himself in 1957, the magnitude of Suslov's skill in stealthily building his majority becomes evident. Suslov was by no means eager to enhance the power of the Central Committee, which has not had as much to say since that date. Details of Suslov's actions have not been available, but his political premises may be surmised.

Suslov represented continuity with Stalin's last period, with its rout of the great economic wizard Vosnesenskii but also with its defense of the primacy of the *sovkhoz* and of heavy industry, and with its broad vistas of advance of the international communist movement through a process of war and revolution.[104] With Khrushchev, he had helped remove police hegemony over the party through the Beria affair and defended heavy industry and internationalist optimism in the face of threatening nuclear war against the innovations of the 'Bukharinist' Malenkov. He had sought to maintain the rectitude of the break with Tito and the political premises, if not the regime, of the Stalinist group from the twenties. He had resisted Khrushchev's turn to the right after the 1957 crisis. With Molotov, he had opposed Titoite revisionism more than Maoist dogmatism. With the rest of the leadership, including no doubt the closest supporters of Khrushchev, he feared adventurism, subjectism, and 'hare-brained schemes,' especially those which meant war. Suslov could be viewed as a faithful voice of Stalinism without its police regime—that is, Kirovism— and as a savior of the party from 'Bonapartism' in the Zhukov affair. He had helped prevent rehabilitation of the Old Bolsheviks and the disgrace of his whole generation of Stalinists. Suslov had also defended the party from a new Stalin, the de-Stalinizer Khrushchev, who had to be defeated by re-Stalinization. Thus the tortured course of Stalin's heirs, led by Suslov's centrism, maintained continuity and stability of cadres. Suslov's centrism, so different from that of Lenin and Stalin, was to prove remarkably durable.

Kremlinology and the Russian Question

The triumph of Suslov's third centrism in 1964 may also be seen as a refutation of the thesis of a Soviet Thermidor in the form of Socialism in One Country. Suslov was by no means the practical engineer-statesman one would have expected to hold the reins of a rational bureaucratic state once it had renounced the sins of October. On the contrary, he was for his contemporaries an indispensable resource for a party whose founder had intended it to be a vessel of theory. Lenin had dominated Bolshevism not only because of his organizational ruthlessness but also for his grasp of theory and his skill at polemics. Suslov sought to be just such a leader. That he was entrusted with the correspondence with China, once conflict with Maoism had broken out, shows that his colleagues considered the polemical defense of the party's Leninism a sine qua non of its success. Like its action in subordinating the police and reviving the party after the death of Stalin, dependence on Suslov was an ideological reflex of a regime that not only ruled Russia but hoped to dominate a historic international movement as well.

Deutscher preferred to think of the Khrushchev leadership as occupying the center of that movement, with Mao on the left and Tito, Togliatti, and others on the right. This characterization most nearly resembled the views of Communists such as Gomulka. Deutscher thought that the threefold division replicated the situation of the twenties, with Stalin between Bukharin on the right and Trotsky on the left. That is, Mao was occupying the same ideological ground as Trotsky. Deutscher tried to make this clear by claiming that 'the basic antagonism between the Chinese revolution and the Soviet bureaucracy is four decades old,' thus linking Mao's revolt against Khrushchev with the Left Opposition of 1926–1927.[105] This was probably also the view of Suslov, as expressed in his speech to the January 1964 Central Committee plenum. There he accused the Chinese Communists of 'rehashing Trotskyism' with a position that recalled Permanent Revolution and Neither War nor Peace.[106] Special attention was drawn to the writings of J. Posadas, a Latin American Trotskyist who advocated preventive nuclear war. This was the most lurid case, but support for Maoism among Trotskyists was not uncommon.[107]

Souvarine, who had contributed at least as much to Western understanding of the succession struggle of the twenties as Deutscher, made no such comparison of the positions of Trotsky and Mao. He remained skeptical about divisions in Communism based on ideology, convinced at bottom that a struggle among individuals 'artificially accumulated' ideological clothing post factum. Souvarine's views clashed violently with those of Nicolaevsky in a debate in the pages of *Sotsialisticheskii vestnik* at the end of 1963. The occasion was a difference in interpretation of the Twenty-Second Congress, but more general themes were sounded which gave Souvarine and Nicolaevsky a forum to compare their approaches to the study of Soviet reality.

Souvarine objected to Nicolaevsky's assumption of a 'ferocious struggle for power,' with inevitable links to the struggle in world communism between the Chinese and Soviet parties. He had never shared Nicolaevsky's views about the power of Soviet ideologues such as Suslov. He disagreed with writers such as K. S. Karol and Ferenc Feijto, who speculated about Khrushchev's indisposition after the affair of the Anti-Party Group and about the power of the 'theoreticians and doctrinaires.'[108] For Souvarine, the 'implacable Suslov' was a myth of Western sovietologues. The Soviet Union had been ruled since Stalin's death by a collective leadership in which Khrushchev was *primus inter pares*. 'Khrushchev leaves for weeks at a time and the machine works well without him,' he wrote to Volskii, 'and the Central Committee deliberates like a little consultative parliament.'[109] Souvarine was prepared to recognize that Khrushchev had achieved a certain primacy, but not the 'personal' (*edinolichnyi*) power described by Nicolaevsky. 'I'm as struck as you by the fact that he is the only one who speaks freely,' he told Volskii. The only explanation Souvarine could offer was that Stalin had shot all the men of talent and that it would take time for new ones to emerge.

Nevertheless, he argued against Nicolaevsky, there was no really conclusive evidence of a struggle between the Khrushchev and Suslov factions, nor was this ineluctably linked to the quarrel between Moscow and Peking, as 'the Great Boris' had asserted. It was like the legend of a struggle between Socialism in One Country and Permanent Revolution, with the sage and reasonable Stalin pitted against the perverse and hysterical Trotsky 'seeking to enflame the four corners of the earth.'[110] Western experts wanted to see Khrushchev as the man of peace and Mao as the incorrigible prophet of war-revolution. In reality, Souvarine maintained, neither China nor the Soviet Union wished peace and both feared war with the West, so that they maintained the traditional position of espousing an intermediate form of aggression, as in the old days with Neither War nor Peace. It was absurd, thought Souvarine, to find anything socialist or Marxist in their regimes or policies. The Chinese might rail at Khrushchev for betraying Marxism, encouraging him to take on the imperialists and at the same time cultivating their relationship with the American ally, Pakistan. For Souvarine, talk among Western observers of an ideological split could only encourage concessions to one or another of the Communist giants.

Nicolaevsky was also against Western concessions. Yet he could not see how the rational observer could fail to note a struggle and regroupment, usually connected to programmatic issues, within the totalitarian Soviet system. If one argued, as did Souvarine, that both Khrushchev and Mao feared all-out war with the West, it was the same as saying that there was really no war danger, a ludicrous position in view of the tumultuous events of 1961–1962. Souvarine's theory of collective leadership, argued Nicolaevsky, also raised the image of an inscrutable Communist monolith, impervious to external pressure, before which one could only make concessions.[111] It was unconscionable for a political man to maintain such agnosticism. Nicolaevsky seemed to be implying the possibility of a kind of Western intervention in Soviet factional politics.

According to Nicolaevsky, the differences between him and Souvarine were summed up by examining their views of the Beria affair, an issue that had come up frequently in current discussions between them. Souvarine believed that the execution of Beria had meant little more than that the Soviet police chief had refused, in the wake of Stalin's death, to cede to the principle of collective leadership. It had been a matter of the Regime Question, pure and simple.

Nicolaevsky argued that on this view, which presented the liquidation of Beria as an act in the struggle against Stalinist terror, there was a consensus in the Western press, to which the interpretation in his own articles constituted the sole exception. The central point had not been the Regime Question, wrote Nicolaevsky, but a matter of program, in particular, foreign policy:

> We now know that the real reason for the liquidation of Beria was his attempt to re-orient the foreign policy of the Soviet dictatorship towards accord with the West.[112]

It was necessary, insisted Nicolaevsky, to look more closely at the collective leadership and recognize within it a recurrent tendency to lessen the aggressive anti-Western element in Soviet foreign policy. Lenin had made some effort in this direction late in his life, but he had had neither the time nor, perhaps, sufficient desire. Beria had taken up the task in 1953, and Khrushchev, who had led the campaign against Beria, was now himself making the same attempt. Such were the ironies in the 'dialectic of history.'

Nicolaevsky was taking note of the Moscow line. Souvarine was sounding a note from his 1929 debate with Trotsky and insisting on the importance of the Regime Question. Yet, if there were only the Regime Question and no opposition of programs, one could hardly account for the changes of line that have marked Soviet history. In order to avoid this difficulty, it seems necessary to identify individuals with programs, but the turns they make from one program to another then become incomprehensible. Perhaps some way out may be suggested by taking the turns themselves, Nicolaevsky's 'ironies,' to be part of the energy of the Soviet political system. This is what is meant by the idea of alternance.

9

Epilogue: Suslov and Alternance, 1964–1982

La Russie ne boude pas,
la Russie se recueille.
(Russia is not sulking, but collecting herself.)
— A. M. Gorchakov, Foreign Minister to Tsar Aleksandr II

Whoever is the cause of another's coming to power, falls himself, for power is built up either by art or force, both of which are suspect to the one who has become powerful.

— Niccolò Machiavelli

SOVIET RUSSIA'S MOOD after the Cuban missile crisis might be compared to the reflux of Imperial Russia after the Crimean War, her expansionary ambitions in the Near East having proved to be premature. During the following fifteen years, Russia introduced far-ranging internal reforms and annexed vast territories in the Caucasus, Central Asia, and the Far East. After her neutrality in the wars of German unification, she appeared again, replenished, as a major factor in the European balance. Post-Khrushchev Russia also appeared to contemporaries to be sinking within herself, but was really repairing the deficiencies that a policy of bluff and intimidation had sought unsuccessfully to hide. By the end of the 1960s, with the Vietnam War having altered the relations among the powers, she too reappeared on the international scene with renewed confidence.

The achievements of Soviet arms-building could be considered a result of the equilibrium of the party regime. Under the rubric of 'stabilization of cadres,' Suslov set about ordering an oligarchy that might tame the excesses of the Soviet policy debate and master the alternance through a finely calibrated collective leadership. While observers such as Deutscher at first expected this regime to enjoy only a short lull, it proved to be a satisfactory, while probably less than permanent, prophylactic against the extremes of factional struggle.

This involved a different approach to the mediation of opposed ambitions and views. The candidates for the Stalin succession had themselves

201

tried to find the center position. Malenkov sought to avoid the fate of Beria, beginning with a consumerist and pro-détente assertion and ending as an ally of Molotov. Khrushchev was a Leningrader as long as it took to defeat Malenkov, after which he moved more to the right. Suslov, like Stalin in 1922–1927, was most reliable and least threatening, and profited from resistance to the bold initiatives of others. Where Khrushchev took positions in the expectation of dislodging those who opposed, and dealt as capriciously with people as he had with issues, Suslov and Brezhnev would move more carefully, apparently on the assumption that less shifting of individuals in and out of the Politburo (for so it would be again called by 1966) would make for more all-around security for collective leadership.

That Brezhnev remained at the top without degrading his associates seemed a violation of all the rules of Communist succession, as Myron Rush has suggested.[1] There was no denying that, in terms of individual movement of leaders, the Brezhnev years presented less for Kremlin watchers to watch. Yet from the perspective of this study, it would seem that alternance was not destroyed in the Brezhnev years, but only subjected to restraint.

Suslov Rebuilds

The first order of business was a series of sweeping counterreforms designed to dismantle the results of Khrushchev's 'hare-brained schemes.' These latter included the *sovnarkhozy*, division of the party into industrial and agricultural branches, the dissolution of the Machine Tractor Stations, the vast and open-ended scheme of foreign-aid commitments to Third World neutrals, and other measures, such as canceling the vital incentive pay for Siberian technical jobs. Where Khrushchev had depended on a minimum nuclear deterrent, his successors opted for broad development of all the armed forces, perhaps in imitation of the U.S. 'triad.' This included not only the missile program, but also manned bombers, a vast increase in ground forces, and a surface fleet. This may have been connected to the failure of the new leadership to reopen dialogue with China. The worsening of Sino-Soviet relations would have its own pressure on Brezhnev arms budgets, by necessitating a huge land army in the Soviet Far East and other areas bordering China. The Brezhnev Politburo seemed willing to bear the necessary costs in this and other areas to avoid another fiasco comparable in scope to the Caribbean crisis.

De-Stalinization was virtually brought to a halt, and the basic Kirovism of the leadership was not deepened by further rehabilitations of the Old Bolsheviks. Khrushchev's formula, that the victims of the terror of the thirties had been wrong politically but not dangerous enough to execute, preserved the political charter myth of Stalinists who had enjoyed the ride up with Stalin prior to 1934, but who found the rigors of High Stalinism too nervous-making. Pressures on the intellectuals, for whom this was not a satisfactory solution, would continue. Abram Tertz and Nikolai Arzhak (Andrei Siniavskii and Iulii Daniel) would be sent to prison in 1966 for their literary work criticizing the Stalin cult and Socialist Realism, but no return to the Stalin terror materialized. The operative idea of Kirovism—that Stalinism could be administered *doucement*—seemed to serve in dealings with the intelligentsia, which, it was found, could be discouraged by methods short of shooting.

The destruction of the *sovnarkhozy* reinstated the power of the Moscow economic bureaus. In general, this seemed to work to the advantage of Kosygin, who, as head of the state machinery and in the absence of a leadership with strong economic ideas, drew all of the reins of the Soviet economy together. It was no surprise that the heir of Rykov and Malenkov should make a demonstration on behalf of the classical Moscow line in 1965, when he raised claims for the Soviet consumer as against the defense budget. Kosygin was really in no position to assert himself in any other cause, and Suslov's professed ignorance of economic affairs may have been encouraging. However, his protest served only as a prelude to the budget commitment to defense which emerged by the end of 1965.[2] Suslov apparently threw his weight into the struggle on behalf of the pro-defense line.

But Kosygin was not banished; nor was Podgornii, who would continue to argue the same line, perhaps out of genuine conviction, after Kosygin had relented. Had this occasion seen a struggle among vested interests of a pluralistic bureaucracy, as is sometimes supposed in the West, it might have been suspected that Aleksandr Shelepin would have benefited from the defeat of Kosygin and Podgornii. Shelepin had been a key link in the cabal which overthrew Khrushchev, despite his having been a former protégé of the deposed. He had employed the intelligence forces to plan the choreography of the plot. He was known, as well, as a bright and energetic man, clearly more dynamic, some thought, than Brezhnev. He also had as good a record on de-Stalinization as anyone in the leadership, certainly better than that of Suslov, who was again in the position of having to oppose what he considered a new Stalin, who was yet a de-Stalinizer. Shelepin's excellent connections with the military must have reinforced his ominous image as a possible new Khrushchev.

By posing this threat, Shelepin had, as it turned out, suffered a decisive *defeat* from which he would not recover. But he could not have been aware of it, since he remained in the Politburo and the Secretariat, merely losing control over the Party and State Control Commission. He still retained a powerful supporter in the KGB, Semichastnyi, and other friends in the Moscow party apparatus. Yet from this point on, the 'shrinking of Shelepin' would be an inexorable process.[3]

Suslov and Brezhnev held on against threats from right and left, while they themselves espoused a synthesis that, in domestic affairs, was quite left. Nevertheless, the foreign policy position had to be a quiet one, in view of the resolve of the leadership to eschew adventures until the Soviet military regime was in a better position vis-à-vis the United States. In this period that meant something very close to behaving like a second-rate power, and that was indeed the way de Gaulle actually described the Soviet attitude. The French President judged that, with the United States bogging down increasingly in Vietnam, more freedom of action would be available to powers such as France and China. The Chinese were attempting to make themselves a center of gravity for what they saw as a rise of worldwide revolutionary movement, which meant for them armed struggle in Asia and Latin America, and radical popular movements in the West, especially the United States. De Gaulle saw this as an opportunity for France. 'The rise of a powerful China,' said de Gaulle, 'causes the Soviets to inject a note of sincerity into the couplets they periodically devote to a peaceful coexistence.' For him, the chastened state of Soviet foreign policy offered a chance to bring about the Europeanization of Russia. Thus, while he began to puncture the American dollar by calling for gold in exchange for French holdings of dollars, he set about the task of reconciliation with the Soviet Union.

The Soviet leaders were delighted to watch what they perceived as a disintegration of NATO, caused by French withdrawal from the alliance's integrated command in 1966. They were thus induced to tolerate Romania's attempt to mediate between them and China. Actually they would follow Romania in developing cooperation with West Germany in the same way that the United States was eventually to follow West German *Ostpolitik* in developing and generalizing détente with them. The statement of European Communist parties assembled at Karlovy Vary in 1967 made it clear that the initiatives of de Gaulle and of West German *Ostpolitik* would be welcomed.

Diplomatic maneuvers were at the time widely considered an outward manifestation of the inexorable tendency toward the dissolution of the European blocs. As an exchange student in Warsaw, I was told often that the Soviets had lost their capacity to discipline their eastern empire in the Stalinist manner, in the same way that United States could no longer control affairs among its allies. While student and labor ferment rose up in Western Europe, the same process would liberate the East from tutelage to Moscow. The Poles hoped that they would not again be in the lead, as in 1956—they were only partially correct, as the Warsaw student rising of March 1968 would show—and they looked instead to Prague. Brezhnev's consolidation of power after the struggle of 1965, his instinct for the center position, and the feeling he and Suslov might have shared that a lossening of bonds between fraternal parties was in the air—all this must have contributed to a permissive attitude toward the emergence of the Dubcek experiment in Czechoslovakia.

Yet the loosening of bonds proved to be intolerable. Even while the Soviet leaders tried to make Dubcek aware of the dangers of, for example, secret ballot elections to party posts (a key demand of the opposition in 1927–1928), they could not convince the Czech leader that the reform course endangered the Soviet Union. That point was made by Ukrainian party head Shelest, who naturally feared the spillover effect, and by Defense Minister Grechko, in place after the death of Malinovskii in 1967, who feared a general mutiny in the Warsaw pact in imitation of Romania. East Germany's Walter Ulbricht encouraged this reaction, while apparently Brezhnev and Suslov, fearful of the impact on the international Communist movement, wrung their hands and temporized.

When Brezhnev did decide to carry out the invasion of Czechoslovakia, the impression was created that the Shelest-Grechko-Ulbricht combination had forced his hand. It was known that Suslov and Shelepin, and perhaps Kosygin, had hoped for conciliation. Later Ponomarev, head of the International Department, tried to create the impression that these 'progressives' were outvoted by dogmatic and 'semi-fascist' elements in the Politburo, including 'centrists' of the Brezhnev type 'who had kept their district secretary mentality.'[4] Gomulka, who had suppressed the March demonstrations in Poland with extreme severity and a hysterical denunciation of 'Zionist influences,' had also given his support to the hard-liners. Shelest-Grechko-Ulbricht reminded many of Khrushchev-Zhukov-Ulbricht in the years after Stalin's death. Now that they were running into serious foreign problems, Brezhnev and Suslov seemed vulnerable before such combinations led by more dynamic leaders of the Shelpin and Shelest type.

The question of Brezhnev's leadership was thus continually forced onto the agenda at a time when all the basic relations among the powers were being transformed. Most important for Soviet policy was the ripening of the antagonism with China, visibly dramatized by the armed clashes at Damanskii/Chenpao Island in March 1969. As important as the fighting itself was the war of nerves conducted by the Soviets in accompaniment of their search for talks with the Chinese. This included threats against the Chinese nuclear facilities at Lop Nor in Sinkiang province,[5] and ultimately revival of a 'Free Turkestan' movement to 'liberate' Sinkiang. No doubt these Soviet actions moved along the diplomatic revolution which would result in normalization of Chinese relations with the United States. This process was already well in train, however, and had perhaps already been given a decisive push by the events of 1968. American response to the Tet Offensive had showed the Communist world that 'U.S. ruling circles' had lost their enthusiasm for the Vietnam War. The Nixon Doctrine on Vietnamization would underscore that impression, which served, as far as the Chinese were concerned, as the fundamental premise for their turn toward the United States.[6] The Chinese could hardly have helped but be impressed with the contrast between the Nixon Doctrine and what they called the 'Brezhnev Doctrine.' Moreover, the May–June events in Paris had crushed Gaullism; nor could German *Ostpolitik* take over in its stead. Thus the Europeanization of the Soviet Union seemed largely a failed project. The premise of the sixties, that the superpowers were receding before revolutionary forces and innovative middle-rank nations, had been exploded. The West had been weakened, but the Soviet Union had emerged more robust than ever.

This impression extended to the radicalism of the period, for which the Chinese press had given much support. In the United States, the Black Panther party came more and more under the influence of pro-Moscow Communists and was itself used as a battering ram to split the largest American student organization, Students for a Democratic Society, when the latter threatened in 1969 to come under the pro-Chinese leadership of the Progressive Labor party. One may interpret many such Soviet actions in terms not merely of general assertiveness and desire to liquidate a false premise of the sixties—that the U.S.S.R. had become a second-rate power—but also as a service to the developing détente. However, the Chinese must have viewed this and related developments with alarm. Chou En-lai told Henry Kissinger that the Soviets had attacked Damanskii Island to divert attention from the East German failure, in a concurrent mini-crisis involving harassment of Western access routes, to prevent the West German presidential election from taking place in West Berlin. The Soviets attacked China, said Chou, 'to escape their responsibilities over Berlin.'[7] Chou's perspective serves as well as a possible setting for explaining the Chinese motives on Damanskii Island, and may have been a preview of later Chinese encouragement of NATO. Kissinger reported that he disagreed with Kremlinologists who reasoned that any attempts to better U.S.-China relations would ruin relations with the Soviets. He thought that alignment with the weaker of two powers would restrain the stronger.[8] Here one can hear Bismarck's injunction that in any alliance it is better to be the rider than the horse. It is probable that the Chinese felt the same way.

Suslov and Brezhnev

The transformation of the world setting signaled in a sense the end of Brezhnev's apprenticeship as dispatcher of the collective leadership. It was precisely the Politburo divisions over the invasion of Czechoslovakia that permitted Brezhnev the opportunity to rise above his colleagues. The skirmish opened in the spring of 1969 when Suslov, along with Shelepin and Mazurov issued a challenge to Brezhnev's economic policy. Shelepin had little to lose by this time; his man Semichastnyi had lost the KGB to Iurii Andropov in 1967, and shortly thereafter Shelepin had been demoted further, losing his position as head of Party–State Control. The complaint about economic policy was broadening into a general warning about the threat to collective leadership, a warning to Brezhnev by the 'democracy of the eleven.'[9] Kosygin was caught in the crossfire and offered to resign, a proposal which introduced a more prickly question: Would Brezhnev replace him as head of the state machinery? If not, Polianskii was the agreed alternative, but he was as much anathema to the heavy-industry lobby as anyone in the Politburo. There was no other way than to require Kosygin to stay on.[10] Brezhnev could have his victory on a Leningrader approach to the economy, but he could not yet have the state machinery. Moreover, his victory on the 'issue' was ephemeral. When Polish strikes and riots forced Gomulka's resignation in 1970, Brezhnev switched to a pro-consumer line more in keeping with the views of Kosygin and Polianskii.

Perhaps there had been a desire to restrain Brezhnev after the invasion of Czechoslovakia, in a general mood of caution as in 1964. If this were so, Suslov appeared to have applied the restraints moderately and cemented his partnership with Brezhnev. The conflict nevertheless strengthened Brezhnev. He turned inexorably toward détente, signing the Treaty of Moscow with Willy Brandt in August 1970. It will be recalled that this issue had assisted in the ruin of Beria in 1953. The 'hards' of 1968, Shelest-Grechko-Ulbricht-Gomulka, might have been expected to counter it, but Brezhnev assiduously cultivated his link to Grechko, accepted Gomulka's resignation in 1970, and eased Ulbricht into retirement in 1971. Shelest's turn would also come. Unable to break with the conventions of the third centrism, Brezhnev did not shake up the Politburo as Stalin had in 1952, but instead expanded it to fifteen members at the Twenty-Fourth Party Congress. The four new members, Shcherbitskii, Kunaev, Kulakov, and Grishin, were expected to be reliable Brezhnevists and with the possible exception of Kulakov, all proved to be such.

Potential criticism of détente was weakened but not silenced completely. Shelest would continue to oppose, and within the consensus on détente there could still be fissures as to the emphasis on the various aspects of the new relationship with the United States. The expansion of trade and the promise of technology transfer eased the position of Brezhnev on the economy and probably pleased Kosygin. The American idea was to enmesh the Soviets in a web of economic relationships, thus to provide an incentive for moderation of Soviet activity in the Third World, but time would tell, a Brezhnevist could argue, just who would be enmeshed. This and Soviet interest in arms limitation might also constrain initiatives in support of wars of national liberation, it was hoped in the West. Yet the

Soviets always insisted that détente would not lessen their interest in 'progressive' causes. It was a contest to see whose definition of détente would prevail. The elevation of Grechko, Gromyko, and Andropov to membership in the Politburo in April 1973 indicated the rise to influence of the 'national security' group in the Soviet leadership. The concurrent removal of Shelest from the Politburo further strengthened Brezhnev's hand.

Therefore the continuing tension between Suslov and Brezhnev should not be interpreted as a struggle over détente itself, but rather as an attempt by Suslov to defend collective leadership (the Regime Question again) and to maintain the revolutionary momentum of Soviet policy despite and within détente. This came to be represented institutionally as a struggle between the International Department of the Central Committee and the Ministry of Foreign Affairs. Thus, while SALT I and the ABM treaty were being signed and the way was being prepared for the crowning achievement of détente, the Helsinki Final Act of 1975, Suslov was asserting counterpoint.

Conflict between the Politburo and Suslov must be inferred, not only from quarrels over Suslov's views on nationality policy (he advocated redrawing boundaries for republics on the basis of economic factors rather than ethnic ones) but also from reminders of Suslov's Stalinist past. In September 1974, a biography of Voznesenskii was published, with a *Pravda* review honoring and praising the Leningrad economist shot by Stalin.[11] The Voznesenskii affair had already been used by Khrushchev and Adzhubei to embarrass Suslov, who was depicted as Salieri to Voznesenskii's Mozart. The further rehabilitation of Voznesenskii at this time could only serve to make Suslov squirm. The *Pravda* review, however, was written by a certain G. Sorokin, who had also been attacked by Suslov in his denunciation of Voznesenskii in 1952.

Nevertheless, Suslov continued to press the point that, détente or not, the world revolution would continue. In a series of speeches in 1973–1974, Suslov insisted on an analysis which could also be found in speeches and articles by Ponomarev, Zarodov, Timofeev, and others associated with the periodical *Problems of Peace and Socialism*. According to this analysis, the quadrupling of the oil price by OPEC in the wake of the Yom Kippur War had reversed the financial lead held by Europe over the United States in recent years, at least since the run on the dollar at the time of the Tet Offensive. Now the Eurodollars would become petrodollars, flowing into OPEC coffers. Europe would be severely shaken, and its economic crisis would be offering big opportunities for the Communist parties in coming years. The Brezhnev leadership had never before shown such sanguine expectations for European Communism.

Most striking was the activity of the Portuguese Communists under

Alvaro Cunhal, who, when the Caetano dictatorship collapsed in April 1974, proclaimed openly his intention to conquer power in alliance with the pro-Communist Armed Forces Movement, even if that meant suppressing democracy.[12] Fears that Cunhal's tactical line would be generally prescribed for all the Western Communists impelled criticism from the Italian Communists and eventually from other parties, some of whom hated to risk their electoral positions for what must have looked like a repeat of the Canton Commune of 1927. Resistance to the Cunhal line was severely denounced by Suslov. The Western Communists were forced to resort to what became known as Eurocommunism. Suslov denounced Eurocommunism as well.

Suslov's 'Comintern' policy was causing friction in the leadership, but he does not appear to have sought to supplant Brezhnev. Curiously, just as Shelepin was being forced out of the leadership for good, with no real contender coming up to take his place, Brezhnev suffered a stroke which took him out of action for several months. Suslov was now put into the position of having to save Brezhnev, since a too-rapid succession bringing in a younger man would have ended his career as well.

No effort was spared, therefore, to provide Brezhnev with every laurel of victory. The Helsinki Final Act of 1975 could with justice be described as a triumph for Soviet diplomacy, since it achieved recognition of the existing East European frontiers which had been challenged in the West since 1945. Suslov no doubt found it useful to depict Brezhnev as the architect of détente, a product of wise arms policies pursued since 1964. At the Twenty-Fifth Congress in March 1976, Grigorii Romanov of the Leningrad organization was brought into the Politburo, as was Dmitri Ustinov who, on the death of Grechko, became defense minister. Brezhnev's protégé and aide, Konstantin Chernenko, became a Central Committee secretary. He would be a candidate member of the Politburo by 1977 and a full member by 1978. Podgornii, who had resisted Brezhnev's heading the party and state simultaneously, was removed, and Brezhnev was made president although he was denied the premiership.

In thus honoring Brezhnev, Suslov was also celebrating the great strides being made by the Communist idea since the outbreak of the Portuguese revolution. These included the triumph of Communist forces in Vietnam and Laos and victory for Leninists in Angola, Mozambique, and Guinea-Bissau. That these events caused the Ford-Kissinger leadership in the United States to drop the word 'détente' from its vocabulary they could regard as an advance in the struggle to force the Americans to accept the Soviet definition, without linkage. As it became clear to all who saw him in public that Brezhnev was not well, major changes in the world 'balance of forces' seemed to vindicate the prognoses of Suslov and the International Department.

Brezhnev and Chernenko

The climax came in 1978–1979. Somalia's failure to take the Ogaden desert from an Ethiopia increasingly influenced by Soviet and Cuban advice showed the onset of grave problems for détente. In April, the Daoud regime in Afghanistan was overthrown by a coup which installed the Marxist-Leninist Khalq (People's) faction of Noor Mohammed Taraki, whose pro-Soviet character unnerved Western observers. The same month saw an invasion of Zaire's mineral-rich Shaba (formerly Katanga) province by former followers of the Katangese separatist Moishe Tshombe, perhaps assisted by Cuban and Angolan forces.[13] The Parisian *Les Echoes de Paris* guessed that this might be the opening shot in the 'Third World War for the resources of the world.'[14] President Carter dispatched his national security adviser to China in May amid talk of 'playing the China card.' The principal result of this mission was the unblocking of Chinese-Japanese treaty talks, stymied by Japanese trepidations about what they considered a too obviously anti-Soviet 'anti-hegemony' passage in the Chinese draft. American persuasion permitted a treaty between the two Asian giants.

The extreme tension continued. In June an internal struggle in South Yemen was won by Fatah Ismail, reportedly with the help of Cuban and Soviet troops flown in from Ethiopia. His regime signed a treaty with the Soviet Union the following year, and by 1981 would be party to a defense pact with Ethiopia and Libya. The great fear in the West was that Saudi Arabia would be pressured by this and Soviet activity in North Yemen into an accommodation with the Soviets. In the fall a Soviet-Vietnamese pact served as a prelude to the Vietnamese invasion of Cambodia. The Chinese were resolved to counter this, Deng Xiaoping told Carter and Brzezinski on his visit to the United States in January 1979, by teaching the Vietnamese a lesson. Yet the lesson turned out to be different from that expected. China failed to restrain the Vietnamese by force or otherwise. Moreover, in the same month the government of the Shah of Iran collapsed. The Soviets could reflect that the positions so laboriously maintained by the Western policy of containment were falling rapidly. Summer 1979 saw the victory of the Sandinistas in Nicaragua. In the fall, all hope that radical Islam might be mobilized against Soviet expansion was dashed by the seizure of the American embassy and the taking of its personnel as hostages. In December, the Soviets invaded Afghanistan.

The Soviet leaders seem to have calculated that their Western counterparts would be forced by the need to preserve détente into a policy of adjustment to the march of 'progressive forces'—a march actively supported by a vigorous Soviet policy. At the same time, despite the fact that Brezhnev' health appeared worse to all who saw him, he continually bolstered his personal position. This affected his Politburo colleagues most sharply in regard to the positioning of an eventual successor. In 1979 no one in the West doubted that it would be Andrei Kirilenko, Suslov being judged too old and others such as Tikhonov and Grishin seeming to lack the stature and preparation for the job. Andropov seemed far down the list.[15] It was noted that the KGB had grown in prominence in the preceding years, having been 'liberated' from its nominal subordination to the Council of Ministers and called simply the Committee for State Security of the U.S.S.R. This apparent slight to the state machinery implied conflict between Brezhnev and Kosygin. Yet it also suggested that the KGB, and not Andropov, was being promoted. In fact, Andropov was hemmed in by his immediate subordinates, Tsvigun, Tsinev, and Chebrikov, who were regarded as close Brezhnev supporters. Tsvigun, the most prominent among them, was Brezhnev's brother-in-law, having married the sister of Brezhnev's wife.

Thus, Brezhnev must have thought that he had a free hand to designate his successor. Increasingly, Brezhnev gave indications that he hoped that successor would be, not Kirilenko, but Chernenko. The latter was widely regarded as a parvenu whose chief distinction was his closeness to Brezhnev, not so much as an associate but as an aide. Suslov was not blind to the fact, but there is reason to suppose that he promoted the eclipse of Kirilenko by Chernenko perhaps because of Kirilenko's resistance to a planned reduction in the growth of the economy, as Myron Rush has suggested.[16] At the Central Committee plenum of April 1979, Kirilenko's protégé Yakov Riabov lost his position as a Central Committee secretary. The official announcement hinted that Suslov had played at least as important a role in formulating the Politburo's proposals to the plenum as had Brezhnev.[17] Suslov probably supported the advance of Chernenko. The decline of Kirilenko's health, which paralleled his political decline, left Suslov with no other option, unless he were to promote a younger man. This seems never to have been considered; rule by the elders was the watchword. When Kosygin retired in 1980, the elderly Tikhonov moved into his place as chair of the Council of Ministers.

With Brezhnev's work schedule cut down to accommodate his weakness, Chernenko was called upon to chair Politburo sessions. Thus the entire oligarchy was given a preview of what life would be like under Chernenko. Apparently they disliked what they saw. This was especially the case with the 'national security' group, including Ustinov and Gromyko, who could not have considered Chernenko to be bright enough to handle the responsibilities of the leader of a nuclear superpower. But could they oppose Chernenko against the wishes of Suslov? If Brezhnev were to die before Suslov, which appeared likely, the latter would no doubt be excellently placed to defend Chernenko as successor. Some break would have to be made with Suslov-Brezhnev *before* Brezhnev's passing from the scene. Like Stalin in 1951–1953, Brezhnev was resolved to hold on to power until the last and to heap upon himself every decoration, every prize, every last token of compulsory adulation. This fact precluded an orderly succession, since a consensus on an acceptable successor would be a temptation toward an early transfer of power. Against this horrifying possibility, Chernenko seemed the only insurance.

Andropov's Tour de Force

The revolt against Brezhnev finally came in the beginning of 1982, with the affair of Boris the Gypsy. According to reports from Soviet sources made available to foreign correspondents, a vast scandal was about to engulf the Brezhnev clan. Boris Buriatiia, originally a star with the Moscow Gypsy Theater and currently a singer at the Bolshoi Theater, was said to be at the center of an illegal trade in diamonds and hard currency. Boris was also the lover of Brezhnev's daughter, Galina. Her husband was General Iurii Churbanov, a deputy minister of the Interior. The scandal apparently also touched Demichev, Minister of Culture, and Kolevatov, the director of the state circus. The stories that were circulated attempted to explain the death in January, perhaps by suicide, of General Tsvigun, Brezhnev's KGB ally and brother-in-law. These suggested that Tsvigun had, when confronted with the case, attempted to make arrests on his own—that is, that this ally and relative of Brezhnev had turned against his patron.

It was not difficult to imagine a KGB-led revolt against the Brezhnev regime, but how to account for the role of Tsvigun or, if the stories circulated were not false, for his motive? Since any move against Brezhnev was more pointedly a move against Chernenko, was there a reason for Tsvigun to fight Chernenko? As a speculation, one could go back to the period of Chernenko's rise and the decision to invade Afghanistan. If the defecting KGB major Vladimir Kuzichkin is to be believed, the KGB had warned Brezhnev repeatedly against the invasion, and earlier, at the time of the coup of 1978, against installing Taraki and the Khalq faction.[18] Their preference was for Babrak Karmal of the Parcham (Flag) faction, according to Kuzichkin, a KGB agent of long standing. But Brezhnev had insisted on Taraki and, even after Karmal was sent off to Prague as ambassador and Taraki was eclipsed by Hafizullah Amin, Brezhnev continued to favor Amin over the KGB candidate. Then, when fear arose that Amin might be unreliable, an 'Afghan Tito,' only then did Brezhnev turn to Karmal.[19]

The preparations for the coup that accompanied the invasion were made by MVD deputy chief Viktor Paputin, under the guise of shaping up the personal security arrangements for Amin. That the MVD was given this mission may have been continued evidence of Brezhnev's bypassing the KGB, and a source of anxiety for both Tsvigun and Andropov. The MVD was in the hands of the grouping of Brezhnev supporters and cronies who attached themselves to him when he was party head in Moldavia in the early fifties. One member of the Moldavian faction was Nikolai Shchelokov, whom Brezhnev brought to Moscow to be Interior Minister. Another was Chernenko. It is not unreasonable to suppose, then, that Brezhnev had attempted to divide the police power in something like the same way Stalin had at the end of his reign. Some evidence for the thesis of the Chernenko–MVD–Moldavian faction is given by the fact that one of Andropov's first acts on succeeding Brezhnev was to replace Shchelokov as the head of the MVD with a KGB professional, Vitalii Fedorchuk.

The invasion of Afghanistan appeared to be the last chapter of the saga set in motion by the playing of the China card. Brzezinski's China trip had been answered by the invasion of Cambodia; Deng's attack on Vietnam by the invasion of Afghanistan. Yet somehow Afghanistan could not be digested. Civil war raged on. American public opinion, as reflected in the mood of the United States Senate, also began to weary of the results of détente. By the fall of 1980, all hope for the ratification of the SALT II treaty evaporated. This cannot have been taken lightly by the opponents of Brezhnev and Chernenko. Moreover, in the summer, Poland had erupted with the emergence of the *Solidarność* trade union organization, whose potential threat to the Soviet internal order cannot be overestimated. It must have seemed that the fortunes of Soviet foreign policy, which had risen constantly throughout the seventies, had reached their apogee and that the curve was now pointing sharply downward.

The Polish problem seemed almost as severe as Hungary in 1956. Especially vexing was the effect on the Polish Communist party, which increasingly established 'horizontal structures' for the review and discussion of decisions coming from the top. By August 1981, the Polish party had actually held a democratic Party Congress, in the sense that the Soviets had not known since the twenties. To be sure, the Poles endorsed a man originally favored by Moscow, Stanisław Kania, who had already replaced Edward Gierek, but at the same time a new political bureau was elected from below and the dread chief of the political police, Mieczysław Moczar, was removed from the leadership altogether.

The irony of the Polish Communists' action against Moczar was that it was probably not directed against the Soviet Union. This was the same Moczar who had directed Gomulka's anti-Semitic campaign against the Polish students in 1968, but Moczar had since helped in the removal of Gomulka for Edward Gierek in 1970. Pushed into obscurity with Gierek's consolidation of power, he had to side with Gierek's critics, Stefan Olszowski and Tadeusz Grabski, in order to return to prominence. This had been accomplished by the crisis in which Solidarność emerged and Gierek fell. Moreover, Moczar had taken, during spring and summer of 1981, a moderate position on the changes in the Communist Party and endorsed the 'socialist renewal' which culminated in the Ninth Extraordinary Congress of August. Moczar's campaign for compromise had been conducted against Olszowski and Grabski, who staked a claim for the support of the Kremlin by charging that *Solidarność* was controlled by anti-Soviet radicals and was bent on establishing 'dual power' in the country, that is, on breaking the power of the party. The party itself, pressured by reform sentiment in the ranks, had seemed on the verge of dismissing Olszowski and Grabski in the first months of 1981, but an urgent telegram from Brezhnev had saved them. The same Extraordinary Congress that removed Moczar had freely elected Olszowski to the Politburo. The party's 'socialist renewal' thus sought a visible symbol of reconciliation with Moscow.

Nevertheless, Moscow persisted in the view that the Polish party had relinquished its 'leading role.' In March, the Soviet Politburo had set it as the Polish party's principal task to 'reverse the course of events.' There followed immediately an incident in which some *Solidarność* officials were beaten in Bydgoszcz, considered a stronghold of Olszowski and the pro-Moscow group. The 'Bydgoszcz incident' was widely interpreted as a provocation, perhaps coordinated by Moscow, against a government considered too weak to act against *Solidarność*. The party was sharply divided, with a majority critical of Olszowski's refusal to compromise with *Solidarność*. Yet the majority refused to remove Olszowski from the leadership, knowing what that would signal to Moscow. Suslov paid a surprise visit to Warsaw in April. On his return, the Soviet press stridently charged that 'revisionist' elements were influential in the Polish party. At the same time, the army's paper, *Zolnierz wolnosci*, took a hard line against the threat of 'dual power.' Few understood it at the time, but this was a suggestion that the army might eventually have to replace the party.

Suslov undoubtedly thought that the Polish party was in need of a thorough housecleaning. Yet the coup by the army in December 1981 could not have been a palatable alternative and must have made those responsible for relations with ruling Communist parties appear to have lost everything. This may have been regarded as a major defeat for Suslov. The Olszowski group in Poland was thought to be close to Romanov and the Leningrad machine in the Soviet party. It may not be too farfetched to suppose that Romanov, who had been active in relations with foreign Communist parties, supported Olszowski and a Polish party revival and therefore came to regard Suslov's policy as a failure. Vadim Zagladin of the International Department gave an interview at the time of the coup, to the Rome Communist paper *Paese sera*, in which he defended the right to use force in defense of the 'gains of socialism' but also held that there would be no more interventions 'from the outside,' since that task could now be left to local armies.[20]

Perhaps Romanov considered this resort to 'Bonapartism' as the appropriate occasion to begin the break with Brezhnev-Suslov-

Chernenko. In December 1981, the Leningrad literary magazine *Avrora* carried a heavy-handed 'satirical' article about a superannuated writer (Brezhnev had lately been celebrated for his writings and had received a Lenin Prize for his memoirs) whose death, eagerly awaited, never seemed to come, to the disappointment of his admirers. 'But I think that he will not keep us waiting very long. He will not disappoint us. We all believe in him. We want him to finish those labors that he has not yet finished, and hasten to gladden our hearts.'[21] The article could not have been published without the approval of Romanov, who must have had broad encouragement to undertake such a perilous step, even in such an indirect manner. If Tsvigun had been the one who initiated the arrests in the affair of Boris the Gypsy, as the circulated stories indicated, perhaps he had come to suppose that the campaign against Brezhnev had already begun.

The stories that were circulated connected the death of Tsvigun and the death of Suslov with the affair. According to one, Suslov confronted Tsvigun and informed him that, in view of the damage that the arrests would do to the Brezhnev regime, Tsvigun's political career was over and there was no alternative to shooting himself. Whereupon Tsvigun took the advice. The confrontation so shook Suslov that he suffered a stroke from which he died days later. Tsvigun's role in the affair is underscored by the fact that Brezhnev did not sign Tsvigun's obituary, as was customary and certainly expected with regard to his own brother-in-law. Some stories suggested that Tsvigun was not a suicide, but the essential point of the events of January 1982 remains: The affair of Boris the Gypsy had removed at one blow the major obstacles in the KGB and Politburo to the ascent of Andropov.

From Andropov to Gorbachev

The passing of Suslov was an important watershed in the history of Soviet succession politics. He had represented genuine continuity with the Stalin era. He had suppressed criticism of the Cult of the Personality and promoted an essentially positive assessment of Stalin's career. He had defended the heritage of Stalinism in the programmatic and factional sense and, while he had permitted criticism of certain of its excesses, had also taught the leadership to proscribe excesses in the criticism. As had Stalin, he had developed the notion that the struggle against opposition represented intellectual and theoretical gains that had to be defended. Suslov was, after all, regarded as the party's best Marxist, and he preferred to think that the Khrushchev era, even more than the Stalinist bloodbath of the thirties, was the aberration. He had seemed to be able to freeze the alternance along with the extremes of faction, with Brezhnev and Kosygin personifying a synthesis of the Moscow and Leningrad lines. The essential question posed by his death was whether he had provided an institutional framework to ensure continuity or merely a holding action against the processes let loose by Khrushchev.

The individual who benefited most from the subtraction of Suslov was Andropov. This was not generally recognized at the time. Western observers commonly suggested Chernenko, Kirilenko, or even Grishin as likely heirs. Andropov was thought to be too closely associated with the police to permit trust. The Beria analogy dominated assessments of Andropov. There was reason for this: Beria had also represented a 'national security' candidacy, with his far-flung connections in intelligence matters, East European regimes, and the nuclear program. Yet the analogy halts there.

Western analysis failed through its inability to assess the intellectual qualities of the individual leaders. There was ample respect for the factor of toughness and the role played by fear in the machinations of the Politburo, but there was no way of assessing who had made the crucial inputs in political and foreign policy matters, and Western observers really had no idea who the Politburo members considered to have the best grasp of theory. We now know that the most highly regarded individual was Andropov. His 'national security' credentials were not overshadowed by fear of his policies or his apparatus, as was the case with Beria. Andropov had originally been a protégé of Kuusinen, since the twenties an arch-political Stalinist who sensed that the spread of Communism in the era of Stalin would come not by revolutionary but by 'political' methods.[22] Andropov also proved able to get along with Suslov for the entire period of his tenure at the KGB since 1967. He apparently delivered on expectations that he would be an anti-Shelepin. He proved to all that he was capable of both employing the KGB for its various murky purposes and preventing its becoming a rogue elephant in factional politics.

It became obvious that, in order to succeed Brezhnev, Andropov would have to take Suslov's place in the Secretariat and assume the role of ideological watchdog. The 'ideological post' was the institutional center of the Suslov legacy. But it had always indicated, at least outwardly, *désintéressement* with regard to the top job. Now it had become a stepping-stone to supreme power. This was a distinct sign that the Suslov system was no longer in operation. Under Suslov it had produced a kind of elective monarchy which was supposed to limit the authority of the general secretary. But if it were to work properly, the ideological post must be held by someone without personal ambition, or at least without realistic hopes. At this writing, however, no less than three candidates have used it to get to the top. Andropov was the first.

He profited from support by the military, delivered by Defense Minister Ustinov and probably by Chief of Staff Ogarkov as well, perhaps because of the latter's link to Romanov, who had opened the campaign against

Chernenko. After Andropov had been named to replace Suslov at the May plenum, rumors circulated to the effect that Brezhnev was finished. The military chiefs held press conferences without party participation. Western commentators actually wondered if a struggle might break out between the party and the army, so cavalierly did the military men treat the fading Brezhnev. After his stroke in February or March, he appeared increasingly feeble. His death in November brought the election to Andropov. Had Brezhnev died in January and Suslov in November, Andropov's fate might have been quite different.

The Western press speculated on Andropov being a 'closet liberal,' who sipped Scotch, read English novels, and enjoyed the records of Glenn Miller and Peggy Lee. His *moderantisme* was already legendary, partly because of the claims of Boris Rabbot, a political adviser to the moderate Aleksei Rumiantsev, an editor of *Pravda* in the sixties. After Rabbot's defection, he had depicted Andropov as one of the two 'politically literate' persons in the leadership (the other was Gromyko), whose 'liberal views . . . would surprise people in the West.'[23] Harrison Salisbury's novel, *The Gates of Hell* (1975) described extended Politburo debates in which Andropov, a leading character in the novel, usually defended a humanistic position against apparatchiks such as Shelest. A great deal of commentary, however, suggested that this was all disinformation and that Andropov was and remained a Stalinist.

Yet it was clear that Andropov was a man of important intellectual gifts. His first meetings with foreigners, moreover, promoted the expectation that he would break with many of Brezhnev's policies. German foreign secretary Hans-Dietrich Genscher came away from a meeting with Andropov convinced that the Soviet leader was searching for a way to quit Afghanistan. It was suggested that Andropov might prevail upon the Polish military regime to give more authority to Mieczysław Rakowski, who seconded the Gdansk agreement with Solidarity in 1980 and who enjoyed a reputation for favoring 'socialist renewal' in the party. Andropov may have deliberately floated these rumors in order to give himself an air of moderation, an asset in negotiation with the West.

Even had he been of such a temperament, Andropov did not have a great deal of room for maneuver. He faced pressure from elements among the officer corps for a greater assertion of Soviet strength. This may have been particularly pressing in view of the miserable performance of Soviet equipment during the Lebanon war in 1982, especially surface-to-air missiles and tanks. Chernenko was said to have support, in his criticism of Andropov, from the commanders of the air force, air defense forces, strategic rocket forces, and electronic warfare command.[24] In revenge, Andropov was able to secure the appointment of his ally, General V. I. Petrov, to command of the army's ground forces, to replace General Ivan Pavlovskii, who was forced into retirement. Pavlovskii had commanded the 1968 invasion of Czechoslovakia and had enthusiastically supported the Afghanistan war. He was also thought to be an ally of Chernenko.

Andropov was not willing to force a showdown with Chernenko and the Brezhnevists that would have had to be decided in the Central Committee. Instead he preferred to use his power to undermine them by increments. The anticorruption campaign served as a lever to dislodge Brezhnevists from local party offices. The purge in Moldavia was particularly extensive and followed the logic which had led Andropov to replace the Chernenko supporter Shchelokov at the MVD. Andropov's own health was not robust, and he seemed to be in a hurry to establish Mikhail Gorbachev as his principal deputy and Geidar Aliev as president in place of Tikhonov. By August, Andropov had disappeared from public view, never to resurface. But the December, 1983, Central Committee plenum made sweeping personnel changes according to his plans.

The changes reinforced the idea of a campaign against the Brezhnevists. Three full members of the Politburo and two candidates were named. Geidar Aliev, a KGB veteran, had come up by way of posts as head of KGB, then party chief, in Azerbaijan.[25] The Azerbaijani are a Turkic-speaking people of Shia Moslem faith and Persian culture. Aliev's background suggested that he would arouse enthusiasm among Soviet Moslems and that he might be useful in dealing with West Asian affairs. He was designated for a special mission to Syria in February 1984 (Syria's Assad is an Alawite, a Shia sect). Mikhail Solomentsev had been in Kazakhstan, before being demoted by Brezhnev in favor of Kunaev. Brezhnev no doubt remembered that Solomentsev had been a supporter of his 1961–1962 opponent, Frol Kozlov. With this past, Solomentsev could hardly be counted a friend of the Brezhnevists and he and Kunaev would not likely be found on the same side on many issues.[26] Vitallii Vorotnikov had been close to Kirilenko and had been 'exiled' to the embassy in Cuba with the rise of Chernenko in 1979. Andropov had brought him back to replace the Brezhnevist Medunov in Krasnodar in 1982.

Nominees for candidate membership were of the same cloth. Victor Chebrikov had spent fourteen years in the leadership of the KGB. He had been appointed to head the KGB in December 1982 when Fedorchuk was moved out and given the MVD. Egor Ligachev, regarded as a man of cultivation and political gifts, nevertheless had languished in Tomsk since 1965. Andropov made him Central Committee Secretary for Organizational and Party Work. Except for Aliev, the appointees of the December plenum had all suffered from the Brezhnev-Suslov 'stabilization of cadres.' The plenum published a list of Politburo members out of alphabetical order, that is, in order of rank: Andropov, Tikhonov, Chernenko, Grishin, Ustinov, Romanov, Vorotnikov, Gorbachev, Gromyko, Solomentsev, Shcherbitskii, Kunaev, Aliev. An Andropov 'faction' might have included Gorbachev, Vorotnikov, Solomentsev, and Aliev, with

Romanov allied. Ustinov and Gromyko could be regarded as Andropov supporters. That left a Chernenko group with Tikhonov, Grishin, Kunaev, and perhaps Shcherbitskii. Andropov could be said to command a slim but robust majority, as long as Ustinov and Gromyko cooperated. Aside from Andropov and Chernenko, the only Politburo members in the Secretariat were Gorbachev and Romanov.

These two ambitious and able younger leaders seemed to personify the Moscow and Leningrad division, description of the dynamics of which has been one of the main burdens of this study. Had Andropov lived to replace the remaining Brezhnevists in the leadership, sorting out this potential and logical rivalry would have been his next order of business. Because Andropov did not return to action—his death came in March 1984—the task fell to Ustinov and Gromyko, in view of their swing vote between Andropovism and Brezhnevism.

By the time of Andropov's death, his major foreign policy initiatives had ended in failure. Instead of quitting Afghanistan he ended by sending fresh troops. Nor did he make progress in Poland. What appeared to be his most important project, arrival at an agreement on theater nuclear forces that would have prevented the installation of ground-launched cruise missiles and Pershing II missiles in Western Europe, also ran aground. And, while the negotiations were being prepared, quantity, as the Soviets like to say, turned into quality. President Reagan announced, in March 1983, his Strategic Defence Initiative. Up to this point, the Euromissiles had held center stage in Soviet propaganda, but by the first deployment in November, the Soviets had given up the preliminary talks and turned immediately to a campaign to stop the SDI. Andropov's illness was apparently advanced by this time. Gorbachev was filling some of his functions, and Chernenko was doing his best to play the role of the new Suslov.

Andropov's death in February 1984 thus occurred at a moment when his work had been undertaken but by no means completed. Ustinov and Gromyko found themselves *in media res* with regard to the succession. Should they promote Gorbachev at the risk of opening up the Romanov-Gorbachev struggle prematurely or at the risk of dispatching the older Brezhnevists too hastily? Perhaps they hoped to establish the 'ideological post' as the anteroom to the chairmanship of the party. Or perhaps they felt it necessary to sort out the rivalry between Chernenko and Romanov while Gorbachev was eased into the ideological position and prepared for the top job. Lacking more definite information about the bizarre choice of Chernenko, we are forced into these speculations.

The most appealing speculation was that they sought a bloc between Gorbachev and the Andropovists on the one hand and Chernenko and the Brezhnevists on the other, a bloc for the purpose of reducing Romanov's power to more manageable proportions. This hypothesis seemed to fit the subsequent appearances. Amazingly, the party chairmanship was turned over to Chernenko, who, even at this supreme moment in his political career, seemed ill at ease and out of his depth. His election hardly improved his comrades' estimation of his talents, as 'praise analysis' showed. Andropov had been commonly praised as a man with a talent for politics and an aptitude for theory, a man who had made contributions to foreign policy and to the solution of 'topical problems of socialist construction.' Chernenko, by contrast, even in triumph, was praised as a 'faithful propagandist of Communism' or as a 'tireless fighter for the Leninist cause.' The exception was Grishin, who extolled Chernenko effusively, no doubt because he realized that his own career was tied up with Chernenko's longevity, or that longevity itself had become the highest virtue. Perhaps because of a prior deal, Gorbachev assumed the 'ideological post.' In his first speeches, Chernenko vowed to continue the anti-corruption campaign but pathetically sought to blunt it by invoking a 'distinction between economic and party structures.' Apparently he hoped that the purge could be diverted from Andropov's purpose, that of dismantling the Brezhnev machine, to the more banal declared purpose of disciplining this or that corrupt manager.

Chernenko was unable to halt the momentum. It might even be said that his elevation to chairmanship of the party was the last and deepest stage of his degradation. Foreign visitors reported that he was treated with scorn even by Soviet officials, who often paid no attention when he spoke. Some Western observers had actually expressed hopes for initiatives in East-West relations on the basis of Chernenko's previous speeches in favor of Brezhnev's détente policy. Soviet sources, on the other hand, broadly indicated that they would await the outcome of the American November elections. The high standing of the American president in opinion polls may have caused a reconciliation, for at the end of June they offered to reopen negotiations, perhaps to 'intervene' in a close race. There is little reason to suspect a special Chernenko input there. Gromyko would stress that these were to be absolutely new talks which would include all topics, from 'Star Wars' to the fourteen American aircraft carriers.

Little is known of Gorbachev's work with ideology, but in July an extraordinary, even gratuitous, step was taken with the readmission to the party of Molotov, at the age of 94. This deeply symbolic act was not easy to explain. Was the Chernenko-Gorbachev Politburo signaling approval of the positions Molotov had taken in his long career? Was it appreciating the Third Period line, the reconciliation with Hitler, intractability toward Tito, or Molotov's favorable attitude toward Mao? Molotov had been driven from the party by Khrushchev in the early sixties, so the Politburo may have been underlining its opposition to Khrushchevism in general. Molotov and Suslov had been shown with all their warts in Roy Medvedev's 1983 book *All Stalin's Men*, so the leadership may have intended this as a defense of Stalinism and a rebuke to Medvedev, especially in view of the latter's oft-proclaimed enthusiasm for Khrushchev.

In September the point of Gorbachev's alliance with the Brezhnevists became clearer. Romanov was sent to Ethiopia to oversee the founding of its Communist party. The Soviets had been trying to get the Ethiopian Dergue to transform itself into a Marxist-Leninist party, and Romanov's trip accomplished the task, a feather in the cap of one who would not have minded the appearance of being able to step into Suslov's shoes. While Romanov was gone, however, the Politburo demoted his ally, Chief of Staff Ogarkov. This appeared to be the last political act of Ustinov, who died in October. In subsequent months the fall of Ogarkov was attributed to a 1979 speech in which he seemed to endorse nuclear war-fighting, his enthusiasm for the deployment of SS-20 missiles in Eastern Europe, his urgent calls for Emerging Technology conventional weapons (long-range sensors and 'smart' munitions), his defense of the shooting down of KAL 007, or his stridency during the period of Brezhnev's imposture in 1982. The Politburo may have judged that the Romanov-Ogarkov combination looked too much like Khrushchev-Zhukov. It is not unreasonable to suppose that Gorbachev himself saw this, or that the Politburo acted with Gorbachev in mind. Chernenko would have lacked little in motivation to deflate Romanov, whom he would have remembered as an opponent, with the 'steel-eaters,' of Brezhnev's populist 'Food Program' of 1981, and the man who opened the anti-Brezhnev floodgates at the end of that year.

Everything seemed to strengthen Gorbachev. Gromyko was to remark later that, as Chernenko's health faded, Gorbachev chaired Politburo sessions 'in a brilliant manner.' The Chernenko interlude appeared to be a finishing school for Gorbachev. Thus on Chernenko's passing, in March 1985, the election of Gorbachev was almost simultaneously announced. Still, there was some suggestion of conflict in the election. Gromyko, who nominated Gorbachev, remarked shortly afterward that by reason of his, Gromyko's, responsibilities (for foreign policy) he had perceived 'perhaps more clearly than certain other comrades' Gorbachev's aptitude to guide the Soviet Union in the international arena. The precise identity of the 'certain other comrades' was not obvious.[27] One could reflexively assume that Tikhonov, Grishin, and the remaining Brezhnevists were still resisting, but it seems more likely that opposition came from within the camp of Andropov appointees.

This might be easier to fathom if the holder of the 'ideological post' were clearly determined at that time, but such was not the case. Romanov, who had been permitted to announce that Ogarkov had not been banished but instead given a new, unspecified command, was also permitted to greet some heads of foreign Communist parties. Various incidents, including the murder of the pro-Solidarity priest Father Popiełuszko, continued to occur in the Bydgoszcz area, identified as a stronghold of the diehard pro-Moscow party revivalists associated with the names of Olszowski and Romanov. Romanov might even have been thought a possible new Suslov, considering his work in Ethiopia, but his disappearance from view in the spring made it seem more that he was at the end of his rope or that, like Shelepin, he was going to be removed from influence by stages. A gain in Aliev's stature was suggested by his delivering the address commemorating the one hundred fifteenth anniversary of the birth of Lenin, 'The Historical Validity of the Ideas and the Cause of Lenin,' on 22 April. He also took part in the important meetings with Nicaragua's Daniel Ortega at the end of the month.

A Central Committee plenum, held in April 1985, further strengthened Gorbachev by making Ligachev, Chebrikov, and Nikolai Ryzhkov full Politbureau members. Ligachev was said to be a man with a capacity for theory whose ideas were in tune with those of Gorbachev. He seemed prepared to give life to Gorbachev's promise that there would be more and better information forthcoming. Ryzhkov, a former associate of Kirilenko, had been brought into the Secretariat by Andropov. His rise showed how carefully the Andropovists had cultivated the Kirilenko men. Moreover, since both Ligachev and Ryzhkov were already in the Secretariat, their appointment to the Politburo made them two of the four enjoying that exalted dual status. The other two were Gorbachev and Romanov.

Gorbachev was extraordinarily well ensconsed, better certainly than was Zinoviev in 1924, Malenkov in 1953, or Brezhnev in 1964. One could attribute this to the genius of the Suslov system, except for the fact that the succession from Brezhnev to Andropov to Chernenko seemed to have the effect of liquidating the Suslov system. Gorbachev had not, however, established himself as anything more than a spokesman for the collective leadership; nor had he brought forward policies that could be associated with his name. His leadership in fact gave the appearance of being provisional.

Western observers nevertheless expected Gorbachev to effect vast changes in the Soviet system, in the direction of those being pursued in Hungary and in China.[28] Mention was made of the program of the Novosibirsk academician Tatiana Zaslavskaia, who not only provided theoretical underpinning for a call to renovate the Soviet economy but also identified the social layer most likely to resist the needed changes: in her view, middle management.[29] It was even said that Gorbachev protected the Novosibirsk school because his sensibilities were very much in tune with theirs. Gorbachev's inclinations were compared with those of Khrushchev and it was remarked that the leader himself did nothing to discourage the comparison.[30] The changes that were suggested amounted to a new NEP.

That sort of reform was very much within the capacities of the newly unleashed Andropovists, if they were of one mind. Reform in the opposite spirit was no less so. Ligachev, in his years at Tomsk, formed close relationships with the Novosibirsk scholars, apparently Zaslavskaia among them. As he assumed the ideological post, the expectation was that large-scale purges in the state and party machinery would continue. But these could not be assumed to favor the unleashing of market forces beyond an attempt to bring illegal economic life within the scope of taxation. To judge by the Novosibirsk document, Tatiana Zaslavskaia was actually calling for a 'shaking up' of the cadres from above. Soviet leaders who wanted to make big changes had before them not only the neo-NEP models of Hungary and China but also a centralized model such as East Germany. This was another refraction of the Moscow-Leningrad dualism.

After Suslov

We have become accustomed to associating the advocacy of reform with the impulse to de-Stalinization. The corollary puts Suslov as a 'conservative' and Khrushchev as the reformer, the latter seen only in the phase of his activity when he championed the consumer. By extension, it becomes normal to tie Khrushchev to the idea of a neo-NEP and to the fight against Stalinism historically projected across the entire canvas of Soviet history. This view of things may be made to save the appearances, but it is uneconomical, since it requires the assumption of de-radicalization: that the Stalinist revolution from above has been transformed into Suslovist 'conservatism'—still, however, requiring reform. It seems less of a strain on the available language to view Stalinism not as a program but as a regime, capable of adopting a Bukharinist program or a Zinovievist one, by turns. Suslov was an heir of this regime who sought to lessen the friction between the competing programmatic options. A complete de-Stalinization, such as that, for example, advocated by Zhukov, would mean the rehabilitation of the whole Lenin Politburo and would immediately suggest a second look at the programs offered by Bukharin and Zinoviev. It makes no sense to make either of these programs essential to a definition of Stalinism, unless we suppose that the struggle at the Fourteenth Congress of 1925 was a struggle between reform and Stalinist 'conservatism.' This study has argued instead that an alternance between Moscow and Leningrad lines emerges from different constituencies and from the confrontation between revolutionary ideology on the one hand and the Russian and international reality on the other. The pervasive idea that the Russian Revolution long ago passed through its Thermidor with the promulgation of the idea of Socialism in One Country, may have obscured for us the dynamic of Soviet Communism.

In any case Gorbachev seemed little disposed toward de-Stalinization in 1985. Gorbachev's speech to assembled war veterans on the occasion of the anniversary of V-E day paid a fulsome homage to the wartime leadership of Stalin, the mention of whose name prompted demonstrative applause. It may be that Gorbachev was only responding in kind to the visit of President Reagan to the Bitburg cemetery, where some Nazis are buried. And praise for Stalin's war leadership is not the same as praise for the regime of 1937. Yet a certain homage to Stalin spoke defiance to Soviet anti-Stalinists and accorded well with the rehabilitation of Molotov, undertaken while Gorbachev was in charge of ideology.

It would not be in keeping with the approach employed in this study to attribute to Gorbachev a policy program in the abstract. It would also be well to bear in mind the highly contentious nature of life at the top of Soviet politics and the near-certainty that major departures call forth opposition. Thus Gorbachev would have been unlikely to get the kind of accompanying cast he required without making major changes. In the manifesto of the Movement for Socialist Renewal (*Dvizhenie Sotsialisti-cheskogo Obnovleniia*), a protest document made public in Leningrad in November 1985, one could already see the maximum program for a socialist opposition outside the party: a neo-NEP in the economy, a free press, and an end to one-party rule. This program could never make headway inside the party, but it was significant that the slogan 'socialist renewal,' promoted by the extraordinary Congress of the Polish Communist party in August 1981, had found an echo in the Soviet Union. It was no less significant that Gorbachev's campaign for *glasnost*, *perestroika*, and *demokratizatsiia* (openness, restructuring, democracy) gathered steam at this time. It was a superb vehicle for isolating potential opponents and casting new leadership.

The replacement of cadres from the previous era proceeded on a grand scale. Romanov was removed in July 1985. Epishev, head of the MPA since 1962, followed. Then the plenum of October 1985 removed Tikhonov; purges of the armed forces followed in January 1986, with the father of the Soviet navy, Admiral Gorshkov, and the head of the strategic rocket forces, General Tolubko, being retired. Kapitonov, Rusakov, and Zimyanin were removed from the secretariat. Broad restructuring was undertaken in the party organs in Uzbekistan, Kirghizia, Turkmenia, and Tadzhikstan at the same time that Grishin retired at the Twenty Seventh Congress in February 1986. A kind of climax came with the removal of Kunaev in Kazakhstan for a great Russian, Gennadi Kolbin, in December. Riots broke out in Alma Ata and appear to have had a nationalistic flavor. The central press blamed the trade unions and educational institutions for doing nothing to suppress the outbursts of hostility to Moscow, an indication that students, workers, and perhaps even ex-soldiers were involved. This dampened enthusiasm for the removal of the Ukrainian

Shcherbitskii at the central committee plenum of January 1987. Gorbachev frankly admitted that he faced opposition at the plenum and even in the Politburo. Speculation about its composition centered around Ligachev, who, holding the ideological post, was necessarily at the fulcrum of the Politburo balance; whatever his inclinations, he would have been forced to act as a Suslov. Yet he called for continued restructuring in the Ukraine after the plenum, and the Lvov and Dnepropetrovsk secretaries, Dobrik and Boiko, were ousted in March. Gorbachev's struggle was bound to continue.

It was hard to imagine that a leader of Gorbachev's standing and undoubted gifts could live permanently with the heritage of the Brezhnev regime. This would also include the foreign policy of Brezhnev's last years at its most fatuous, with military rule in Poland and the seemingly endless war with Afghanistan. Initiatives to liquidate these problems seemed to comprise a good platform on which to base restructuring the leadership.

Moreover, it might be observed that a new generation of leaders would be judged unworthy in the scales of history if it proved incapable of taking de-Stalinization any further than did Suslov. At a minimum, it could permit a renewed and franker discussion of Soviet history, of the episodes discussed in this volume and the many unmentionable names. The pall on the mind of the Soviet Union is in no small measure an inheritance from the Stalin era, and in turn a reflection of the mediocrity of Stalin. Now that the Soviet Union has leaders whose mental world is not so narrow — who presumably enjoy the esteem of their colleagues for their intellectual capacities — is it not possible to hope that they can do something to lift that pall?

10

Conclusion

Oh, happy who still hopes to rise
Out of this sea of errors and false views!
What one does *not* know, one could utilize,
And what one knows one cannot use.

—Goethe, *Faust*, after Walter Kaufmann

A NARRATIVE must have its lessons, or so we are accustomed to think. Actually a good case might be made for the opposite view, that no reading of facts can ever be properly encapsulated by maxims. Nevertheless, one studies Soviet affairs not only to establish historical points but also to address a serious general reader who wants to understand what is happening to his world. The questions asked of Soviet experts by media people, whenever there is a summit or a funeral in Moscow, show that it is not enough for the experts to explain what has happened. They must tell the public what is going to happen next. After all, the scientist studies in order to predict. With regard to the Soviet Union, along with the desperate need for usable knowledge goes the feeling that, lacking the knowledge and failing to address the East-West relationship properly, we may all perish. Yet the demands made on Soviet experts are surely too exacting; in foretelling the future all, or very nearly all, are out of their depth. What can the student of Soviet affairs report that will pass the test of relevance? What can elevate musings about the connections between odd facts to the level of wise counsel about the nature of Soviet politics? For this, it seems that only rules of thumb about Soviet behavior will do. Everyone who works in the area has them, while not everyone writes about them. To be useful, they must be in the present tense and describe observable recurrent phenomena.

A few observations of this type emerge from this study. The first is that succession struggles have not been interruptions in an otherwise routine bureaucratic life, but climactic moments of an ongoing contention which is itself the norm.[1] While it cannot be said that policy programs have been unimportant, too close a commitment by a Soviet leader to a program has apparently not been an asset. Those whose names personify definite policy positions (Zinoviev, Bukharin, Zhdanov, Malenkov, Romanov) have usually not been successful, while the winners have espoused various programs and have succeeded by virtue of being centrists. There have been numerous cases where an opponent's line is expropriated, after his defeat for advocating it. Patronage tends to be personal rather than linked to advocacy of issues. It even appears to be the case that individuals are often as not chosen to be part of a given coterie by virtue of their animosities. Stalin collected Gusev for his grudge against Trotsky; Andropov picked Solomentsev and Ligachev for their anti–Brezhnevism. Stalin seems to have promoted strife among his closest associates, apparently for the increased leverage that it afforded him.

The atmosphere of contention is apparently not simply a product of Stalin's peculiar leadership style but is built into the method of Russian Communism. It is assumed that disputes in the party are not simply over the merits of a given measure but reflect in some way class pressures on the vanguard party, so that every struggle inside it is a kind of class struggle. Comrades are sometimes criticized for being 'politically naive' or 'gullible' because they were too attracted by the merits of a case and neglected this larger picture. Moreover, a defeated minority is expected to defend the victorious majority platform publicly, while keeping secret under discipline its own role in the debate. It becomes difficult to build a constituency. And it can destroy an existing bloc, as when the majority compels the minority to break with an associate. Thus Zinoviev was compelled by the course of 'normalization' (criticizing his 'ultra-left' position) to remove his client Ruth Fischer from leadership of the German Communist party. Zhdanov and Beria had to perform similar ablutions. Or a published self-criticism may be necessary.

Soviet Communists see the party not as a grouping of friends permeated by a 'family spirit' but as an arena of struggle for the correct ideas. Democratic Centralism, the 'law of party life' is possible only with 'inner-party democracy,' and alone ensures 'monolithic unity with the people,' proletarian internationalism, and the handling of 'complex relations with fraternal governments.'[2] In Lenin's time there was some truth in this characterization, with contestants able to publish documents and propagate views, presumably to change the party's mind. Platform documents of this type have been illegal since 1921. Even under 'Leninist norms' political struggle was often imposed from above. The majority usually used every administrative trick at its disposal to get its way between congresses, but Politburo members felt obliged to explain their individual views and published articles in the press, a practice which has virtually disappeared. Under Stalin and his successors, the 'struggle for ideas' has had a terroristic aspect, all the more so when a fight takes place in a large meeting. There is what a Polish Communist called in 1981 'the dread bandwagon,' when someone is being denounced and no one knows what to say, but everyone looks around for cues. Someone you trust chimes in, then another, perhaps one to whom you owe a favor, and soon you yourself are calling for measures against the dangerous deviation. Central Committee plenums, especially ones in which a leader's fate is decided, such as the 1957 plenum that saved Khrushchev or the 1964 plenum that retired him, are thus highly explosive affairs.

This is not to say that Democratic Centralism will always exist in the same form. On the face of it, the Bolshevik theory of organization prescribes only that, after a democratic discussion, the defeated minority will not obstruct execution of the majority line. This would be similar to what is expected, or hoped, in Western political parties. At times the discussion at congresses has been extremely animated and even quite open. The debate on the trade unions in 1920 entertained no less than eight platform factions. Today perhaps only Italian political parties could match this fine subdivision of constituencies. A return to a more open party life would, of course, be scarcely less explosive than today's norm. And it cannot be completely excluded that party practice could change. The Polish Communist party had an open and democratic congress in 1981 which it considered a monument to Democratic Centralism. Four months later, however, the party was overtaken by a military coup. Perhaps change will come only in the fullness of the twenty-first century. One is reminded of Kafka's 'there is really infinite hope, but not for us.'

Guidelines for understanding the struggle for power have been provided in the West by those whose speciality is what has been called 'esoteric political communication.' Following the Communist press in a crisis would be difficult if one did not know, for example, that 'dual power' means the army may not be loyal, or that 'fetishizing the law of value' is an accusation made against the right rather than the left. It also helps to know what historic errors are called to mind by mention of the names of Lassalle, Akselrod, or Tomskii. Most of the closest students of this communication acknowledge some manner of debt to the writings reviewed in these pages. People such as Souvarine and Nicolaevsky were in some measure progenitors of professional Soviet studies whose work, while by no means the last word, has provided a certain illumination for historians. This may be said for Souvarine on the early Stalin era and Nicolaevsky on the Stalin succession. The preceding pages have given my own differences, often substantial, with their views. Yet their debates on Russian affairs have provided some valuable signposts.

Souvarine's dispute with Trotsky in 1929 began with Trotsky's pro-scription of the Regime Question. One could question Stalin's policy but not his use of patronage, party rules or police. 'One can put up with any regime as long as it accomplishes some purpose.' Trotsky was only stating his availability for a bloc with Stalin against Bukharin, as Zinoviev and Bukharin had already done against him. These three were always ready for a bloc with Stalin against one another. Stalin was attractive to them because of his power; they were attractive to Stalin because of their animosity toward one another. Had they been more serious about the 'issues' that they used to attack one another and less cynical about the Regime Question, they might have combined against Stalin, who may not have been easily beaten, even in 1923, but whose path to power might not have been as smooth as it was with their help. Stalin was assisted by his ability to make turns and to maneuver his opponents into an 'unprincipled bloc' of two opposed programs hoping only for a freer regime. These turns, as a means of building Stalin's patronage assets, were essential to his rise to power.

Instead of the Regime Question, Trotsky suggested the Russian Question: What is the nature of the Soviet state? Souvarine had said that it was 'state capitalist.' Trotsky insisted that the Soviet state had not yet undergone its Thermidor, that it was still essentially proletarian and deserved loyalty. He was avoiding a real discussion of the rise of Stalin and the roles of Zinoviev, Bukharin, Trotsky, and others, by questioning Souvarine's Soviet patriotism. Trotsky thought that he was taking a short cut: The only worth of discussing the Lenin succession was to determine loyalty or disloyalty to the regime. However, if one has to prove in advance the worth of the discussion, one has to know in advance its conclusions. It should have been enough to ask 'How did it happen?' without any doctrinal anticipations. Straightening out Trotsky's messy ad-hoc pronouncements on the events of 1923 would have shown that the 'issues' had come out of the faction fight rather than the reverse. Moreover, they could not have been such life-and-death matters as to justify recourse to the Stalin regime. Thus the losers were in the ludicrous position of being forced to crawl back later to an 'unprincipled bloc' (that is, a bloc) on the Regime Question (that is, on Stalin) in 1932. Or, they could avoid such contamination, call for one another's deaths, and have their wishes accommodated.

The defeated and the disgraced, if they lived, were forced to pose the Russian Question, now: What is the nature of the Stalinist system? This study has devoted a good deal of attention to the answers. Even for those who were free to view Stalinism frankly, the Russian Question again became a means of avoiding discussion of the top leadership. Usually theories of Soviet degeneration were influenced by the phase of the alternance, as with Trotsky's Thermidor and the Second Five Year Plan or Hilferding's Totalitarian State Economy and the Hitler-Stalin pact. Disputes about the degenerate workers' state or state capitalism or New Class largely concerned the relationship between elite and society. Usually the matter hinged not on the Stalin tyranny but on the betrayal of the revolution inherent in its economic and social policies. The resultant sociological photo almost invariably produced the same image: a society of white-collar workers, professionals, civil servants, and administrative and technical personnel as the ruling class usurping the place of the enslaved blue-collar worker. Nineteenth-century anarchism had warned about this and leftist opponents of the regime claimed it had come to pass. Craipeau spoke of 'bureaucratic collectivism,' then Rizzi and others of a 'bureaucratic revolution.' After the war, theories about a Soviet New Class resurfaced in Western social science literature concerned with the problem of analyzing Soviet bureaucracy.[3]

When the Soviets appeared to withdraw from active participation in world politics after the Cuban missile crisis of 1962, these theories were bolstered by the thesis of Soviet de-radicalization to suggest a 'convergence' of the social systems of the two superpowers. Today this suggestion is denied vehemently, largely because it is alleged to promote the supposition (which I admit to be misguided) that East-West differences are a matter of misunderstanding. Yet convergence, despite its extravagance, was a way of realizing that the technical and administrative tasks of modern society produce some social similarities. The vogue for the idea was usually accompanied by the view the Auguste Comte, the prophet of the managerial intelligentsia of the nineteenth century, had proven superior to Marx. Writers such as Raymond Aron argued this way. The argument would have been more attractive had *dirigisme* held sway in the West and the managerial elements dominated Soviet politics. On the Soviet side this would have assumed that the Moscow line, a Soviet Bukharinism, was in control of affairs. And of course, if this were so, the prospects for peaceful coexistence would be brightened. There are indeed communities in both countries who may see international relations similarly.[4] Nevertheless this thesis cannot account for the recurrent element of Soviet leftist dynamism. Inquiries into the nature of the Soviet state and society have also had the effect of denying the importance of political struggles in the Soviet leadership. Souvarine, in his debate with Nicolaevsky in 1962, argued that recognition of these differences amounted to pleading on behalf of a good Khrushchev against a bad, pro-Chinese Suslov. He had arrived at a position analogous to Trotsky's of 1929, using the Russian Question as a substitute for the study of the leadership, in this case by Nicolaevsky and Western Kremlinology. In this volume, I have tried to demonstrate some of the merits of Kremlinology and to defend it against grander ideological formulations, which of course have their own value and fascination but which can never replace empirical study of leadership conflict.

It would be ludicrous to describe the course of Soviet history as a relentless path toward bureaucratic ossification, and far better to recognize an oscillation between periods of relative stability and consolidation on the one hand and willful transformation on the other. The model for the opposition of the two tendencies, Moscow and Leningrad, is the clash between Bukharin and Zinoviev at the Fourteenth Party Congress in 1925.

Echoes of this clash have been found in the conflict between Bukharin-Ordzhonikidze and Molotov; Malenkov and Zhdanov; Malenkov and Khrushchev; Khrushchev and Kozlov; Kosygin and Brezhnev; Brezhnev and Kirilenko; and Gorbachev and Romanov. The idea of alternance seems the best way to describe the swings of the Soviet pendulum through its history.

At the turn of the century Lenin was alarmed by the ascent to power of the Australian Labour party, knowing that this would not mean the dictatorship of the proletariat but only observation of the 'Anglo-Saxon alternance.' The same fear was expressed by Communist critics of Eurocommunism in 1976–1978. Alternance is correctly perceived as central to the political system of the West. Hence it has been fought relentlessly in the East. The swings of the pendulum have become less violent and the center has become stronger. So even the idea of alternance, the centerpiece of this study, has not depicted a single, continuous, repetitive event. The struggle of Zinoviev and Bukharin was not exactly rerun by Brezhnev and Malenkov. Aside from the changes in circumstances and policy challenges, one can also assume that the Soviet leadership is aware of this tendency and doing its best to overcome it. There would be little point in excluding the possibility that it may indeed do so.

But since evidence does not suggest this but rather the opposite, the continued existence of conflict and even its necessity in a party that places such emphasis on dialectic and political struggle, the question arises whether outside forces can intervene in the process. It would seem that some kind of outside intervention has already been made at various points in Soviet history. Britain and France seemed on the verge of affecting internal Soviet policy in 1921–1922. Fischer and Maslow did so in 1923. The 'counteroffensive' of resistance to world communism after the British General Strike of 1926 certainly strengthened the Leningrader line and may have promoted the turn of 1927. Some Western opportunity to bolster the opponents of Khrushchev may have been present in 1953. The Chinese opposition to Khrushchev had an impact in 1960–1961. And the response of the Kennedy administration to the Berlin crisis of 1961 and the Cuban crisis of 1962 undoubtedly shortened the career of his 'adventurism and subjectivism.' There seems, therefore, little reason for the assumption, made in 1982–1985 by American officials, that no significant policy actions could be undertaken vis-à-vis the Soviet Union until the Brezhnev succession was completed.

Nor is there reason to assume that the results of such interventions can be easily predicted. It may be said, however, that every action of the West has its effect on the Soviet policy agenda. This fact would seem to be of special importance in the realm of ideas. There has been a kind of 'learning curve' along which some Soviet strategic conceptions have occasionally and temporarily moved into line with Western ones.[5] No doubt other fields will be susceptible to the influence of new ideas. It need not be assumed that the Soviets share with the West a spiritual kinship, or that we all want the same thing. Even if the Soviet leaders sincerely hoped for a routinized bureaucratic political life and the foreign policy of a status quo power, the heritage of the revolution and the changing conditions of world politics would act against these hopes. However, one cannot exclude the possibility that the Soviet Union will change and one must assume that change can result from internal conflicts and shocks. Alternance may help to understand the rhythm of changes in the Soviet past. Knowledge of the past, along with the perspective it provides, should also promote recognition of the new. 'Twas ever thus' is not a maxim for historians.

Notes

Preface

1 T. H. Rigby, 'Crypto-Politics,' in Walter Z. Lacqueur and Leopold Labedz, eds. *The State of Soviet Studies* (Cambridge, Mass., MIT Press, 1965), 144–145; Robert Conquest, 'In Defense of Kremlinology,' ibid., 129; Michel Tatu, 'Kremlinology: The Mini-Crisis of 1970,' *Interplay*, October 1970, 19.
2 Myron Rush, *How Communist States Change Their Rulers* (Ithaca and London, Cornell University Press, 1974), 18.

Chapter 1

1 As Walter Duranty of the *New York Times* put it, in his 1929 interview with Stalin. See *The Kremlin and the People* (New York, Reynal and Hitchcock, 1941), 33–34.
2 Louis Fischer, *The Soviets in World Affairs* (London, Jonathan Cape, 1930), vol. 11, pp. 822–823. The same view will be found in Michael T. Florinsky, *World Revolution and the USSR* (New York, Macmillan, 1933), 127, 137; Henri Barbusse, *Stalin* (New York, Macmillan, 1935), 170–172; Sidney and Beatrice Webb, *Soviet Communism: A New Civilization?* (London, Longmans, 1935), 1103–1104; Bernard Pares, *Russia* (London and New York, Allen Lane, 1940), 140–141; Samuel Harper, *The Government of the Soviet Union* (1938; Toronto, New York, and London, Van Nostrand, 1949), 272; Nicholas Timasheff, *The Great Retreat: The Growth and Decline of Communism in Russia* (New York, E. P. Dutton, 1946), 155–158; and in a number of contemporary textbooks.
3 An American visitor, Thomas Donald Campbell, interviewed Stalin on 28 January 1929 and gave a rosy description of Stalin's moderation in *Russia: Market or Menace?* (London and New York, Longmans, 1932). But Stalin objected to Campbell's judgment that 'Trotsky believed in universal Communism, while he (Stalin) worked to confine his efforts to his own country,' calling it 'nonsense.' See 'Mr. Campbell Stretches the Truth,' 23 November 1932, in *Works* (Moscow, 1955), vol. 13, pp. 148–150.
4 Isaac Deutscher, *Stalin: A Political Biography* (New York, Vintage, 1961), 339–340. See also E. H. Carr, *The October Revolution Before and After* (New York, Vintage, 1971), 173–175.
5 See E. H. Carr, *Socialism in One Country, 1924–1926* (Baltimore, Penguin, 1970), vol. 2, p. 45, where it is claimed that Trotsky accepted the antithesis between Socialism in One Country and Permanent Revolution. This is done by quoting Trotsky's polemic against Radek, *The Permanent Revolution* of 1928. Trotsky, however, made no such public claim between 1924, when Stalin argued it first, and his expulsion from the party at the Fifteenth Congress. Textbooks commonly assume an open debate on the two theories between Trotsky and Stalin. See, for example, Georg von Rauch, *A History of*

Soviet Russia (New York and London, Praeger, 1972), 168–170; and M. K. Dziewanowski, *A History of Soviet Russia* (Englewood Cliffs, N.J., Prentice-Hall, 1979), 175–179.

6   J. P. Nettl, *The Soviet Achievement* (London, Thames and Hudson, 1967), 251. World War II, argues Nettl, 'was an unfortunate interruption to the active development of Socialism in One Country which Stalin had pursued so laboriously from 1925 onwards, at home and abroad' (176).

7   Stephen F. Cohen, *Bukharin and the Bolshevik Revolution: A Political Biography, 1888–1938* (New York, Knopf, 1975), 362–364. 'Bukharin, what he represented, and his allies, were more important in Bolshevik politics and thinking than Trotsky or Trotskyism' (xvi). As to program alternatives, 'If "ism" is to be affixed, there was no Stalinism, only Bukharinism and Trotskyism.' Stephen F. Cohen, 'Bolshevism and Stalinism,' in Robert C. Tucker, ed., *Stalinism: Essays in Historical Interpretation* (New York, Norton, 1977), 22. See also *Bukharin*, 390, citing E. H. Carr as a forerunner. Carr denies the role in 'The Myth of Bukharin,' *Times Literary Supplement*, September 20, 1974, 989–991.

8   Richard B. Day, *Leon Trotsky and the Politics of Economic Isolation* (Cambridge Univ. Press, 1973), 119–126. Suggestions also appear in Deutscher, *The Prophet Unarmed: Trotsky, 1921–1929* (London, Oxford Univ. Press, 1959), 212; Florinsky, *World Revolution*, 129–130; and Barbusse, *Stalin*, 170–172, the last representing Trotsky as a disciple of German Socialist economist Rudolf Hilferding, thus a believer in the primacy of the world market. I have no wish to refute this thesis, except as a presumed position of principle defended publicly, for which the evidence is lacking. See chap. 5.

9   That was in 1927. By 1930, he claimed that a central fault of Socialism in One Country was that it 'imposes upon revolutions in backward countries the task of establishing an unrealizable regime of democratic dictatorship.' *Permanent Revolution* (New York 1969), 280. He was referring to Chiang Kai-shek in China and Marshal Piłsudski in Poland.

10   Victor Serge and Natalia Sedova Trotsky, *The Life and Death of Leon Trotsky* (New York, Basic Books, 1973), 252.

11   Robert Wohl, *French Communism in the Making, 1914–1925* (Stanford, Stanford University Press, 1966), 76–78.

12   Souvarine to Trotsky, 8 May 1929, Trotsky Exile Archive, $T_2$5332. Rosenthal recalled to Trotsky that Souvarine had lost none of his old powers: 'His erudition was considerable, vigorous, critical, *pointilleuse*. . . Small, fragile, and resolute, with a countenance, under his large myopic's glasses, and a visage to which age would later lend rather an Asiatic turn, almost always irritated, sombre in his prognostications, refined in his pleasantries, delicate in his amities and implacable in his aversions, he was infinitely seductive. An excellent writer, clear and classical, and a redoubtable polemicist, he spared no denunciation of the crimes of Stalinism. His intransigence had isolated him, or more exactly, he had been isolated for his intransigence.' *Avocat de Trotsky* (Paris, R. Laffont, 1975), 67–68.

13   L. Trotsky, 'Groupings in the Communist Opposition,' 31 March 1929, in *Writings of Leon Trotsky, 1929* (New York, Pathfinder, 1975), 80. (Hereafter, *WLT*).

14   Quoted in Deutscher, *The Prophet Unarmed*, 428.

15   In light of what they called a 'regroupment of forces' since the Fifteenth Congress and the new efforts toward 'socialist reconstruction' in opposition to the Right Danger, Rakovskii and the other signatories declared themselves

ready to dispense with 'factional methods' and submit to party discipline. Text in *La Vérité*, 1 October 1929, 2–6. Trotsky's 'Open Letter' in the same issue suggested that the cooptation of left slogans by the Stalin center 'facilitates in great measure the reconstitution of unity on a Leninist basis.' The essential problem of the October Revolution was 'the transformation of the bourgeois society into a socialist society.' 'A Marxist can refuse to sign your declaration only in the case that he concludes that Thermidor is accomplished, the party is a cadaver, and the road to the Dictatorship of the Proletariat can be found only by a new revolution' (6). Trotsky would arrive at a variant of that view, declaring Thermidor an accomplished fact, by 1935.

16 *Avocat de Trotsky*, 74.
17 Trotsky to Souvarine, 25 April 1929; text in Boris Souvarine's collection of documents, 'Une Controverse avec Trotski, 1929,' in Jacques Freymond, ed., *Contributions à l'histoire du Comintern* (Geneva, 1965), 149.
18 'Une Controverse,' 150.
19 Trotsky to Souvarine, 10 May 1929, ibid., 154.
20 Souvarine to Trotsky, 8 June 1929, Trotsky Exile Archive, T_2 5335.
21 Ibid.
22 Here Souvarine was extending a contemporary criticism, that of the extreme Left Communist Karl Korsch, who sought the source of the degeneration of Communist ideology in the special impact of Russian Marxism, through Plekhanov, on the Marxism of the Second International. Korsch quoted for support Trotsky's article on the twenty-fifth anniversary of *Neue Zeit* on Russian Marxism's role in establishing international Social Democratic orthodoxy. See 'The Present State of the Problem of Marxism and Philosophy: An Anti-Critique,' in *Marxism and Philosophy* (1930; London, NLB, 1970), 123.
23 Souvarine to Trotsky, 8 June 1929, Trotsky Exile Archive, T_2 5335.
24 The passages to which Souvarine referred were from 'Tradition and Revolutionary Policy,' not published originally in *Pravda* but included in *The New Course*. The German party, argued Trotsky, 'proved unable to free itself, at the beginning of the new phase (May–July 1923), from the automatism of its preceding policy. . . It would have been the same with us if our party had not made its leap in April 1917 and then taken power in October. We have every ground to believe that the German proletariat will not pay too dearly for its omission, for the stability of the present German regime, resulting above all from the international situation, is more than doubtful.' L. Trotsky, *The New Course* (1924; Ann Arbor, University of Michigan Press, 1965), 50.
25 'Une Controverse,' 192.
26 Ibid.
27 Ibid., 207.
28 Trotsky to Souvarine, 3 July 1929, ibid., 208.
29 Ibid., 209. This is only one illustration, among many that could be cited, of Trotsky's pride in his contribution to Soviet industrialization under Stalin. Richard B. Day's excellent study of Trotsky's ideas on economic isolation thus claims too much: 'Only in the limited sense that Stalin was reviving War Communist policies can it be said with Deutscher that Trotsky was the inspirer of Soviet industrialization. Still concerned with the paramount problem of isolation, Trotsky himself would have greeted such faint praise with total disdain.' *Leon Trotsky and the Politics of Economic Isolation*, 187.

Chapter 2

1   *Polnoe sobranie sochinenii* (Moscow, 1960), vol. 11, p. 54.
2   Robert Wohl, *French Communism*, 146–148.
3   Christian Gras, *Alfred Rosmer et le mouvement révolutionnaire internationale* (Paris, François Maspero, 1971), 110–113.
4   Alfred Rosmer, 'La Conférence de Zimmerwald,' *Lettres aux abonnés de la 'Vie ouvrière'* (Paris, 1915), 11, 24. Trotsky would nevertheless later hold up the early ILP as a model for British Communists in their work inside the Labour party. See *Where is Britain Going?* (1925; London, New Park, 1960), p. 127.
5   *Nashe slovo*, 4 June 1915, quoted in Alfred Rosmer, *Le Mouvement ouvrière pendant la première guerre mondiale: De Zimmerwald à la révolution russe* (Paris, 1959), p. 104.
6   G. Zinoviev, 'Rossiiskaia sotsial-demokratiia i russkii sotsial-shovinizm' (1915); text in *Protiv techeniia!* (Petrograd, 1918), 245, 251. Lenin used the epithet 'liquidator' to describe how those Mencheviks who saw no need for an illegal organization of Social Democrats in Russia, and even those such as Iulii Martov, who, while not himself a 'liquidator,' had sought equality of status between the legal and illegal party organizations.
7   Groupe des Temps Nouveaux, *Un Désaccord: Nos Explications* (Paris, 1916), 55–57. Faure adhered to the position of the *International Anarchist Manifesto on the War*, signed by Alexander Berkman, Emma Goldman, Errico Malatesta, Domela Niewenhuis, Alexander Shapiro, and others; text in *Freedom*, March, 1915, 21.
8   Wohl, *French Communism*, 141–142. Russian anarcho-syndicalists had also seen the Soviets as 'production-consumption communes' and voted with the Bolsheviks in the factory committees, viewing them as allies against the Mensheviks, who stood for state control of industry. Péricat was, with Guy Tourrette of the *Vie ouvrière*, a signatory of the *Temps nouveaux* manifesto against the war. *Movement ouvrière*, 112–113. Left-wing Socialist Raymond Lefebvre also spoke of the mystique created by the word 'soviet,' which could permit 'a posthumous triumph of Marx and of Bakunin, reconciled on the pedestal of the Russian Revolution.' Quoted in Annie Kriegel, *Aux origines du communisme français* (Paris, Flammarion, 1969), 62.
9   On the persecution of the Russian anarchists, see Anatolii Gorelik et al., *Goneniia na anarkhizm v Sovietskoi Rossii* (Berlin, 1922).
10 G. P. Maksimov, *Sovety rabochikh, soldatskikh i krestianskikh deputatov: Nashe k nim otnoshenie* (New York, 1919), 2; Augustin Souchy, *Wie lebt der Arbeiter und Bauer in Russland und in der Ukraine?* (Berlin, n.d. [1922?]), 27.
11 *Pervyi kongress Kominterna, Mart 1919 g.* (Moscow, 1933), 116–117.
12 The veteran American Communist William Z. Foster developed his idea of 'boring from within'—expounded to generations of American Communists—from his trip to France in 1910. He met Jouhaux, Monatte, and other syndicalist leaders, read the classic anarchist blueprint of Pouget and Pataud, *Comment nous ferons la révolution*, and expressed admiration for the anarchist 'raid' on the reformist CGT during the 1890s. *From Bryan to Stalin* (New York, International Publishers, 1937), 48–49.
13 Rosmer reports an exchange of this kind in 1920 with the German Communist Paul Levi. *Moscou sous Lenine: Les Origines du communisme* (Paris, P. Horay, 1953), 102.
14 Leon Trotsky, *Communism and Syndicalism* (London, 1968), 24. At the Second Comintern Congress, Lenin had told Jack Tanner of the British Shop

Stewards: 'Your conscious minority of the working class, this active minority which has to guide its action—well, that's the party, that's what we call the party. . . But for that the minority must organize, it must create a firm organization, and must impose discipline based on the principles of democratic centralism.' Quoted in ibid., 101.

15 On this, see Wohl, *French Communism*, 70.

16 Pannekoek reported this conversation to Franz Borkenau. See *World Communism* (Ann Arbor, University of Michigan Press, 1962), 191.

17 Herman Gorter, *Réponse à Lenin* (Paris, 1920), 12, 28. Pannekoek's parallel theory of antiparliamentary 'mass action' dominated the thinking of the American Communists in the early days. See Theodore Draper, *The Roots of American Communism* (New York, Viking, 1957), 88–91. For Pannekoek's theory, see *Bolschewismus und Demokratie* (Vienna, 1919), especially his denial of a role for a party: 'The Soviet is posed against party organization and other varieties of parliamentary filth: party discipline, profiteering and maneuvering behind the scenes, intrigue and endless debate' (7).

18 Leon Trotsky, 'Réponse au Camarade Gorter,' report from a session of the Comintern executive, 24 November 1920; text in *Bulletin communiste*, 18 August 1921, 566.

19 See Adolf Sturmthal, *The Tragedy of European Labor* (New York, Columbia Univ. Press, 1943), 3–16, for the argument that Marxist class theory induced paralysis in the parliamentary arena and resulted in impotence, as with Rudolf Hilferding's refusal to countenance countercyclical action by the German government after the 1929 crash: '[Those who] think they can mitigate a depression by public works, they are merely showing they are not Marxists.' Quoted in W. S. Woytinsky, *Stormy Passage: A Personal History* (New York, Vanguard, 1961), 465. See also the discussion of this point in Charles P. Kindleberger, *The World in Depression, 1929–1939* (Berkeley, University of California Press, 1973), 171–177.

20 'Réponse au Camarade Gorter,' 565.

21 Ibid., 569.

22 Leon Trotsky, *Na proizvodstvennyi put!* (Moscow, 1921), 5, 12.

23 'Un Discours de Trotski à la conférence des transports,' *Bulletin communiste*, 27 January 1921, 53–54.

24 Trotsky's version of this is in *My Life* (1930: New York, 1970), 466. His views on 'Mobilization of labor' may be found in RKP(b), *Deviatyi s"ezd rossiiskoi kommunisticheskoi partii: Stenograficheskii otchet (29 marta–4 aprelia 1920g.)* (Moscow, 1920), 79–99, and in the Trotsky Archive, T-468.

25 Leon Trotsky 'Labor Control in Russia,' *Living Age*, 26 January 1920, 754.

26 Leon Trotsky, 'Nouvelle période, nouveaux problèmes,' *Bulletin communiste*, 3 February 1921, 66.

27 'In his economic thinking, Trotsky was the earliest Stalinist.' Robert V. Daniels, *The Conscience of the Revolution: Communist Opposition in Soviet Russia* (New York, Simon & Schuster, 1960), 122. As will become clear, I do not share the view that Stalin was attached on principle to any line of economic thinking. Trotsky's followers have continued to insist that 'mobilization of labor' and 'militarization of the economy' were always mere expedients. See the exchange on this between Raya Dunayevskaya, criticizing Trotsky, and Ernest Mandel, defending, in *Studies in Comparative Communism*, Spring–Summer 1977, 169–173, 180.

28 *Congrès anarchiste tenu à Amsterdam, août 1907* (Paris, 1908); Errico Malatesta, 'Syndicalism and Anarchism,' *La prensa* (Rome), 15 December 1925; text in *Road to Freedom*, January 1931, 1.

29   Trotsky to Monatte, 13 July 1921, Pierre Brové, ed. *Le Mouvement communiste en France, 1919–1939* (Paris, 1967), 113.
30   On the Mannheim declaration, see Carl Schorske, *German Social Democracy* (Cambridge, Mass., Harvard Univ. Press, 1955), 49–53; Selig Perlman, *A Theory of the Labor Movement* (New York, A. M. Kelly, 1928), 100.
31   Paul Delesalle, 'Front unique et syndicalisme,' *Bulletin communiste*, 16 February, 1922, 132.
32   *Bulletin communiste*, 7 July 1921, 458.
33   *Bulletin communiste*, 21 September 1922, 728.
34   'This kind of violence compels capitalism to restrict its attentions solely to its material role and tends to restore to it the warlike qualities which it formerly possessed. A growing and solidly organized working class can compel the capitalist class to remain firm in the industrial war; if a united and revolutionary proletariat confronts a rich bourgeoisie, eager for conquest, capitalist society will have reached its historical perfection.' *Reflections on Violence* (1908; New York, 1950), 92.
35   V. I. Lenin, *Sochineniia* (Moscow, 1929), vol. 4, p. 366.
36   See the discussion of the Russian syndicalist Takhtarev, in J. L. H. Keep, *The Rise of Social Democracy in Russia* (Oxford Univ. Press, 1963), 60–61.
37   Her case against Polish 'social patriotism' may be found in the German Social Democratic organ *Neue Zeit*, no. 6 (1897–1898), 164–176, with an appended disavowal by Karl Kautsky. For a reply by a supporter of the PPS (the orthodox Polish Socialist Party), see Res (Feliks Perl), *Kwestya polska w oświetleniu Social-demokracyi polskiej* (Warsaw, 1907), 12–20.
38   A. Volski (J. W. Machajski), *Umstvennyi rabochii* (Geneva, 1905), pt. 1, pp. 41–49; *Burzuazyjna rewolucya a sprawa rabotnicza* (Geneva, 1905), 4–5. For Trotsky's appreciation of Machajski, see *My Life* (New York, 1929), 129; and *On Lenin* (1924; London, 1971), 31–32. For an elaboration of Machajski's thought, see Anthony D'Agostino 'Intelligentsia Socialism and the "Workers' Revolution": The Views of J. W. Machajski,' *International Review of Social History* (Amsterdam), vol. 14, pt. 2 (1969).
39   For Akselrod's influence on Trotsky, see Abraham Ascher, *Pavel Akselrod and the Development of Menshevism* (Cambridge, Mass., Harvard Univ. Press, 1972), 200–201, 238–239. Ascher suggests that Akselrod anticipated Trotsky's notion that the workers could skip the stage of subordination to bourgeois democracy. Trotsky envisioned the Russian Labor party of the future as 'one powerful union.' 'The Russian word *stachka* (strike),' Trotsky thought, 'fully corresponds in the most precise sense with foreign words for "coalition," "agreement," "understanding," or "union."' *Borba*, no. 3 (April 12, 1914), 12.
40   The nationalization process in Russia was not complete until the fall of 1918, with the Bolsheviks already in power and by no means leading the way. Lenin, in fact, preferred an imitation of Walter Rathenau's German war economy to large-scale nationalizations, and dated the transfer from the democratic revolution to the proletarian from the compulsory grain requisitions of spring, 1918. Thus a socialist dictatorship of the proletariat, for him, could employ 'state capitalism' as a policy. For Trotsky's Permanent Revolution, see Alain Brossat, *Aux origines de la révolution permanente: La Pensée politique du jeune Trotsky* (Paris, F. Maspero, 1974); Baruch Knei-Paz, *The Social and Political Thought of Leon Trotsky* (London, Oxford Univ. Press, 1979); Guido Vestuti, *La rivoluzione permanente: Uno studio sulla politica di Trotsky* (Milano, 1960). Brossat follows Michel Lowy, *La Théorie de la révolution chez le jeune Marx* (Paris, F. Maspero, 1970), in drawing a straight line between Marx's *Address of the Central Authority to the Communist League*

(1850) and Permanent Revolution. Denise Avenas, *Trotsky Marxiste* (Paris, 1970), perhaps too ambitious, already has the 1905 prognosis connected to a theory of imperialism in decline. Brossat and Knei-Paz see Permanent Revolution as an idea with universal application for a social science of backwardness. In this respect they take the idea much further than Trotsky. My interpretation of the succession struggle, as will be indicated, does not hold Permanent Revolution to be of central importance.

41   Not only Trotsky's formula but Lenin's as well. In a speech on the fourth anniversary of the revolution, Lenin recalled that 'we decided the questions of the bourgeois-democratic revolution in passing, as a "by-product" of our main and genuinely *proletarian*—revolutionary socialist activities.' *Sochineniia* (Moscow, 1950), vol. 33, p. 32. A socialist Russia, according to Permanent Revolution, could be truly safeguarded only by 'state support' from a major Western country, made possible by a socialist revolution there. In this, Trotsky did not differ from Mensheviks and Bolsheviks who thought only 'state support' of this kind could protect Russian democracy. See the argument in Keep, *Rise of Social Democracy*, 274–277.

42   V. I. Lenin, *Sochineniia* (Moscow, 1930), vol. 26, p. 67.

43   *Deviatyi s"ezd RKP(b) Mart. Aprel 1920 goda: Protokoly* (Moscow, 1960), 417.

44   'K organizatsiiam RKP po voprosu o poriadke dnia partiinogo s"ezda,' in ibid., 494.

45   V. I. Lenin, *Sochineniia* (Moscow, 1930), vol. 26, p. 67.

46   *Desiatyi s"ezd rossiiskoi kommunisticheskoi partii: Stenograficheskoi otchet (8–16 marta, 1921g.)* (Moscow, 1921), 190.

47   Ibid., 193.

48   Ibid., 191.

49   N. N. Krestinskii, a Bolshevik since 1905, had come into the Central Committee in July, 1917, and had been its sole secretary in 1919–1920. E. A. Preobrazhenskii, a Bolshevik since 1904, an early supporter of Lenin's *April Theses*, had been in the Central Committee since August 1917, and was secretary in 1920. L. P. Serebriakov, a Bolshevik since 1905, entered the Central Committee in 1919 and the Secretariat in 1920. V. M. Molotov (Skriabin), a Bolshevik since 1906, established a Central Committee bureau in Petrograd in 1916. After 1917 he worked in Petrograd and Nizhni Novgorod, and in 1920 he was a secretary for the Ukraine. He became a candidate member of the Central Committee in 1920. Emelian Iaroslavskii, a Bolshevik since 1903, candidate member of the Central Committee in 1919–1920, was later an official historian of the party. V. M. Mikhailov, a Bolshevik from 1915, had been an official in the Moscow Printers' Union, then chairman of the Moscow raion cheka.

Chapter 3

1   Albert Mathiez, *Le Bolchevisme et le jacobinisme* (Bologna, 1920), 3.

2   Mathiez was attacked by pacifist leftists in the surrealist review *Clarté*. Romain Rolland criticized the 'savant archpriest of the Church of Robespierre.' 'L'Élite Européenne et la terreur,' *Clarté*, 1 July 1922, 372. Mathiez asked Rolland: 'Do you believe that deep in my heart I don't have reservations about certain acts of the Russians? But one cannot live on sentiment.' Trotsky was also impatient with 'Rollandist humanism,' which he said one found in 'all the art and literature of the French counterrevolution, from the men of

Thermidor to Aristide Briand.' 'Le Drame du prolétariat français,' *Clarté*, 1 October 1922, 508–510.

3   See Mikhail Agursky, *Ideologiia natsional bolshevizma* (Paris, YMCA, 1980), 62–64; Otto-Ernst Schuddekopf, *Linke Leute von rechts: Die national-revolutionären Minderheiten und der Kommunismus in der Weimarer Republik* (Stuttgart, W. Kohlhammer, 1960), 110–112. The Hamburg 'National Bolsheviks' Heinrich Lauffenberg and Fritz Wolffheim were expelled in 1919 from the KPD, then led by Paul Levi, not because of their ideas about a national rally against the Entente but for their too great enthusiasm for the movement of workers' councils, which Levi labeled 'syndicalism.'

4   N. V. Ustrialov, 'Fragmenti: O razume prava i prave istorii,' *Smena vekh*, 29 October 1921, 6.

5   N. V. Ustrialov, 'Natsional-bolshevizm,' *Smena vekh*, 12 November 1921, 13–16.

6   A. Lunacharskii, 'Smena vekh intelligentskoi obshchestvennosti,' *Ob Intelligentsii. Sbornik statei* (Moscow, 1923), 46.

7   Ibid., 47. See also A. Lunacharskii, 'Intelligentsiia i ee mesto v sotsialisticheskom stroitelstve,' *Revoliutsiia i kultura*, 15 November 1927, 23–29, for the distinction between 'old' intelligentsia, including the *smenavekhovtsy*, who were only temporarily necessary, and the 'new,' currently being trained in Soviet institutions.

8   See Agursky, *Ideologiia*, 251–327, for an alternative view, in which the adaptation of nationalism to Bolshevik ideology had resulted in the more or less complete absorption of the latter. Russian National Bolshevism can thus confront the National Communism of the oppressed nation, from the Hamberg Communists to Tito and Mao.

9   Victor Serge thus reassured the French comrades that Ustrialov had been wrong to say that NEP was an 'evolution' rather than a 'tactic.' It was, Serge insisted, citing Bukharin, a framework for 'prolonged struggle' against a lower middle class which in France provided a basis for a future fascist movement. Hence the danger was great in Russia. See 'Les Classes moyennes dans la révolution russe,' *Clarté*, 15 September 1922.

10 For a discussion of these congresses as 'a final and elaborate recapitulation of the differences between western and Russian socialism,' see Albert S. Lindemann, *The 'Red Years': European Socialism Versus Bolshevism, 1919–1921* (Berkeley, University of California Press, 1974), 249 and *passim*.

11 *Pervyi kongress Kommunisticheskogo Internationala: Protokoly zasedanii v Moskve so 2 po 19 marta 1919 goda* (Petrograd, 1921), 284–285.

12 On the factory committees in Italy, B. R. Lopukhov, *Obrazovanie italianskoi kommunisticheskoi partii* (Moscow, 1962), 63–64. Lopukhov describes the Turino councils as 'factory-plant councils' (*fabrichno-zavodskie soviety*), effecting a verbal composite of the 'factory-plant committees' (*komitety*) and 'soviets.' A. M. Pankratova, *Fabzakomi v borbe na sotsialisticheskuiu fabriku* (Moscow, 1923), 175–180, illustrates the old distinction.

13 Trotsky thought of factory committees as 'elements of dual power in the factory' and 'schools for planned economy.' He imagined, at the time of the German rising of October 1923, that factory councils might take the place of soviets. See *The Death Agony of Capitalism and the Tasks of the Fourth International* (1938; New York, 1970), 14, 29. Zinoviev wrote that in the German situation in October, 1923, 'the functions performed in Russia by factory committees and soviets were performed in Germany by factory committees alone.' 'Problemy germanskoi revoliutsii,' *Kommunisticheskii Internatsional* (December 1923), 7507, 7514.

14 Bordiga to ECCI, 11 January 1920, quoted in Donald W. Urquidi, 'The Origins of the Italian Communist Party, 1918–1921' (unpublished doctoral dissertation, Columbia University, 1962), 111.

15 Antonio Gramsci, 'The Factory Council,' 5 June 1920, in *Soviets in Italy* (Nottingham, 1972), 9.

16 'Two Revolutions,' 3 July 1920, in ibid., 26.

17 Curiously, Angelica Balabanova, who was in political sympathy with Serrati, suggests that Lenin actually assessed the Italian situation pessimistically in their meeting of 20 September: 'What about bread, what about coal? How long could the workers resist such a blockade? No, we don't want a repetition of the Hungarian defeat.' *My Life as a Rebel* (New York, Harper & Bros., 1938), 284–285. Yet Comintern directives were emphatic in urging the PSI to broaden what they described as a revolutionary movement. See Urquidi, 'The Origins,' 298–299.

18 Session of the German Zentrale with ECCI representative 'Comrade Max' (Radek); text in Milorad M. Drachkovitch and Branko Lazitch, eds., *The Comintern: Historical Highlights* (New York, Washington, and London, 1966), 286.

19 As had his archenemy Bordiga, chiefly through mental reservation, as Bordiga did not want to emphasize any greater variance with Comintern positions than necessary. He later counted it a mistake to have betrayed the 'fundamental Marxist line' on the peasantry in order to construct 'a Bolshevism as a revolutionary ideology of the proletariat allied with the peasants, *à la* Zinoviev.' 'Lenin sur le chemin de la révolution,' Rome Conference of PCI, 24 February 1924; text in *Lutte des classes*, June, 1928.

20 Quoted in Urquidi, 'The Origins,' 369.

21 *Bulletin communiste*, 23 March 1922, 234.

22 N. Bukharin, 'De la tactique offensive,' *Bulletin communiste* 31 March 1921, 219.

23 'Le Récit du "camarade Thomas,"' in Freymond, *Contributions*, 5–28.

24 Thalheimer to Central Committee, 16 June 1921, Trotsky Archive, T-681.

25 Ibid.

26 Subsequent accounts have not agreed on its origin. Borkenau (*World Communism*, 213–214) ascribes responsibility to Zinoviev and to Béla Kun, the latter dispatched to Germany to create a diversion from the developing Kronstadt rising in Russia. Writing about the March Action in 1928, Trotsky asserted that 'the guiding thought of the German Central Committee in this was to save the Soviet Republic.' *The Third International After Lenin* (New York, 1970), 87. This version appears in Walter Krivitsky, *In Stalin's Secret Service* (New York, Harpers, 1939), 32, and Ossip K. Flechtheim, *Die KPD in der Weimarer Republik* (Frankfurt-am-Main, Europäischer Verlagsanstalt, 1969), 159. Reviewing these and other sources, Werner T. Angress, *Stillborn Revolution: The Communist Bid for Power in Germany, 1921–1923* (Princeton, Princeton Univ. Press, 1963), 120–121, casts doubt on this theory but finds no other satisfactory. E. H. Carr, *The Bolshevik Revolution, 1917–1923* (Baltimore, Penguin, 1953), vol. 3, p. 334, concludes that, since Kun must have left Russia around March 1, before the Kronstadt rising, the theory must be rejected. However, he accepts the possibility that, once in Germany, Kun may have referred to the danger in Russia. When one considers that the already desperate situation of general strike in Petrograd had resulted in martial law by the end of February, the problem in the dating seems to disappear. Lenin's confident and brutal debriefing of Kun at the Third Comintern Congress in June–July, resulting in the latter's heart attack, suggests that he may not have

dispatched Kun directly. But 'Le Récit du "camarade Thomas,"' in Freymond, *Contributions*, 24, insists that Kun had a blank check from Lenin and used it to overrule 'Thomas' (Vladimir Degot), Warski (Warszawski), and Lapinski (Levinson), who objected to the action.

27   *Bulletin communiste*, 4 August 1921, 528.

28   Ibid., 531. This after Klara Zetkin had pointedly demanded of the Third Congress that treatment of Levi be at least as gentle as treatment of Zinoviev and Kamenev after October, 1917.

29   Lenin, 'Report to German Comrades,' *Bulletin communiste*, 29 December 1921.

30   L. Trotsky, 'La Révolution bolchevique s'est accomplie à date fixe,' *Bulletin communiste*, 17 November 1921, 852. This should be distinguished from his call for a 'schedule' for the German revolution of 1923. See L. Trotsky, 'Mozhno–li kontr-revoliutsiiu ili revoliutsiiu sdelat v srok?' *Pravda*, 23 September 1923, 2.

31   Trotsky to Cachin and Frossard, 14 July 1921, Bibliothèque Nationale file 218917.

32   Ibid.

33   L. Trotsky, *Le Salut du Parti Communiste Français* (Paris, 1922), 24–25.

34   Trotsky to 'X,' July 23, 1921, Bibliothèque Nationale file 218917.

35   Ibid.

36   Souvarine singled out Meric, Verfueil, Fabre, and Rappoport, the last the editor of *Le Journal du peuple*, an independent party paper.

37   L.-O. Frossard, 'Contre le front unique,' *Bulletin communiste*, 16 February 1922, 124.

38   Trotsky to 'X,' 2 March 1922; text in Pierre Broué, ed., *Le Mouvement communiste en France, 1919–1939* (Paris, 1967), 166.

39   L. Trotsky, 'Le Front unique et le communisme en France,' *Bulletin communiste*, 6 April 1922, 274. In discussions with the CGT leaders, Frossard had assured them that there would be no *noyautage*.

40   See p. 28.

41   Pierre Monatte, 'Le Syndicalisme: Est-il mort a Saint-Etienne?' *Clarté*, 15 July 1922, 401. Monatte criticized the syndicalist idea of 'unions of affinities' (rather like the Federacion Anarquista Iberica [FAI], by which Spanish anarchosyndicalists grouped in 1926 as anarchists rather than trade unionists), saying that only a party could fill that role. Wohl, *French Communism*, 283, calls Saint-Etienne the Halle of French Communism. Pierre Broué, *Mouvement communiste*, 204n, notes that the unity was still on the syndicalist rather than the Bolshevik ideological basis, because of the autonomy provision. Trotsky, however, had praised the Charte d'Amiens when it implied autonomy from the prewar SFIO.

42   Trotsky to Rosmer, 22 May 1922, Bibliothèque Nationale file 218917.

43   Trotsky to Ker, 6 June 1922, Bibliothèque Nationale file 218917.

44   For a close study of Sokolnikov's ideas and their reception, see Day, *Politics of Economic Isolation*, 59–65.

45   Louis Fischer, *The Soviets in World Affairs* (Princeton, Princeton Univ. Press, 1930), vol. 1, pp. 321–322, reports a conversation even before Cannes between Chicherin and German industrialist Felix Deutsch, in which this idea was broached, only to be summarily rejected.

46   L. Trotsky, 'Un Discours de Trotski aux sections féminines,' *Bulletin communiste*, 13 January 1921, 23.

47   For the argument that this attitude dominated Lenin's Marxism, see Karl Korsch, *Marxism and Philosophy* (1923; New York and London, NLB, 1970), 126–127.

48 Mikhailov and Iaroslavskii were replaced by Stalin and Kuibyshev in 1922. Mikhailov later supported the right against Stalin in 1928–1929, but he was prominent in party work until his arrest and disappearance in 1937.
49 Stalin to Politburo, 27 September 1922, quoted in L. Trotsky, *The Stalin School of Falsification* (New York, 1937), 67. Stalin's shift was clearly to avoid having a vote go against him. Thus he dropped without hesitation his position 'of principle.' 'In a sense,' writes Moshe Lewin, 'the whole of Stalin is contained in this letter.' *Lenin's Last Struggle* (New York, 1968), 53.
50 Lenin endorsed Trotsky's 'exceptionally precise' formulations on the NEP. Lenin to Trotsky, 25 November 1922, Trotsky Archive, T-763.
51 Trotsky to Zinoviev, 22 November 1922, Trotsky Archive, T-759.
52 Trotsky to Zinoviev, 25 November, 1922, Trotsky Archive, T-761.
53 L. Trotsky, preface to *Kommunisticheskoe dvizhenie vo Fransii* (Moscow, 1923), 11.

Chapter 4

1 Trotsky to the Central Committee Secretariat, 28 March 1923, Trotsky Archive, T-792.
2 Trotsky to Stalin, 18 April 1923, Trotsky Archive, T-796.
3 'Mysli o partii,' *Pravda*, 20 March 1923.
4 'Tezisy o promyshlennosti,' 13 April 1923, Trotsky Archive, T-2964.
5 Ibid.
6 Trotsky to Rosmer, February–March 1922, Bibliothèque Nationale file 218917.
7 V. Sorin, *Rabochaia gruppa ("Miasnikovshchina")* (Moscow, 1924), 64, 109. On the New Exploitation of the Proletariat, see the text of the Workers' Group manifesto of February 1923, in Roberto Sinigaglia, *Mjasnikov e la rivoluzione russa* (Milano, 1973), 127–166, especially 128, and Lev Kamenev, 'Le Parti et la démocratie ouvrière,' *Bulletin communiste*, 1 February 1924, 135. On the Workers' Truth, see N. Karev, 'O gruppa "rabochaia pravda,"' *Bolshevik*, nos. 7–8 (1924).
8 L. Trotsky, 'La Greve dans l'état ouvrier,' *Bulletin communiste*, 13 April 1922, 297.
9 L. Trotsky, 1922 preface to *1905* (New York, 1971), vi–vii.
10 G. Zinoviev, *Istoriia rossiiskoi kommunisticheskoi partii (bolshevikov): Populiarnyi ocherk* (Moscow and Petrograd, 1923), 115. Zinoviev soon amplified the Democratic Dictatorship by the slogan 'Face to the Village!' (*litsom k derevne*), telling the Thirteenth Congress that 'we must not be merely a city party.' *Politicheskii otchet Ts. K., XIII s"ezdu R.K.P. (b)* (Moscow, 1924), 58–59. See also *Litsom k derevne: Stati i rechi*, 2 vols. (Moscow and Leningrad, 1925) and *Rabochii klass i krestianstvo* (Moscow and Leningrad, 1925).
11 See p. 44.
12 *Bulletin communiste*, 4 January 1923, 12.
13 Ernst Meyer, 'Les Résultats du IVe Congress de Moscou,' *Bulletin Communiste*, 4 January 1923, 3.
14 L. Trotsky, 'Le Gouvernement ouvrière en France,' *Bulletin communiste*, 8 February 1923, 104.
15 See pp. 43–44.
16 See George D. Jackson, *Comintern and Peasant in East Europe, 1919–1930* (New York and London, Columbia Univ., 1966), 61–62.

17   Pierre Broué, *Révolution en Allemagne, 1917–1923* (Paris, Editions de Minuit, 1971), 319.
18   Michael Karolyi, *Faith Without Illusion* (New York, Dutton, 1957), 153.
19   See Frank Eckelt, 'The Rise and Fall of the Béla Kun Regime in 1919' (unpublished doctoral dissertation, New York University, 1965), 294–322; Ivan Volgyes, 'Soviet Russia and Soviet Hungary,' in Ivan Volgyes, ed., *Hungary in Revolution, 1918–1919* (Lincoln, 1971), 169.
20   For the idea that intervention in the Russian civil war had permitted the survival of the East European states of the *cordon sanitaire*, see Winston Churchill, *The Aftermath* (New York, Scribner's, 1929), 288.
21   Ruth Fischer, *Stalin and German Communism* (Cambridge, Mass., Harvard Univ. Press, 1948), 273–277, presents the most extensive case for this view, but she can cite no instance of opposition to the line by her patron Zinoviev— none, that is, prior to his break with Stalin in 1925.
22   *Bulletin communiste*, 4 January 1923, 13–14. Albert Treint later recalled that Bukharin spoke to many 'in the corridors' about the vast possibilities for 'Red Imperialism.' 'Le Groupe Paz et l'opportunisme électoral,' *L'Unité leniniste*, 5 January 1928, 10–11.
23   Interview with the *Manchester Guardian*, 1 March 1923; text in Jane Degras, ed., *Soviet Documents on Foreign Policy* (London, Oxford, 1951), vol. 1, p. 376.
24   Ibid.; see also Marcel Fourrier, 'Les Banquiers, reconstruiront-ils l'Europe centrale?,' *Clarté*, 15 June 1922, 355–358.
25   L. Trotsky, 'De l'opportunité du mot d'ordre: "Les États-Unis d'Europe,"' *Bulletin communiste*, 26 July 1923, 416.
26   H. Pogge von Strandmann, ed., *Rathenau, Tagebuch, 1907–1922*, entry of 13 February 1912, quoted in Fritz Fischer, *War of Illusions: German Policies from 1911 to 1914* (1969; New York, Norton, 1975), 137.
27   See p. 21.
28   L. Trotsky, *The Third International After Lenin* (New York, Pathfinder, 1970), 120. In view of Trotsky's subsequent position, Isaac Deutscher, researching his Trotsky biography, could not account for Trotsky's defense of the 'Workers' and Peasants' Government' slogan. Deutscher to Alfred Rosmer, 22 May 1954, Deutscher Archive.
29   Pogany-Pepper's 'August Theses' of 1923, containing his assessment of the political power of a farmer-labor alliance, incurred the opposition of William Z. Foster, after 1928 the major leader of the American Communists, and James Cannon, future leader of American Trotskyism. In 1923 Foster and Cannon thought the American party must turn away from the foreign-language federations, which had played a prominent role up to then, and toward the 'native' worker. Foster was closest to S. Lozovskii of the Profintern. Both denounced Trotsky in 1924 and helped expel the only supporter of Trotsky's views, Ludwig Lore of the *New Yorker Volkszeitung*. 'We took the Comintern's political criticism of Lore, like its other pronouncements, for good coin,' wrote Cannon later, 'and thought that it was up to Lore to straighten himself out with the Comintern.' *The First Ten Years of American Communism* (New York, Pathfinder, 1962), 190. Lore later assisted the exiled Trotsky to form an American faction in 1928–1929. Speculation that Lore was employed throughout by the GPU may be found in Daniel Bell, *Marxian Socialism in the United States* (Princeton, Princeton Univ. Press, 1967), 134. Pogany-Pepper, considered an adept of Zinoviev in 1923–1924, supported Bukharin in 1925 and was made chief of the ECCI Information Department. His attack on the Trotsky–Zinoviev opposition of 1926 is in Jane Degras, ed.,

The Communist International, 1919–1943: Documents (London, Oxford Univ. Press, 1971), vol. 2, p. 328.

30 L. Trotsky, *The Third International After Lenin*, 121.
31 L. Kamenev, 'Le Parti et la Démocratie ouvrière,' *Bulletin communiste*, 1 February 1924, 135.
32 M. K. Dziewanowski, *The Communist Party of Poland* (Cambridge, Mass. Harvard Univ. Press, 1959), 105–107. Perhaps the Comintern was preoccupied with plans for a Bulgarian rising, announced to the Bulgarian party leaders on 5 August and staged unsuccessfully in September. The post-mortems made by the Bulgarians emphasized that they had put too much faith in mobilizing the peasantry and had neglected the cities! See Joseph Rothschild, *The Communist Party of Bulgaria: Origins and Development, 1883–1936* (New York, Columbia Univ. Press, 1959), 133, 145.
33 A paraphrased account of the letter appeared in the Menshevik *Sotsialisticheskii vestnik*, 28 May 1924, 9–10, with a Politburo response calling it a plan for 'a dictatorship of Trotsky in economic and military affairs.'
34 Ibid., 10.
35 'V politburo TsK RKP,' 15 October, 1923, Trotsky Archive, T-802.
36 Ibid.
37 *Bulletin communiste*, 8 February 1924, 149.
38 Trotsky to Bukharin, 8 January 1926, Trotsky Archive, T-2976.
39 G. Zinoviev, 'Problemy germanskoi revoliutsii,' *Kommunisticheskii Internatsional*, December 1923, 7487–7514; see above, ch. 3, n. 13. *Betriebsrat*, 'factory council,' corresponds to the Turino *consigli di fabbrica* of 1920 and the Russian factory committees of 1917.
40 L. Trotsky, 'Mozhno-li kontr-revoliutsiiu ili revoliutsiiu sdelat v srok?' *Pravda*, 23 September 1923, 2.
41 See Carr, *Interregnum*, 240–241; Fischer, *Stalin and German Communism*, 779–783.
42 August Thalheimer, *1923, Eine verpasste Revolution? Die deutsche Oktoberlegende und die wirkliche Geschichte von 1923* (Berlin, Juniusverlag, 1931), 20–21. Thalheimer did not mention the Schlageter line in spring and summer, 1923.
43 *The Third International After Lenin*, 112.
44 L. Trotsky, 'Greetings to *La Vérité*,' *WLT 1930*, 367.
45 Trotsky to SAP, 11 January 1934, Trotsky Archive, T-4990.
46 Quoted in Rosenthal, *Avocat de Trotsky*, 74. Trotsky spoke at Prinkipo in the summer of 1929.
47 Trotsky's exclusion from deliberations of the troika, expanded to a group of seven is described in Souvarine, *Stalin*, 341. Rosmer claimed to Deutscher that Trotsky was also excluded from military preparations, a suggestion that Deutscher found 'incredible.' Deutscher to Brandler, 26 June 1954; 19 February 1955, Deutscher Archive. This was all the more incredible in view of Trotsky's later admission that he had insisted against Stalin in November that Soviet 'representatives' be recalled. 'O Brandlere,' March 24, 1927, Trotsky Archive, T-3082. Nevertheless, Deutscher finally described the Comintern postmortems on, *inter alia*, Trotsky's role in evasive language: 'Radek conveyed the protest [of Brandler's demotion], but being mainly interested in defending his own and Brandler's policy, he gave the Executive the impression that Trotsky associated himself with that policy; and this enabled the Triumvirs to link Trotsky once again with the "right wing" in the German party. In truth, Trotsky never ceased to be critical of Brandler's conduct. . .'

The Prophet Unarmed, 145. The operative words in this account would seem to be 'policy' and 'conduct.' Even if it were difficult to disavow the policy, Trotsky could disavow its conduct. Deutscher had already written to Brandler: 'I am ready to admit that he was unjust to you in connection with the crisis of 1923.' Deutscher to Brandler, 19 July 1952.

48   Deutscher's notes on a conversation with Brandler, February 1948, Deutscher Archive.

49   Stenographic record of a discussion of Trotsky and C. L. R. James, Trotsky Archive, T-4559.

50   L. Trotsky, 'O Brandlere,' 24 March 1927, Trotsky Archive, T-3082.

51   For example, Shachtman to Trotsky, 13 January 1933, Trotsky Exile Archive, $T_2$5066; C. L. R. James to Trotsky, 24 June 1936, Trotsky Exile Archive, $T_2$2068.

52   L. Trotsky, *Kak vooruzhalas revoliutsiia*, vol. 3, pt. 2, (Moscow, 1925), 122. He compared it to the Bolshevik offer of a bloc with the Mensheviks and SRs against Kornilov in August 1917.

53   Ibid., 132, 133, 149.

54   Most explicit about this was Chicherin's close friend, Brockdorff-Rontzau. See Kurt Rosenbaum, *Community of Fate: German–Soviet Diplomatic Relations, 1922–1928* (Syracuse, N.Y., Syracuse Univ. Press, 1965), 60. More exaggerated, but not wholly fantastic, variations on this theme may be found in Ypsilon (Karl Volk and Julian Gomperz), *Pattern for World Revolution* (Chicago and New York, Ziff-Davis, 1947), 76–89.

Chapter 5

1   J. V. Stalin, 'O zadachakh partii,' December 2, 1923, *Sochineniia* (Moscow, 1947), vol. 5, pp. 369–370.

2   G. Zinoviev, 'Les Intellectuels et la révolution,' *Bulletin communiste*, 27 December 1923. The Bolsheviks' strikebreaking activity against the 'intelligentsia counterrevolution' had also greatly impressed Jan Wacław Machajski; see *Rabochaia revoliutsiia*, 1918, 2.

3   G. Zinoviev, 'L'Internationale communiste et le Parti Communiste Italien,' *Bulletin communiste*, 22 March 1923, 184.

4   *Bulletin communiste*, 22 February 1924, 209. Earl Browder applied the doctrine to the American scene. Referring to the negotiations of 1923 with Chicago labor leaders for a Farmer-Labor party ticket, he suggested that these 'American union bureaucrats have vivid sympathies for fascism. . . . If Mussolini had found the time to come to America, he would have found himself—amazing spectacle—at the side of Gompers.' 'Le Fascisme,' *Bulletin communiste*, 8 February 1924, 160.

5   L. Trotsky, 'Groupements et fractions,' *Bulletin communiste*, 18 January 1924, 82.

6   This despite his continuing feud with Souvarine. Trotsky's letters to Treint are in Bibliothèque Nationale file 218917.

7   Treint criticized Fischer-Maslow for 'the error of reviving the charge of National-Bolshevism.' *Bulletin communiste*, 2 August 1923, 456.

8   Albert Treint, 'Dans la voie tracée par Lénine,' *Bulletin communiste*, 28 March 1924.

9   Quoted in Jedermann, *La 'Bolchevisation' du Parti Communiste Français* (Paris, F. Maspero, 1971), 67.

10 Trotsky to Krasin, 18 June 1924, Trotsky Archive, T-812; *Izvestia*, 5 August 1924, English translation in the pamphlet *Europe and America* (New York, 1971).

11 Albert Treint, 'Contre Trotsky,' *Cahiers du Bolchevisme*, 28 November 1924, 72, 77–78.

12 L. Trotsky, *The Third International After Lenin*, 96.

13 *Sochineniia* (Moscow, 1947), vol. 6, p. 282.

14 See Daniels, *Conscience of the Revolution*, 254.

15 G. Zinoviev, *Bolshevizm ili trotskizm?* (Leningrad, 1925), 16.

16 J. V. Stalin, speech to the Central Trade Union Council, 19 November 1924, in Ibid., 28. The center was, according to Central Committee minutes of 16 October 1917, attached to the Military Revolutionary Committee, of which latter Trotsky was chair. See L. Trotsky, *The Stalin School of Falsification*, 14–15. For a discussion of the latter, see Alexander Rabinowitch, *The Bolsheviks Come to Power: The Revolution of 1917 in Petrograd* (New York, Norton, 1978), 266–267, and 'Lenin and Trockij in the October Revolution,' in Francesca Geri, ed., *Pensiero e azione politica di Lev Trockij* (Florence, Leonardo Olschki, 1978), 199–208.

17 J. V. Stalin, *Sochineniia*, vol. 6, pp. 374–375.

18 Souvarine reported this from Moscow. Souvarine to Rosmer, December 8–15, 1924, Monatte Archives, cited by Wohl, *French Communism*, 419. Humbert-Droz criticized Treint's views on the united front, and his 'too personal methods' without defending the *Gauche ouvrière*: 'Rosmer and Monatte's only political statement is an act of faith in Trotsky. They go the way of Serrati and Levi and pass over to the camp of the enemy.' 'Mise au point nécessaire,' *Cahiers du Bolchevisme*, 23 January 1925, 679.

19 This rendering was preserved in Stalinist accounts. See *History of the Communist Party of the Soviet Union (Bolsheviks): Short Course* (New York, 1939), 273–275, and the distressingly similar view in Roy Medvedev, *Leninism and Western Socialism* (London, Verso, 1981), 179–181.

20 As, for example, in L. Trotsky, 'Vers une culture nouvelle,' *Clarté*, 15 August 1923, 346.

21 Trotsky's account is in *Proletarskaia revoliutsiia*, no. 3, (1922), 246.

22 'Tov. Stalin o perspektivakh GKP i o bolshevizatsii,' *Pravda*, 3 February 1925, 1.

23 J. V. Stalin, 'O Chekoslovatskoi kompartii,' *Sochineniia*, vol. 7, p. 63.

24 J. V. Stalin, speech to the Fourteenth Congress, *Sochineniia*, vol. 7, pp. 379–380.

25 Stalin to Maslow, 28 February 1925; text in *Bulletin communiste*, April–June 1927, 296.

26 The Politburo did not have a high opinion of their 'friend,' the 'little fool' Ramsay MacDonald. According to Stalin's secretary Bazhanov, Bukharin jokingly 'nominated' Tomskii as British prime minister and 'appointed' Ramsay MacDonald to a post in an obscure rural Russian province. The document was drawn up and signed, amid much gaiety. *Avec Staline dans le Kremlin* (Paris, 1930), 156–157.

27 See Fischer, *Stalin and German Communism*, 493, 553.

28 L. Trotsky, *Where Is Britain Going?* (1925; London, n.d.), 4–6.

29 Marxism would be for the proletariat what the doctrine of predestination had been for the seventeenth-century revolution. Ibid., 36.

30 For Tomskii's clash with Lozovskii on Britain, see David Langsam, 'Pressure Group Politics in NEP Russia: The Case of the Trade Unions' (unpublished doctoral dissertation, Princeton University, 1974), 182–186.

31   Ibid., 127. The tactics of the Trotskyist groups in the Labour Party thus stem from Trotsky's reading of the history of the ILP rather than from the later tactic of 'entrism.'

32   L. Trotsky, 'Un Discours aux sections féminines,' *Bulletin communiste*, 13 January 1921, 23. When Armand Hammer visited Trotsky in December 1921, he found the War Commissar enthusiastic about trade with the United States, and inquiring about the American bankers' interest in possible loans. When the revolution came to America, he reportedly assured Hammer, those who had invested in Russia would find that their agreements still held and they would therefore 'be in a more flexible position than the rest of their fellow capitalists.' Bob Considine, *The Remarkable Life of Armand Hammer* (New York, 1975), 38–39.

33   See p. 40.

34   L. Trotsky, *Whither Russia?* (1925; Colombo, Ceylon, 1973). 70–71.

35   *Ekonomicheskaia zhizn*, 16 February 1926; text in R. Chappell and Alan Clinton, eds., *Collected Writings and Speeches on Britain* (London, 1974), vol. 1, p. 161.

36   L. Trotsky, 'The Russian Position,' *Current History*, February 1926, 618.

37   Ibid., 621. Trotsky's position on concessions was not one he could maintain indefinitely. Harriman later met with Trotsky in December 1926, during the caesura between the opposition struggle of that year and the one of 1927. Trotsky was cold and wary. 'He behaved as if our conversation was being heard and he was taking no chances that his talk with me would add to his troubles.' William Averell Harriman, with Elie Abel, *Special Envoy to Churchill and Stalin, 1941–1946* (New York, Random House, 1975), 49.

38   Trotsky's French supporters were at a loss to interpret *Whither Russia?* in terms of a presumed opposition struggle. 'In point of fact, no one reading it could find any challenge to the Stalinist theses and to the general line the Russian Communist party was following.' André Thirion, *Revolutionaries Without Revolution* (New York, 1972), 122.

39   Quoted in Claude Lefort, 'La Contradiction de Trotsky et le problème révolutionnaire,' *Les Temps modernes*, December 1948–January 1949, 52.

40   Boris Souvarine, 'Exclus, mais communistes,' *Révolution prolétarienne*, 23 October 1925, 5.

41   L. Trotsky, 'Déclaration,' *Révolution prolétarienne*, October 1925, 6.

42   'La Réponse du 'Noyau' à deux demandes de Trotsky,' *Révolution prolétarienne*, October 1925, 5.

43   Zinoviev, they decided, was a Lassallean, referring to the German labor leader of Marx's time who described all but the proletariat as 'one reactionary mass.' See Trotsky Archive, T-851, T-852, T-854.

44   Rosa Meyer-Leviné, *Inside German Communism* (London, Pluto, 1977), 92.

45   In which Ustrialov, too, claimed to be a Leninist, rhapsodizing about 'Lenin, our own Lenin, special son of Russia, its national hero alongside Dmitri Donskoi, Peter the Great, Pushkin and Tolstoy.' *Pod znakom revoliutsii* (Harbin, 1925), 244. This from an obituary of January 1924. Zinoviev's critique is in 'Filosofia epokhi,' *Pravda*, 19 September 1925, 2–3; 20 September 1925, 2–3. Bukharin's view of Ustrialovism is in a book-length review of *Pod znakom revoliutsii* in which Ustrialov's admiration for the philosophy of Machiavelli and the figure of Il Duce is described as 'a theory of the strategy and tactics of Russian fascist Caesarism.' *Tsezarizm pod maskoi revoliutsii* (Moscow, 1925), 44.

46   *XIV s"ezd vsesoiuznoi kommunisticheskoi partii (b): stenograficheskii otchet* (Mos-

cow and Leningrad, 1926), 102. Zinoviev's Leningrad associate, Petr Zalutskii, raised the question of state capitalism earlier in the year, in *Voprosy partraboty i zvenievye organizatori* (Leningrad, 1925), but denied at the congress that he saw a Thermidorean degeneration in the Central Committee. *XIV s"ezd*, 230.

47 *Pravda*, 27 November 1925, 6; for Bukharin's theory of European state capitalism, see Cohen, *Bukharin and the Bolshevik Revolution* (New York, 1971), 254–258.

48 Lenin's widow Krupskaia apparently made the first charge against Bukharin's 'un-Leninist' peasant policy, perhaps with the encouragement of Zinoviev and Kamenev, in July, 1925. See Robert McNeal, *Bride of the Revolution* (Ann Arbor, Univ. of Michigan Press, 1972), 250–251; Carr, *Socialism in One Country*, vol. 2, pp. 70–71.

49 J. Stalin, *Sochineniia*, vol. 7, pp. 364–365. Stalin's view of the matter thus harmonized with that of Bukharin and Trotsky. See Trotsky Archive, T-2974. Day, *Politics of Economic Isolation*, 117, considers Sokolnikov's views the reason for Trotsky's adherence to Stalin–Bukharin against Zinoviev.

50 For Kirov's warnings about White émigré hopes for a split between Moscow and Leningrad, see *XIV s"ezd*, 367.

51 *Bulletin communiste*, 8 January 1926, 183.

52 *Bulletin communiste*, 25 December 1925, 149.

53 *Bulletin communiste*, 22 January 1926, 216.

54 Trotsky to Bukharin, 9 January 1926, Trotsky Archive, T-2926.

55 Ibid.

56 Ibid.

57 Trotsky to Bukharin, 4 March 1926, Trotsky Archive, T-868.

58 Meyer-Leviné, *Inside German Communism*, 94. Meyer-Leviné puts this exchange in March, 1925. Trotsky (*My Life*, 522), dates his departure for Berlin from mid–April. The latter would place the discussion in Berlin after preliminary queries about a bloc from Kamenev.

59 In his private writings of 1925 there occur certain references to the impossibility of complete national self-sufficiency. In an unpublished memorandum of 22 December 1925 (Trotsky Archive, T-2975), attacking the Leningraders, he referred disapprovingly to a 'closed national economy,' but usually, as in *Whither Russia?*, he spoke of 'socialism in our country,' or 'socialism in a backward country,' never in a manner to suggest deviation from the general line. Nevertheless, the idea has persisted that Trotsky opposed Socialism in One Country at this time. See, for example, Richard B. Day, 'Socialism in One Country—New Thoughts on an Old Question,' in *Pensiero e azione politica di Lev Trockij*, 311–330, relying on the evidence of the unpublished memorandum cited above.

60 L. Trotsky, 'Notes on Economic Questions,' 2 May 1926, in Naomi Allen and George Saunders, eds., *The Challenge of the Left Opposition, 1926–1927* (New York, 1980), 57.

61 The Polish leaders Warski and Walecki were not chastised until the ECC1 Polish Commission of 2 July. See Trotsky Archive, T-2995, T-3024; *Biulleten oppozitsii*, September, 1932.

62 J. V. Stalin, *Sochineniia* (Moscow, 1948), vol. 8, pp. 171–172.

63 Trotsky Archive, T-880a.

64 J. V. Stalin, *Sochineniia*, vol. 8, pp. 209–213.

65 Statement signed by Zinoviev, Kamenev, Piatakov, Sokolnikov, Trotsky, and Evdokimov, dated 16 October 1926; text in *Pravda*, 17 October 1926, 1.

66   Speech to the Fifteenth Conference, 1 November 1926. *Pravda*, 6 November 1926, 5.

67   Trotsky Archive, T-941.

68   Zinoviev's apposite comparison of Chiang Kai-shek and Kemal Pasha is in his 'Theses on the Chinese Revolution,' in L. Trotsky, *Problems of the Chinese Revolution* (New York, 1932), 310–311. The chief Comintern agent in China had been Mikhail Borodin, who had also been Lenin's chief agent in Turkey. See Conrad Brandt, *Stalin's Failure in China, 1924–1927* (New York, 1958), 14–15.

69   Brandt, *Stalin's Failure*, 80.

70   Trotsky Archive, T-941. 'We approve of Communist support,' Trotsky had said in 1924, 'for the *Kuomintang* party in China, which we are endeavoring to push forward.' 'Perspektivy i zadachi na Vostoke,' *Pravda*, 1 May 1924, 5.

71   'From the beginning, we, representatives of the International Left Opposition, the Bolshevik–Leninists, were against entering the Kuomintang and for an independent proletarian policy,' 'Manifesto on China of the International Left Opposition,' September 1930, text in *WLT 1930–1931* (New York, 1973), 15.

72   Trotsky to Shachtman, 10 December 1930, *Problems of the Chinese Revolution*, 13.

73   'Voprosy nashei politiki v otnoshenii kitai i iaponii,' 25 March 1926. Trotsky Archive, T-870.

74   Interview with C. L. R. James, April 1939. Trotsky Archive, T-4559.

75   *Problems of the Chinese Revolution*, 137–138. In 1928 he would write to Ivan Smirnov that, after May 1927, the Democratic Dictatorship slogan had been just as harmful as in Russia in 1917. Trotsky to Smirnov, 10 March 1928; text in *La Lutte des classes*, August–September 1928, 163–164. See also Trotsky's complaint in 1930, that 'the formula of the democratic dictatorship opens the gates to a new deception of the workers and the peasants by the bourgeoisie.' Manifesto on China of the International Left Opposition, September 1930, in *WLT 1930–1931*, 20.

76   Fischer, *Stalin and German Communism*, 451–452; Meyer-Leviné, *Inside German Communism*, 86–87.

77   Theodor Draper, 'The Strange Case of the Comintern,' *Survey* (Summer 1972), 109–111.

78   Serge to Trotsky, 7 July 1927. Trotsky Archive, T-974.

79   Chên Tu-hsiu was not a Trotskyist at the time, but became one after his dismissal in August 1927, apparently until his death in 1942. He continued to oppose policies associated with the primacy of agrarian revolution, unsuccessfully demanding a discussion in 1929. He later kept contact with the Trotskyists and supported a 'national and democratic' struggle led by the proletariat. He was reported to have spoken in favor of a capitalistic development for China and preferred Western democracy to Stalinism. On Chên, see the correspondence from China in the Trotsky Exile Archive, $T_2$1421–1426.

80   Quoted by Stuart Schram, *Mao Tse-tung* (Baltimore and Harmondsworth, Penguin, 1967), 120.

81   Karl Textor, 'La Crise du P. C. Allemand,' *Bulletin communiste*, December 1927, 410–411. Hostile maneuvers of Stalin against Bukharin in the U.S. party are described in Joseph Zack, 'The Methods of Stalinism,' *The Militant*, 29 December 1934, 3.

82   For Bukharin's campaign of resistance, see Cohen, *Bukharin and the Bolshevik Revolution*, ch. 9.

83   Perhaps because of charges made by Timofei Sapranov, V. M. Smirnov, and

the Democratic Centralist group in their 1928 platform, *Before Thermidor*, to the effect that the German managers in the Donbas coal industry had got considerable support from the party right in their handling of strikes. Text in *La Lutte des classes*, April 1928, 1–2. Souvarine, on the contrary, was convinced that, despite the Shakhty trial's anti-intelligentsia and anti-Bukharin implications, it was Bukharin who insisted, against Stalin, that some of the convicted be shot. See Souvarine, *Stalin*, 483. Also Kamenev's notes from the 1928 meeting with Bukharin, Trotsky Archive, T-1897.

84 Nikolai Ustrialov, *Na Novom etape* (Shanghai, 1930), 8, arguing against émigré critics, whom he called a 'cacistrocracy' (*kakistokratiia*) — rule by the worst.
85 See discussion in Cohen, *Bukharin and the Bolshevik Revolution*, 290–291.
86 'Iulskii plenum i pravaia opasnost,' 22 July 1928. Trotsky Archive, T-3126.
87 Naville to Paz, *La Lutte des classes,* July 1928, 129–130.
88 *La Vérité*, 11 October 1929, 4–6.
89 Ibid.
90 Souvarine borrowed Bakunin's phrase for the Bismarckian regime — the 'Knuto–German empire' — and arrived at the 'Knuto–Soviet' state. *Stalin*, 500.

Chapter 6

1 Trotsky to comrades, 21 October 1928. *La Lutte des classes*, February 1929, 221.
2 Trotsky, 'Answers to Questions from the USSR,' *WLT 1930*, 132. Centrism was also made into an international category, not easy for his French supporters to comprehend. The syndicalists were centrists 'moving to the right,' while the Stalinists were centrists zigzagging left. The latter motion was called admirable but only preparatory to a lurch back to the right, as in the Soviet Union. See Trotsky, 'Qu'est-ce que le centrisme?' *La Vérité*, 27 June 1930, 1.
3 *La Vérité*, 13 September 1929, 2.
4 'K Kapitalizmu ili k sotsializmu?' *Biulleten oppozitsii* (May 1930), 8. Like Trotsky, Rosmer thought Voroshilov the most likely candidate. 'Echéance du plan quinquennal,' *Le Communiste*, 1 November 1932, 2. In the salon of N. N. Sukhanov, accused in the trial of the Menshevik 'Union Bureau' in 1931, talk centered on General Blücher, who would be shot in 1937. See Victor Serge, *Memoirs of a Revolutionary* (Oxford Univ. Press, 1963), 252. Ustrialov remarked that 'Klim (Voroshilov) is really only believable as Napoleon the Third, while Trotsky himself would be a match for the first.' *Hic Rhodus, Hic Salta!* (Harbin, 1929), 10.
5 See p. 104.
6 Trotsky, 'Zashchita sovetskoi respubliki i oppozitsiia: Kakov put lenin-bunda?' 7 September 1929, Trotsky Archive, T-3234.
7 'Sovetsko- Kitaisko konflikt i zadachi oppozitsii,' *Biulleten oppozitsii*, September 1929, 2–3. 'If one cannot say that Thermidor is accomplished,' Trotsky complains of Urbahns, 'then one cannot say that the policy of the Soviet Union is capitalist or imperialist.'
8 *Imperialisme et nationalisme* (Paris, n.d. [1929]), 26.
9 Robert Louzon, *La Déchéance du capitalisme* (Paris, n.d.), 8.
10 Robert Louzon, 'La Conquête de l'Europe,' *Révolution prolétarienne* (February 1925), 20.

11 *Imperialisme et nationalisme*, 39.
12 Ibid., 32. See also the review of *Imperialisme et nationalisme* by F. Gérard, *La Lutte des classes*, May 1929, 277–278. Marcel Fourrier, who had edited *Clarté* with Pierre Naville, strongly defended the cause of Alsatian autonomy, which was also dear to the Brandlerists. See Nathaniel London, 'The National Question and the Left Opposition in France, 1928–1930,' Memoíre de maîtrise, Université de Paris VIII, 1977. Naville clung to a special reading of the Permanent Revolution theory which excluded support for the autonomists, on the assumption that the Treaty of Versailles had solved the last nationality problems in a Europe which did not need further 'Balkanizing.' See Georges Haupt, Michel Lowy, and Claudie Weill, *Les Marxistes et la question nationale* (Paris, 1974). The dispute was extended to cover Brittany, Catalonia, Indochina, and even the American black 'nation.' Zinovievists such as Treint were usually with Trotsky against Naville.
13 Leon Trotsky, 'Razoruzhenie Soedinennye Shtaty Evropy,' *Biulleten oppozitsii* (October 1929), 12.
14 Interview with the *Manchester Guardian*, 27 March 1931, 9. Stalin's preference was exactly opposite. Trotsky accused him of placating American interests in supporting the Kellogg–Briand pact of 1928. Stalin held that the United States had 'better grounds' for trade contacts with the Soviet Union than any other country. He told an agreeing Raymond Robins in 1933 that only Britain hindered such relations. *Sochineniia* (Moscow, 1951), vol. 13, pp. 271–272. That reversed the positions of 1925, when Stalin based his hopes on British 'moral support' and Trotsky on concessions agreements with the United States.
15 'K 12-i godovshchine oktyabria,' Trotsky Archive, T-3245.
16 See pp. 97–100.
17 The Monopoly of Foreign Trade, Trotsky held, was at the same time the last rampart against Thermidor.
18 Leon Trotsky, *The Permanent Revolution* (1930; New York, 1969).
19 Albert Treint, 'Le Suicide de Ioffe,' *L'Unité léniniste*, 5 January 1928, 13. Pierre Naville, who endorsed Permanent Revolution, considered it an error for Trotsky to have joined with Zinoviev in 1926–1927. Naville to Paz, *La Lutte des classes*, July 1928, 129–130.
20 Amadeo Bordiga, 'Lenin sur le chemin de la révolution,' speech of 24 February 1924, text in *La Lutte des classes*, June 1928, 126–127.
21 Paolo Spriano, *Storia del partito comunista italiano: Da Bordiga a Gramsci* (Torino, 1967), 429–456; John E. Chiaradia, 'The Spectral Figure of Amadeo Bordiga' (unpublished doctoral dissertation, New York University, 1972), 2–12; Silverio Corvisieri, *Trotskij e il movimento comunista italiano* (Rome, 1969), 10–17; Giuseppi Berti, 'Trenta anni di vita e di lotte de PCI,' *Rinascita*, 1951, 60.
22 Bordiga to Trotsky, 2 March 1926, Tasca Archive; text in *Annali Feltrinelli* (Milano, 1966), 271–273.
23 Leon Trotsky, 'Pismo italianskim levym kommunistam,' 25 September 1929. Trotsky Archive, T-3240.
24 The correspondence is in the Trotsky Exile Archive, $T_2$2644-2726.
25 Corvisieri, in *Trotskij e il movimento comunista italiano*, argues against the identification of Trotsky and Bordiga, as found in Berti's analysis, rejecting it for a more interesting amalgam. Since he holds Gramsci's fight against Bordiga to contain the 'essence of anti-Stalinism' (21), Bordiga becomes the Italian Stalin. Roberto Massari also speaks of a 'Gramscian patrimony' of the

NOI which matches that of the Trotsky opposition. See the introduction to *All'opposizione nel PCI con Trotskij e Gramsci* (Rome, 1977).

26 Frazione Sinistra to Trotsky, September, 1930; text in Corvisieri, *Trotskij e il movimento comunista italiano*, 252–262.

27 Leon Trotsky, 'Italia e Spagna,' *Bolletino dell' opposizione comunista italiano*, 5 August 1931, 10. *Prometeo* was the group of Bordiga.

28 'Souzo' (Leonetti), statement on Bordigism and Trotskyism, 15 March 1932. Trotsky Exile Archive, $T_2$2675. See also NOI to Trotsky, 12 November 1931, $T_2$2670.

29 Corvisieri, *Trotskij e il movimento comunista italiano*, 31.

30 Gramsci saw Trotsky's argument as part of the 'stabilization' prognosis. See Alastair Davidson, *Antonio Gramsci: Towards an Intellectual Biography* (London, 1977), 217–218.

31 Isaac Deutscher regarded Gramsci's letter to the Soviet Politburo on the opposition as a sign of defense of Trotsky against Stalin. See *The Prophet Outcast*, 31. Actually, Gramsci thought Zinoviev and Trotsky the source of difficulties and hoped only to quiet the controversy. See John M. Cammett, *Antonio Gramsci and the Origins of Italian Communism* (Stanford Univ. Press, 1967), 181–182, and Davidson, *Antonio Gramsci*, 239. Gramsci supported both Zinoviev's 'Bolshevization' and Bukharin's 'Normalization.'

32 NOI to Trotsky, April–May 1930, *Annali Feltrinelli 1966*, 1034–1035.

33 'Perche il bolletino?' *Bolletino dell'opposizione comunista italiano*, 10 April 1931, 1.

34 See Giuliano Procacci, 'Trotsky's View of the Critical Years, 1929–1936,' *Science and Society* (Winter 1963), 62–69, for the PCI view that Trotsky was right on the Third Period and wrong (opposing) on the Popular Front. Leonetti could not tolerate Trotsky's 1934–1935 line of entry into the Socialist parties: He returned to the PCI and eventually fought in the resistance (See Corvisieri, *Trotskij e il movimento comunista italiano*, 158), forgetting his earlier denunciation of 'Menshevik formulas' for a 'united anti-fascist front.' See 'Il partito comunista al lavoro,' *Lo stato operaio*, July 1927, 517. Much later he judged the whole issue of democratic dictatorship versus Permanent Revolution to have been 'artificial.' See *Trotski e il trotskismo ciò che è vivo e ciò che è morto* (Rome, 1973), 486.

35 See Isaac Deutscher, 'La Tragédie du communisme polonais entre les deux guerres,' *Les Temps modernes*, March 1958, 1657–1658; also E. H. Carr, 'The Communist Party of Poland and the May Error, 1926,' *Annali Feltrinelli* (1972), 155–171. Trotsky's view is in the Trotsky Archive, T-2995 and T-3024; also *Biulleten oppozitsii*, September, 1932, 20–24.

36 Deutscher, 'Tragédie,' 1663.

37 Deutscher to Dziewanowski, 21 June 1952, Deutscher Archive.

38 Ludwik Hass, unpublished manuscript (in Polish) on Polish Communism; letter to author, 8 September 1978.

39 For the Balham group, see Trotsky Exile Archive, $T_2$1111, $T_2$1686; Reg Groves, *The Balham Group* (London, Pluto, 1974). The British Trotskyists began resistance to the transitional left-Bukharinist 'class against class' line in late 1927.

40 The phrase is that of Bertram Wolfe. See Robert Alexander, *The Right Opposition: The Lovestoneites and the International Communist Opposition of the Nineteen-Thirties* (Westport, Conn., Greenwood, 1981), 190.

41 Nín to Trotsky, 18 September 1931, *Bulletin internationale*, April 1933. The file

of Trotsky–Nín correspondence is in the Trotsky Exile Archive, and parts of the correspondence may be also found in other periodicals, bulletins, and circulars.

42   Rosmer and Naville considered Molinier an *homme d'affaires*, and a somewhat shady one, who had run roughshod over the intellectuals in the French opposition. 'With us,' he is said to have remarked, 'it's Trotsky for the doctrine and Stalin for the method.' Rosenthal, *Advocat de Trotsky*, 225. James Cannon, of the American Trotskyists, was quoted similarly: 'Trotsky for the program, Zinoviev for organization.'

43   *La Vérité*, 16 February 1930, 4.

44   'Ekonomicheskii avantiurizm i ego opasnosti' (written 13 February 1930), *Biulleten oppozitsii*, February–March 1930, 8. Trotsky's right turn began in Comintern affairs with 'Tretii period oshibok Kominterna' (The Third Period of Comintern Mistakes) occupying the whole January issue of *Biulleten oppozitsii*. The 'Dizziness with Success' article of Stalin was widely rumored to be the result of army pressure to ease the collectivization drive. See Jonathan Haslam, *Soviet Foreign Policy, 1930–1933: The Impact of the Depression* (London, Macmillan, 1983), appendix 1, citing information from Italian diplomatic sources.

45   Leon Trotsky, 'Le Plan quinquennal et la chômage mondiale,' *La Vérité*, 28 March 1930, 5. For the similarity between these views and Bukharin's 'Notes of an Economist,' see Moshe Lewin, *Political Undercurrents in Soviet Economic Debates* (Princeton, 1974), 68–72.

46   For Stalin's dicta, see *Sochineniia* (Moscow, 1951), vol. 13, p. 67; on Machajski, see N. Syrkin, *Makhaevshchina* (Moscow and Leningrad, 1931).

47   *Sochineniia*, vol. 13, pp. 90–91. On the Russian setting of the dispute with *Proletarskaia revoliutsiia*, see Robert C. Tucker, 'The Rise of Stalin's Personality Cult,' *American Historical Review* (April 1979), 347–366.

48   Tasca to Gramsci, 15 August 1926, *Annali Feltrinelli* (1966), 296–299. Victor Serge thought that Mussolini had learned something from Zubatovism, the Tsarist experiment in police trade unionism. See *Vie des révolutionnaires* (Paris, 1929), 27.

49   Annali Feltrinelli (1966), 471.

50   Leon Trotsky, 'The Key to the International Situation,' 8 December 1931, *Germany, 1931–1932* (London, New York, 1970), 19.

51   Leon Trotsky, 'Hitler e gli insegnamenti dell'esperienza italiano,' *Bolletino dell'opposizione*, 15 February 1932, 7. For the German Trotskyists, see 'O politike levoi oppozitsii v Germanii,' 30 September 1929, T-3241; and the considerable correspondence in the Trotsky Exile Archive, especially T$_2$2530–2593. Trotsky was in touch with a Wedding-Pfalz group (a Berlin suburb), which dated its opposition from 1925; also with members of Urbahns's Leninbund. Stalin's agents were also active; see G. Vereeken, *La Guepeou dans le mouvement trotskiste* (Paris, 1975), 28–42.

52   See, for example, Borkenau, *World Communism*, 339; Flechtheim, *Die KPD*, 249–251.

53   See Haslam, *Soviet Foreign Policy*, 98–99. For the presumed harmony of the Third Period ('social fascism') line and National Bolshevism, see 58–59. E. H. Carr, *Twilight of the Comintern, 1930–1935* (New York, Macmillan, 1982), 25, however, finds them to be contradictory.

54   See Aino Kuusinen, *Rings of Destiny* (New York, William Morrow, 1974), 81.

55   Interview with C. L. R. James, 1939. Trotsky Archive, T-4559.

56   Waltraudt Ireland, 'The Lost Gamble: The Theory and Practice of the German Communist Party Between Social Democracy and National Socialism, 1929–

1931' (unpublished doctoral dissertation, Johns Hopkins University, 1971), 199–207, 436; E. H. Carr, *Twilight of the Comintern*, 29–31.

57 See Abraham Ascher and Guenter Lewy, 'National Bolshevism in Weimar Germany,' *Social Research*, Winter 1956, *passim*.

58 L. Trotsky, 'Protiv natsional-kommunizm!' *Biulleten oppozitsii*, September 1931, 7.

59 See Schuddekopf, *Linke Leute von Rechts*, 286–306.

60 See 'Lost Gamble,' 658.

61 On this, see Karl Dietrich Bracher, *The German Dictatorship* (New York, Praeger, 1970), 200. Moscow's analysis was that Strasser was still seeking a legal path to power and would have been satisfied to participate in a non-Nazi government, while Hitler wanted power 'on Italian terms.' A. Gartman, 'Germaniia nakanunie novykh klassovykh bitv,' *Pravda*, 11 September 1932, 3.

62 Walter Krivitsky, *In Stalin's Secret Service* (New York, Harper & Row, 1939), 5; Ypsilon, *Pattern for World Revolution*, 164–165; Boris Nicolaevsky, 'Stalin i ubiistvo Kirova,' *Sotsialisticheskii vestnik*, December, 1956, 240. For Stalin's confidence in Schleicher, as well as Neurath and Blomberg, see the letter of German ambassador Dirksen to Bulow, 31 January 1933, *Documents on German Foreign Policy, 1918–1945* (Washington, D.C., 1957), series C, vol. 1, 14–15.

63 See Roy Medvedev, *Let History Judge: The Origin and Consequences of Stalinism* (New York, Knopf, 1971), 111–123; Avtorkhanov, *Stalin and the Soviet Communist Party* (New York, 1959), 28–31.

64 The Prompartiia (Industrial Party) trial of 1930 concerned Professor L. K. Ramzin, a leading Soviet specialist on heat engineering, and seven other high officials allegedly wrecking and spying for the French government. There were death sentences, but none was shot, and Ramzin was shortly returned to work.

65 Leon Trotsky, 'Les Enseignements du procès des saboteurs,' *La Vérité*, 5 December 1930, 2. Stalin's clemency, and his fears, may have been influenced by these remarks.

66 Bessedovskii Papers, Hoover Institution.

67 Serge, *Memoirs*, 258–259.

68 Kh. Rakovskii, 'O Kapituliatsii i kapituliantakh,' *Biulleten oppozitsii* (November–December 1929), 7.

69 *Pravda*, 6 October 1930, 3. Riutin's name was connected to two other expelled 'plotters,' Nusinov and Kavraiskii, who were said to be showing signs of 'Kondratievschina,' and 'Sukhanovshchina.' L. Averbach, 'O dvurushnichestve,' *Pravda*, 30 October 1930, 4. Kondratiev, later known in the West for his famous 'long wave' theory of business cycles, had criticized the relative paucity of investment in agriculture. See E. H. Carr and R. W. Davies, *Foundations of a Planned Economy, 1926–1929* (Harmondsworth, Penguin, 1974), vol. 1, pp. 777–779. Zinoviev had already denounced 'Kondratievshchina' in 1927. Kondratiev was said to be, not merely a 'neo-narodnik,' but the leader of the 'Toiling Peasant Party.' Together with Sukhanov (the historian of the revolution) and his 'Union Bureau' of Mensheviks, he was said to be in a bloc with the 'Industrial Party' of Professor Ramzin.

70 'O Termidorianstve i bonapartisme,' *Biulleten oppozitsii* (November–December 1930), 31.

71 R. W. Davies, 'The Syrtsov-Lominadze Affair,' *Soviet Studies* (January 1981), 31–32.

72   See p. 101.
73   Leon Trotsky, 'What Next in the Campaign Against the Russian Right Wing?' *WLT 1930–1931*, 64.
74   On these, see Medvedev, *Let History Judge*, 111–137, with depositions and memoirs of the accused.
75   Medvedev, *Let History Judge*, 140–141; Avtorkhanov, *Stalin and the Soviet Communist Party*, 195–201; Robert Conquest, *The Great Terror: Stalin's Purge of the Thirties* (New York, Macmillan, 1968), 253–254. Em. Iaroslavskii, 'Put VKP(b) ot Oktiabria ko vtoroi piatiletka,' *Bolshevik*, 1 November 1932, 44–45; Ciliga to Trotsky, 14 May 1936, Trotsky Exile Archive, T_2573.
76   *KPSS v rezoliutsiiakh i resheniiakh* (Moscow, 1953), vol. 2, 742.
77   Serge, *Memoirs*, 258–259; Anton Ciliga, *Au pays du grand mensonge* (Paris, Gallimard, 1938), 228–229. Boris Nicolaevsky, 'Letter of an Old Bolshevik,' in *Power and the Soviet Elite* (Ann Arbor, Univ. of Michigan Press, 1975), 26–68.
78   *Sotsialisticheskii vestnik*, 26 September 1932, 20. The report was dated 7 September.
79   Ibid., 21. For the origin of the *Letter of An Old Bolshevik*, see p. 143.
80   'Pismo iz Moskvy,' *Biulleten oppozitsii*, November 1932, 23.
81   'Besposhchadnyi otpor vragam leninskoi partii,' *Pravda*, 11 October 1932, 5.
82   Others called rightists were P. A. Galkin, M. S. Ivanov, P. M. Zamiatin, B. I. Demidov, and M. I. Mebeli. Trotskyists were B. M. Ptashnyi, N. I. Vasilev, and V. B. Gorelov. P. P. Fedorov was described as an ex-SR, V. N. Kaiurov as an ex-member of the Workers' Opposition, and G. Rokhkin as a Bundist. The others, V. N. Kaiurov, A. V. Kaiurov, S. V. Tokarev, N. P. Kaiurov, K. A. Zamiatin-Cherny, and H. I. Kolokolov, were simply described as 'distributors of counter-revolutionary literature and supporters of counter-revolutionary groups.' Ibid., 2.
83   *WLT 1932*, 71.
84   Trotsky to Wicks, November, 1932. Trotsky Exile Archive, T_28114. Wicks had been expelled from the British Communist Party with Reg Groves and the Balham Group in August.
85   Trotsky to Sedov, n.d. (November 1932). Trotsky Exile Archive, T_213095.
86   Ko. ('Kolokolnikov'—I. N. Smirnov), 'Khoziaistvennoe polozhenie Sovetskogo Soiuza,' *Biulleten oppozitsii*, November 1932, 18–20.
87   Sedov to Trotsky, n.d. (October–November 1932). Trotsky Exile Archive, T_24782, written in invisible ink. It was discovered by a research team including Pierre Broué, Michel Dreyfus, Alain Calvic, Jean-Pierre Joubert, Isabelle Lombard, and Katia Sich. See P. Broué, 'Trotsky et le bloc des oppositions de 1932,' *Cahiers Leon Trotsky*, January–March 1980, 5–37.
88   In a separate category, with Uglanov, Petr Petrovskii, and M. E. Ravich-Cherkasskii, suspended from the party 'pending a review of the decision and their future conduct.' *Pravda*, 11 October 1932, 2.
89   Sedov to Trotsky, 12 October 1932, Trotsky Collection, Nicolaevsky Archive, series 231. I am indebted to Elena Danielson of the Hoover Achives for giving me access to this collection prior to its being opened to the public.
90   Ibid.
91   Trotsky to Sedov, 17 October 1932, Trotsky Exile Archive, T_210247. See also 'Signal trevogi,' *Biulleten oppozitsii*, March 1933, 9.
92   Sedov to Trotsky, 27 June 1932, Trotsky Collection, Nicolaevsky Archive, series 231.
93   Trotsky to Sedov, 30 October 1932, Trotsky Exile Archive, T_210248.

94 *Pravda*, 12 October 1932, 2.
95 *Pravda*, 14 October 1932, 3.
96 V. M. Molotov, 'K redaktsiiu zhurnala 'Kommunist,' *Kommunist*, September 1955, 127–128.
97 Elizabeth Lermolo, *Face of a Victim* (New York, Harper & Row, 1955).

Chapter 7

1 'A Letter to the Politburo,' 15 March 1933, *WLT 1932–1933*, 141. See also Robert McNeal, 'Trockij and Stalinism,' *Pensiero e azione politica di Lev Trockij*, 381.
2 Albert Treint, 'Pour déchiffrer l'énigme Russe,' 27 March 1933, Archives Spartacus/René Lefeuvre.
3 Ibid.
4 'Ou sommes nous?' July 1933, Archives Spartacus/René Lefeuvre.
5 Urbahns's declaration, 27–28 August 1933. Archives Spartacus/René Lefeuvre. For the efforts to unite the Trotskyists with other left parties, see Michel Dreyfus, 'Bureau de Londres ou Quatrième International?' (thèse de doctorat, 3ème cycle, University of Paris X), November 1977.
6 Albert Treint, 'Capitalisme d'état et Quatrième Internationale,' 18 January 1934. Archives Spartacus/René Lefeuvre.
7 Treint charged, accurately, that Trotsky misrepresented Lenin on this score, Trotsky holding that Lenin had only used 'state capitalism' with the inverted commas.
8 'Capitalisme d'état.'
9 The German and French Zinovievists, at the time of the Zinoviev-Trotsky opposition, had shared some of the thinking on Russia of those to their left. Karl Korsch and the bimonthly *Kommunistische politik*, in sympathy with the *Révolution prolétarienne* syndicalists and with the Bordigists, called Russia 'state capitalist,' but their critique of Leninism was unacceptable to Urbahns. The Schwarz group and *Entschiedene Link* argued similarly, continuing their sympathy for the KAPD tradition. The Katz group was close to the blend of Communism and anarchism offered by Franz Pfemfert's *Die Aktion*. Treint's *L'Étincelle* published the writings of Miasnikov.
10 Lucien Laurat, *L'Accumulation du capital d'après Rosa Luxemburg* (Paris, Rivière, 1930), 165. Bukharin was encouraged, thought Laurat, by Luxemburg's translator, S. Dvolaïtskii, and his reinstatement of the Hilferding tradition, with its emphasis on the wedding of the finance and trustified industry, having its upper 'limit' in a 'general cartel.'
11 Hilferding and Luxemburg thus came to symbolize right and left economic analyses, or 'stabilization' and 'crisis.' On this, see Fritz Sternberg, *Der Imperializmus* (Berlin, Malik-verlag, 1926), and Richard B. Day, *The 'Crisis' and the 'Crash': Soviet Studies of the West, 1917–1939* (London, NLB, 1980), ch. 4.
12 Lucien Laurat, *L'Économie sovietique* (Paris, Valois, 1931), 42. This was related to Machajski's 'perpetual incommensurability of social product and social income.' *Umstvennyi rabochi* (Geneva, 1905), p. 2, p. 18.
13 *L'Économie sovietique*, 105.
14 Lucien Laurat, *Cinq Années de crise mondiale* (Paris, Nouveau Prométhée, 1934), 92–93. For the argument that Marx and Rodbertus were actually both

---

defenders of 'perpetual national capital,' see Machajski, *Umstvennyi rabochi*, pt. 2, p. 4.

15 For the polemic on Proudhon's theory of 'constituted value,' see Anthony D'Agostino, *Marxism and the Russian Anarchists* (San Francisco, Germinal, 1977), 30.

16 Lucien Laurat, *Économie dirigée et socialization* (Paris, 1934), 64–65.

17 Max Nomad (Max Nacht), 'Le Socialisme des intellectuals,' *Révolution prolétarienne* (November 1933), 420. The editors appended this note: 'False. The author confuses Marx with Stalin's interpretation of Marx.'

18 Simone Weil, 'Allons-nous vers la révolution prolétarienne?' *Révolution prolétarienne* (25 August 1933), 312.

19 Jean Prader, 'Comment il ne faut pas faire une nouvelle Internationale,' *Le Travailleur* (17 January 1934), 3.

20 Leon Trotsky, 'Klassovaia priroda sovetskogo gosudarstva,' *Biulleten oppozitsii*, October 1933, 6–7.

21 The unfinished fragment in which he attempted to define the term breaks off just as he appears ready to grant it to 'physicians and officials.' K. Marx, *Capital* (Moscow, 1966), vol. 3, p. 886. See the discussion in Jean-Yves Calvez, *La Pensée de Karl Marx* (Paris, Éditions du Seuíl, 1970), 108–113.

22 Krivitsky, *In Stalin's Secret Service*, 9–10, reports Radek tailoring every phrase to suit Stalin, and assuring that the new line was not serious, in view of the still extensive Soviet contacts with German business and military circles.

23 Cohen, *Bukharin and the Bolshevik Revolution*, 355.

24 Trotsky remembered that during the period of Stalin's encouragement for Béla Kun's pan-European trade union alliance in 1926 Kaganovich had urged links to the Amsterdam trade union international, a position he had to disavow when the line changed.

25 Jane Degras, ed., *Soviet Documents on Foreign Policy*, vol. 3, p. 184. Also, Robert Slusser, 'The Role of the Foreign Ministry,' in Ivo Lederer, ed., *Russian Foreign Policy* (New Haven, Conn., Yale Univ. Press, 1962), 218–219: and Cohen, *Bukharin and the Bolshevik Revolution*, 360.

26 See pp. 39–41.

27 For Bolshevism described as the bearer of the 'general-democratic and political tendencies' of the Russian revolutionary movement, in the Jacobin sense, Theodore Dan, *Origins of Bolshevism* (New York, Schocken, 1970), 259.

28 Platform of the Fifteen, 27 June 1927, Trotsky Archive, T-964. For Stalinism as the 'peasantization of Bolshevism,' see N. Vakar, *The Taproot of Soviet Society* (New York, Harper, 1961), *passim*.

29 See 'Maretskii o Termidore,' Summer 1926, Trotsky Archive, T-878; and Trotsky to Comrades, 21 October 1928, text in *WLT 1928–1929*, 270.

30 1 March 1931, Trotsky Archive, T-4983.

31 'Rabochee gosudarstvo, termidor i bonapartizm,' *Biulleten oppozitsii*, April 1935, 8.

32 *Biulleten oppozitsii*, nos. 17–18 (1930), 11–19. For an appreciation of Rakovskii's insight, see Alec Nove, 'A Note on Trotsky and the "Left Opposition," 1929–1931,' *Soviet Studies*, October 1977, 585.

33 On first hearing the news, he claimed that the act could have but one goal: 'to clear the way for Bonapartism and fascism in the soviet Union.' 'Meunier,' 'L'Assassinat de Kirov,' *La Vérité*, 15 December 1934, 1.

34 *Sotsialisticheskii vestnik*, 25 May, 1933, 16.

35 Ibíd., 10 February 1934, 17.

36 Ibid., 22 December 1936, 20–33, and 17 January 1937, 17–24. English translation in *Power and the Soviet Elite* (Ann Arbor, 1975), 26–68.

37   See pp. 122–129. Numerous loose ends in the account show that it was not a verbatim interview but an assemblage of Nicolaevsky's gleanings from Bukharin and others.
38   Tibor Szamuely, 'The Elimination of Opposition Between the Sixteenth and Seventeenth Party Congresses of the CPSU,' *Soviet Studies* (January 1966), 326.
39   *Sotsialisticheskii vestnik*, 25 April 1934, 15.
40   Ibid., 10 November 1934, 16.
41   For the right course considered as Stalin's own preference, see J. Arch Getty, *Origins of the Great Purges: The Soviet Communist Party Reconsidered, 1933–1938* (Cambridge Univ. Press, 1985), 94.
42   'Kuda stalinskaia biurokratiia vedet SSSR?' *Biulleten oppozitsii*, February 1935, 3.
43   Karl Radek, 'Zhest pontiia pilata,' *Izvestiia*, 6 June 1934, 2.
44   'Resultaty konferentsii v streze,' *Izvestiia*, 16 April 1935, 2. See also Evgenii Gnedin, *Iz Istorii otnoshenii mezhdu SSSR i fashistskoi germaniei* (New York, Khronika, 1977), 21–23.
45   'Plan i nashi zadachi,' *Pravda*, 11 January 1936, 3.
46   Ibid. A sentiment strongly echoed in a Maslow-Fischer document of 16 October 1935, which may have come to Stalin's attention. Trotsky Exile Archive, T$_2$15967. See also Maslow, 'Zum abessinischen Krieg,' 1935, T$_2$17028.
47   See Cohen, *Bukharin and the Bolshevik Revolution*, 360–361.
48   *The Case of the Trotskyite–Zinovievite Terrorist Center* (Moscow, 1936), 11, 56, 176.
49   Ibid., 24, 150.
50   Ibid., 28.
51   *Sotsialisticheskii vestnik*, 10 October 1936, 24.
52   N. I. Bukharin, 'Surovye slova,' *Izvestiia*, 22 December 1934, 2.
53   Manuscript on the Zinoviev-Kamenev trial, 16 September 1936, Trotsky Exile Archive, T$_2$15888. Bukharin, in testimony at his own trial, would be at pains to deny that the confessions were attributable to 'l'âme slave.'
54   Ibid.
55   Alexander Uralov (Abdurakhman Avtorkhanov), *The Reign of Stalin* (London, Bodley Head, 1959), 223; but see the discussion among Avtorkhanov, John Armstrong, Robert Slusser, and George Kennan, in *Slavic Review* (December 1967), 665–677.
56   Text in *Crimes of the Stalin Era* (New York, 1962), 23. It has been assumed by Boris Nicolaevsky and many others that Stalin referred to the Riutin program of 1932. Pierre Broué, 'Bloc des oppositions,' 23 assumes Stalin to mean the bloc of 1932 as well. Getty, *Origins of the Great Purge*, 246, curiously insists that Stalin meant the bloc of 1932, and not the Riutin platform. For Iagoda's connection with Bukharin, see Robert Conquest, *Inside Stalin's Secret Police: NKVD Politics, 1936–1939* (Stanford, Hoover Institution Press, 1985), 11–13.
57   A. A. Gromyko and B. N. Ponomarev, *Istoria vneshnei politiki SSSR, 1917–1980* (Moscow, 1980), 325, date the arrival of Soviet equipment from October. David Cattell, *Soviet Diplomacy and the Spanish Civil War* (Berkeley, U.C. Press, 1957), 32, puts the decision in the last week of August or first week of September.
58   *The Case of the Anti-Soviet Trotskyite Center* (Moscow, 1937), 5, 10, 458, 543.
59   Ibid., 109.
60   Ibid., 444.

61 His name had appeared on the victims 'honor list' at a November trial in Novosibirsk.
62 'Stalin in Partial Retreat,' *New York Times*, 30 January 1937; text in *WLT 1936–1937*, 168–170. See also *'Prigovor Bol'shevizma,'* *Sotsialisticheskii vestnik*, 11 February 1937, 1. General Kostring, the German military attaché, who would have been hard to ignore in all this plotting with the Germans, was nevertheless not declared persona non grata. See Conquest, *Great Terror*, 218.
63 *Great Terror*, 168; Hryhory Kostiuk, *The Fall of Postyshev*, Research Program on the USSR (New York, 1954), 18–23.
64 See Krivitsky, *In Stalin's Secret Service*, 147–171, for the denunciation of Iagoda. Trotsky thought Iagoda's later trial testimony extraordinary for its candor in admitting the GPU role in the murder of Kirov. See 'Rol Genrika Iagoda,' *Biulleten oppozitsii*, April, 1938, 10; also *Sotsialisticheskii vestnik*, 27 April 1937, 22.
65 George Kennan, *Russia and the West Under Lenin and Stalin* (Boston, Little, Brown, 1961), 310.
66 Krivitsky, *In Stalin's Secret Service*, 211–213; Conquest, *Great Terror*, ch. 7.
67 'Obezglavlenie Krasnoi Armii,' *Biulleten oppozitsii*, July–August 1937, 4–6.
68 *The Case of the Anti-Soviet Bloc of Rights and Trotskyites* (Moscow, 1938), 51. For the enormous reputation of Polish intelligence among Soviet leaders, see Ypsilon, *Pattern for World Revolution*, 225–245.
69 Ibid., 294.
70 See the survey in *The Times* (London) for 20 April 1933, 10–11. Also Walter Duranty, 'Soviet Prosecutor Clears One Briton,' *New York Times*, 18 April 1933, 1, 7.
71 For this, see Raymond Sontag, 'The Last Months of Peace,' *Foreign Affairs* (April 1957), 507–524; and Anthony D'Agostino, 'Trotsky on Stalin's Foreign Policy,' in *Pensiero e azione politica*, 405–415.
72 Khrushchev's complaints about Pavlov are in *Khrushchev Remembers* (New York, 1971), 185–187. 'Victor Alexandrov' concocts an imaginary conversation between Stalin and Radek, ending with Stalin's advice that the icebreaker theory, not Litvinov's policy, is 'true Marxism.' *The Tukhachevsky Affair* (London, MacDonald, 1963), 28.
73 'A–propos de la politique extérieure de la bureaucratie staliniste,' *La Vérité*, 19 May 1933, 1. Ustrialov had early concluded that Hitler and Stalin would produce a 'synthesis of Bolshevism and fascism,' which would campaign against the Anglo-Saxon plutocracy. See *Germanskoi natsional-sotsializm* (Harbin, 1933), 83.
74 'Nationalism and Economic Life,' *Foreign Affairs* (April 1934), 402.
75 The Second Five Year Plan is also the starting point for the postwar thesis of Nicholas S. Timasheff, *The Great Retreat: The Growth and Decline of Communism in Russia* (New York, Dutton, 1946).
76 Yvan Craipeau, 'Contre-rapport pour le congrès du POI,' *Bulletin internationale (POI)*, 30 October 1937, 3, 11.
77 Speech to POI conference, 1937, in *Défense du Marxisme* (Paris, 1972), 319.
78 Discussion on tasks of Fourth International, *Quatrième Internationale*, September–October 1938, 176.
79 Yvan Craipeau, 'Sur l'URSS, le défaitisme cosmique et le défaitisme tout court,' *Bulletin internationale (POI)*, 21 January 1938, 4.
80 James Burnham, 'On the Character of War and Perspectives of the Fourth International,' *Interim Bulletin ORSCPC*, December 1937, vol. 3, p. 9; Bill Cohen, 'On the Nature of the Russian State,' in ibid., 10. M. Glee and Daniel Eastman (son of Max Eastman) complained that Trotsky tried to argue that

the Moscow trials had been primarily against the left, but in fact the 'target' was the whole spectrum of Communist opinion. After Max Shachtman had broken with Trotsky on the Soviet war with Finland, a tendency in his Workers' Party would conclude that 'Socialist totalitarianism is not better but worse than bourgeois democracy.' The Sherman Group, 'Defining a Tendency,' *Bulletin WP*, April 1941, 7.

81 Leon Trotsky, discussion on the Russian Question, 25 March 1938, Trotsky Archive, T-4334.7.
82 Rizzi to Trotsky, 12 December 1938, Trotsky Exile Archive, T₂4267; 19 June 1939, T₂4270-2.
83 Bruno R. (Rizzi), *La Bureaucratization du monde: Le Collectivisme bureaucratique: Quo vadis America?* (Paris, 1939), 25.
84 Ibid., 89, 103.
85 Ibid., 135, 167.
86 Ibid., 293.
87 Ibid., 295–296. Ustrialov had noted in 1933 that the Black Hundred counter-revolutionists of 1905 had been both anti-Semitic and anticapitalist. Thus there was affinity in the Russian tradition for Nazism. See *Germanskoi natsional-sotsializm*, 16.
88 *La Bureaucratization du monde*, 324.

Chapter 8

1 *Memoirs of Marshall Zhukov* (New York, Delacorte, 1971), 180.
2 Max Shachtman, *The Bureaucratic Revolution: The Rise of The Stalinist State* (New York, 1962); James Burnham, *The Managerial Revolution* (New York, 1941), chs. 14 and 15, in which a German victory is assumed.
3 Stenographic draft of a discussion with Trotsky, 12 June 1940, in *WLT 1929–1940*, 56. On the 'defeatism' slogan, see Anthony D'Agostino, 'Ambiguities of Trotsky's Leninism,' *Survey*, Winter 1979, 200–203.
4 Leon Trotsky, 'L'Union soviétique et la révolution internationale,' *La Vérité*, 8 November 1935, 2.
5 Leon Trotsky, 'Independence of the Ukraine and Sectarian Muddleheads,' 30 July 1939, in *WLT 1939–1940*, 44–54.
6 Observation on Trotsky's 1939 essay, 'The Soviet Union in War, in *Annali Feltrinelli 1968*, 706.
7 Dan, *Origins of Bolshevism*, 440.
8 Boris Nicolaevsky, 'O "pilotovskom voprose,"' *Sotsialisticheskii vestnik*, 8 May 1943, 112.
9 Boris Nicolaevsky, 'Vneshnaia politika moskvy,' *Novyi zhurnal*, 1942, no. 1, 241.
10 Lucien Laurat had suggested a law of accumulation for the Soviet economy in *L'Accumulation du capital d'après Rosa Luxemburg* (1930), then denied it in *Le Marxisme en faillité* (1939).
11 Rudolf Hilferding, 'Gosudarstvennyi kapitalizm ili totalitarnoe goskhoziaistvo?' *Sotsialistcheskii vestnik*, 25 April 1940, 118–120. Boris Nicolaevsky, 'Teoreticheskoe zaveshchanie R. Gilferdinga,' *Sotsialisticheskii vestnik*, January–February 1947, 18–22. See also the remarks of George Denicke on the voluntarist nature of totalitarianism, in Carl Friedrich, ed., *Totalitarianism* (New York, 1964), 75. The weakness of the Soviet managers is also stressed in Jeremy Azrael, *Managerial Power and Soviet Politics* (Cambridge, Mass., 1966), 174–175.

12 Boris Nicolaevsky, '"Termidor" russkoi revoliutsii,' *Sotsialisticheskii vestnik*, 6 September 1945, 171–175. See also Rafael Abramovitch, 'Dall'utopia socialista all'impero totalitario,' *Critical sociale*, 1 and 16 December 1947, 490–492 and 462–464; and Michael Karpovich, 'Russkii imperializm ili Kommunisticheskaia agressia?' *Novyi zhurnal* (1951), 243–263.

13 See p. 66.

14 *Sochineniia* (Moscow, 1932), vol. 17, pp. 425–474.

15 See pp. 110–252. Boris Nicolaevsky, 'Crux of Soviet Foreign Policy was Creation of a Reich Army of Revenge to Destroy the West,' *New Leader*, 19 July 1941, 4.

16 Boris Nicolaevsky, 'Elimination of Bolshevik Old Guard Was Hitler's Price for Stalin Pact,' *New Leader*, 30 August 1941, 5. Nicolaevsky claimed that Rosenberg had sent Stalin a list of prominent Bolsheviks who were an obstacle to the improvement of Nazi–Soviet relations, a list which comprised the names of the defendants in the Moscow trials.

17 Boris Nicolaevsky, 'Soviet Secret Policy Turned Pro-Nazi in 1934,' *New Leader*, 23 August 1941, 4–6.

18 Harry Hopkins, 'My Meeting with Stalin,' *American Magazine*, December 1941, 114; Boris Nicolaevsky, 'The Crisis in the German High Command,' *New Europe*, April 1942, 8.

19 Boris Nicolaevsky, 'Smeshchenie feld marshala Braukhicha,' *Novyi zhurnal*, no. 2 (1942), 226.

20 Boris Nicolaevsky, 'SSSR i Kitai,' *Sotsialisticheskii vestnik*, May 1955, 79–82.

21 Jonathan Harris, 'The Origins of the Conflict Between Malenkov and Zhdanov: 1939–1941,' *Slavic Review*, June 1976, 296–297; Gavriel Ra'anan, *International Policy Formation in the USSR: Factional 'Debates' During the Zhdanovshchina* (Hamden, Conn., Scarecrow, 1983), 12–16.

22 See Robert McNeal, 'Decisions of the CPSU and the Great Purge,' *Soviet Studies* (October 1971), 178–179.

23 Harris, 'The Origins of Conflict,' 288–295; Vladimir Rudolph, 'Agencies of Control,' in Robert Slusser, ed., *Soviet Economic Policy in Postwar Germany*, Research Program on the USSR (New York, 1953), 19–45.

24 Nicolaevsky to Uriel Weinreich, State Department, 15 May 1952, Nicolaevsky Archives. This is in dispute. Gunther Nollau, in *International Communism and World Revolution* (New York, 1961), 212, maintains that Zhdanov was in charge. Aleksandr Shcherbakov has also been suggested. See the discussion in Robert Kitrinos, 'The International Department of the CPSU,' *Problems of Communism*, September–October 1984, 49. 'Alfred Burmeister,' a Polish Communist who was in 'Institute 205' (the Comintern's 1941 name) in Engels in the former Volga German capital, says that Dmitrov, Manuilskii, and Shcherbakov gave theoretical lectures but that Zhdanov had no influence. *Dissolution and Aftermath of the Comintern, 1937–1947* (New York, 1955), 10–25. This makes sense in view of the prominence of people such as Wilhelm Zaisser and Bedrich Geminder, later associated with Beria, whom Nikolaevsky has taking over the apparatus with the fall of Malenkov in August, 1946.

25 The term used by Hugh Seton-Watson, *The East European Revolution* (New York, Praeger, 1956), 169.

26 'A signal to the Communist parties of the west that they should recover their identity, it was Moscow's alert to Communists everywhere that they should prepare for new policies in the postwar world.' Arthur Schlesinger, Jr., 'Origins of the Cold War,' *Foreign Affairs* (October 1967), 43. The term 'party

revival' for the CPSU is used by William McCagg, *Stalin Embattled, 1943–1948* (Detroit, Wayne State Univ. Press, 1978), 98.

27 German Trotskyists had come to this conclusion in 1941, noting the utopia of hoping to replace the fascist regimes with socialist ones and the importance of 'national liberation' and 'democratic revolution.' *Three Theses* (IKD), Dossier Quatrième Internationale, Bibliothèque de Documentation Internationale et Contemporaine, Nanterre.

28 Eugen S. Varga, *Izmeneniia v ekonomike kapitalizma v itoge vtoroi mirovoi voiny* (Moscow, 1946), 226–268; also *Anglo-Amerikanskie ekonomicheskie otnosheniia* (Moscow, 1946), 17–18.

29 For a discussion of this National Bolshevik line, which may have included preference for a German flag in black, white, and red (colors designed to appeal to the Bismarck tradition and Hohenzollern nationalism) rather than the republican black, red, and gold, see Ra'anan, *International Policy Formation*, 95–99.

30 Nicolaevsky to Weinrich, 15 May 1952, Nicolaevsky Archives.

31 Werner Hahn's useful study of the press for this period, the central argument of which is a denial that Zhdanov carried the 'Zhdanovshchina' any further than literature and culture— that is, not to 'moderates' in politics and ideology—does not deny the importance of the tie between the Leningraders and Titoists. See *Postwar Soviet Politics: The Fall of Zhdanov and the Defeat of Moderation, 1946–1953* (Ithaca, Cornell Univ. Press, 1982), 94, 99, 113.

32 Zhukov mentions disputes with Zhdanov during the seige of Leningrad. *Memoirs of Marshall Zhukov*, 212. Also, see Boris Nicolaevsky, 'Opala marshala zhukova,' *Sotsialisticheskii vestnik*, 20 August 1946, 171.

33 See N. S. Patolichev, *Measures of Maturity: My Early Life* (Oxford and New York, Pergamon, 1983). Patolichev was brought from Cheliabinsk into the Secretariat by the Central Committee plenum of March 1946, which also brought into the Orgburo Kuznetsov from Leningrad, Rodionov from Gorky, and Suslov from Stavropol. For Patolichev and Suslov as part of a 'third force' independent of Malenkov or Zhdanov, see Arnold Beichman and Mikhail Bernstam, *Andropov* (Briarcliff Manor, N.Y., Stein & Day, 1983), 85–87.

34 Vladimir Dedijer, *Tito* (New York, Simon & Shuster, 1953), 297. See also Eugenio Reale, *Avec Jacques Duclos au banc des accusés* (Paris, Plon, 1958), 35.

35 Milovan Djilas, *Conversations with Stalin* (New York, Harcourt, Brace, 1962), 143.

36 Boris Nicolaevsky, 'How Malenkov Triumphed,' *New Leader*, 30 March 1953, 15–19. Souvarine's critique of this argument is in 'L'Ordre des préséances au Politburo sovietique de 1945 à 1952,' *BEIPI*, 16–30 June 1953, 1–5.

37 Ypsilon, *Pattern for World Revolution*, 433.

38 Phillipe Devillers, *Histoire du Viet-nam de 1940 à 1952* (Paris, Éditions du Sevil, 1952), 454–455. Mao's occupation of the South China provinces in December 1949 strengthened the position of left critics of Ho such as Truong Chinh. See Paul Isoart, *Le Phénomène national vietnamien* (Paris, 1961), 396. The French Communists had abstained on the vote for war credits for Indochina in March 1947, and the Communist cabinet ministers had voted with the government. At Sklarska Poręba in September they were accused of 'parliamentary cretinism.' See Reale, *Avec Jacques Duclos*, 36.

39 Boris Nicolaevsky, 'Mao Checks Khrushchev,' *New Leader*, 16 January 1961, 15–17. Wang Ming, *Mao's Betrayal* (Moscow, 1979), 63–64.

40 Lazar Pistrak has suggested that he was a Trotskyist at the Moscow Higher

Technical School in 1923–1924. See 'Malenkov: The Man and the Myth,' *New Leader*, 16 March 1953, 6–8.

41   Boris Nicolaevsky, 'Stalin's Secret Sickness,' *Cleveland Plain Dealer*, 7 November 1948, 15.

42   *Khrushchev Remembers* (New York, 1970), 294–301.

43   Ibid., 266–269.

44   Ibid., 271–272.

45   This possibility is pursued by Ra'anan, *International Policy Formation*, 128–129.

46   According to accounts published during the mood of de-Stalinization after the Twenty-Second Congress, when Khrushchev wanted to embarrass Suslov for his persecution of Voznesenskii. Summarized in Hahn, *Postwar Soviet Politics*, 130–135.

47   Abdurakhman Avtorkhanov, 'Suslov, the Kremlin's Chief Ideologist,' *Bulletin of the Institute for the Study of the USSR* (February 1968), 6.

48   J. V. Stalin, *Economic Problems of Socialism in the USSR*, supplement to *New Times*, 29 October 1952, 1–2.

49   Enver Hoxha, *With Stalin: Memoirs* (Tirana, 1979), 30–31. Djilas reports that this was exactly Stalin's offer. *Conversations with Stalin*, 143.

50   This was, according to Khrushchev, especially the case with the imprisonment of Gomulka by his factional opponents Berman and Minc, *Khrushchev Remembers: The Last Testament* (New York, 1974), 204–205. 'He was victimized,' Berman said of Gomulka in a recent interview, 'by the fact that he had not, as we had, lived longer in the Soviet Union.' Teresa Torańska, *Oni* (London, Aneks, 1985), 299.

51   For the Soviet policy change on Israel as the result of growing Anglo–American cooperation, see Yaacov Ro'i, *Soviet Decision-making in Practice: The USSR and Israel, 1947–1954* (New Brunswick, N.J., Rutgers Univ. Press, 1980), 274–275.

52   Andrei Sakharov, 'How I Came to Dissent,' *New York Review of Books*, 21 March 1974, 11.

53   *Khrushchev Remembers*, 400–401. At the end of January, the Soviets followed the Chinese lead and recognized Ho Chi Minh's government in Vietnam, where General Giap was managing the transition from guerrilla warfare to mobile warfare, according to the formula of Mao, as explained to General Giap by Liu Shao-chi. See Devillers, *Histoire du Viet-nam*, 454–456.

54   Truman's removal of General MacArthur is said to have prompted agonized second thoughts by Mao. See Wang Ming, *Mao's Betrayal*, 186.

55   Boris Nicolaevsky, 'The New Soviet Spy Directors,' *New Leader*, 21 June 1954, 17–18.

56   Boris Nicolaevsky, address to the American Committee for the Liberation of the Peoples of Russia, 23 January 1953. Nicolaevsky Archive; 'Porazhenie Khrushcheva,' *Novyi zhurnal*, no. 25 (1951), 226.

57   Boris Nicolaevsky, 'Party Men and Managers,' *New Leader*, 29 July 1957, 8–10.

58   The term used by Myron Rush to designate the role of Brezhnev in Khrushchev's regime of the late fifties. See *How Communist States Change Their Rulers* (Ithaca, Cornell Univ. Press, 1974), 196.

59   *Khrushchev Remembers*, 298.

60   Ibid., 338.

61   Text of Churchill's speech, *New York Times*, 12 May 1953, 8.

62   Deutscher to Astor, 7 August 1949, Deutscher Archive.

63   Isaac Deutscher, *Russia After Stalin* (Oxford, 1953), 122.

64 Isaac Deutscher, 'The Legacies and Heirs of J. V. Stalin,' *Reporter*, 14 April 1953, 14–15.

65 Deutscher to Brandler, 3 January 1955, Deutscher Archive. See also the correspondence with R. N. Carew Hunt, Jane Degras, Carr, and George Lichtheim. 'If one wishes to assess the historical significance of the Russian Revolution in terms of the influence exercised by it,' wrote Carr, 'productivity, industrialization, and planning are the key words.' 'A Historical Turning Point: Marx, Lenin, and Stalin,' in Richard Pipes, ed., *Revolutionary Russia* (New York, 1969), 364.

66 N. V. Volskii, *Vstrechi s Leninym* (New York, 1953), translated (by Paul Rosta and Brian Pearce) as *Encounters with Lenin* (London, Oxford Univ. Press, 1968).

67 N. Valentinov (Volskii), 'Deux Marxismes,' *Contrat social*, January 1959, 29.

68 N. Valentinov, 'Le Complexe byzantin dans la conscience russe,' *BEIPI*, 16–29 February 1956, 5–10. Against this argument, see Karpovich, 'Russkii imperializm,' 252.

69 N. Valentinov, 'Un Caligula à Moscou: Le Cas pathologique de Staline,' supplement to *BEIPI*, 16–30 November 1953, 1, 3–6, 15. This idea is also pursued by André Visson, *Le Grand Mystère du Kremlin* (Paris, 1953).

70 *The Secret History of Stalin's Crimes* (London, 1953), 265–269.

71 Boris Meissner, 'Die neue Parteiführung,' *Osteuropa*, April 1953, 108. Meissner had thought Molotov a more likely successor than Malenkov since 1951.

72 Robert Conquest, *Power and Policy in the USSR* (New York, Macmillan, 1961), 210.

73 Bertram D. Wolfe, 'The Death of Stalin' (unpublished paper for U.S. Department of State, April 1953, Wolfe Collection, Hoover Institution).

74 Boris Nicolaevsky, 'Sovetskaia diktatura i germanskaia problema,' *Sotsialisticheskii vestnik*, November 1955, 209–210. For the idea of a political struggle between Stalin and Beria on the national minorities and foreign policy, see A. Avtorkhanov, *Zagadki smerti Stalina: Zagovor Beria* (Frankfurt-am-Main, Possev, 1976), 134, 143–145.

75 See Raymond L. Garthoff, *Soviet Strategy in the Nuclear Era* (New York, 1962), 23–24.

76 Boris Nicolaevsky, 'Rasstrel Riumina,' *Sotsialisticheskii vestnik*, August–September 1954, 155–157.

77 Boris Nicolaevsky, 'Delo Abakumova,' *Sotsialisticheskii vestnik*, January 1955, 3–6.

78 Isaac Deutscher, 'How the Russians Bet a Little in Asia to Win a Lot in Europe,' *Reporter*, 23 September 1954, 19.

79 George Modelski, *Atomic Energy in the Communist Bloc* (Melbourne, 1959), 181–184.

80 'A,' 'Report on Yugoslavia,' September, 1950, *Dossier Quatrième Internationale*, BD1C.

81 The opposite of Djilas's later formulation, in *The New Class* (New York, Praeger, 1957), according to which the USSR was dominated by a new bureaucracy. Djilas did not recapitulate the theory of Machajski, but argued that the new class had not existed before 1917, having developed exclusively from the Communist party. He did not agree with Laurat's description of collectivization as an imperative for the new class, part of its need to multiply industrial cadres. Dedijer thought some of Djilas's views to be influenced by the 'state capitalism' theory. See *The Battle Stalin Lost*, 294.

82   See Franz Borkenau, 'Conflict in World Communism,' *New Leader*, 23 January 1956, 11–12.
83   Molotov's letter in *Kommunist*, September 1955, 127–128.
84   Boris Meissner, 'Die Sowjetführung am Vorabend des xx Parteikongresses,' *Osteuropa*, February 1956, 27.
85   *Khrushchev Remembers*, vol. 1, p. 412; Seweryn Bialer, 'Three Schools of Kremlin Policy,' *New Leader*, 29 July 1957, 11–12.
86   No doubt an extension of Khrushchev's animosity toward Beria, a supporter of the pact who had been able to place a protégé, V. G. Dekanosov, as Ambassador to Berlin. Dekanosov had played a role in the negotiations in 1939. Litvinov told Edgar Snow that Molotov relied so heavily on Dekanosov that he, not Molotov, was really responsible for the pact. Snow to Bertram Wolfe, 6 May 1956, Wolfe Collection, Hoover Institution. Dekanosov was appointed Interior Minister of Georgia during Beria's heyday in spring 1953 but was dismissed at the end of the year when Beria fell.
87   Isaac Deutscher, 'Communist Party Congress: The Break with Stalinism,' *Reporter*, 22 March 1956, 32. This was also Souvarine's opinion. See 'Le XXe Congrès: Le Stalinisme sans démence,' *Est et ouest*, 1–15 March 1956, 5; and 'Khrouchtchev confirme le BEIPI et persiste dans le stalinisme,' *Est et ouest*, 1–15 April 1956, 1–4.
88   For the distinction between Polish 'domesticism' and Hungarian 'national communism,' see Zbigniew Brzezinski, *The Soviet Bloc: Unity and Conflict* (Cambridge, Mass., 1960), 260–265.
89   Conquest, *Power and Policy*, 318.
90   Wolfgang Leonhard, *The Kremlin Since Stalin* (London, 1962), 249. The speech was said to have been cut. The text in *Pravda*, 15 July 1957, 2, and *Leningradskaia pravda*, 14 July 1957, 1–2, calls for 'monolithic unity' in support of the June plenum condemning the Anti-Party Group, without any emphasis on the 1930s. But an article by A. Velikanova, 'V edinstve—sila partii' (In unity is the strength of the party), accused the Anti-Party Group of 'fighting against the course of the Twentieth Congress' and quoted a worker who had fought their kind for 'thirty years.' *Leningradskaia pravda*, 18 July 1957, 2.
91   Isaac Deutscher, 'Did Zhukov Carry De-Stalinization Too Far?" *Reporter*, 14 November 1957, 15. But see Timothy Colton, 'The Zhukov Affair Reconsidered,' *Soviet Studies*, April 1977, 190, casting doubt on the idea that Zhukov was a potential 'Bonaparte.' Veljko Micunovic, *Moscow Diary* (Garden City, N.Y., Doubleday, 1980), 309, says the October plenum that ousted Zhukov was shown films in which he was mounted on a white horse outside the Brandenburg Gate.
92   As did Velikanova, 'V edinstve,' *Leningradskaia Pravda*, 18 July 1957, 2. In August, the army paper *Krasnaia zvezda* rehabilitated Marshal Blücher, shot in 1937. For Zhukov's refusal to criticize Yugoslav Revisionism, see Micunovic, *Moscow Diary*, 233.
93   Conquest, *Power and Policy*, 324.
94   Boris Nicolaevsky, 'Khrushchev protiv "ideologov,"' *Sotsialisticheskii vestnik*, June 1958, 109.
95   Sidney I. Ploss, *Soviet Politics Since the Fall of Khrushchev* (Philadelphia, Univ. of Pennsylvania Press, 1965), 4–6; Carl A. Linden, *Khrushchev and the Soviet Leadership, 1957–1964* (Baltimore, Johns Hopkins, Univ. Press, 1966), chs. 4 and 5; Michel Tatu, *Power in the Kremlin: From Khrushchev to Kosygin* (New York, 1970), 69–78. For a critique of the above on behalf of a more complex formula, see George W. Breslauer, *Khrushchev and Brezhnev as Leaders: Building Authority in Soviet Politics* (London, Allen & Unwin, 1982), x–xii.

96   *Khrushchev Remembers*, 569.
97   *Khrushchev Remembers*. Ibid., 294–296. For Khrushchev's promise of a bomb prototype and technical data at the November, 1957, meeting, see Alice Langley-Hsieh, *Communist China's Strategy in the Nuclear Era* (Englewood Cliffs, N.J., 1962), 100.
98   Removed were Aristov, Furtseva, Ignatov, Kirichenko, and Pospelov. Kozlov was added.
99   Robert Conquest, 'Khrushchev's "Conservative" Opposition,' *New Leader*, 27 November 1961, 20; Linden, *Khrushchev and the Soviet Leadership*, 133; but doubted by Robert Slusser, *The Berlin Crisis of 1961: Soviet–American Relations and the Struggle for Power in the Kremlin, June–November, 1961* (Baltimore, Johns Hopkins Univ. Press, 1973), 342. Slusser argues that during Khrushchev's absence from the Kremlin, 22–31 August, his opponents took over and brought the United States and the Soviet Union to the brink of war. He compares Kozlov's actions in 1961 to those of Ordzhonikidze and others in September, 1936, bringing the Soviets, in the absence of Stalin, into the Spanish Civil War.
100 Arnold L. Horelick and Myron Rush, *Strategic Power and Soviet Foreign Policy* (Chicago, Univ. of Chicago Press, 1965), 93.
101 *Khrushchev Remembers*, 546–547.
102 The phrase of William Hyland and Richard Shryock, *The Fall of Khrushchev* (New York, Funk & Wagnells, 1968), 70.
103 See ibid., 151–156.
104 For Suslov's emergence in Stalin's last years, see Boris Nicolaevsky, 'M. A. Suslov. Opyt biograficheskoi spravki,' *Sotsialisticheskii vestnik*, November 1960, 208–209; Hans-Jurgen Eitner, 'M. A. Suslov,' *Osteuropa*, June 1960, 405.
105 Isaac Deutscher, 'Three Currents in Communism,' *New Left Review*, January–February 1964, 6.
106 Text in *FBIS Daily Report*, supplement, 6 April 1964. Tatu reports (*Power in the Kremlin*, 367), the rumor that Suslov was forced to read this report by Khrushchev, who had commissioned one of his own ideologists to write it. Tatu also cites the corroboration of an 'east European personality,' perhaps the same one who gave information on the later plenum that ousted Khrushchev. Suslov's views on Trotsky and Mao are repeated in later works by Soviet writers, such as Sergei Ogurtsov, *The True Face of Neo-Trotskyism* (Moscow, 1973), 50–51.
107 For example, see Michel Raptis (Pablo), 'A la défense de la révolution chinoise!' 10 November 1959, *Dossier Quatrième International*, BDIC, supporting the Chinese on Tibet and against India. See also Deutscher's statement in Yvan Craipeau, Pierre Cot, Lelio Basso, and Jacques Vergès, *Que se passe-t-il dans la mouvement communiste international?* (Paris, 1965), 12, 44.
108 Boris Souvarine, 'Khroutchev et la direction collective,' *Est et ouest*, 1–15 July 1958, 5–8.
109 Souvarine to Volskii, 1 April 1960, Nicolaevsky Archives.
110 Boris Souvarine, 'Ot Neozhidannosti k neozhidannosti,' *Sotsialisticheskii vestnik*, November–December 1963, 160.
111 Boris Nicolaevsky, 'O Sushchestve spora,' *Sotsialisticheskii vestnik*, November–December 1963, 162.
112 Ibid.

Chapter 9

1   Myron Rush, *How Communist States Change Their Rulers* (Ithaca, Cornell Univ. Press, 1974), 18.
2   For an argument relating the Soviet decision to American action in Vietnam, see George W. Breslauer, 'Political Succession and the Soviet Policy Agenda,' *Problems of Communism*, May–June 1980, 38–39.
3   The phrase is Harry Gelman's. See *The Brezhnev Politburo and the Decline of Detente* (Ithaca, Cornell Univ. Press, 1984), 76.
4   Pavel Tigrid, *Why Dubcek Fell* (London, MacDonald, 1969), 86, 127–128; Jiri Valenta, *Soviet Intervention in Czechoslovakia, 1968: Anatomy of a Decision* (Baltimore and London, Johns Hopkins, 1979), 102, 186. Michel Tatu was told by his sources of a Soviet internal party document which named Suslov, Kosygin, and Ponomarev as having 'underestimated the danger of counter-revolution in Czechoslovakia.' 'Intervention in East Europe,' in Steven S. Kaplan, ed., *The Diplomacy of Power: The Soviet Armed Forces as a Political Instrument* (Washington, D.C., Brookings, 1981), 228.
5   H. R. Haldeman, *The Ends of Power* (New York, Times Books, 1978), 90–91; Henry A. Kissinger, *White House Years* (Boston, Little, Brown, 1979), 183–185.
6   Kissinger, *White House Years*, 689.
7   Ibid., 145–146, 172–173.
8   Ibid., 178.
9   See Michel Tatu, 'Kremlinology: The Mini-Crisis of 1970,' *Interplay*, October 1970, 19. Tatu stresses the continuous struggle of a leader in Brezhnev's position to bolster his power—in this case, to subvert the Kosygin reforms and strive for more party input.
10 *Politicheskii dnevnik*, vol. 1 [1964–1970] (Amsterdam, Fond imeni Gertsena, 1972), 657–658. John Dornberg, *Brezhnev: The Masks of Power* (New York, Basic Books, 1974), 248–249; Christian Duevel, 'Marginal Notes on a Leadership Crisis,' *Radio Liberty Research*, CRD 272/70, 23 July 1970; Gelman, *The Brezhnev Politburo*, 128–129.
11 V. V. Kolotov, *Nikolai Alekseevich Voznesenskii* (Moscow, n.d.), 174, reviewed by G. Sorokin, *Pravda*, September 1974. Terry McNeill, 'The Spector of Voznesensky Stalks Suslov,' *Radio Liberty Research*, 338/74, 11 October 1974.
12 Intervention in disputes in the officer corps was strongly advised in a conference on tactics held with representatives from the Communist parties of East Germany, Bolivia, Brazil, Indonesia, and Iraq. See 'Whom Does the Army Serve?' *World Marxist Review*, April 1974, 43–59.
13 This remains murky. Some claim has been made that the expedition was encouraged by Belgian conservatives unhappy with President Mobutu, whom they saw as a French puppet. See Bernard Veillet-Lavalée, 'Pourquoi les Belges sont furieux du "coup" français,' *Le Matin*, 20 May 1978, 13.
14 For the chain of responses linking Kolwezi to China and Japan, see Zbigniew K. Brzezinski, *Power and Principle* (New York, 1983), 208–209, 211, 216.
15 An exception was Zhores Medvedev, 'Russia Under Brezhnev,' *New Left Review*, September 1979, 28, who gave Andropov the best chances.
16 Myron Rush, 'The Soviet Policy Favoring Arms over Investment since 1975.' Paper prepared for the U.S. Congress, Joint Economic Committee, *Soviet Economy in the 1980s: Problems and Prospects*. Cited in Gelman, *The Brezhnev Politburo*, 176–177. For the implications of Gorbachev's collection of Kirilenko supporters, see Jerry Hough, 'Gorbachev's Strategy,' *Foreign Affairs*, Fall 1985, 41.

17 Christian Duevel, 'Suslov's Role at the Central Committee Plenum and the Supreme Soviet Session,' *Radio Liberty Research*, R 137/79, 2 May 1979, 2.
18 Interview with Kuzichkin, *Time*, 22 November 1982, 33–34.
19 See the discussion in Anthony Arnold, *Afghanistan's Two-Party Communism: Parcham and Khalg* (Stanford, Hoover Institution, 1983), 88–98.
20 Quoted by Arrigo Levi, in *The Times* (London), 11 February 1982.
21 Viktor Goliavkin, 'Iubileinaia rech,' *Avrora*, December 1981, 75.
22 Aino Kuusinen, *Rings of Destiny* (New York, 1974), 81. Communism would advance, as Kuusinen's wife reported him predicting, by 'armed forces and conquest.'
23 Boris Rabbot, 'A Letter to Brezhnev,' *New York Times Magazine*, 6 November 1977, 55.
24 *Foreign Report* (1766), 3 March 1983, 5.
25 For Aliev's anticorruption campaigns as rehearsals for the affair of Boris the Gypsy, see Bernard Feron, 'Un Pouvoir fondé sur l'ambiguïté,' *Le Monde*, 9 February 1984, 2.
26 Solomentsev's post as head of the Control Commission made his political grudge important and recalled the role of Gusev, with his grudges, in 1922.
27 For speculation about Aliev and Vorotnikov, see Dominique Dhombres, 'M. Gromkyo a lancé une mise en garde,' *Le Monde*, 15 March 1985, 2.
28 Seweryn Bialer, 'How Gorbachev Can Get His Country Moving Again,' *Washington Post*, 6 May 1985, 23.
29 Text in *Survey*, Spring 1984, 88–108.
30 K. S. Karol, 'Le Gamin de Moscou,' *Le Nouvelle Observateur*, 15 March 1985, 33.

Conclusion

1 'The main determinant of scope for policy maneuver,' according to the description of Sidney Ploss, 'The Case for Studying Soviet Politics,' *The Soviet Political Process* (Waltham, Mass., Toronto, and London, Ginn, 1971), 16. 'Over time,' writes Carl Linden, 'it has been the political struggle that has shaped Soviet institutions rather than the other way around.' *Khrushchev and the Soviet Leadership*, 7.
2 'Dostovernye dokumenty epokhi' (review of a three-volume edition of Suslov's speeches), *Kommunist*, no. 8 (May 1983), 122.
3 They remain topical. For example, Michael Voslensky, *Nomenklatura: The Soviet Ruling Class*, Eric Mosbacher, trans. (Garden City, N.Y., Doubleday, 1984), 3–5, citing Djilas and arguing against the theory of the 'state of all the people.' Also, Alexander Shtromas, 'How the End of the Soviet System May Come About,' paper presented to a meeting of the Professors' World Peace Academy, Geneva, August, 1985, describing the Soviet New Class as the gravedigger of the party and state leadership.
4 Both 'moderates' and 'hawks.' See Alexander Dallin, 'Domestic Sources of Soviet Foreign Policy,' in Seweryn Bialer, ed., *The Domestic Context of Soviet Foreign Policy* (Boulder, Colo., Westview, 1981), 383–386.
5 Roman Kolkowicz et al. *The Soviet Union and Arms Control: A Superpower Dilemma* (Baltimore, Johns Hopkins Univ. Press, 1970), 34–37. Lawrence Freedman, *The Evolution of Nuclear Strategy* (New York, Macmillan, 1981), 257.

Index